Grounds of the Immaterial

For Laura, Luca, Mylan & Elena

Grounds of the Immaterial

A Conflict-Based Approach to Intellectual Rights

Niels van Dijk

Postdoctoral Fellow, Research Group on Law, Science, Technology & Society, Vrije Universiteit Brussel, Belgium

Edward Elgar
PUBLISHING

Cheltenham, UK • Northampton, MA, USA

Published by
Edward Elgar Publishing Limited
The Lypiatts
15 Lansdown Road
Cheltenham
Glos GL50 2JA
UK

Edward Elgar Publishing, Inc.
William Pratt House
9 Dewey Court
Northampton
Massachusetts 01060
USA

A catalogue record for this book
is available from the British Library

Library of Congress Control Number: 2017931768

This book is available electronically in the **Elgar**online
Law subject collection
DOI 10.4337/9781786432506

MIX
Paper from
responsible sources
FSC® C013056
FSC
www.fsc.org

ISBN 978 1 78643 249 0 (cased)
ISBN 978 1 78643 250 6 (eBook)

Typeset by Servis Filmsetting Ltd, Stockport, Cheshire
Printed and bound in Great Britain by TJ International Ltd, Padstow

Contents

Preface

Semper ad eventum festinat et in medias res.[1]
(Horace)

It is with a slight feeling of alienation mixed with nostalgia that I am writing this preface to a work before you and now behind me. The process of its genesis has been a curious adventure. It truly took off in the middle of things, *in medias res* so to say, in what was meant to be an orienting internship period at a law firm in order to become familiar with the legal regime of intellectual rights. This internship became the starting point for an interest in the workings of legal practice. I blew the dust off my old philosophical interests in Actor-Network Theory, acquired as a student of philosophy of science, and engaged in an empirical study of a patent dispute that was at stake in the law firm. The resulting textual account became the first writing and the median chapter of this book. Having started this journey into the workings of legal practice, it seemed only logical to follow it through to the end. I therefore decided to also move my research to court and study how legal disputes arrive at judgment.

While these accounts were being written down, the difficulties started heaping up. By that time, I had become further versed in the doctrine, histories and philosophies of intellectual rights and theories on their role in the information society. How does one proceed from the accounts at the law firm and the court to these theories that often seemed so far away from the perspective of practice? How to establish relations between such seemingly disparate exercises, or worse, how to establish a unifying thread throughout all of these?

In this period, I often cursed the exigencies of the monograph, with its assumption of a complete treatise on a single subject. How can one be faithful to the very different issues encountered in each study when one has to unite them in a single subject? Should each chapter not find a voice of its own in order to speak for itself and, if so, how does a writer deal with such polyphony? The challenge of the mono*graph* for my research thus became

1 [Trans.] *He always hurries to the event and in the middle of things.*

to come up with a singular way of writing, which at the same time avoided being mono*tonous*.

How strange and unexpected the helping hands of the muses can be! Since music has been the sole continuous companion throughout the whole exercise of writing down this text, it was probably bound to have an impact of some sorts. At first the playing of music in between writing episodes served as a source of creativity that is constantly needed for the arduous work of constructing textual accounts fuelled with the vitality of practice and action (instead of being the result of habitual writing routines that one constantly risks slipping back into). Eventually, it however also provided the kind of dynamic solution required for the monographic problem sketched above. After having repeatedly listened to Mussorgsky's *Pictures at an Exhibition*, I realized the character of Mussorgsky's work was a solution to a (musical) problem comparable to the one I was faced with. Mussorgsky links a series of very different musical impressions of paintings together in one composition. He creatively uses the 'promenade' as a connecting device, triggered by the distance of the two paintings between which it moves. The concept provided inspiration for linking the seemingly disparately different investigations in this book together without having to resort to the format of a philosophical 'album'. This promenadology allowed for experiments with a way of thinking not so much primarily addressed by the different topics studied in the distinct chapters (legal doctrine, history, philosophy and practice), but by the tensions and distances between these different topics as itself a theme for separate study. Such an interludic movement, a 'turn' in this case, made possible a compositional solution to the problem of connecting the different accounts of legal theory and legal practice.

This dynamic way of thinking from the 'between' had been set in motion and gradually each median movement attained its own (musical) character, sometimes a prelude, an interlude, a transposition, a reprise, a movement, or a coda. Only much later did I realize that the character of these movements of thought (*denkbewegingen*) had philosophical implications and that the way in which the philosopher approaches legal phenomena is intricately entangled with the eventual account of these phenomena. This became the basis for several tentative explorations, which, as a series of Satie-esque coda, would bring this book to its end.

***

Along this whole journey, I can only be extremely grateful for all the help and support that I have received.

I owe great gratitude to Serge Gutwirth in multiple ways: as facilitator of the spaces for an academic freedom and 'slow thinking' that is becoming increasingly rare, but also for suggesting an internship at a law firm, a decision that would turn out to have quite unexpected consequences. I owe equal gratitude to Mireille Hildebrandt. Her close critical reading and her capacity to always ask the right question that digs straight down to the core have forced me to think about the consistency of the strange planes explored.

I wish to thank Mrs Blanchard, the attorney who allowed me to perform such extensive studies at her law firm. Only throughout the course of my work did I grow to appreciate the willingness to have around an observer that might even put her work at risk. I also wish to thank the president of the Belgian Court of Commerce for allowing me to conduct my studies there.

Thank you to Katja for being an academic companion and friend throughout the curious trajectories through European projects, conferences and teaching course, and for the endless discussions. These allowed me to thoroughly test many ideas on a daily basis, which is really where the most important research work often takes place. I would like to thank Sari whose legal expertise so greatly helped me in finding my way in intellectual rights, and Dani for his corrections and extensive discussions and for sharing a 'gusto' for Belgian beer. Furthermore, I wish to thank the whole LSTS team for providing such a lively research environment.

A special word here about the processes of anonymization. A very strange and unexpected side-effect of adequately anonymizing textual accounts about intellectual creations that contain so many identifiable technical and artistic details, was that I had to myself engage in creative acts and become an author of works, an inventor of inventions and a designer of models and trademarks (and a forger of signatures). Within these processes, I owe great thanks to Antonio, Mike and Laura for helping me with the laborious and demanding work of inventing a new kind of machine that would fit all the legal arguments *and* be technically plausible, and to Laura for helping me with the designs of the oil spouts.

Thanks to all my friends and family: Peter and Jean-Louis, for keeping on coming to Belgium to visit me and relieve me from my work. Thanks to my parents for always being there and for their groundwork invested in me. Thanks to Rutger for tailoring the design of the original 1883 drawing used as frontispiece, to the contents of the book through digital filtering and colouring. Words fail to express my gratitude to you, Laura. Not only for the help you have given me by your work on images, anonymization, layout and planning, but moreover for your unceasing support and love along the entire journey. Thanks to you, my dear Luca, whose joyful arrival on this world relieved me of so much of the mental stress that would have otherwise accompanied the final stage of this research.

Acknowledgments and sources

Front Cover: Courtroom fight at Yavapai County Courthouse, Prescott, Arizona, 3 December 1883 (adapted by Rutger van Dijk and the author).

Images, pp. 77–8: Three box-filling machines (Laura Muiño and the author).

Image, p. 121: Fragment from Michelangelo's *Last Judgment*, 1541.

Figure 4.1, p. 126: Monadic court architecture (author).

Images, pp. 152–3: Four olive oil spouts (Laura Muiño and the author).

Image, p. 179: Two marks of trade (author). The image of the electric plug above the DEQU letters is created by qubodup. The image of the crystal above the DQ letters is created by Dennis J. Kincaid.

Figure 4.2, p. 207: Tarpaulin of D as depicted in drawing 3 of European Patent 1405804.

Figure 4.3, p. 207: Tarpaulin of A as depicted in the judgment by the court [anonymized].

Figure 4.4, p. 210: Fragment of tarpaulin of D as depicted in drawing 3 of European Patent 1405804.

Figure 5.1, p. 242: Life of the legal dispute (author).

Introduction

'What is an idea?'
'What is the relation between an idea and a concept?'
'In what sense are they immaterial?'

It might seem that by positing these questions, we have initiated a philosophical discourse and in a certain sense we have. Many philosophers will find themselves engaged by these questions. We could turn to several of the great treatises that have been written throughout the history of philosophy in order to find tentative responses to these questions. The question of the Being of Ideas for instance could be tackled by giving an exposition of the metaphysical theories of Plato, Descartes, Locke, Leibniz, Hume or Kant about these issues. It could for instance also be dealt with philosophically by setting up a new environment of thought in which the idea is constituted in its being or its becoming. A question can evoke and be evoked in multiple ways however. Posed in the same grammatical form these questions could also engage a jurist in the course of working within the legal regimes of patent law or copyright. The mode of engagement will obviously be very different in each case. By way of illustration, let us evoke one of these phrases again:

'What is an idea?'

The short question uttered by a slightly agitated female voice, resounds against the walls of a courtroom in Brussels. The question is raised by the attorney, Mrs Blanchard, in the closing remarks to her plea before the judges of the court. The atmosphere has become quite heated at the closing of the morning session of the Court of Commerce. The nature of ideas has become an issue in the complex patent dispute that she has worked on for the last few years. The attorney of the adverse party had just, a few minutes ago, called the invention she has been advocating a mere 'idea'. Her question is a response to this disqualification. The fact that we are dealing with a specific legal question becomes clear by her subsequent question: '*What is not susceptible of protection?*' or when she asks whether the matter of dispute is '*an "idea" in the sense of patent law or intellectual property law?*' The being of ideas is here raised in a specific legal way. The question evokes a host of similar matters of dispute that have been authoritatively qualified as ideas and inventions in other court cases, and through which the meaning of these concepts has itself come to be reconstituted. In this sense, an 'idea' or an 'invention' is a *legal concept* that obeys specific conditions different from the ones in other disciplines and in everyday speech. Legal concepts are imbedded in a web of different spaces, places, actions, objects, people, conditions, procedures and other concepts. In order to understand the use of legal concepts like 'idea', 'concept', 'intellectual creation', 'invention', 'work' or 'sign', we have to turn to the specific practices of intellectual rights in which they are deployed and where they are constituted as *immaterial* entities. We first have to get familiar with the modes of operation of the practices of copyright, patent and trademark law in order to be able to grasp their meaning.

***

This is a book in between law and philosophy; or rather, it is an experiment with positions and movements in a philosophical thinking that is addressed by the legal regime of intellectual rights. We cannot call this book a philosophy of law in the sense in which it is regularly practiced. It contains rather the thoughts of a philosopher evoked by a confrontation with the peculiarities of this legal regime moving past, through or in divergence from several legal positions. These movements of thought first have to be engaged in – doing philosophy – in order to show what thinking could be in a legal-philosophical sense, without directly grasping and locating it according to the co-ordinates of existing legal theory.[1] This approach is partly borne out of a lingering dissatisfaction with the existent approaches to law and the laws of intellectual property more specifically. It is dissatisfaction with the distant abstract treatment and theoretical fixation of both the legal doctrine and the philosophy of intellectual property, but also dissatisfaction with the critical analysis of intellectual property with regard to the calculation of its economical and societal effects in the information society, or the unmasking of its hidden presumptions. Their explanations often get before, after, above or below the objects of intellectual rights that they investigate in order to explain them, but they never get to the middle of things – *in medias res* – where IP is still a vital event (*eventum*) that is in the process of happening. We could thus ask in what way they have managed to *approach* the matters of intellectual rights at

---

[1] We will return to these relations between law and philosophy in Chapter 6.

all. This book will endeavour to provide such an approach by engaging in a *trans-versal* philosophy, understood as a '*turn*' and change in the orientation of legal thinking, which moves '*across*' the legal matters that it is engaged by (not to be confused with trans-cendence as a 'jumping over'). Thus oriented we will find a very specific kind of encounter between two regimes: How do practitioners of intellectual rights deal with conflicts about technologies and render them solvable?

In order to arrive *in medias res* we are however required to cover quite some distance and, in contrast to Horace's adage, we will not hasten our path to the events. Chapter 1 will first treat the history, philosophy and doctrine of intellectual rights in order to understand the existing theoretical positions on intellectual property. We will discuss the historical developments of copyright, patent and trademark laws, the discourse on intellectual property, the theory of immaterial goods and its culmination into information goods in the knowledge economy. After discussing some of the problems with several of the theoretical 'approaches', Chapter 2 will provide an outline of a transversal approach to law mentioned above. It will explore a path towards intellectual rights in action by investigating a practice turn in law and (legal) theory. Only then will we relocate our research within the legal practice of law firms and courts in Chapters 3 and 4 respectively, where extensive empirical case studies have been conducted. Here we can once again take up the questions posed at the start and begin anew our investigations. Legal concepts like 'idea', 'concept', 'work', 'invention' and 'sign' will be studied as they are evoked by legal practitioners in the proceeding of a concrete dispute. Things play an important role in this process. As *matters of dispute* they are the occasion for the legal process. We will closely follow such a matter of dispute on its proceedings from technological or commercial sites of enterprises, through the offices of law firms, the court registry, the courtroom, the judge's office, until we finally arrive at judgment. Throughout these processes, non-legal matters of dispute will slowly be *grounded* as immaterial ideas, concepts, works, inventions or signs by the ceaseless operations of legal practitioners. This legal grounding requires a lot of work and will be the topic of the present study. The focus will be on the ways in which this immateriality is constituted when a matter of dispute passes through the legal instruments and vocabulary of intellectual rights practices, to be transformed in a *matter of fact* before becoming an immaterial *legal object* of intellectual rights. This leads us to the formulation of a first research question, addressed in Chapters 1, 3 and 4: '*How is immateriality constituted in intellectual rights?*'

In addition to the issues and problems that arise within the legal regime of intellectual rights, these studies will also be occupied with creating a setting in which a new philosophical approach to law could become possible. The two strands are two sides of the same coin. One cannot dissociate an investigation of the nature of fundamental concepts and distinctions of intellectual rights from the specific legal practices in which they are deployed and from the way these practices and concepts are approached by the researcher. This leads us to formulate a second objective of exploration: '*How to approach legal phenomena as a philosopher?*' This question will first be addressed in sketching the transversal approach to legal practices of intellectual rights in Chapter 2. It will be taken up again in the discussion about the relations between law and philosophy in a set of coda to this book (Chapter 6), through a double analysis of the juridical features in philosophical thought (Plato, Bacon, Kant, Freud) and the approaches to law and legal practice in legal theory (Hohfeld, Holmes, Hart, Dworkin). These theories will be confronted with the transversal approach to law and the case study findings in Chapters 3 and 4.

In this way, these investigations might provide the groundwork for the construction of a different legal philosophy. The term 'philosophy' here refers not so much to a disciplinary demarcation of an intellectual territory, but to the different movements of thought performed throughout and between the chapters. Here, along a range of different sites, a series of different encounters take place between philosophy and law that could send them off on a path of mutual becoming, both with regard to the manner in which legal practices deploy their own operations and theories on questions of philosophical interest and to the different ways of becoming-legal of philosophy itself. Finally, along these journeys through law, several phenomena of possible interest to philosophy are encountered, each time from different directions depending on the matter of investigation. The index to this book registers and links the different occurrences of these phenomena at various sites. These hyperversal connections make visible certain characteristics, which are offered for further exploration.

1. Legal theory: from intellectual property to informational goods

Patents and copyrights approach, nearer than any other class of cases belonging to forensic discussions, to what may be called the metaphysics of the law, *where the distinctions are, or at least may be, very subtle and refined, and, sometimes, almost evanescent.*

(*Folsom v. Marsh*, C.C.D.Mass. 1841, No. 4,901)

What is this intellectual property or what are these intellectual rights? In what does their intellectuality consist? How should we understand the division between the intangible immateriality of the created work or the innovative invention and their embodiments in tangible material objects? What is an idea in the sense of patent and copyright law? In this chapter, we will deal with some of the answers given to these questions about this 'metaphysics of the law', along with a host of different theoretical positions. By way of a prelude to our topic, we will start here with an encounter with the issues that intellectual property rights raise in what is called the information society. In section 1.2, we will provide the concise kind of introductory view on intellectual property that we get by reading the textbooks on the matter and the articles in which the polemics about the use of the term are discussed. In section 1.3, we will engage with studies of the historical development of intellectual property and show the philosophical positions that have been used to ground this legal regime. In section 1.4, we will engage with the shifts in legal doctrine from intellectual property, through immaterial goods to informational goods. The accounts provided here do not aspire to be exhaustive of these subsequent topics. This would have required a different kind of book. They will instead rather serve to introduce the broad themes and developments of the distinct regimes of intellectual rights. They will also provide an opportunity to study different approaches in explaining concepts of intellectual property.

1.1 INTELLECTUAL RIGHTS IN THE INFORMATION SOCIETY

Intellectual rights have become a prevalent legal regime in modern society. A frequent glance at the technology sections in newspapers generally gives a good impression. We read about lawsuits of copyright organizations against file sharing sites like the Swedish 'Pirate Bay' and against internet providers for hosting connections to all kinds of movies, images and films. We further read about the founding of European Pirate parties that protest against excessive copyright protection and urge the protection of the public domain. There are also several property controversies about online social network site Facebook, ranging from its assertions to possess rights to all the users' photos and videos, to Russian hackers offering 1.5 million Facebook profiles for sale on the black market. There are also some interesting articles about two Dutch court cases on affairs of theft of virtual property, judging that virtual items have been stolen within an online computer game and a virtual world. Apart from copyright and information technologies, there are also several articles about biotechnology and patent law. The practice of patenting genetically modified products, including living organisms, cell lines and genes, has spurned a controversy in the US, sometimes resulting in court cases.[1] Patents on nanotechnologies seem to be next in the line of fire. The latest development of 3-D printing is also bound to give rise to a whole new dimension of copyright issues.

All these issues have to do with intellectual rights and the emergence of new information technologies. Information has fast become an organizing concept of the international economy and its control and ownership channels important power relations in society.[2] The last decade has seen the emergence of a discourse on the convergence of technologies. Formerly separate domains like nanotechnology, biotechnology, information and communication technology and neuro-technologies are coming together in a single paradigm of engineering of information in which the material medium becomes an interchangeable carrier of intangible information.[3] This convergence had its precursors in discourses on media and information technologies. Some theorists of media described how different media with their own autonomous data format,

---

[1] *Diamond v. Chakrabarty*, 447 US 303; *Association for Molecular Pathology v. Myriad Genetics*, No. 11–725.

[2] The question about the legal status of information thus becomes all the more relevant (Gutwirth, 1993).

[3] Nordmann, 2004.

like writing, film, photography and phonography, were transformed by the advent of digitization through which they all converged into the single bit format. Different media have become interchangeable carriers of informational codes (Kittler, 1986). The medium might have become the message, but the only message is that the medium has made itself irrelevant.

In this context, some have spoken about the 'homologization of information', which unites contemporary problems of ethnic cultures, software industries and the human genome project and results in an increasing decontextualization of information from its particular medium and location (Boyle, 1996). In Big Data 'informatics', raw data are turned into meaningful information through data mining algorithms. In molecular biology discourses, genetic issues have also been restated in terms of information. Through the mobilization of book metaphors the reproduction of DNA has been framed as a bio-material variant of printing in which an intangible informational code is transferred from one material medium to another (Pottage, 2009).

This framing of informational issues has pushed the regimes of intellectual rights centre stage. The difference between immaterial information and material mediums or carriers is precisely the kind of difference on which these regimes are grounded.[4] Intellectual rights protect intangible inventions or works that have become expressed in tangible objects (like amino acids and hard disks). This has provided an ideal basis for using these legal regimes to regulate information technologies. If information has become the organizing concept of knowledge-based economies, intellectual rights have become its legal 'property' regime, 'intellectual property is the legal form of the information age' (Boyle, 1997, p. 90). The ontological framing here turns into 'ontological politics',[5] or rather ontological juridics. Some have pushed the boundaries of the frame, or have even inverted the relation between frame and framed in claiming that that 'each work has the character of information'. Both are immaterial goods with a structured form of expression capable of transmission for communication (Hugenholtz, 2005).

---

[4] For a critique of the attempts to frame information as immaterial and an account of the material histories of computing, see Blanchette, 2011. Stiegler is more sweeping when, in the context of the web as a medium, he states that 'nothing is immaterial' (Stiegler, 2012, p. 5). This statement cannot serve as a point of departure, since immateriality is dismissed *tout court* at the outset.

[5] Mol & Law, 1994.

1.2 INTELLECTUAL PROPERTY AND ITS CRITIQUE

The rhythm of the information society is one of increasing speed in striving towards the ideals of real-time reaction and future anticipation. It is time to decelerate in order to find a closer resonance with the rhythms more proper to legal discourse. Law slows things down, it temporizes. This is not an expression of its incapacity, the fact that it is badly organized, or that it continuously is lagging behind the developments of society. It is an expression of its own mode of operation.

We will start with a first introduction to intellectual property, the kind that we get when reading legal textbooks or encyclopedias. Although these are always situated in a particular legal tradition, they often introduce the field in general terms in ways that provide a unification of the subject matter at hand. Intellectual property, *geistiges Eigentum, propriété intellectuelle*, is a term that is used to group together legal regimes like patent, copyright and trademark law. In the next section, we will see how the term served as a rallying cry for the establishment of a new legal regime when the first copyright laws were enacted at the end of the eighteenth century. Whether the term 'intellectual property' really ever established itself as a *legal concept* in the legislations, jurisprudence or legal theory of the nation states in the following centuries up until the mid-twentieth century is controversial.[6] Nevertheless, with the founding of the World Intellectual Property Organisation (WIPO) in 1967 these different legal regimes merged under the sole header 'intellectual property', which installed the term as a general overarching concept in international law. The term was fortified by the Treaty on the Trade-Related aspects of Intellectual Property Rights (TRIPS) in 1994 and, from then on, further trickled down into European law and national legislations. The different legal regimes of copyright, patent and trademarks are all said to belong together, because they all grant exclusive rights on the 'creations of the human mind'.[7] The purpose of all these rights is to protect 'the integrity of intellectual objects'.[8]

Critics have pointed out that there is a problem with the use of the word

---

[6] With regard to European law Goetting, 2006 supports this thesis, whereas Peukert, 2011 rejects it.

[7] See for example the textbook of Wichers Hoeth, 2007 on intellectual property. This view is acknowledged by WIPO.

[8] Spinello & Bottis, 2009, p. 4.

'property' for referring to the regimes of copyright and patent. There are significant differences between property and intellectual property with regard to the kind of right and the object of the rights. Property rights are conceived as the most absolute exclusive right of a person on a thing. The rights granted in patent law or copyright however are more limited in duration and scope, and for this reason they have also been called temporary intellectual monopolies instead of property rights. Furthermore, in criminal law there are also important differences between intellectual rights and property rights. Contrary to common language a violation of intellectual rights does not constitute 'theft'. The insistence on such terms as 'property' and 'theft' reveals a certain rhetoric of propertization, which is fed by the content industries and their representative author organizations[9] and by WIPO itself. In this way, a whole range of issues is located within a discourse of appropriation and its concepts are employed to remove the limitations of such 'intellectual' objects.

Furthermore, it has been pointed out that the legal objects of property rights and intellectual property rights are fundamentally different. The object of property rights (in Continental law) is a material thing, a *Sache, zaak, chose, corpus mechanicum*. The object of intellectual rights is a *corpus mysticum* or *Immaterialgut*. Contrary to tangible property like land, intangibles are non-rivalrous. A work or an invention can be made available to third parties without diminishing their use value. Thomas Jefferson already remarked that ideas are 'like fire, expansible over all space, without lessening their density at any point, and like the air in which we breathe, move, and have our physical being, incapable of confinement or exclusive appropriation. Inventions then cannot, in nature, be a subject of property' (Jefferson, 1813, p. 333).[10]

The legal regimes of copyright law and patent law are thus very different from the legal regime of property, both qua incorporeal object and qua limited nature of the granted rights. These regimes however also have important differences from each other, which oppose their assimilation to a singular regime of 'intellectual property'. The term lumps together fields of rights that each had their independent historical trajectories and involve very different sets of law. Each of these legal regimes has had to invent its own techniques for the demarcation of

---

[9] Lemley, 1997.

[10] This is also the reason the infamous 'tragedy of the commons', which occurs when a common resource like land is overused due to the fact that too many people have entitlements in it, will not take place with intangibles. In fact in some fields, granting too many intellectual rights has resulted in a 'tragedy of the anticommons' (Heller & Eisenberg, 1998, p. 698).

its intellectual object. All these differences are obscured by the use of this general term 'intellectual property'.[11] Curiously, whereas the notion of 'property' is heavily debated, what is little or not discussed is the notion of 'intellectuality'. 'Intellectuality' and 'immateriality' have played an important role both in the conceptualizations of the legal regimes of copyright and patent law and to a certain extent also in that of trademark law. By focusing on the specificities of these regimes, we can come to understand the figures of intellectuality at stake in creation.

1.3 HISTORICAL AND PHILOSOPHICAL DEVELOPMENTS OF INTELLECTUAL PROPERTY

The author has played the role of the regulator of the fictive, a role quite characteristic of our era of industrial and bourgeois society, of individualism and private property.
(Foucault, 1979, p. 159)

Gutenberg's invention of the printing press with movable type around 1440, and the subsequent spread of printing presses to urban centres throughout European countries, has had important consequences. It enabled what has been called the 'Gutenberg Galaxy' (McLuhan, 1994) or the 'printing revolution' (Eisenstein, 2005), which led to transformations in many disciplines amongst which are law and its many regimes.[12] The printing press mechanized the mode of book production and led to an enormous increase in output. There was a marked proliferation of copies of works on the market and an expansion of a reading public. In order to safeguard printers and also authors against these practices of copying, a system of printing privileges was created modeled on the old legal figure of commercial monopolies in the fiteenth and sixteenth centuries. These monopolies were granted by the state on all printing

---

[11] Stallman, 2006.

[12] Eisenstein describes the many consequences of the shift from the technology of script (manual copying) to print. The possibility of producing more uniform texts and distributing these over large areas influenced law, language, science, education, memory and art. Access to the same legal codes made it possible to apply the 'same' law on a more broad scale, unifying the legal regime within a certain territory. The quantity of available texts revealed conflicts between texts and spurred a process of cataloguing, indexing and rationalization leading to the extension of old criteria of consistency and unity (Eisenstein, 2005).

activities and did not discriminate between classical works, dictionaries, calendars and new creations. They also led to state censorship of works. In the seventeenth century, the system of privileges became untenable. The demand for books had risen dramatically, partly due to a growing literacy in the middle classes. The existing system of privileges limited the supply of books that was available at the time. The result was an emergence of illegally printed books that flooded the market. This problem became very prevalent in the eighteenth century as a problem that required solution.[13] A public of differently affected groups in different countries and of different professions – lawyers, writers, printers, thinkers and politicians – were engaged by this problem and formulated their wide-ranging responses. In Germany, they ranged from Luther, Putter, Kant, Fichte, Hegel to Schopenhauer and further included Diderot, Voltaire and Condorcet in France and Young and Blackstone in England.[14] Eventually, the idea of intellectual property became decisive for the abolishment of the privilege system and for the development of authorial rights. The act of copying of works was no longer only seen as a moral offensive, as it was in the time when Luther compared the illegal printers of his bible translations to thieves and robbers in the sixteenth century, but was now seen as an infringement of the law, the legal source in question being the natural law.[15]

In order to understand these European developments in more detail, we will turn to historical accounts of the role of the 'author function' in the emergence of copyright in England, France and Germany,[16] which transforms discourses of writing into objects of appropriation and ownership (Foucault, 1979).[17] In this context, we will study several thinkers whose works have been an event in this emergence of intellectual property, and

---

[13] Eisenstein states that since 'early printers were primarily responsible for forcing definition of literary property rights, for shaping new concepts of authorship, for exploiting bestsellers and trying to tap new markets, their role in this celebrated quarrel should not be overlooked' (Eisenstein, 2005, p. 96). By providing access to more identical copies of texts, the printing technology mediated a sharper distinction between 'the fresh and original as against the repeatable and copied' (p. 58).

[14] For an account of the 'prehistory' of the development of intellectual property before these times, see Buydens, 2012.

[15] Ulmer, 1960, pp. 49–50.

[16] For an account of the emergence of copyright in the US, see Jaszi, 1991.

[17] Barthes had proclaimed that writing implies the destruction of its point of origin, which would provide a certain unity to the work, i.e. it implies 'the death of the author' (Barthes, 1977). Foucault responded to this disappearance of the subject in writing in order to analyze the space hereby left empty.

follow how they constitute these rights in intellectual works in response to the problems of illegal printing practices.[18]

Copyright in England

The concept of the modern proprietary author in England has been described as a contraction of three different developments: the fact that there was sufficient economic demand for books on the market to commercially uphold a system of continued book production; the presence of the concept of the romantic author as the originator of works; the presence of a Lockean labourer's discourse on property (Rose, 1988). The 'English struggle over copyright' took place through polemical pamphlets and some landmark legal court cases. The pamphlet writers were engaged by the struggle about the nature of copyright and literary works between upcoming provincial booksellers and London booksellers who wanted to maintain their dominant position in English book trade. The London booksellers wanted to establish that copyright was like a perpetual property right in corporeal things recognized under common-law, whereas the provincial booksellers denied this position. These tensions were eventually solved in the important court cases *Millar vs. Taylor* and *Donaldson vs. Beckett*, in which the judges acknowledged the common law right of the author to control his publication, but rejected a perpetual copyright. Within this landscape, we will follow the course of this debate and how the problems of authorial creation and illegal printing were dealt with in the *Tonson v. Collins* case in 1762, and how the author's rights on literary composition were herein constituted either as a property right on an incorporeal entity, or as a right to perform certain actions with regard to a text.

The issue at stake in *Tonson v. Collins* was the reprint by Collins of *The Spectator* by Addison and Steele, once printed by London bookseller Tonson.[19] Tonson's attorney, the famous jurist Blackstone, argues that the author of a literary work has the exclusive right to make copies of

[18] Diderot makes an interesting orienting remark about the nature of such problems: 'We must not imagine that things happen without cause, or that wise men are unique to our own age, or that the public interest was less well-known or less highly-esteemed by our predecessors than by ourselves. Seduced by systematic ideas, we attack their behaviour, and we are all the less inclined to *recognize their prudence* because the *problem which they solved by their legislation no longer affects us*' (Diderot, 1763, my accents). This provides an orientation for how to approach the writings of the thinkers mentioned above: we will look at the traits of the problems of illegal printing in different countries and how these thinkers formulated their conceptual distinctions as responses.

[19] For a more thorough exposition of this case, see Deazley, 2008.

this work. In order to institute this right he refers to the Lockean argument for justifying property rights. Locke has argued that since man has a property in his own person and thus in his bodily actions, by his bodily labour, man mixes a part of himself with things in their natural state and thereby appropriates them.[20] Blackstone extends Locke's argument to literary works: permanent property rights may be acquired both through occupancy by bodily labour as by mental labour. There is thus the 'same right of occupancy in ideas as in a field, a tree, or a stone'. He continues by introducing the following differentiation:

> A literary composition, as it lies, in the author's mind, before it is substantiated by reducing it into writing, has the essential requisites to make it the subject of property. While it is dormant in the mind, it is absolutely in the power of the proprietor. He alone is intitled to the profits of communicating, or making it public. The first to which, is cloathing our conceptions in words, the only means to communicate abstracted ideas (Court of King's Bench, 1762, *Tonson v. Collins*, 322–3).

By publication the author does not relinquish his right to make profit by his work, merely the exclusive privilege to be the only person to orally recite the work 'to the Ear'. Instead, by the acts of writing or printing that substantiate his ideas in paper and ink, the author 'has constituted a substitute in his stead, which speaks perpetually to the eyes of every reader' (p. 324). Blackstone later condenses several of these elaborate case-based arguments in the famous 'Commentaries', his systematization of English common law (Blackstone, 1897). Both copyright and patents are here categorized under the chapter 'Title to things personal by occupancy', together with property in corporeal things like goods, movables, light, air, water, animals or fruits.

Yates, Collins' attorney, to the contrary emphasizes the specific nature of this mental property that is in dispute. He compares it with the known species and principles of property and finds it lacking. First, this mental property is incapable of separate and exclusive enjoyment (the argument of non-rivalrousness) and it is not capable of possession. The books published by Collins – the 'paper and ink' – never belonged to Tonson, merely the ideas which the book communicates and these ideas, upon publication, have become in possession of everyone 'like land thrown into the Highway'. The author thus merely has property in his private 'incorporeal ideas' before publication. Furthermore, this mental property lacks the essential requisites of real property since it is neither visible nor

---

20 Locke, 2005, §27.

material, whereas it 'should be something, that may be seen, felt, given, delivered, lost or stolen' (*Tonson v. Collins*, p. 338). Yates thus obstructs Blackstone's attempts to make a literary work into a separate kind of incorporeal entity that can be occupied and possessed and could constitute the subject matter of a property right. Instead, we are here not dealing with property rights to things, but with rights to perform certain actions: to publish ideas to the public. In this sense they resemble temporary privileges like patents, since 'both are the productions of genius, both require labour and study, and both, by publication, become equally common to the world' (p. 339).

In his reply, Blackstone denies this comparison. He states that the identity of the literary work resides in its 'style and sentiment', whereas the 'paper and print' are mere accidents. 'Every duplicate therefore of a work, whether ten or ten thousand, if it conveys the same style and sentiment, is the same identical work' (p. 343). By requiring that the subject of property has to be substantial, palpable and visible, Yates has failed to distinguish between corporeal and incorporeal rights that can both be the basis of property. Later in his Commentaries, he consolidates this distinction. Interestingly, he describes incorporeal hereditaments as 'something collateral' to corporate things:

> Corporate hereditaments are the substance, while incorporeal hereditaments are but a sort of *accident*, which inhere in and are supported by such substance, and may or may not belong to it, without any visible alteration therein. Their existence is merely in idea (Blackstone, 1897, p. 174, my accents).

Although Blackstone has constituted literary works as incorporeal entities subject to property rights, he still assigns them a rather marginal status in the property spectrum in relation to corporeal substances.[21]

Droit d'Auteur in France

In France, there was a different mix of historical developments. Although there also was a great market for commercial book trade, the concept of the proprietary author arose in the period in which France politically moved from an absolute monarchy to the French Revolution (Hesse, 1990). Under the Old Regime, printing privileges had been granted to certain publishers, which also functioned as a censoring device. In the French Revolution, the system of privileges of the Old Regime was

[21] In Chapter 6, we will see how Hohfeld criticizes Blackstone's distinction, stating that all legal interests are incorporeal.

overthrown. This resulted in a wild growth of pirated and libellous publishing. Laws were passed that made it compulsory for authors to sign their texts in order to be held accountable for their contents. Limited rights of literary property were initially created for these purposes. Only later, when the issues of literary property and libel were separated, could the former be represented as promoting public enlightenment. Furthermore, this concept of literary property emerged within a discourse on property that diverged from the one in England. Although, the debate on literary property was also based on the Lockean conception of property, it capitalized upon the tension between the labourer's conception of appropriation and the Lockean proviso of the commons free for all to use.[22] These two opposite positions were taken by d'Héricourt and Diderot, who defended an eternal property right on ideas as natural creations by the individual mind, and by Condorcet, who defended a conception of a public domain of ideas discovered in nature by the senses.

These writers were also engaged with the French version of the 'battle of the booksellers' of provincial booksellers against the literary monopolies of royal printing privileges held by Parisian booksellers. At stake in this debate are the relation of privileges on literary works to property rights in land and goods on the one hand and notions of the public interest on the other. D'Héricourt, jurist and attorney of the Parisian faction, argued in a letter that the author's rights on his literary work could not be distinguished from a property right on land, houses or movables, but are 'of the same nature' and thus 'subject to the same Laws' (d'Héricourt, 1725). Both rights are justified by the Lockean argument as fruits of the (creative) labour of the author. Royal privileges did not constitute the author's right, but merely served as 'authentic authorizations' of pre-existent works. Diderot, who was asked to advocate the Parisian cause, further develops d'Héricourt's distinction between literary property and landed property in a famous passage:

> Indeed, what can a man possess, if a *product of the mind*, the unique *fruit of* his education, his study, his efforts, his time, his research, his observation; if the finest hours, the finest moments of his life; if *his own thoughts*, the feelings of his heart, the most precious part of himself, that part which does not perish, that which immortalizes him, cannot be said to belong to him? What comparison can there be between a man, the *very substance of a man, his soul*, and a *field, a meadow, a tree or a vine* which, at the beginning of time, *nature* offered equally to all men, and which the *individual claimed for himself only by cultivation*, the first legitimate means of possession? *Who has more right than the author* to use his goods by giving or selling them? (Diderot, 1763, my accents).

22 Locke, 2005, B II, Ch XXVII, §27.

Diderot uses a cultivation argument for acquiring property in land and goods and applies it to products of mental labour. This justification could be seen as an epitomization of Locke's labourer theory of property, the backbone of which was a personhood based argument. In contrast to the things of external nature ('a field, a meadow, a tree or a vine') that first have to be mixed with personhood, a literary work is the direct product of mental thoughts and ideas that make up the very substance of human personhood. Therefore, the Lockean argument applies even more forcefully to literary works.

Condorcet introduces a different position on the battle of the booksellers based on the freedom of the press. He argues that the regulation of book printing by royal privilege and preceding censorship restricted the way in which ideas and truths could freely circulate amongst the reading public and thus hampered the progress of Enlightenment:

> it is thus only for the *expressions*, for the sentences, that privileges exist. It is not for the issues, the *ideas*: it is for the words, for the *name of the author*. Hence their objective is not to preserve for an inventor the price of the useful *discoveries* he has made, but to put it up for sale at a higher price with the *agreeable appearances* which he has imagined (Condorcet, 1776, p. 311, my accents).

Ideas and truth inhere in nature and can be discovered by different people and thus do not merit legal protection by privileges.[23] Only the particular linguistic expression given to those ideas by the author can be protected. This personal expression of the author is rather negatively seen as an 'agreeable appearance' to drive up the price of the work in relation to its 'natural price' obtained in unhampered free circulation.

The eventual law passed by the legislative assembly in 1793 during the French Revolution can be seen as a compromise between the positions of Diderot and Condorcet (Hesse, 1990). On the one hand, the law recognized the inviolable rights of an individual on his creation. On the other hand, this right was temporally limited instead of eternal since in the final instance such works served to promote Enlightenment, which could only be achieved by a free circulation of ideas and knowledge.

Urheberrecht in Germany

Germany had its own mix of developmental lines that were contracted in the concept of the proprietary author: a romantic conception of the originary author (vs. craftsman or divine inspiration/gift), an unauthorized

---

[23] Hesse, 1990.

market of commercial reprinting of books, a transition from authors writing under limited patronage to writing as a separate occupation under the democratic patronage of the marketplace. This was a gradual transition, no revolution as in France, within a nation scattered over many different states that all came up with their own copyright laws. The practices of book piracy, actively supported by mercantilist economic policies of the German states, eventually spawned the 'debate over the book' in a period between 1773 and 1794 in which lawyers, publishers, poets and philosophers were all engaged. The new concept of the proprietary author emerged exactly at this interplay of the economic-legal and the esthetic-philosophical levels of discourse (Woodmansee, 1984).[24] Mercantilists emphasized that a book was not an ideal thing that could be owned by its author, but was a physical thing of ink and paper owned by its publisher. In order to ground property claims of the author on his creation, it was thus necessary to constitute the book as something immaterial. This brings us to the romantic concept of the originary genius. In the Renaissance, the figure of the author was an instable marriage between the incompatible concepts of the craftsman and of the divinely inspired. The author was here seen as a vehicle of creation, rather than as someone personally responsible for it. In the eighteenth century this divine source of inspiration became internalized in the new concept of the creative genius and the original work (Panofsky, 1968). This was to an important extent due to the reception of the ideas of Young in Germany, which answered to the need of German writers to establish ownership through copyright laws.[25] They also enabled theorists and philosophers of the genius period to effect a new conception of composition. In this context, we will treat the positions of Fichte and Schopenhauer within the debate on illegal printing and the immaterial nature of the work.

Fichte responds in an essay to the question of the legitimacy of book copying raised in a journal article by publisher Mr Reimarus. At stake is the issue of determining whether a writer has an exclusive property right to the book he wrote, which Reimarus denies. Fichte, considering

---

[24] Woodmansee does not really treat the legal aspects of the debate. According to Ulmer, the property discourse on natural law formed the background for the development of copyright or intellectual property doctrine more generally (Ulmer, 1960), perhaps with the exception of Kant, 1785 who argued authorial rights are personal rights.

[25] Rose has commented on how Young's ideas had not yet been present-at-hand in England itself when the struggle over copyright was performed, withholding the possibility of offering lines of argumentation based on his romantic conception of the creative author (Rose, 1988, pp. 61–2).

the difficulty that no similar situation exists, takes up the challenge by introducing some crucial distinctions with regard to books. First, he distinguishes between their physical (*körperliche*) aspect as printed paper and their intellectual (*geistiges*) aspect. The ownership of the printed paper is indeed transferred upon the purchase of a book. The question is whether the same applies to the intellectual aspect. To answer this question, Fichte further divides the intellectual aspect of the book

> into a *material* (*materielle*) aspect, the content of the book, the ideas it presents; and the *form* of these ideas, the way in which, the combination in which, the phrasing and wording in which they are presented (Fichte, 1793, p. 447).

These are crucial distinctions which have come to dominate much of copyright doctrine. Not only can one distinguish a physical side of the book consisting in its paper and ink, but one can also distinguish its content consisting of ideas, and its form consisting in the way these ideas are combined and presented. Whereas ownership of the physical book can be transferred by purchase, the ideas a book contains are common property due to their ideal nature and cease to be the author's exclusive property upon publication. The form of ideas however can never be appropriated because everyone has their own way of making and connecting them and it is highly improbable that two persons will follow the same course of ideas (*Ideeengang*). This remains the exclusive property of the writer.

It is interesting to also look at Schopenhauer's writings on genius and author's rights, since he provided inspiration for Kohler's theory of immaterial goods, which will be treated in the next section. In a very short piece, Schopenhauer argues that the work of ideas (*Gedankenwerk*) is, if anything, the property of the author, which is to be protected by law. Since this property is not physical, but intellectual or immaterial, it cannot be treated according to the rules that apply to physical property. The author must be free to communicate his work, without seeing his property rights endangered. Since this communication can only happen through material means which expose his property to theft, this has to be prevented by laws with a special character. Their object in this singular case is an intangible property which remains the same throughout the material media of communication, which they enter merely '*per accidens*' (Schopenhauer, 1864). This view of the work as an immaterial object has to be understood in the light of Schopenhauer's philosophical writings on art and genius. In his vision, art, being the work of genius, repeats the eternal Platonic Ideas as the original unchanging forms. Through the process of contemplation that is essentially perceptive, non-conscious and organic, the genius retains the

Ideas and repeats them in an original work.[26] The being of the work of art thus consists in the repetition of eternal ideas, which themselves remains unchanged in this process. These works, as individual things, relate to an Idea 'as an archetype to its copies' (Schopenhauer, 1954, Book III).

In the course of a century, the issue of the legality of book printing had spawned ongoing debates about the nature and legal protection of literary works, in which they gradually became constituted as full-fledged substantial incorporeal entities with their own legal regime of protection. In Blackstone, literary works as incorporeal entities became the subject of property rights, but were still deemed collateral accidents to corporeal substance that formed the basis of the property regime. Through the arguments of d'Héricourt and Diderot the rights of the author on his work become subsequently levelled in importance with regard to corporeal property rights and even exceeded the latter. In Schopenhauer, this reversal becomes complete: the incorporeal work of ideas becomes the substance, whereas the material medium of communication has become a mere accident.

Patents

The discourse on intellectual property mainly developed in the context of the emergence of copyright. Patents and trademarks had different independent paths of historical development. In order to understand why these legal regimes were later also considered intellectual property, we need to focus on those aspects that make this inclusion intelligible. The transition from privileges on machines to patents on inventions was a complex phenomenon that involved the demise of political absolutism, development of liberal economies and the emergence of the modern political subject. To this historical mix of lines of development we can add the important role of textual patent requirements (Biagioli, 2006) and scale models of inventions (Pottage & Sherman, 2010) in mediating the crucial distinction between immaterial inventive idea and its embodiment in the material artifact.

The modern conception of patent law emerged in the course of the eighteenth century and resulted in the passing of the first patent laws in France, England and the US. There was a shift from the old system of privileges

---

[26] This view of genius echoes Edward Young's conjectures about the nature of originality more than a century before, who stated that an 'original may be said to be of a vegetable nature; it rises spontaneously from the vital roots of genius; it grows, it is not made' (Young, 1918, p. 7).

granted by the sovereign, to patents as a kind of contractual right between the individual inventor and the public. Under the privilege system the machine that was the object of legal protection was an actual device situated at a specific location. The privilege contained some brief working requirements for the factual and technical examination of this machine. In the new patent rights system however, the patent document needed to contain extensive textual and pictorial specifications that no longer served for the examination but for the construction of the invention.[27] The invention hereby became conceived as a publication, i.e. a tool for the disclosure of new knowledge so that the (skilled) public could study and repeat it. The object of legal protection was hereby transformed from an actual spatiotemporal material machine into an immaterial invention as a possible machine.

> [These specification requirements] created the conditions of possibility for treating the actual material invention (the entity that used to be protected by early modern privileges) as separate from its 'idea' (the entity that would become protected by patent law). It was a paper item – the specification – that eventually put the 'intellectual' into 'intellectual property'. Allowing for the emergence of the idea as a distinct entity, specifications made possible for that idea to become the immaterial essence of the invention. This in turn recast the material invention (which previously had been the sole instantiation of the invention) as just one of the possible (and therefore inessential) embodiments of such an idea (Biagioli, 2006, p. 1143).

The immaterial idea and material embodiment of the invention thus become first constituted through the mediating role of legal specification requirements and the resulting descriptions and depictions in the patent document. In later developments, this immaterial essence of the machine becomes formulated as its 'principle' that could become embodied in several possible material machines.[28] This notion served to distinguish the invention from abstract ideas in the philosophical sense, from principles discovered in nature in the scientific sense, and from concrete manufactured machines in the sense of engineering.[29] The necessity to work out this principle eventually led to a need for lawyers to visually observe the material machines or their scale models in order to extract their immaterial 'mode of operation'.[30]

---

[27] These specification requirements are first introduced in the United States Patent Act of 1790 and the French Patent Law of 1791.

[28] The notion of the principle of the machine is first introduced in the United States Patent Act of 1793.

[29] Biagioli, 2006, p. 1143.

[30] Scale models of the invention have played a crucial mediating role similar to that of textual specification requirements. During patent disputes in court

The shift towards the patent regime had further effects: it also transformed the figure of the inventor itself. Throughout the privilege regime the ideas which an inventor may have had about his invention were considered irrelevant for granting legal protection to machines, whereas in the patent regime these ideas become the essence of his invention. The inventor is hereby displaced away from the figures of the importer and the engineer who produce a material artifact or machine, towards the figures of the author and the genius who create an idea and its specifications. This transformation can be compared to the transition between printing privileges and copyright, with the difference that literary works had existed in textual form before the enactment of copyright laws, whereas inventions attained their textual form precisely due to the enactment of the patent laws and their specification requirements.

Trademarks

Trademark law is another legal regime that is classified as intellectual property. As a separate legal regime, trademark law historically developed considerably later than patent and copyright law and in more explicit relation to these other regimes. Whereas the use of marks of trade is usually dated all the way back to biblical times, the emergence of the modern regime of trademark law conceptualized as property rights took shape in the nineteenth century in Europe and the USA. These developments occurred in a period in which processes of industrialization were well underway and in which there was a slowly growing use and recognition of marks in practices of trade. More and more marks were put on products in order for the consuming public to unambiguously identify their producers and to distinguish them from both generic goods and the products of other producers. These developments fuelled an increased demand for the legal protection of trademarks as a separate legal regime. This led to a discussion on the nature of the legal trademark[31] and several countries passed their first trademark laws,[32] installed systems of registration and engaged in international treaties. Of special interest here are the relations with the regimes of copyright and patents throughout these discussions in Great Britain and the USA, in which there were pressures from different sides to include trademark within the framework of intellectual property.

---

or the examination at the patent office, they enabled the extraction of the principle out of a material machine as its immaterial essence (Pottage & Sherman, 2010).

[31] Bently, 2008.

[32] France in 1857, Great Britain in 1862, USA in 1870 and Germany in 1875.

Patents and copyrights also provided an important point of comparison in the process of formulating and interpreting trademark rights and, in the lack of any trademark-specific legislation, these regimes also provided the legal basis for pursuing court cases.[33]

Some commentators would however come to argue that there are important differences between these legal regimes, since trademarks had little to do with creation. The US lawyer Upton stated that:

> The exclusive right of multiplying copies of original productions of the mind, whether in the form of books, maps, engravings, designs or other of the manifold emanations of human thought, expressed by words or symbols—bears no appreciable resemblance to a right of property in a mere name, figure, letter, mark, device or symbol—when used as a designation of a thing (Upton, 1860, p. 14).

There is no similarity between these regimes since copyrights deal with 'original productions of the mind' that did not exist before and the right granted is 'a property in the thing itself'. Trademarks on the other hand are merely words or images which were already in existence in common public use and are re-appropriated as 'a means of designating things'. These signs are thus not protected in themselves but in so far as they designate something else: a certain trade product. Upton states that a trademark 'has no existence apart from the thing designated'. Furthermore, it was also argued that trademarks had more to do with laws of forgery, fraud and unfair competition than with the protection of intellectual property. In this context it is interesting to see that Upton did speak about 'this peculiar character of property' in the well-earned reputation of trademarks.

This focus on reputation already indicates a later transition in trademark law and the function of trademarks as a 'salesman',[34] which would occur with the increase in importance of advertising.[35] In an important article Schechter argued that the injury to trademark infringements does not necessarily consist in the creation of confusion for consumers that diverts trade to another producer. Instead, the real injury

> is the gradual whittling away or dispersion of the identity and hold upon the public mind of the mark or name by its use upon non-competing goods. The

---

[33] Sherman & Bently, 1999, pp. 168–72.

[34] Schechter, 1927, p. 815.

[35] Drescher calls this the change from the trademark as a sign that identifies and distinguishes its producer as the origin of a product, to the trademark as a symbol as 'a device to express the intangible values and attributes of a product' (Drescher, 1992, p. 339).

> more distinctive or unique the mark, the deeper its impress upon the public consciousness and the greater its need for protection against vitiation and dissociation from the particular product in connection with which it has been used (Schechter, 1927, p. 825).

The immaterial character of the trademark is here thus not located in the mind of its creator (like in copyright and patent law) but displaced and installed in the mind of the public. Schechter even speaks of the 'psychological hold on the public' which no longer depends only on the quality of the products but on the uniqueness of the mark and the advertising efforts of the trademark holder. He also introduces an element of creativity in trademark law. By the continued use of and investment in the trademark, the trader gains a favourable impression in the public's mind. Just as an author creates a work, a trader creates goodwill or reputation. Furthermore, a mark will only have a unique identity when it is original to the extent that its wording has been 'added to rather than withdrawn from the human vocabulary' (p. 829).[36] On this conception a trademark is no longer devoid of a separate existence as Upton still maintained, but has become 'an agency for the actual creation and perpetuation of good will' (Schechter, 1927, p. 818).

A Note on Legal Approaches

Copyright laws emerged as a convergence of different historical developments: the dispersion of the invented printing press throughout European countries, the proliferation of copies on an economic market of growing literates, the systems of printing privileges of the old legal regimes, natural law theories on property, the romantic philosophies of authorship and political events like the French Revolution. The figure of the author hereby came to serve as a proprietor of a special kind of commodity: his work. The distinction between immaterial form and material embodiment played a comparable role. This *immaterialization function* is a vector of appropriation for literary creation or technological invention, both of which necessarily always occur outside of the law. It serves to internalize these creative movements and make them legally manageable by abstracting an immaterial identity and retroactively grounding this as a legally protected work or invention. The law can hereby come to govern localizable material entities now qualified as material embodiments or reproductions of an immaterial template.

---

[36] For a critical discussion of these arguments, see Bently & Sherman, 2009, pp. 717–18).

Before we conclude this section, a short note on theoretical or methodological positioning is warranted, in order to understand the approaches pursued in explaining intellectual property concepts. Rose, Woodmansee, Hesse and Jaszi work out a certain historical nexus in which the figure of the author arose and attained a function of appropriation. Law was an instrumental strand in this contraction.[37] Rose is the most engaged with this role of law by focusing on the legal debates on authorship and literary property in English courts in the eighteenth century. He gives account of the intra-legal arguments about 'the great cause concerning literary property' by which the new figure of the author arose. Woodmansee is concerned with Foucault's author function and the development of the concept of the author in the eighteenth century. Law here forms but a few footnotes in a complex web of philosophical, political, economic and esthetic strands. Hesse is much interested in 'the relationship between authorship and the law', this relation is however discussed in terms of extra-legal causalities. She states that the political event of the French Revolution 'reshaped the legal and political identity of the author' and that the concept of the author as proprietor arose 'as a result of the commercialization of the book trade' (Hesse, 1990, pp. 109–10). This kind of theoretical positioning comes out most explicitly in Jaszi. He is interested in how the notion of authorship influenced the law in the USA and tries 'to show how copyright received a constructed idea of "authorship" from literary and artistic culture' and how 'this "authorship construct" has been mobilized in legal discourse'. Jaszi performs an analysis from an 'external perspective' that takes its bearings from deconstructivism and post-structuralism in literary theory, in trying to reveal the concealed interests in the discussions on intellectual property. On this account, authorship is nothing but a 'culturally, politically, economically, and socially constructed category' with a set of values that derive from Romanticism (Jaszi, 1991, pp. 455–9).

There is an important difference on this point with the approaches by Biagioli and Pottage & Sherman to the history of patent law. Whereas for the former the distinction between material and immaterial used in the law was (externally) imported from Romanticist philosophy, for the latter it is the product of an 'internal logic' of legal regimes and the mediating role of certain items and techniques like textual patent specifications and models of inventions.[38] The strands of politics, economics and philosophy

---

[37] The different roles these authors assign to law might also relate to the differences between Anglo-Saxon common law and Continental civil law systems.

[38] Something similar pertains to Bently & Sherman who argue that the historical legal changes in trademark law should not be conflated with the historical socio-commercial practices of applying marks to goods (Bently & Sherman, 2009,

do enter the picture here, but in a different, less determinative way. In our empirical analysis of intellectual property in technological inventions in the next chapters, we will focus on these mediating items for constituting patents as ideal templates that become distinguished from their material reproductions.[39]

1.4 LEGAL DOCTRINE: FROM IMMATERIAL GOODS TO INFORMATION GOODS

In this section we will discuss the further developments of the incorporeal things that are the subject 'matter' of copyright and patent laws, by treating some of the seminal works in legal doctrine on the theory of immaterial goods. This theory is both a continuation and a critique of the theory of intellectual property. We will start with Josef Kohler's initial framing of *Immaterialgüterrecht.* We will study how the theory consolidated in later doctrinal texts in which the immaterialization function achieved its most explicit formulation (Troller) and in which there eventually is a shift from immaterial goods to informational goods (Hugenholtz). The focus will be on the idea/expression or content/form distinctions and the corporeal/incorporeal, tangible/intangible or material/immaterial distinctions.

The Staging of Immaterial Goods

Kohler developed his legal theory of immaterial goods in order to overcome some of the problems of the theory of intellectual property (Kohler, 1894). He argues that the term 'property' is limited to corporeal things, either movable things like commodities or unmovable things like parcels of ground, and cannot be easily transferred to incorporeal goods. In contrast to corporeal goods with their fixed borders, the scope of an original idea is not easily demarcated, which makes a different legal treatment necessary. The good created by the author (*Autorsgut*) has to be distinguished from the ideas that are already available and from productions without original character. But wherein resides the distinctive criterion of the quality of this *Autorsgut*, this object of the author's rights? Kohler responds to this question on a

p. 711). They accuse Schechter (1927) and Drescher (1992) of committing such a conflation.

[39] In this context, it is interesting that Pottage and Sherman speak about the 'limitations of a speculative historical enquiry' for understanding the role of things in the overall historical ensemble of developments. They instead advocate an ethnographical method. Here a turn to legal practice becomes relevant.

meta-level of doctrinal creativity, by extracting four legal stages of authorial creation from different art forms and places them in a hierarchy. Each implies a different relation between author and idea and increasingly grasps the essence of authorial quality (Kohler, 1880, pp. 166–77).

The first stage concerns the oral representation of ideas (*Ideeendarstellung*) externalized in language or another means of communication. The bound, measured way in which thoughts are shaped and expressed in a lecture can here be distinguished from the unbound, loose usage of everyday speech. The artistic quality of a work however, does not merely reside in linguistic form, but also has an inner form of shaping ideas (*Ideeenbildung*), which forms the second stage of authorial quality.

> The most essential form is the *inner form*: the way the author approaches his ideas, how he *groups* them as main- and side-*figures* and *stages* them. It is the *coloring* under which the ideas stand out, like the figures in a painting, sometimes in clear contours, sometimes in the chiaroscuro of the more stimulating and suggestive, as executive and demarcating styles, sometimes in flash, sometimes in gentle *lighting*, with more or less clarity and perspective, with bigger or smaller distinction of the essential from the inessential background: this is the secret of every author, this is the atmosphere of his shaping of ideas [*Ideeenbildung*] [. . .] This form is not the inner form of language, but the *form of the sequence of ideas, the grouping of ideas and the movement of ideas*, the peculiar nature of the *association, connection, and rejection of ideas*, about the individual particularity of the *mental mechanics* in general (Kohler, 1880, p. 168, my accents).

The relation between author, creation and ideas is here transposed from oral speech in which the author represents an idea on the external plane of language in the clear and bounded form of its grammatical rules and vocabulary, to the plane of composition on which the author 'approaches' his ideas by their figural staging, lighting and colouring. The author function of creation has here changed from the art of oration to the arts of painting and theatre direction, and the relation between author and idea has changed from linguistic expression of ideas to their internalization as acting figures within a composition. Different artistic techniques are employed for these purposes. The author situates his ideas in relation to other ideas as main actors or side-figures, places them against a certain background and in a certain light, so that the idea is made to stand out. Ideas here attain the form of figures. Kohler calls the results of these 'mental mechanics' of artistic creation, the 'atmosphere of shaping ideas'.[40] Through the author's compositional activities of association, connection

---

[40] This concept is similar to what Benjamin calls the 'aura' or 'atmosphere' of the work (Benjamin, 2008).

or rejection of ideas, these ideas will form certain sequences and groupings and even dynamic developments, which constitute the artistic form of the work; its inner form.

The creations of poetic fantasy are located on a higher, third stage of authorial quality. Authentic creation does here not consist in the formation of external materials like the facts that scientists are often forced to treat in their works, but this material itself is the free creation of poetic fantasy. Great writers like Turgenjev, Homer and Shakespeare have created new images of life that undergo all kinds of psychic development. Not only the inner and external forms of the work, but also its individual content of ideas (*Ideeeninhalt*) are thus the object of authorial rights. Kohler calls this the imaginary image (*imaginären Bild*), which is the individual inner core of the work of art. This core lies behind the veils of speech and remains constant throughout the many changes in its subsequent adaptations and translations. Finally, the highest, fourth stage of authorial quality is musical. Kohler follows Schopenhauer in stating that where the other arts get their idea-elements (*Ideeenelemente*) from empirical perception of the objects of experience, music gets its ideas from the immediate intuition of a higher realm of existence beyond sensation.[41]

Kohler concludes that the rights of the author are not his *intellectual property*. It is a property-like right on an immaterial good: the imaginary idea-image, just like a patent right, is an *immaterial good right* (*Immaterialgüterrecht*) on inventive ideas.[42] This link to patent law is not coincidental, since Kohler first formulated his theory on immaterial goods in his writings on patent law and later transferred it to copyright. In this theory, there is a distinction between the material thing (the book or machine) that is the object of property and the immaterial good that is the object of copyright and patent law.

The Axiology and Power of Immaterial Goods

The intellectualization of the legal object in Kohler's theory of immaterial goods has formed the basis for much of (Germanic) legal doctrine. The theory has found its full extrapolation in the voluminous

---

41 Schopenhauer elevated music to the highest form of art as 'a copy of the will itself', whereas all the other arts are copies of certain (Platonic) Ideas (Schopenhauer, 1954, p. 257).

42 Ulmer calls Kohler's theory of immaterial goods incomplete, since a work does not only have a relation of economic utility with its author, but also has an ideal tie with the author as its brainchild. It thus has a relation of paternity (Ulmer, 1960).

Immaterialgüterrecht (Troller, 1983) by Troller and its condensation in his *Kurzlehrbuch des Immaterialgüterrechts* (Troller, 1978). We will study these doctrinal developments and touch upon the approach to legal phenomena they imply.[43] Troller starts his 'general dogmatic considerations' with the position that the fixed points of legal order are legal subjects and legal objects, and that the legal game of rights and claims moves between the two. Within this traditional dogmatic framework however, immaterial goods behave with a certain resistance to being classified as legal objects and force the legal scholar to think about things unfamiliar to legal theory. The legal objects of immaterial goods are different from other legal objects due to their common character as intellectual things. Law has always recognized corporeal things as legal objects, for instance of property law. Incorporeal things however have never been protected to the same extent. One of the main tasks of *Immaterialgüterrecht* therefore is to determine whether technical and artistic achievements and distinctive signs can attain protection as a legal object according to general categories.

These preliminary remarks have already sketched a whole image of law and have paved the doctrinal path for the analysis of intellectual rights. According to Troller the legal continuum can be ordered according to an axis between the two extremes of legal subjectivity and legal objectivity. On the basis of this axis the whole dynamics of disputes, claims and rights can be assigned its legal co-ordinates, giving rise to the order of law.[44] Within this order, the task of legal doctrine is to classify such claims and rights according to their object and subject. Troller is aware however, of a certain resistance of the objects of intellectual rights against such classification. Instead of taking this resistance as a theme for concrete investigation however, he makes it into a common trait of all these objects – their intellectual nature – in order to determine this nature after general categories.

Troller first compares immaterial goods to the *res incorporales* of Roman law in order to demonstrate the clear and distinct intellectual nature of the former. *Res incorporales* are rights or collectives of things that have corporeal things as their immediate substrate, or things equivalent to money or certain achievements. These things (*res*) only acquired 'incorporeal' quality through techniques of legal abstraction. All the

---

43 Whereas Kohler's writings are characterized by a certain fluidity of writing with creative excursions, Troller wants to institute immaterial goods as a doctrinal legal system.

44 With Deleuze and Guattari we can call this an arborescent schema of law in which all the movements of legal practice are subjected to a line drawn between two pre-fixed points, instead of passing in the middle between such points (Deleuze & Guattari, 1987, pp. 292–6).

goods designated by the term '*res incorporales*' are submitted to the laws of the corporeal world and are thus limited in time and space. On the contrary, the term 'immaterial good' refers to things of an intellectual nature like artistic works, technical rules, models or distinctive signs, and neither represent corporeal things on a conceptual level nor through legal techniques. These categories of immaterial goods have in common their independence in relation to space and time.[45]

The establishment of the intellectual nature of immaterial goods has important consequences. According to Troller, their independence from corporeal fixation assures these goods a 'particular power' and provides them with a potential ubiquity. An invention can serve in all countries as a rule for the unlimited fabrication of merchandise or execution of activities. A literary, musical or artistic work can be represented in different places in the world at the same moment. The use of a distinctive sign of an enterprise reinforces its capacity as authoritative referent. All immaterial goods can quantitatively be indefinitely repeated in space and time and 'can be communicated without losing in substance and quality, no matter where, when or how often one submits them to the aid of sensorial perceptible signs' (Troller, 1978, p. 34). The corporeal thing is a mere medium for the transmission of the self-identical immaterial good that itself remains unaffected by this process. We could call this the strong position on immateriality, which also presupposes particular theories of communication and representation.

After having established their common intellectual nature, Troller can enter into the particularities of the different kinds of immaterial objects. He observes that not all kinds of immaterial goods (scientific discoveries) merit legal protection and that it is therefore necessary to understand each of these subcategories precisely. Discoveries, technical works and esthetic works all constitute immaterial goods, but have to be clearly distinguished. The particularity of each of these objects resides in their material fundaments and legal nature. Troller notes that there is a 'difficulty' here relating to the fact that legally protectable immaterial goods do not correspond to corporeal objects or even to purely intellectual objects in an extra-legal sense. The concepts for these immaterial objects are not taken from the domains of technique or art, but are established by law itself. Whereas in many legal fields the legal definition of concepts is sufficient to

45 It does not become clear how these immaterial goods acquired independence from corporeality and how *res incorporales* did not. This is unfortunate since the distinction is crucial for the success of the theory of immaterial goods. We will see that such a comparison might backfire by making the immateriality of these goods also dependent on legal techniques dealing with spatiotemporal matters.

determine the relevant legal aspects of things without recourse to experts, this is not the case in the law of immaterial goods. Here, the lawyer is often not able to determine the essential attributes through legal method, but has to address experts in the profession in question, like technicians in the case of patents. Thus, 'it is indispensable that lawyers, within the law of intellectual property, possess the faculty to understand the techniques, commercial acts or the characteristics of esthetical creations. Only the one who satisfies this qualification can find access to the material fundaments' (Troller, 1978, p. 59) of these immaterial goods.

Troller again runs into a 'difficulty' when working out the commonality between all immaterial goods, which is related precisely to the fact that here we are situated on the plane of law with its specific legal exigencies in dealing with the specific materialities of conflicts. On this plane we will not find immaterial goods, but just 'works', 'inventions', 'trademarks' which are *legal concepts.* When immaterial goods are first made totally independent from everything including law and material fundaments, but are then installed as legal concepts, one will indeed confront an insurmountable problem of correspondence between these concepts and supposed extra-legal things. Experts would then indeed be called for to bridge this gap of correspondence from the outside. In the end, it is indeed indispensable for lawyers to acquire an understanding of the 'domains' under their consideration. The 'difficulty' thus lies elsewhere in the theoretical pre-positions. Troller's foundational moves start from commonality between these domains: the postulated shortcut to the existence of immaterial goods and their common character as intellectual things fixed between the two juri-axiomatic points of legal subjectivity and legal objectivity. In this way one presupposes what would still have to be investigated and established when one sets out to constitute the theory of immaterial goods. The ones who should actually acquire a sense for the concrete materiality and legality are the legal theorists not the legal practitioners! Only in this way can the legal theorist have access to the material fundaments of these immaterial goods.

The Work as Information Good

The theoretical developments of immaterial goods can be pursued a step further into the domain of the information society, with regard to the relation between intellectual rights and information. In his dissertation Hugenholtz, confronted with the ubiquity of information[46] and its

---

[46] He even states 'our life depends on information. Information determines our actions and our total existence' (Hugenholtz, 2005, p. 1).

economic value, sets out to determine whether factual information can be protected by copyright, 'since information is preeminently a copyable immaterial product' (Hugenholtz, 2005, p. 4). Considering that the term information has a range of different meanings, Hugenholtz proposes to interpret it in its classical semiotic sense as a message that is communicated through a physical medium and increases knowledge in the receiver. Information is hereby fixed under the threefold structure of syntax, semantics and pragmatics as: formal arrangement, meaningful content and practical effect.

Hugenholtz argues that works can also be interpreted in this way and that from this perspective it has several elements of form: a transmission form determined by the type of communication; a syntactical form as a specific configuration of signs (letters, words, symbols); a semantic form as the reference of the work to its content; and a pragmatic form that determined how the work is appreciated by the receiver. He proposes to replace the duality between content and form of classical copyright theories (like Kohler's) by the semiotic threefold of sign, reference and referent. This distinction can hereby be reconceptualized as a difference between information and data developed in (semiotic) information theory. Copyright thus does not protect data or facts but only information and this leads Hugenholtz to assert that 'each work has the character of information' (Hugenholtz, 2005, p. 60). Both work and information are immaterial objects. The immaterial good that Kohler and Troller referred to actually *is* information and we should henceforth better speak of *information goods*.

***

This section focused on the grounding of immateriality or intellectuality in the development of the theory of immaterial goods. Different disciplines, models and figures were resorted to in order to constitute and work out the immateriality of intellectual goods. We have seen the first figural staging of these immaterial goods by Kohler in a correction of the theory of intellectual property. He developed the qualitative forms of authorial creations by passing through models from the arts: speech for the work's outer form; painting and theatre for the work's inner form; poetry for the imaginary image of the work; music for the creative intellectual intuition. These different forms of artistic creation were then subjected to a hierarchy based on gradients along the sensation-intellection axis, the so-called stages of authorial quality. Furthermore, Kohler grounds the central distinction between the material representation and immaterial being of the work on (Schopenhauer's) philosophical theories.

These figures of authorial creation, which were still dynamically staged in the writings of Kohler, became condensed into static forms of doctrinal statement in the legal theory of Troller. Immaterial goods were assigned their location on the axis of legal order through a range of doctrinal pre-positions, suppositions and positions. The common trait between the different subcategories of immaterial goods – works, inventions and trademarks – was their intellectual nature. Immaterial goods acquired an independence from spatiotemporal corporeal things and gained a force of proliferation through representation and communication.

In Hugenholtz the intellectual work of copyright becomes itself transformed into information within the exercise of determining the relation between copyright and information. The immaterial good turns out to be an information good. This change was achieved through the semiotic concepts of the communication of information in which information is taken as a structured sign (or a message) which is communicated through a physical medium, has a signification for a receiver within a certain context and refers to a signified in the non-communicable outside world. Under the threefold aegis of syntax, semantics and pragmatics, the distinction between content and the different forms of the work of copyright theory is transformed into the distinction between the facts and information of information theory.

2. Interlude ~ turning to legal practice: outlines of a transversal approach

For a philosopher many of the discussions about the foundational concepts of intellectual property or immaterial goods might seem somewhat surprising. Within contemporary philosophy concepts like 'author' and 'originality' and distinctions between nature-human, body-mind and material-immaterial have all been severely criticized, deconstructed and rejected. Nevertheless, they still give guidance to the law in an unfazed way. It is no wonder therefore, that such criticisms have been extended to legal practices. Although very interesting and revealing, they only tell us a part of the story, since they usually stop short at the point where such concepts are introduced into the law. Critics account for this introduction in terms of forces that are outside of law itself, which is supposed to be a sufficient explanation. We could deconstruct the concept of an idea, but have we thereby also deconstructed ideas '*in the sense of patent law or intellectual property law*'? From a legal perspective, something important is missing here: these accounts lack a dimension of legal specificity.[1] From the moment these concepts have become instituted in law, they have undergone an important transformation. As *legal concepts* they respond to very different conditions and forces.[2] Also, legal concepts have very different ways of working within the practice of law when compared to their use in everyday life or in other professional practices. To understand the *modi operandi* of these concepts one has to take a closer look at these specific workings. This requires a turn away from legal theory to legal practices and a study of intellectual rights in action.

This is not as easy to accomplish as it may sound. We first need to inquire what such a turn requires: why and from what it wants to move away (theoretical axiologies), what it wants to move towards (practices),

[1] At most, they can provide insight into the nature of *legislative* concepts, which do not necessarily coincide with *legal* concepts (Gutwirth, De Hert & De Sutter, 2008).

[2] This 'force of law' or these 'legal conditions' are very different from the social, economic, political or materialistic forces and conditions claimed to govern legal processes.

how this is done (practice theory vs. practice approach) and what to look out for when making the turn (hesitations, non-humans, networks of distributed cognition). This chapter will explore the possibility of a transversal approach to legal practices and in this sense provides a first response to the question how to philosophically approach legal phenomena. The outline sketched will provide an orienting guide for the empirical studies of legal practices of intellectual rights (Chapters 3 and 4) and will provide important ingredients for a confrontation with the way legal theory has approached law and legal practice (Chapter 6).

We will first treat Wittgenstein's philosophical investigations of mental phenomena (2.1) where many of the lines of this book come together. Wittgenstein criticized the classical philosophies of mind on which legal theories of intellectual property and immaterial goods were based. In his approach there is a convergence between the way intellectuality is constituted in practice and the philosophical approach to phenomena through his empirical language-game method. We will subsequently discuss the practice turn in contemporary theory in which these investigations have been worked out in a research programme (2.2). An important methodological difference is made between practice theories and practice approaches to networks of distributed cognition in which hesitations and non-humans play an important role.

2.1 PRACTICAL TECHNIQUES OF MENTAL TALK

Wittgenstein was an important thinker in the 'turn to practices' and the move away from the philosophical theories on which the legal theories of intellectual property and immaterial goods were grounded. At stake in his writings are many philosophical topics like the conception of the mind and the mental, the status of intellectual objects and their relation to material bodies. His approach is not theoretical but is rather steeped in a way of thinking that is deeply practice-oriented. Instead of providing a classical philosophical account, with thoughts that proceed in a well-ordered linear sequence from theme to theme, the practical nature of the objects (*Gegenstande*) of his investigation forced him 'to travel criss-cross in all directions through a wide field of thought' and thus provide 'a number of sketches of landscapes which were made on these long and meandering journeys' (Wittgenstein, 2009, p. 3e). The philosopher is here presented as a thinking traveller on a journey in transit, who moves through a field with dispersed problematic points, and whose rough travel sketches rather resemble a philosophical 'album'. Since later commentators (like Schatzki) have cast his thinking into a more solid theoretical form, it is worthwhile to be thoughtful of these dynamics in the treatment of these themes.

The 'nature of the investigation' can best be understood as a criticism of the philosophical tendency to approach things with the *a priori* demand that all their manifestations necessarily must have something in common which is their essence. In this approach philosophy is caught by a certain 'image of thought'. It is thereby led to a very one-sided view of the phenomena investigated and many other aspects remain obscured. Wittgenstein's methodology is aimed at de-idealizing this use of language and images in favour of empirical investigation. Instead of looking at a general rational form that we claim *must* be the same for all phenomena, he invites us to actually look (*schau!*) at the many different everyday practices in which we engage with these phenomena and use language about them (§65–6). We have to 'look at particularities of events, to *consider* what is happening *from close by*' (§51). This is an essential ingredient in the philosophical turn to practices.

One of the main phenomena to which Wittgenstein devoted such investigations is of particular interest here: the status of intellectual or mental objects and their relation to empirically observable bodies. He reacts against the classical view that takes the mental as a kind of privileged site of special abstract, non-spatiotemporal ideas or images, which would determine the meaning of our linguistic behaviour and the objects we use. This mentalist image of thought has captivated much of philosophical thinking.[3] As a cure, he conjures up a plurality of different images of thought in much more concrete practices of 'mental talk' like in contexts of logic, experimental psychology, painting, playing chess and education. For Wittgenstein our bodily and linguistic behaviour is not a representation of previous mental ideas or images, but is itself a constitutive trait for what we call 'ideas', 'intentions', 'mental states' or 'the mental' within the context of these practices:

> But didn't I already *intend* the whole *general form* of the sentence (for example) at its beginning? So surely it already existed in my mind before I uttered it out loud! If it was *in my mind*, still it would not normally be there in some different word order. But here again, we are forming a *misleading image* of 'intending': that is, of the use of this word. An *intention* is *embedded* in a *setting*, in human customs and *institutions*. If the *technique* of the game of chess did not exist, I *could not intend* to play a game of chess (Wittgenstein, 2009, §337, my accents).

---

[3] Rorty crucially relied on Wittgenstein in asserting that '[t]he picture which holds traditional philosophy captive is that of the mind as a great mirror, containing various representations' (Rorty, 1980, p. 12).

An intention is not a private inner object that pre-exists in the mental realm and determines the meaning of things. Instead, such mental phenomena are constituted within concrete practices like the playing of chess, with its specific figures and board, the techniques for using these figures and the rule of the game. Different practices all have their separate techniques for the activities that are carried out within them and for the ways mental phenomena are constituted. We could even say that these techniques constitute the very being of mental operations.[4] It is thus within such a distributed setting that having certain intentions becomes possible at all. Wittgenstein thus directs the attention away from the deeply misleading mentalist image of language and action and towards practical settings and their techniques and elements: images, figures, apparatuses, people, human bodies, objects, words and concepts. He hereby also contributes to a new conception of the status of mental phenomena. The distinctions between tangible and intangible or material and immaterial are constituted within the enactment of these techniques in diverse practices.

From this perspective, Kohler's foundational distinction between the imaginary image, the inner form as the composition of ideas and the outer form as linguistic expression has become displaced close to the point of a full reversal. Bodies, objects and linguistic expressions are not the mere external representations or tangible copies of an intangible composition of mental elements or an imagined mental image. Instead they constitute these mental forms within the context of concrete practices with distinct techniques. 'The concept of an "inner picture" is misleading, since the model for this concept is the "outer picture"'.[5] The so-called material models that are supposed to be the copies, are instead the grounds for the imaginary image that is considered the immaterial essence of the artistic work.

2.2 PRACTICE THEORY AND NETWORKS OF DISTRIBUTED COGNITION

> As anthropologists have tirelessly shown, actors incessantly engage in the most abstruse metaphysical constructions by redefining all the elements in the world. Only a researcher trained in the conceptual calisthenics offered by the philosophical tradition could be quick, strong, daring and pliable enough to painstakingly register what they have to say (Latour, 2005, p. 51).

---

4 Wittgenstein, 2009, II. xi.
5 Wittgenstein, 2009, II. xi.

We have treated Wittgenstein's investigations of mental phenomena and his focus on the constitutive role of techniques within practices. Now the important question is in which ways these practices, especially legal practices, are to be approached, which is not a *straightforward* matter. How could the researcher get closer to them in a way that discloses what law requires? How do we address law in the nearness of its peculiarities? Where do we begin? Some authors have taken Wittgenstein's dispersed thought travels on practices and the mental, and first worked them out into philosophical positions (Schatzki, 1996) and later taken them as an ancestral component for a full-fledged programme coined 'the practice turn' (Schatzki, Knorr Cetina & von Savigny, 2001). Practice theorists concur in the view that many phenomena like knowledge, meaning, action, the mental and language are not determined by the macro level of abstract structures or systems.[6] There are no hidden structures that will explain things, just a social theory of the visible. Neither can things be explained by resorting to the micro level of the individual and his or her intentions.[7] There are also no hidden mental states that can be invoked for explanation. Practices are not reducible to these two levels, but are rather situated on a 'meso' level that, from the perspective of the other two, is situated 'in between'. Phenomena are here conceived as components of the practices in which they take place.

One could have both a certain sympathy and a hesitation towards this project. A lot depends on the ways in which we 'turn' to these practices.[8] This point can best be brought out by having a look at the programme's mission statement: 'The "practice approach" can thus be demarcated as all analyses that 1) develop an account of practices, either the field of practices or some sub domain thereof (e.g. science), or 2) treat the field of practices as the place to study the nature and transformation of their subject matter' (Schatzki et al., 2001, p. 2). There are thus two distinct turns at stake here, which are not that easily thrown together under one banner. The first is called 'practice theory' and aims at developing a 'general and abstract account' of practices. There is something deeply problematical about this juxtaposition of the contradictory terms 'practice' and 'theory' going back to the Greek opposition between *praxis* and *theoria* or between prudence (*phronesis*) as a concernful action

---

[6] Hereby going against structuralist sociology (Durkheim) or systems theory sociology (Luhmann).

[7] Hereby going against interpretative hermeneutics and *verstehende* sociology (like Schleiermacher, Dilthey and Weber's methodological individualism).

[8] Stengers remarks that in this turn, the direction that is to be abandoned is much clearer than the direction that is to be taken (Stengers, 2006).

(*praxis*) with and among things (*pragmata*), and knowledge (*ephistemi*) as making objects present by giving them a theoretical standing over against oneself (the German *Gegen-stand*).[9] In developing an abstract theory one assumes a general position on practices as an object of investigation put at a distance. From this perspective practices are treated as if endowed with a certain identity like 'Science', 'Law', 'Art' or 'Technology' that defines its actions and in terms of which these practices can be compared. This theoretical positioning contrasts with approaching practices in a way in which the researcher lets him or herself be addressed by the proximity of the peculiarities of the movements that traverse each practice.[10] This second orientation to practices more merits the designation of a 'practice approach'.

These remarks on prudence disclose some lines of approach on practice (and legal practice more particularly).[11] It orients us to several activities in which practitioners might be engaged with and among a host of things. We have to be careful how to proceed from this orientation. According to the programme of the practice turn most practice theorists coincide in conceiving of practice as arrays of human activity. Human action has to do with knowing how to proceed in certain situations based on one's domination of certain presuppositions, skills and tacit knowledge. Practical actions can either be interpreted as behavioural regularities described from the point of view of an observer, or they can be interpreted as subjected to norms which justify such behaviour and by which its correctness is measured and sanctions are administered.[12]

On this framing of practices, the philosopher is presented through the figure of the teacher who knows the meaning of things and how to

---

[9] The obvious reference here is Heidegger's distinction between ready-to-handness (*Zuhandenheit*) of a thing (*Ding*) that we work with in practice, and the present-at-handness (*Vorhandenheit*) of an object (*Gegenstand*) in theory. 'The Greeks had an appropriate term for "things": *pragmata* – that is to say, that which one has to do in one's concernful dealings (*praxis*). But ontologically, the specifically "pragmatic" character of the *pragmata* is just what the Greeks left in obscurity; they thought of these "proximally" as "mere things"' (Heidegger, 1962, pp. 96–7). In his later work, characteristically titled *The Thing*, Heidegger worked out this 'pragmatic' way of being of things. We will come back to this point in the next chapter.

[10] See Stengers' crucial distinction between identity and belonging in addressing practices in this regard (Stengers, 2006, p. 17).

[11] We could also here make a link to Deleuze's concept of jurisprudence that never departs from the generality of the law, but always from the proximity of a singular issue (Deleuze, 1995, p. 153).

[12] Rouse has explicitly distinguished these two 'concepts of practice' in his contribution to the practice turn (Rouse, 2001).

correctly proceed with them,[13] and the role of the social theorist assuming the figure of the legislator who identifies and codifies the norms and rules that govern a practice.[14] Such a position assumes that practitioners possess a certain mastery of the situation and that we know how to recognize a normal or an abnormal occurrence, *i.e.* it assumes that practices are given.[15] In legal theory, we will encounter this position when discussing the work of H.L.A. Hart (Chapter 6).

Hesitations: Not Knowing-How

Can we really say that a practice is truly ever given? Can its normative identity be ascertained so easily? And by who exactly? In what way is the thinker legitimated in assuming the role of the teacher who claims to know what is happening? Why postulate the foundational *a priori* requirement that behaviour has to be measured by norms as correct or incorrect? We have to be careful in setting up observer positions that let thought pass by conceptual figures like the Teacher or the Legislator,[16] but rather be attuned to the painstaking efforts it takes practitioners like jurists to set up stable observer positions on things in the first place.

An approach implies a certain opening that is obstructed by such normative requirements. Instead we are interested in observing how certain constraints might be brought to bear upon a course of events within a practice by the work of practitioners. When norms come up it is always within a certain practice in the course of some-thing the practitioners are concerned with: a task, a challenge, an issue, a problem, a controversy or a conflict. In the course of these events the question 'How to proceed from here?' is posed. At stake here is not the identification of a norm by which one knows how to behave correctly in this situation, but what can be done and risked within the field of constraints to solve the issue at stake without betraying the obligations that the practice poses. This is not a situation of certainty in which the practice determines the behaviour and one knows

---

[13] Deleuze opposes the figure of the idiot to this figure of the teacher, in not managing to know what everybody knows or recognizes (Deleuze, 2004a, pp. 165–6).

[14] On this role of the sociologist as legislator, see Bauman, 2003; see also Turner's concept of the sociologist as imposing a tacit book of rules on practices (Turner, 2001).

[15] Wittgenstein also referred to this givenness of practices (Wittgenstein, 2009, pp. 210e, 238e).

[16] Deleuze & Guattari, 1994, p. 69. The role of the figure of the legislator, but also that of the super-judge in approaching legal practice will be discussed when dealing with the legal theories of Hart and Dworkin respectively (Chapter 6).

how to proceed, but rather one in which the practitioners argue, consult or discuss with one another and hesitate about which course to take. This also leaves open the possibility of practitioners not knowing how to proceed, where they hesitate with regard to what obliges them.

A practice approach does not produce a general account of the behavioural regularities in which practitioners engage or identifications of the norms to which they are subjected in their actions, but rather turns to the production of a transversal account of the practice that lets itself be addressed by the kind of constraints that make a practitioner hesitate in order to do his or her work well, especially in situations of conflict or controversy. The concept '*trans-versal*' is introduced here in its etymological sense of a 'turning across'. It highlights that a turn towards practice is a way of thinking that endeavours to establish new connections with practitioners, in our case the jurists. This is different from what we could call an *ablational* turn to practices that tries to abstract and carry away a general account from practices. It is a way of thinking that tries to attach to the concrete conditions that constrain the actions of practitioners and make them hesitate. This means such an approach will not endeavour to explain their practice by external factors, be they political, economic, psychoanalytical or historical. Furthermore, it will not satisfy itself with doctrinal theoretical fixations that locate these practical movements between the fixed points of law (Troller), and neither will it content itself with a philosophically abstract treatment. Practices consist in being practiced, just as actions consist in being enacted. They are ongoing processes in the making, whose dynamic character prevents them from being taken as ready-mades without losing much of their vitality.[17]

Pragmata: What Things Make Us Do

This way of thinking can be dubbed pragmatic to the extent that it takes a certain 'attitude of orientation' towards practices taking account of the matter of concern that its practitioners are dealing with and of the possible consequences of their actions.[18] It also implies an orientation of prudence,

---

[17] As Stengers says, 'nothing is "all made". Everything is to be negotiated, adjusted, aligned, and the term 'practice' means the manner in which these negotiations, adjustments, alignments constrain and specify individual activities without determining them' (Stengers, 2006, p. 62, my translation).

[18] In this sense, it has some familiarities with the pragmatism of William James whose orientation also already foreshadowed the 'practice turn', since the pragmatist 'turns away from abstraction and insufficiency, from verbal solutions, from bad *a priori* reasons, from fixed principles, closed systems, and pretended

i.e. a focus on the concernful action of practitioners with and among *pragmata* or things. Science and technology studies have provided crucial insights into the role of things in enabling all kinds of practical action.[19] We will focus here on the actor-network approach as has been advocated by Latour. First, Latour, like the practice theorists, also argues against structuralist and critical sociologies that explain phenomena or actions by abstract structures (like belonging to a certain social class and invisible economic hands) or external causes (like financial calculations, political strategies and unconscious psychoanalytical desires). Such preassembled aggregates are not causes for explanation, but have to themselves be explained by tracing how they become assembled in the first place through the work of many different actors.[20]

In contrast to most practice theorists, Latour has a conception of action that cannot be reduced to human behaviour and social ties only. Social skills and links are too weak to stabilize society or 'social' practices. This function has instead been delegated to non-humans: in practice things stabilize society and enable the actions of practitioners. Non-humans are normally neglected in sociological accounts and considered mere means or intermediaries for the realization of human actions. Things are the 'missing masses' of social theory without which social explanations run the risk of remaining 'without object'.[21] In legal theory this is the case in the anthropomorphic (or de-reified) theories of law and society of Legal Realists like Hohfeld and Holmes (Chapter 6).

Non-humans have agency too in the sense that they make us do things

---

absolute origins. He turns towards concreteness and adequacy, towards facts, towards action, and towards power' (James, 1995, p. 20). For James, pragmatism is a method or an attitude rather than a theory.

[19] 'Science studies is [defined . . .] by the emphasis on the local, material, mundane sites where sciences are practiced. Thus the word "practice" identifies types of studies that are exactly as far from the normative philosophies of science as they are from the usual efforts of sociology. What has been revealed by the study of practice is not used to debunk the claims of science, as in critical sociology, but to multiply the mediators that collectively produce the sciences' (Latour, 1999, p. 309).

[20] Interestingly Latour states that 'law, for instance, should not be seen as what should be explained by social structure in addition to its inner logic; on the contrary, its inner logic may explain some features of what makes an association last longer and extend wider. Without the ability of legal precedents to draw connections between a case and a general rule, what would we know about putting some matter "into a larger context"?' (Latour, 2005, p. 7).

[21] See Latour, 2005, pp. 73, 82. We will come back to this problem for an account to be 'without object' in the next chapter, when we deal with legal claims and their conditions for proceeding.

(*faire faire*). The concept of mediation becomes important here. Latour makes a crucial distinction between intermediaries and mediators. An intermediary is a means for transporting something intact, without the transported being transformed. A good example is Troller's conception of immaterial goods and Hugenholtz' conception of informational goods. The same immaterial good could become embodied or represented in an indefinite number of corporeal media at different places and moments without 'losing in substance'. The corporal thing is here a mere medium for the transmission of the self-identical immaterial good that remains intact throughout this process of communication. To the contrary, mediators transform and translate that which they carry across. They make other humans or non-humans do unexpected things and thus should also be attributed a certain capacity for action. When we trace the formations of associations in the unfolding of a controversy, we will encounter a complex network of humans and non-humans. 'Action is simply not a property of humans, but of an association of actants' (Latour, 1999, p. 182).

This perspective makes visible the importance of the median region for the analysis of phenomena. It opens up the *mi-lieu*, literally the middle place, in which things happen. This has important consequences for the status of what was always supposed to be at the beginning and at the end of these chains of associations: origins and ends, ideas and representations. We could say that by changing the means, the ends are also changed, both in the sense of an original goal and the result achieved. Technologies or objects can no longer be seen as mere instrumental means for humans to reach their ends through their actions. When the milieu is indeed the place where controversial phenomena become unfolded through chains of mediators and are transformed at each step along the line, then concepts like 'original idea' lose their 'power of ubiquity' as Troller called it and no longer rule the scene. Instead of being explanatory causal terms 'origins' or 'ideas' turn out to be the result of the purification of these median networks (just like their counterpart terms like 'end' and 'material embodiment'). Meanwhile everything has already happened in the middle between the divides where networks proliferate that always already connect these distinctions. When we focus only on the pure concepts at the end of the lines we miss out on all the ways these distinctions are themselves produced and constituted by the network of translations through the mediators in between.[22]

---

[22] Latour, 1993. We can further turn to Hutchins's brilliant study of distributed cognition in navigational practices as an interesting ally to Wittgenstein's

These insights will be very useful for analyzing the conceptual partitions corporeal-incorporeal, material-intellectual, made in the discourses on intellectual property, immaterial goods and informational goods, when studying the legal practices of intellectual rights in action.

'practices of mental talk' analysis and Latour's approach to networks and matters of concern. He combines a focus on what techniques and things make us do, with an interest in the distribution of cognitive abilities 'in the wild'. Hutchins shows how human cognition and knowledge structures are not so much 'inside' the individual mind, but rather distributed throughout a complex network of devices, spatially organized settings, rooms, ranks and people (Hutchins, 1995).

3. Grounds of invention at the law firm: proceedings of a technological dispute

What is an idea?
What is the relation between an idea and a concept?
In what sense are they immaterial?

These questions can now be posed again. In order to address them research can no longer depart from a theory in which the nature of law or these legal concepts are already given in advance, but will have to turn to these practices and empirically observe all the details of intellectual rights in action.[1] Legal concepts will be studied as they are evoked by legal practitioners in the proceeding of a concrete dispute. In this way we hope to gain insight into what allows practitioners to use these legal concepts this way. We will closely follow every-thing that happens to a matter of dispute from the moment it is first brought into contact with attorneys up to the moment it is decided by the judges. This makes clear the whole antagonistic process in which attorneys render an intellectual rights dispute legally decidable and which normally remains invisible. Grounding an invention requires a lot of work. We need to visualize the ways in which immateriality is formed when a dispute passes through the legal instruments and vocabulary of intellectual property practices. Things play an important role in this process. They are the occasion for the legal process. In their circulation through these processes they gather immateriality through constantly being articulated by attorneys.

This chapter presents the results of a 'case' study at a Belgian law firm in the regime of patent law. It has closely studied the legal processes from the moment when the case entered the law firm until its termination in court and its subsequent decision. In following the central matter of dispute we

[1] This study takes its inspiration from Latour's Actor-Network Theory of practices in action. Methodologically it is closest to his studies on circulating objects in science (Latour, 1999) and thematically to his studies on the making of law in the French *Conseil D'État* (Latour, 2010). For a more ample and critical discussion on this topic, see van Dijk, 2011.

will pass from technological sites of international enterprises, through the offices of law firms and will eventually proceed to court. Along the way something gradually happens. The extralegal matters of dispute slowly become oppositionally grounded as legal ideas, concepts, banalities or inventions through the ceaseless operations of proof, disproof, qualification, disqualification, authorization and unauthorization by the attorneys of both parties and through a host of different procedures, conditions and instruments like office tools, computers, media of communication and documents. We will trace these passages by which the *matter of dispute* proposed in the summons will have to be transformed into a *matter of fact* before becoming a *legal object* (*Rechtsobjekt*) or legal non-object of patent law: the 'invention' or the 'idea'. When we immerse ourselves in the peculiarities of these legal dynamics from this perspective, we will notice that our initial question 'What is an invention?' gradually shifts into the question 'How does some-thing legally become an invention?'

3.1 THE APPROACH

There is a host of peculiarities and constraints that a researcher faces in the light of such a conflict-based approach. How can one give an account of the dynamics of attorneys at work without betraying them? The attorneys put themselves at risk in facilitating a study like this one. The nature of the subject matter of this kind of dispute (involving trade secrets and know-how) places severe restrictions on the kind of descriptive account which can be given of these processes. An account of these processes cannot be accused of the same infractions without making itself untenable. This requires respecting obligations of confidentiality and will necessarily limit scientific exigencies of traceability and transparency. This significantly limits the possibilities for presenting the dispute here. First, all names, dates, places and numbers have been made anonymous. Second, the descriptions of these delicate issues has to walk the fine line of making them unrecognizable by replacing them with others that still fit the legal arguments at stake. Paradoxically, this methodological approach might have less effect on the outcome of the processes studied, than submitting to the requirements of total transparency. We are dealing with a court case in the first instance. Total transparency *about* the case would offer the counterparty arguments they might be able to use when the case went to appeal. Their attorneys could mobilize these arguments *within* the case, thus influencing the outcome to their own benefit. Total transparency would thus constantly run the risk of total betrayal of the actors studied.

At times, taking into account these constraints excluded satisfying the exigencies of justice. When we 'just observe'[2] what goes on in the legal practices at the law firm, this does not imply that our descriptions themselves do justice in living up to fundamental procedural principles like *audi alteram partem* demanded by legal procedure. Parties concerned have not received a fair, equal hearing, or, rather, fair, equal observation.[3] A study of the legal work at both law firms in this conflict is practically impossible due to the exigencies of confidentiality between law firms and towards their clients. This study thus does not strive to give a complete and neutral overview of the conflict. This is also due to the very nature of the object of study: conflicts. One of the characteristics of these legal conflicts is that all attempts to neutrally describe them are themselves continuously disputed. In *iuris*, this is even a requirement of legal evidence: dispute something or face it as a fact. How can the writer thus pretend to do what is itself so heavily disputed, namely to neutrally state what the matter of dispute is?[4] The aim of this study is elsewhere. It wants to understand what engages these legal practitioners, in which situations they have doubts and when they feel confident. Where do they feel constrained in their actions and by what? When do they think they 'have a case'? How do they make their proposals about the conflict factually and legally proceed?

Conflicts are complex even when they have already been translated into a legal claim. The construction of a legal narrative about the conflict is a zigzag movement of mutual attack and defence through a host of documents. The attorneys establish many tentative threads between the

---

2 Latour, 2005.

3 The conception of justice employed in the instruction to 'just observe' is quite different from that of procedural justice (fairness in the processes of how decisions are made) encountered within the legal practices studied. Venturini distinguishes three meanings of 'just' observation according to which the researcher is: not to impose any specific theory or *procedure* but use any tool at hand (v. the specific procedures that are exactly required by procedural justice); not to pretend to be neutral or *impartial* but reaching objectivity by multiplying points of view (v. impartiality as a requirement of procedural justice); to listen more to actors than to his or her own *presumptions* (v. certain mandatory presumptions judges have to make in legal proceedings, like the presumption of innocence) (Venturini, 2010, pp. 2–3).

4 In this context, Venturini remarks that controversies are reduction-resistant. 'In controversies, actors tend to disagree on pretty much anything, including their disagreement itself. That's why issues are so difficult to solve, because they are impossible to reduce to a single resuming question [. . .] The difficulty is not that actors disagree on answers, but that they cannot even agree on questions' (Venturini, 2010, p. 5). Nevertheless, we will see that, in contrast to other kinds of controversies, the conditions of the legal processual dynamics do provide certain requisite procession points that simplify the conflict.

matter of dispute, the facts and the law. Some of these connections are cut and/or reinforced. Other connections are abandoned somewhere in the proceedings. The attorneys might no longer deem them important for the way the case has come to unfold in light of the weight of new facts, arguments or qualifications proposed by the adverse party. Relevance is a shifting matter. One attorney even explained that, normally, everything only falls into place at the day of the pleas in court, when it becomes clear what the important points have been. The research account will follow this lead and focus on the threads that retroactively made possible the eventual legal passage of the matter of dispute. This sometimes means the neglect of the dead ends of all other threads that would have yielded different dispute proceedings. The main focus in this case is the grounding and articulation of immateriality and everything this implies. This entails observational attention for the acts of qualification according to the vocabulary of intellectual rights. Nevertheless, it is also necessary to articulate some of the many parallel strands that develop as the dispute proceeds. The antagonistic dynamics of the dispute would otherwise be unintelligible, since these strands can have severe consequences for the outcome of the dispute.

This chapter is about law as a process of dealing with conflicts and not a chapter about 'process law'.[5] The codes of procedural law are too static to sufficiently account for the dynamical processes by which a dispute legally proceeds. They do however inscribe many conditions that legal practitioners take into account in organizing their actions and will therefore be mentioned in footnotes. The main focus will be on empirically following the course of the dispute and all things brought to bear to solve it. In order to limit interruptions of the flow of this process, doctrinal or philosophical qualifications of these happenings will also be presented in the footnotes. The legal workflow is already interrupted enough by its own movements. Attorneys work at many different cases in the same period of time and the formal terms for document exchange create large time lapses in which the case temporarily 'comes to rest'. We are thus studying a process of 'punctuated equilibria' of case work, or sometimes even of 'equilibrated punctuations'.[6] Lawyers are so used to interruptions that suddenly come up and disturb the work on a certain case, that they have standardized their ways of coping with these eventualities.

The methodology used includes a mix of document analysis,

---

[5] This is the literal translation of the Dutch word *procesrecht*, normally translated as 'procedural law'.

[6] The term is exapted from Eldredge & Gould, 1972.

ethnographical observations and feedback sessions.[7] The first three parts of this chapter are mainly based on document analysis. Each part is both structured around a main document – summons and statements – and a main theme. Parts four and five are mainly based on ethnographical observational studies combined with the fruits of interviews and literature research.

3.2 SUMMONS: INTRODUCING THE MATTER OF DISPUTE

Begin at the beginning
and go on till you come to the end; then stop.
(Carroll, 1994)

It is difficult to begin at the beginning.
And not try to go further back.
(Wittgenstein, 1975, § 471)

. . .and write with confidence
'In the beginning was the deed'.
(Goethe, 2003, I: 1237)

Initiation of the Legal Proceedings

This case description will be initiated by the first document of legal concern in the official order of proceeding. Proceedings are formally initiated by the document of a summons in which the primary claim is stated. How can one claim that this is effectively the beginning where the inscription of the case should start? What act or deed authorizes the author to write with such confidence these phrases employing all these order words, both temporally and hierarchically? Will we indeed not have to go further back and start with the forms that authorize these initiating acts?

---

[7] These methods are mentioned in the order of importance for the study. When no neutral account of the dynamic of a legal conflict is possible, the question becomes what position can be assumed. The focus has been on finding ways in which the matters of study could maximize their resistance against possible interpretations, thus privileging document analysis over interviews.

CODE OF PROCEDURAL LAW

[. . .]

BOOK II. PROCEEDINGS.[8]

FIRST TITLE. Pursuit of the claim.

FIRST CHAPTER. **Form** in which the primary claim is pursued.

First Part. **Initiation of the legal proceedings by summons**.

This is the authoritative source for our claim: legal proceedings are initiated by summons. A summons is a legal document that per-forms the legal act of officially summoning a defendant to make himself or herself present in court. Book II on proceedings starts with article 700 that states: 'Primary claims are brought before the judge by summons (under penalty of nullity).' The summons is the legal *form* in which the central matter of dispute is pursued and through which it is authorized to enter into contact with a judge. A claim proposed in any other form suffers the penalty of having zero legal effect through the legal automatism of nullity.

We have gone farther back than the beginning of the case, at least as far as 22 June 2007 when the introduced phrase ('under penalty of nullity') in the Belgian Code of Procedural Law attained the force of law. We could go much further, but we have already had a false beginning. We will start with the summons as the first document of legal relevance in the order of proceedings of the case. In this way we will become familiar with the curious legal language and its mode of operation. The document introduces the parties in the conflict. In this case the plaintiff is the Dutch company The Wool Corporation (TWC) represented by its attorneys, Mrs Blanchard and Mr Zomers. The defendant is the Canadian company Gortec Engineering Mechanics (Gortec) represented by its attorneys, Mr Leerbeek and Mr Vetard. Both are enterprises active in the packing industry.

> In the context of her activities defendant [Gortec] has developed a machine (first called 'SPEEDEC', later 'Filomat') for automatically filling boxes of raw material. In this context defendant has filed a Canadian patent application

8 The Dutch word here is *geding* that is commonly translated as 'proceedings'. The word *geding* is a noun relating to a conflict or dispute. The word has the grammatical form of the perfect simple tense of the verb *dingen* that means 'to compete'. In Heideggerian parlance the term *geding* could even be translated as the 'thinging'. The word *ding* as a root noun however means 'thing'. The word *geding* thus could be said to have the composite meaning of the competition for a thing. In a legal context, *geding* refers both to 'the thing competed for' and 'the process of competing'. In the first case we will speak of the 'matter of dispute'; in the second case we will use the translation 'proceedings'.

> (Canadian patent application, no. DX4980) on 16 July 2004 for a **device for automatically filling boxes**.

This is a first formal introduction to several elements that will play a central role in the legal *proceedings* of our case: a patent application, its filing date and registration number, the device it inscribes, the different names for this device and its summoned developer Gortec. After this introduction of the primary parties to the conflict, the text continues with a brief description of the history of cooperation between the two parties. We will later return to this cooperation. Here, we are interested in the central claims.

> The **additions** with regard to Canadian patent application no. DX4980 that defendant has put in her PCT patent application no. PCT/IL2004/001247 and European patent application no. YE672573 come from the plaintiff.
>
> Since the invention claimed in European patent application no. YE672573 is the **result of the cooperation** of defendant [Gortec] with plaintiff [TWC] (especially claims 1,3,5,6,9 and 10), plaintiff is entitled to claim the joint property of the European patent application no. YE672573. **Plaintiff is joint owner** of the **invention described in the patent application**. According to articles 9(2) of the Belgian Patent Act ***juncto*** article 74 of the European Patent Convention, the plaintiff is **entitled to pose a claim** to be **transferred** this **European patent application no. YE672573** as joint rightful claimant.

The peculiar legal technicalities multiply fast now: another patent application, now European; more registration numbers and their relation to the summoning plaintiff TWC. Here we also have the first appearance of the 'claims' in the document. Gortec is accused of having solely appropriated something that, in fact, belongs to both Gortec *and* TWC. By applying for a patent on a device that is the result of their mutual cooperation, Gortec has unlawfully appropriated the additions that come from TWC. TWC claims joint ownership of the invented device and, subsequently, claims the recovery of the patent application. The claims also provide us with the *matter of dispute*,[9] the thing competed for:[10] a European patent application on a device for automatically filling boxes.[11]

We can also observe the first appearance of legal codes in the

---

[9] The term '*matter of dispute*' is a translation for the Dutch term '*voorwerp van geschil*'.

[10] See footnote 62 and the discussion about the notion of a *res* or 'thing' in the next section.

[11] Here we encounter what Latour calls the 'circulating object'. This is the matter of concern for the actors within a certain practice, the proceedings of which we have to follow in order to understand their activities (Latour, 1999).

document. An article of the Belgian Patent Act is inscribed in the text and knit together with an article in the European Patent Convention (EPC). This is done through the legal linking mechanism of the '*juncto*'[12] which aligns different legal sources to authorize a proposition. Article 74 of the European Patent Convention states that 'unless otherwise specified in this Convention, the European patent application as an object of property shall, in each designated Contracting State and with effect for such State, be subject to the law applicable in that State to national patent applications'. Through this article our patent application no. YE672573 is subjected to the authority of Belgian patent law and thereby article 9(2) of the Belgian Patent Act is made to apply to the dispute.

The Proposition of Legal Effects

With the facts about the cooperation between the companies described and connected with two aligned articles of legal code, TWC has now grounded a legal position to state its claim. The introduction of the conflict can now be wrapped up in a legal performative.

> I, undersigned Frank Kouter, bailiff in Brussels, have issued a summons against Gortec Engineering Mechanics
>
> [. . .]
>
> To **appear** before the first chamber of the Court of Commerce of Brussels on Wednesday 02 January 2008. [. . .]
> In order,
> to hear the plaintiff's **claim** being declared **admissible** and **grounded**, ***thereby***:
>
> - To hear **say** before the **law** that **plaintiff is joint inventor** of the invention described in the European patent application with number YE672573 and consequently joint owner of the invention.
> - ***Consequently,*** to hear the **rights** of joint property to the European patent application number YE672573 be **assigned** to plaintiff according to article 9(2). According to article 9(2) of the Belgian Patent Act *juncto* article 74 of the European Patent Convention.
> - To hear **defendant** be **sentenced** to compensate damages suffered by plaintiff due to defendant's illegal appropriation of its know-how, provisionally estimated at 500.000 euros.
> - To hear **defendant** be **sentenced** to legal expenses.
>
> The **claim** is **based upon** the relationship between parties, the motives mentioned in the writ of summons, the laws and decisions concerning the subject matter, as well as any other factual or legal means made to apply in due time during the course of the proceedings.

---

12 The English translation of '*juncto*' is 'in conjunction with'.

The legal process has hardly been initiated or a proposal for its possible termination is already put forward in the form of a legal *proposition*. The company Gortec has now changed capacity, it has become a party in a legal dispute. What was supposed to be a *matter of business* for Gortec – filing a European patent application for an invented machine, has been duly halted and has turned into a *matter of dispute* officially initiated within the legal arena. More precisely, we are here provided with two *matters of claim:*[13] the box-filling device referred to in the European patent application with number YE672573 (the matter of the first claim for co-inventorship) and this European patent application no.YE672573 itself (the matter of the second claim for recovery of the rights of co-property). The last paragraph of the summons contains the many buds for the unfolding of the legal process. It declares that the claim is firmly stated within a fabric of threads that connect and ground it into contracts, facts, laws, judicial decisions, and legal procedures and tools. We will later follow these specific weaving acts by the attorneys in this case.

Here, we will say more about the format of this legal summoning performative. Words apart, different things are done and in a very particular order. The bailiff has let the calling of law announce itself to Gortec through the act of correctly issuing a valid summons. Gortec is now officially summoned to make its presence before the court to hear the judges 'speak the law'[14] and pass judgment on the legal proposition of TWC. This passage of judgment finds its grammatical articulation through a series of phrases in the summons. TWC proposes to hear its claim to joint property of the European patent application no. YE672573 be declared admissible according to the conditions of procedure and *grounded* by the facts and the law. This means that the court pronounces that it is com-

---

[13] The term 'matter of the claim' is a translation of the Dutch term '*voorwerp van de vordering*'. The term is co-extensive with that of the matter of dispute, but the latter is *less fixed* by the former's propositional form. As we will see, the circulation of the matter of dispute in the initial phase of reconstruction of the conflict *precedes* the fixating contraction into the claim, although after this contraction it will become closely tied to it. Furthermore, the matter of dispute can also be *broader* since it is not limited to the plaintiff's claim, but can be transposed in a different counterclaim or different counterqualifications by the defendant. As we will see, a claim can be without matter, but a dispute can never be. The mode of existence of the dispute consists in the way it comes to matter for those concerned. These remarks have some affinity with the procedure that Whitehead describes as the extraction of an object from an event as its 'it' that becomes the matter of consideration (Whitehead, 2004, pp. 8, 142, 144).

[14] This is the literal translation for the Dutch word *rechtspreken*. The prevalent English translation is 'render justice' or 'dispense justice'.

petent to receive and judge such a claim and pronounces the claim to be sufficiently backed up by factual and legal grounds. *By* this declaration we pass further into judgment. TWC itself is hereby *legally qualified* as joint inventor of the patent application. This legal declaration will have all kinds of *effects*. TWC will consequently be imputed rights of ownership; Gortec might be sentenced to compensate for damages and legal expenses, or face whatever other legal effects will be proposed during the legal proceedings of the case. According to J.L. Austin the judicial speech act of passing judgment has both verdictive and exercitive force (Austin, 1976), pp. 151–7) It is verdictive to the extent that the judgment performatively states what is factually and legally the case in the dispute. The judgment is exercitive to the extent that as an official act the judge's ruling also makes law and executes certain acts of legal consequence. These two forces are aligned by the use of conjunctive grammatical markers like 'thereby'[15] and 'consequently'. These markers function as connectives by which the law is carried into its effects. This 'carrying out' or 'carrying into effect' is the etymological meaning of the verb 'to perform'. The act of judicial qualification according to a *legal form* brings about *legal effects*.

There is a very specific notion of *cause* at stake here. The word 'effect' should not be misunderstood by giving an interpretation befitting a scientistic context in which it can objectively be reduced to, and thus explained by a physical cause. Can these legal effects be explained by referring back to a cause? Yes certainly, but they *refer* to a very *specific* cause that is quite at home in a legal context.[16] The Latin word '*causa*' from which the word 'cause' is etymologically derived, has strong ties to legal practices that deal with conflicts. In this context the *causa* is certainly related to the factual existence of a thing (*res*). This thing however is not necessarily some kind of physical object. The *res* is not necessarily something material or objective, but it does *matter* a great deal to the parties gathered around it before a legal institution.[17] '*Res* means first and foremost the process, the affair to

---

15 Austin focuses attention on the similar use of the word 'hereby'. In a legal statement like 'Notice is hereby given that trespassers will be prosecuted', the word 'hereby' in the utterance is an instrument of effecting the act mentioned (Austin, 1976, p. 57).

16 According to Heidegger, the word cause has a primordial belonging in the legal context. 'In its authentic and original sense, this word [*causa*] in no way signifies "cause"; *causa* means the case and hence also that which is the case [*Fall*], in the sense that something proceeds and becomes claimable [*fällig*]. Only because *causa*, almost synonymous with *res*, means the case, can the word *causa* later come to mean cause, in the sense of the causality of an effect' (Heidegger, 2004, pp. 167–8).

17 Heidegger famously stated that the ancient term 'thing' or 'Ding' means gathering; 'a gathering for the trial of a matter [*Angelegenheit*] under discussion, a

be debated. [. . .]. The primitive meaning of *res* oscillates between the ideas of the dispute, the situation of dispute, and the object that provides the occasion for a disagreement' (Thomas, 1980, p. 415[18]). This object is not so much an external object for a legal subject but, before anything else, the matter of a controversy that opposes and reunites two protagonists within the same relation, a *res iuris*.[19] This matter of dispute finds itself posited in this common interiority: *res in controversia posita*, in which it can become a *causa*. The *causa* is the matter of controversy sufficiently backed up by the facts and put in a legal form that constitutes a legitimate reason for initiating a legal process before the court. From there on it can be further articulated by the specific tools and procedures of law (*lis*).[20] This matter which allows the performance of legal acts is called a 'cause of action'. The thing is thereby introduced in the legal arena and transformed into a *matter of legal dispute*. From there on it can be further articulated by the specific tools and procedures of law.

Cause and form are thus closely related in legal practice. We could even speak of a very specific kind of formal cause that is characteristic for law. It is closely related to the notion of a performative. It is *per forma*, through being put in legal form, that a matter of dispute is carried into its legal effects. The forms here point to the forms of action within the practice, or what Austin calls 'conventional procedure'[21] of affixing documentation and filling out constitutive forms.[22] Instead of having the notion of cause

---

contested case [*Streitfalles*]' (Heidegger, 2004, p. 167). In ancient Germany people gathered at sites in the natural landscape with special features in order to administer the law and to settle disputes. These 'thing sites' – the *Thingstätten* – later developed into, natural shelters, half-open structures, multi-purpose buildings and finally into the courthouses of our times (Dölemeyer, 2005).

18 Here and elsewhere in this book, the translations of foreign language texts are my own unless otherwise stated.

19 See footnote 62 in this chapter.

20 On the crucial role of the triad *res-lis-causa* in Roman law, see Thomas, 1978, 1980.

21 Austin thoroughly realized the importance of the practice of law for his model of speech acts. In the many paradigmatic performatives he describes the words uttered within these procedures often come to do things so effectively by having their conventions backed by the force of law. In his articulation of the differences between speech acts, Austin many times refers to law as making an important difference. He says that 'it is worth pointing out – reminding you – how many of the 'acts' which concern the jurist are or include the utterance of performatives' (Austin, 1976, p. 19).

22 This is a very different conception of form than an explanation by a form, idea or intention in the mind of the parties or the judge, or some isolated ideal template for things that would constitute the scene. We could call this an opposition

hijacked by physicalists and reduced to material or efficient causes,[23] we should pay attention to a mode of cause that belongs specifically to law and study how it operates in legal practices.[24]

We could say that the cause in our case is condensed in TWC's statement of the patent claim, namely 'to hear say before the law that TWC is joint inventor of the invention described in the European patent application with number YE672573'. The qualification according to the legal regime of patent law that takes place here has the following grammatical form:

X is the (co-)invention of Y

The conflict finds its most contracted state here. Each subsequent element of this legal 'stick'[25] calls for a distinct articulation during the proceedings of the dispute:

- X: is the matter of the claim: the device for automatically filling boxes described in the European patent application with number YE672573. It is the thing (*res*) that needs to be legally qualified (the *qualificans*) according to the vocabulary of patent law as an invention. What this matter is or whether there exists a matter of the claim at all is not some-thing given or fixed, but needs to constantly be worked out through attaching pieces of evidence and authorizing legal conditions.
- Is: is a grammatical marker of equivalence that *per*forms the qualification of a non-legal matter of dispute X *as* the legal object

between the dispute that comes to *fill in* the blanks of a pre-fixed template and that comes to *fill out* (through) the legal forms as a part of the twofold of ap-plication that extends the corpus of the dispute.

23 Socio-biology (or evolutionary psychology) has tried to reduce human behavioural dispositions to evolved genetic make-up or to strategies aimed at survival. Such explanations have also been attempted for law, by trying to find the 'biological roots of legal institutions' (Yarn, 2000, p. 65) or 'biological imperatives' (Gruter & Bohannan, 1983, p. vx).

24 Stengers proposes to not reduce the concepts of 'cause' and 'explanation' to efficient causality as the proper explanatory modus of scientific practices. Instead, a cause should be understood as that which makes a practitioner hesitate in order to do her work well. It is the event in which the pending issue before her is recognized as something, which engages her as a member of a specific practice. This notion becomes the basis of her philosophical approach of 'thinking through causes' (Stengers, 2006, Chapters 4 & 5).

25 In the next chapter, we will see how an attorney during his pleadings called such a claim that evokes a certain legal regime a 'stick' to hit the adverse party.

of patent law: the invention. It also qualifies the suing party in the dispute as the legal subject of patent law: the inventor. Furthermore, it is also the grafting point for disqualification (X is not an I) and counterqualification (X is an S, Y is a C).

- Co-: is a specific prefix that evokes the legal forms of joint property and joint inventorship and its legal conditions for the required size of the contributions and the factual proof of these contributions.
- Invention: is the main legal concept of patent law. Through this quality the matter of dispute X can be qualified as the legal object of patent law. This legal concept also implies a host of inherent component-conditions like 'inventiveness', 'newness', 'applicability' and 'non-idea' that have to be satisfied.
- Of: is a grammatical marker of possession. It indicates the processes of intellectual origination that connects the matter of dispute X to party Y as a relation between an invention and its inventor. This immaterial relation of invention is established by grounding it in material things and documents with possessive pronouns.
- Y: is the plaintiff – The Wool Corporation – which initiated the proceeding of the legal dispute by summoning its adversary Gortec to appear in court and defend itself. In our case it is the party that asks to be imputed the legal quality of inventor in order to exert its rights on an invention.

This short statement of the elements of the dispute could be deceiving to the extent that it might portray the activity of attorneys as a simple exercise in syllogistic logic in which the concrete complex case is subsumed as a species of a general stable legal form. In the section on qualification we will see that this is not at all the case. Stabilities and simplicities are always local and temporal and quickly become fluid (or rather fluoride as we will see) and complexified, drawn in by the chaotic dynamic movements of the dispute. The claim is the most contracted and simplified state of the conflict that brings together and implicates many heterogeneous elements in one single formula.[26] In this way it gives a primary orientation to the dispute by assigning it a belonging in a certain legal regime: patent law. Within these territories much is still about to happen and the risk of losing one's way is always present even with this orientation. The claim does not

---

[26] With Leibniz we could call this contraction of the infinitely detailed and extensive developments of the dispute in the claim, a little death of the dispute. Leibniz describes death as 'envelopment and shrinking' which he opposes to generation as 'development and growth' (Leibniz, 2010, §73).

yet allow us to understand the more complex dynamic processes through which this contraction has come about and how it will come to unfold.

Reconstructing the Conflict

We have until now studied how our legal dispute was formally initiated through the summons. This document made us more familiar with the specificities of legal speech and the ways in which TWC's attorneys initiated the dispute, claimed what it was about, introduced the parties and actors involved and proposed the effects. Being able to provide such an introductory summary already requires the conflict to have developed to a certain extent. What the conflict is about has already become stabilized. This is not the way a conflict starts when it first enters a law firm and thus provides a misguiding image of the dispute dynamics. We have to get back to the beginning of the process when the conflict was first brought into connection with the law. This is not so easy; origins are always a tricky business shrouded in the mists of time. In these cases, we have to rely on oral recollection, which allows us to evoke a different, less documented and less formalized entrance into the conflict. We return to a time when the summons was yet to be written and the attorneys needed to cooperate with their client in order to reconstruct the conflict.

> *In the beginning of the conflict the client is* ***enthusiastic*** *and fully prepared to cooperate. Cases last for years however, people change roles especially in big companies. Slowly they* ***lose interest****. The cooperation will run less and less smoothly. TWC is not interested, that is why we will lose all their cases. And TWC is a big company with only one lawyer.*
>
> *The client loses pieces of evidence and documents and forgets things. The conflict now happened four years ago. Companies maximally store this kind of information for three months. The truth thus has to be reconstructed on the basis of limited information. Much has been deleted or forgotten.* ***Engineers*** *do not work like* ***lawyers****. They do not* ***write*** *down everything, but do many things* ***orally****.*

An attorney is an advocate for a client. There are certain specific difficulties inherent in this relation of advocacy especially in the representation of big companies. In this sense, the researcher is in a slightly more convenient situation at the law firm than the attorney. He has to reconstruct the legal reconstruction of what happened in this technological dispute. This meta-reconstruction will also have to be based on incomplete information. The attorneys however have at least recorded most things in paper documents, which facilitate our job greatly! The attorney finds herself in a far more delicate predicament. The engineers she has to rely on have not written down things so meticulously. Without such mnemonic devices as paper script, things will not have been stabilized in their memory. When the echo of their pronunciation fades away, their Being slips back into the chaotic plasma of forgetfulness. Nevertheless, even when things have indeed been written down, recorded or incorporated in some way in documents, they have often got lost in the woolly bureaucratic body of the Corporation. Furthermore, this corporation has a wavering interest in the dispute, which is reflected in its lack of enthusiasm for participating in the attorney's reconstructive activities. What a curious world in which an important part of one's job consists in getting and keeping interested the very actors whose claim is at stake!

> *In the beginning of a case the* ***points of dispute*** *are* ***not*** *always immediately* ***clear****. The* ***conflict*** *is often situated at some distant moment in the past,* ***spread out*** *over memories of different people and depending on their role in the conflict. A process of* ***reconstruction*** *starts, guided by the lawyers. The central points of dispute are then articulated.*

In the beginning, for the attorney, the conflict is not given as some-thing immediately apparent, but merely as a conflict she is confronted with. It is not yet clear what it is exactly about; its very about-ness is still a problem to be worked out. The conflict needs to be carefully reconstructed, which requires retracing all the instable memories and lost documents distributed throughout a dispersed institutional network of long gone past situations, role-shifting actors and messy informational archives. On the basis of this preliminary work the attorneys have to search for the *suitable* conditions for the dispute, i.e. the conditions that allow an action of legal suit. All these elements will have to be traced and gathered in order to be contracted into a few central singular points that will constitute the centres from which the conflict will unfold.[27] In our case they have been contracted in claims of co-ownership of a patent application. Such contractions into the central claims of the dispute are important since they will already imply and determine the range of the possible paths through which the dispute might become solved.

We can learn here from Gilles Deleuze's thinking about the 'being of the problematic'. According to Deleuze 'problems must be considered not as "givens" (data) but as ideal "objecticities" possessing their own sufficiency

---

[27] With Deleuze we could call such singular points 'centers of envelopment'. With regard to the relation between the contraction of dispersed elements and claims, he remarks the following. 'Every *contraction* is a presumption, a *claim* – that is to say, it gives rise to an expectation or a *right* in regard to that which it contracts, and comes undone once its *object* escapes' (Deleuze, 2004a, p. 100).

and implying acts of constitution and investment in their respective symbolic fields'. Their 'solution necessarily follows from the complete conditions under which the problem is determined as a problem, from the means and the terms which are employed in order to pose it' (Deleuze, 2004a, p. 198). In our case the objecticity of the problem comes out in the way the issue between TWC and Gortec resisted being treated as a mere matter of business and forced itself upon them as a conflict. It also comes to the fore in the way this conflict resists an easy grasp by the lawyers as to what it is about. The nature of the problem is never totally given. It has to constantly be worked out and each proposed articulation will be objected to and countered with opposed propositions. The dispersed elements remain to be contracted and to be posited as a legal dispute. The symbolic field that we are confronted with is that of law and its means and terms are the legal means of procedure and the legal concepts of the patent vocabulary.

The Attorney, the Detective and the Plumber

The attorney will have to closely cooperate with the client and its engineers in order to recollect all the elements that will allow the constitution of the claim and its further articulation during the course of the dispute. In the process of reconstruction the attorney has a guiding task. The business dispute has been transformed into a legal dispute with its own tools, concepts and requirements. We will later see how these specific legal requirements have to be translated to the engineers to apprehend how to contribute to the reconstruction. The legal objects of patent law are inventions, in our case the matter of dispute is a mechanical apparatus. This means the reconstruction can become quite technical and will almost entirely take place on paper.

> *Working on a file is like writing a novel. The goal is to make it seem like you are the good party.*

The techniques for mechanical and paper construction of machines are very different. The first is the task of the engineer, the second of the attorney. Contrary to the engineers, the attorney's goal is not to make these paper machines progressively pass into real technological objects, but to make them pass as legal objects. The attorneys will have to produce a satisfactory account of what happened when the machine was invented. This account will have to convince the judges of the fact that TWC is the unacknowledged genius/inventor who has been wronged by Gortec. The attorneys rely on narrative techniques for writing such a story. Grammatical markers are used to introduce conditions and requirements (by verbs like 'have to', 'can'), property relations (by possessive pronouns like 'our', 'TWC's'), legal performatives (by conjunctions like 'hereby', 'consequently'), cuts (by negations), or to create rhetorical effect, focus attention on, or qualify the importance of phrases (by punctuation marks, formatting and highlighting). Furthermore, a whole range of metaphors and sayings is used for drawing or disqualifying analogies. Through these acts of writing, formatting, inscribing, quoting, referring, interpreting, (en)listing, highlighting, marking and bracketing, the texture of the lawsuit is gradually constructed. But is this what advocacy is all about? Does it merely deal with making up stories?

> *There is a difference between good and bad attorneys. A good attorney is like a kind of Sherlock Holmes who investigates everything: internet, pictures, documents, etc. A bad attorney doesn't even know her own client.*

The exigencies for good advocacy are drawn more clearly. The construction of a file is not the making up of a fictional novel. As we will see later, fictional accounts of things will easily be punctuated and disqualified by the attorneys of the adverse party. A good account is like a detective novel in which the whole network of dispersed factual elements is re-assembled from many different sources and places. All traces must be followed. Every-thing that is relevant to the conflict must be investigated and be accounted for. This requires intense interaction with clients and ongoing efforts to keep them enthusiastic and involved during the whole process.

In this sense the attorney's job is rather similar to that of the sociologist who has to investigate the course of a technological project and reconstruct the successive stages of existence: from its origination in a creative spark and first ideas, a life size model, a moving prototype, an operating system, to a commercially viable product (Latour, 1996). Curiously, Blanchard and Latour both compare the jobs of the attorney and the sociologist to that of a detective who engages in the reconstruction of the process of invention. Both endeavour to de-scribe the process by which engineers inscribe paper texts, designs and photos in a technological project leading to the invention of a machine.[28] They try to retrieve this technological script in order to identify its authors and their creative contributions.

There are however also important differences between the legal detective and the sociological detective. The attorney/detective engages in a reconstruction of those parts of the process of invention that ground certain positions in a dispute. Her work is oriented towards identifying

[28] For this notion of *de-scription* of technical objects, see Akrich, 1992.

the good party – the unacknowledged genius/inventor – and unmasking the culprit to cut him off from what is legally 'right'.[29] The sociologist/detective aims at a more smooth unfolding of the network of assembled entities without such rash shortcuts.[30] She engages in a reconstruction of the process of invention in order to describe the many different ways in which this project branches out and how many different positions are brought to bear upon it.[31]

Apart from comparing her work on files to that of a detective, Mrs Blanchard often labelled her activities at the law firm as 'plumbing'.

> *By plumbing I refer to the* ***everyday legal practice*** *of* ***applying rules to a case,*** *without thinking about the reasons or goals for these. Just as the plumber has his* ***tools****, the lawyer has certain* ***rules*** *with which to do the* ***handiwork****. Where is the* ***leak****? How do you* ***repair*** *it and with what* ***means*** *and in such a way that it* ***works*** *again?*
>
> *Plumbing also expresses a certain modesty. The work we do is not much more than that. It does not have anything to do with* ***truth****, but is only about* ***fixing a problem by connecting tubes and screws together****.*

This short description raises important questions that sum up an important part of the programme for our investigations. How does this everyday legal practice work? In which ways does this legal handiwork proceed? On which tools does the attorney rely in her plumbing activities? What do attorneys mean when they say they *apply* rules to cases? This provides us with a first lesson for the study of legal practices: 'by-pass the big questions on goals, reason and truth'.[32] These would lead us away from the modest specificities of the intra-legal practice; away from the arduous qualifications of matters through legal means straight to their 'higher' pre-existent goals or 'deeper' abstract truth. The legal handiwork of 'connecting tubes

---

[29] Such cuts in networks of creation are very characteristic for the functions of (intellectual) property rights. 'Where technology might enlarge networks, proprietorship can be guaranteed to cut them down to size' (Strathern, 1996, p. 531).

[30] This approach however also incapacitates the sociologist in reaching any judgment as to the culprit within these processes of technology development. See Latour, 1996, especially the final chapter.

[31] This also has to do with the timeframe available for making the reconstruction. For the attorney the reconstruction has an increased temporal 'urgency that obstructs the horizon of knowledge' gathering. As Derrida states it: 'a just decision is always required immediately. It can't provide itself with infinite information and the unlimited knowledge of conditions' (Derrida, 1992b, p. 255).

[32] Law does not have an ambition for truth, but rather invents a different world through its techniques of putting things at a distance (Hermitte, 1998).

and screws together' would hereby be cut short[33] and we would miss out on what happens on the surface of the text-ure of the lawsuit.[34] We will overlook the kinds of legal fluids that are made to flow through the grid of tubes, once all the tubes have been connected and all the leaks have been closed.[35]

3.3 STATEMENTS: THE FACTS AND FORMS OF THE LAWSUIT

After the first contraction and envelopment in the claims in the summons, the dispute is fully sent off into its antagonist dynamics. It will now enter a phase of rapid extension and development through the interchange of documents called the statement of claim and the statement of defence. The parties are to an important extent legally obliged to organize the antagonistic proceedings of their dispute in accordance with a whole fabric of formal procedures. These documents allow us to understand the way attorneys organize their arguments and how they perform their specific operations.

Gortec, as the summoned party, is granted the opportunity to respond to TWC's accusations by formulating a reply in defence. This document is divided in three sections called 'In fact', 'The matter of the claims', 'In law' and has an appendix with an 'inventory of pieces'. These are the main elements in the unfolding of the legal process. The order shows the central position of the matter of the claims, situated between facts and law and constantly connecting and transforming the two as it proceeds. We can

---

[33] Riles makes a similar comparison. Opposing grand theories on the meaning of law, she draws attention to the everyday 'technical' operations of lawyers in solving problems, which she equates to the 'plumbing of a leaky faucet' (Riles, 2005–2006, pp. 979–80).

[34] See Latour, 2005, pp. 165–72 on keeping the social domain of study flat for purposes of study.

[35] Flows within plumbing grids occupy a position between the notions of 'network' (Latour, 2005) and 'fluid' (Mol & Law, 1994). The network character highlights the amount of work done in the construction of the grid: the preliminary plans and meetings, the design, the assembling of the grid, the attachments of pipes, welding things together and the damage repair. The fluid character puts the focus on what flows in these tubes once all the construction work has been done: the specific legal transformations of a matter of dispute into a matter of fact and a legal object of intellectual property. In this sense, plumbing is closer to a network metaphor than to fluids. In law, the flows are highly *canalized* through the highly exigent weft of formal micro-procedures that governs the construction of all the pipes.

use the term '*affixation*' for these acts of establishing connections between the dispute and all kinds of documents. To affix means both: to secure to something, attach, join one thing to another; but also to impute, attribute, ascribe, assign; and to annex or place at the end. This triple meaning nicely demonstrates the threefold nature of the connection itself (fastening attachments), its indexical location with regard to the documented body text of the dispute (annexes like sources and inventory of pieces) and what happens when these connections manage to hold (assignation).[36] We have to fine-tune this point however, since attachments to different kinds of documents will lead the lawyers in very different directions and set the matter of dispute onto different trajectories of becoming. We will see how the matter of dispute will proceed through mutual transformations into a *matter of fact* and into a *legal object* of patent law.

Stitching and Cutting of Proof

In order to understand the specific notion of the legal fact and the way it works in the dispute dynamics, we need to follow how the central matter of the claim – the machine for automatically filling boxes as described in the patent application – is further *articulated* through the legal procedures of evidence. In the summons TWC claimed the box-filling device described in Gortec's patent application was the result of their joint efforts:

> Many documents demonstrate that direct cooperation between plaintiff and defendant had already begun at the end of 2004.
>
> The cooperation, on part of the plaintiff, consisted in the **communication of its know-how** to defendant in order to **fundamentally improve** the SPEEDEC machine. Because of this contribution of plaintiff, **two major changes** were applied to the device: a **station shift** and a **stapler**. As a result of this improvement the SPEEDEC machine eventually reached a box-filling capacity of 1200 boxes per hour.
>
> 1) Concerning the station shift, the fact that this adjustment comes from plaintiff is *inter alia* **demonstrated by the next documents**:
>   - On 17 September 2004 Mr Mark Graanhof sent an e-mail to Mr Hesse (Gortec) [. . .]
>   - On 20 September 2004 Mr Hesse responded [. . .]
>   - In November 2004 Mr Graanhof sent a letter to defendant that summarized the contents of their meeting in Canada on 15 November 2004 [. . .]
> 2) Concerning the stapler, the fact that this adjustment comes from plaintiff is *inter alia* simply demonstrated by the 'TWC Concept Agreement' signed by

---

[36] The term 'affix' is here not used in its technical legal sense as means of appropriation of something through its attachment to realty.

> plaintiff and defendant on 7 July 2005 in which the stapler of a box-filling device is defined as 'the TWC Concept'.

An important legal condition of proof is that whoever claims something will have to prove it.[37] If TWC claims that it is joint owner of the device, it will, so to say, have to demonstrate how it is joint with the machine. TWC argued that the machine incorporates elements of know-how that originate from its engineers, namely a change of the order of the stations of the machine and the incorporation of a stapler. TWC will have to prove this by *stitching* pieces of evidence to them. The facts inscribed in this case relate to contacts, meetings, negotiations, correspondence, cooperation, contracts and conflicts between Gortec and The Wool Company. The majority of these pieces are documents like e-mails, letters and contracts that inscribe a variety of events, sites, actors, meetings, agreements, inventions and designs. An ongoing part of the work of attorneys consists in obtaining such documents, putting them in the 'Inventory of Pieces', and inscribing sections in the body text of the statement document.

The attorneys of Gortec will endeavour to *cut* as many of those stitches as possible and to do some attaching of their own. Their primary target: TWC's proposition of mutual cooperation.

> In contrast to what TWC asserts, not a single form of cooperation can be deduced from the correspondence of mid 2004 that aims at the mutual development of an improved machine. What can be deduced however, is a mere relation between a manufacturer/salesperson and a potential customer in which the manufacturer adapts the machine to the needs and specifications of the latter.

Cut, cut, cut! All the hard work of TWC's attorneys seems to have been in vain. Not a single form of cooperation aimed at developing an improved machine can be deduced from the documents they so carefully tried to inscribe in their summons. No improvements, no joint ownership. All the relations of mutual invention that TWC deduced from their mutual correspondence are cut by Gortec, and replaced by a new proposal in which their bond is reduced to a mere relation of purchase. Whatever TWC contributed cannot be qualified as anything innovative, but rather as a specification by a customer for a custom-made product. The cause at stake has been transposed from the specific regime of patent law to the general legal regime of sales relations.

---

37 This condition for the burden of proof finds expression in article 870 of the Belgian Code of Procedural Law. 'Each party has to provide the proof for the facts that it brings forward.'

In legal texts these cutting actions can often be identified by the use of negating grammatical markers like 'no', 'not'. The cut plays an important part in law. Derrida pointed out that the legal decision of the judge is marked by a necessary terminating cut. The decision is like the sword of justice that *cuts off* the preceding processes of ongoing deliberation to bring all the possibilities of doing infinite justice to an end (Derrida, 1992b). Strathern transposes this idea to the decisions taken in Patent Offices to grant patents on inventions. These decisions *cut off* a segment of the extensive network of people who have contributed and made possible the invention and officially call the persons in this segment the legal inventors who own the patent (Strathern, 1996). For both Derrida and Strathern, legal decisions figure as a sword that decisively cuts through other unfolding processes in such a way that these are either totally terminated or have crucial parts sliced off. These are macro-cuts cutting things short.[38] *In* our case, the situation is different. The attorneys engage in a constant adversarial process of stitching, cutting and reinforcing through which the weft of links that make up the lawsuit gradually unfolds. These are micro-cuts that are transient and often not terminal. When the severed connections are mended by different attachments and the existent links are enforced, the legal fabric will unfold differently and the dispute will become displaced.

Through these legal operations of stitching and cutting of proof, the matter of dispute is progressively turned into a *matter of fact*. When we speak about what the case is in fact, we have to become familiar with this very specific *legal concept* of proof. Just like with the notions of cause and effect we have to forget all references to science when we want to understand the legal particularity of notions like 'matter of fact' and 'proof'. Attorneys are bound to constraints for providing valid proof that would be very unfamiliar to scientists.[39] Concepts like 'burden of proof', '*evidential value*', '*evidential force*' are very characteristic for the legal mode of proof. Furthermore, a glance at the means of proof allowed in

---

38 In our study of how judges come to their decisions in the next chapter, we will see that this macro image of judgment is itself a short-cut of legal processes through focusing on only one of its moments.

39 For an extensive discussion of this difference, see Murphy, 2003. 'The existence of the law of evidence is one of a number of factors which distinguish a judicial trial from other forms of inquiry into past events [. . .] trials are conducted by a judge using exclusionary legal rules of evidence, the effect of which is to keep from the fact-finders much material which is plainly relevant, and which any rational investigator would wish to take into account in his or her reconstruction of the facts' (p. 2).

general civil proceedings shows them to be utterly strange to science: documents, witnesses, experts, presumptions, oaths, confessions and invoices.[40] What marks the contrast between scientific and legal proof even more is the fact that conclusions or *factual* confirmations by (scientific) experts have the smallest 'evidential *value*' of all means of proof. Article 962 of the Code of Procedural law even determines that the judge is not obliged to follow such conclusions if they conflict with his *convictions*. On the other hand, certified documents which are signed by both parties provide full proof of what they inscribe (agreements). Such a document has 'evidential *force*' which, according to article 1319 of the Civil Code, the judge is obliged to follow even if it would be against his 'conviction'. Is this not most curious from the viewpoint of science or philosophy of knowledge? In court the so called 'subjective' convictions of a judge are valued higher than the 'objective' statements of fact by the expert! And documents with signatures cannot even be valued by the judge but force him to align. The conditions according to which attorneys and judges either have to, or cannot do certain things, characterize the legal mode of proceeding.

Forms of Qualification

In the discussion of the performatives proposed in the summons, we have already made a distinction between the verdictive speech act through which the judge declares what is legally the case and the 'sentence' that proclaims the legal effects that follow from the verdict and are thereby rendered executable. This stating what the case is, *de jure*, is a decisive act in the practice of law. It is an act of translation in which the matter of dispute is put into a legal form (*mise-en-forme*). Only after this translation into legal vocabulary does a certain legal regime become applicable. This characteristic legal act is called *qualification*.

The effects of qualification differ greatly according to the legal actor that performs it. Attorneys make those propositions for qualification that translate the interests of the clients they represent. The word 'advocate' expresses this dimension well: legal practitioners advocating a certain cause and qualified course. In our case TWC proposes translation to the legal vocabulary of patent law. Gortec *disqualifies* this proposition and proposes a *counterqualification* according to the vocabulary of sales. In

---

[40] These means of proof for civil proceedings are exhaustively enumerated in article 1352 of the Belgian Civil Code. In commercial law proceedings like in our case however, there is a full freedom of proof according to article 25 of the Belgian Code of Commerce.

law each qualification is a disqualification of other legal categories either explicitly proposed or possible to propose (Cayla, 1993). This constant *antagonistic* dynamic of qualification-disqualification is characteristic for the legal process of dispute resolution.[41]

When the judge qualifies, something different is at stake. The judge doesn't propose translations for the matter of dispute, but legally performs the very act of qualification through the act of judgment. Through this judgment (*arrêt*) the legal movement of the conflict is brought to a halt (*arrêter*) and the matter of dispute is transformed into a legal object.[42] Their acts of qualification will also constitute a decisive disqualification of the propositions of the losing party and will make the flow of law pass through the tubes of proposition installed by the winning party.

Cayla thinks that since each act of nomination is contaminated by a decision expressing a choice of preference, the decisive act of qualification that constitutes the core mode of existence of law is itself determined by a moment of political will. This is an overly rapid transpositioning into the field of politics. Interests and preferences play a crucial role in the process of law. Clashes of interest of actors will gather around matters of dispute. The procedures for the legal proceedings of cases are designed to channel these very interests and make them pass through many nodes of abstraction that progressively translate the matter of dispute into the language of law in terms of which the complexity of the conflict is rendered legally decidable. The same goes for the preferences and interests of the judge. The possibilities for choice available to a judge are very different from the possibilities for choice of a politician because they are constrained very differently. First, the decisions of the judge, once made, might themselves face the tribunal of the higher courts in which their colleagues preside and face the criticisms of the practitioners of legal doctrine. Second, in reaching judgment the judges are constrained both by the procedures that channel the making of a decision and by the attorneys who, by their many propositions, will endeavour to limit the judge's freedom of appreciation

---

41 Foucault describes the concept of 'agonism' as a contest which gathers and locks the two opponents in a dance of contest in which they reciprocally incite each other and act upon the other's actions, and invent new moves and strategies in function of the actions of the other (Foucault, 1982). See also Nietzsche's use of the Greek concept of ostracism as antagonistic competition against the Romanticist concept of genius and its constitutive relation to Greek art and philosophy (Nietzsche, 2005).

42 This is a termination of the legal conflict to the extent that the parties involved have given up their power of qualification and subjected themselves to the incontestable qualifying power of law and its judges.

as much as possible in favour of their client. Within the field of all these constraints the judges have room for hesitations about how to untie and retie the bonds of the legal fabric in certain directions.[43] Due to the kinds of constraints that operate on the making of a decision, this discretion has a very different character than in politics.[44]

These hiccups in legal decision-making require us to focus on the intra-legal conditions that make judges hesitate in order to reach a good judgment. These obstacles give rise to the whirls and vortexes in the legal fluids that come to flow through the advocated grids of tubes during the process of adjudication. They cannot be accounted for by reducing legal judgment to mechanical application of legal forms or to extra-legal interests and relations of power. Attachment to extra-legal interests is not a problem that should be overcome by cutting oneself free of the ties of preference and hiding behind the mask of 'impartiality'. Rather, it is a question about how, by many ties, to firmly but hesitantly attach a case in the 'right' way to the interests involved, the fact and legal qualifications proposed and the existent fabric of law. Neither can these hesitations be accounted for by presenting adjudication as the automatic application of legal forms to the affair. The attorneys of both parties will make sure they will do everything in their power to not let the judge mechanically apply the legal forms proposed by the other party. Every act of qualification will itself be highly disputed, disqualified and tied to many additional complicating factors proposed to constrain the decision of the judge even further.[45] If both attorneys have done their work well, each act of qualification will be a source of serious doubts, uncertainties and hesitations for the judges and not some automated process like Gortec's invention. 'Good judgment', 'attaching well', 'qualifying rightly', this all sounds rather

---

[43] Latour's ethnographical studies at the French *Conseil d'État* show how the preferences and prejudices of the judges become tied by the existing fabric of legal texts and precedents during deliberations. A judge can create a margin of manoeuvre through techniques of untying and retying these bonds (Latour, 2010, pp. 152–63).

[44] This could imply that in the so-called 'normal case' the judge merely aligns with the translations proposed by the attorneys. If we accept the distinction between 'normal' and 'hard cases' (as made by Dworkin and Hart for instance), this further implies that, normally, the body of law mostly unfolds through the work of attorneys! This gives a new interpretation to Cardozo's statement that 'nine-tenths, perhaps more, of the cases that come before a court are predetermined – predetermined in the sense that they are predestined – their fate established by inevitable laws that follow them from birth to death' (Cardozo, 1924, p. 60).

[45] In the statement documents, there are many occasions in which the judge is explicitly addressed with regard to the work he is supposed to do.

normative. As if in law we only want facts not norms. Actually we want both! And we want them to be tied well together! It is exactly between these two that the particular dynamic of legal conflict resolution unfolds itself, when a matter of dispute has to be tied, cut and retied to a host of pieces of evidence. Within this patchwork of ties that the attorneys have tried to tailor to the matter of dispute, the judges will have to suit their judgment to the conditions that bind the way their judgment will proceed.

On the automatic model of adjudication legal decisions are presented as acts in which the concreteness of a particular case is subsumed under the generality of an abstract rule. This 'image of law'[46] takes judgment as an isolated macro moment which is cut off from all the preceding connections that have rendered a dispute legally decidable. This image obscures all the anterior laborious actions of the attorneys (proof-stitching, qualification, authorization) in constructing the complex grids of connections by which the matter of dispute is slowly but gradually transformed into a legal object for judgment. These are the true pre-judices that the law is supplied with, for they show us all the legal pre-positions that precede judgment and make it possible in the first place. The propositions for legal qualification are the prepositions for judgment. After the preliminary encounter with the conflict and some first facts, the dispute is contracted in the central points of dispute. The attorneys have to connect the dispute to some first legal conditions in a claim. The claim proposed in the summons is the first formal legal qualification of the matter of dispute. This action transforms the conflict into a legal case and initiates the legal proceedings that will lead towards judgment. This proposition is a preparation for the mutual articulation of the factual and legal positions on the dispute.

In this sense application of 'rules' to cases is the work of attorneys not of judges. Etymologically *ap-ply* means 'attach to' or 'fold to' in order to bring something in contact with something else. Attorneys bring heterogeneous elements together when they connect an extra-legal thing to law in order to initiate its proceeding as a matter of legal dispute. During the legal process two different fabrics – the factual patchwork and the legal weft – have to be constantly folded to each other in such a way that they join together and something can proceed.[47] 'Application' does not

---

[46] The 'image of law' is Lefebvre's adaptation of Deleuze's concept of the image of thought. It is a model of adjudication in which judgment is based on the subsumption of cases by identifying them as species of a general rule (Lefebvre, 2008).

[47] We could call this the quilting model of (legal) application, considering that quilting is a technique of joining at least two fabric layers together by stitches. Deleuze & Guattari use quilting as a technology for modeling the relations

have the hierarchical or vertical connotation of 'subsumption' in which a factual matter is transformed by being placed under a form that itself remains unaltered and is merely 'specified'. Instead the term 'application' keeps open the possibilities for the mutual change of both case and rule that might result from the connection of the two. What the case is and what a rule requires is never something given. In a lawsuit both have to be constantly worked out by being connected to each other in a way that is legally tailored to the matter of dispute.[48] The attachment of new evidence to the matter of dispute can give rise to the proposition of new legal qualifications (non-inventive relation of sales) or of counterclaims (property of Gortec). The scope of existing qualifications (co-invention) can themselves also be drawn into the dispute as a point of conflict. Through aligning legal authorities, new legal conditions (of proof) can be validated that require a different, either more or less stringent, evidential grounding of the matter of dispute, which, in turn, will change the way the body of the case will become articulated. In the next section we will see how the proposition of a counterqualification (theft or abuse of procedure) can open up whole new directions in which the dispute will simultaneously come to be unfolded. According to each qualification other avenues are taken and other things become relevant.

Appearance and Reality of the Legal Process

Gortec focused on the fact that the changes made to the machine were part of negotiations aiming at a contract of sales and construction. In the contract TWC will be granted 'exclusivity on the concept changes' under the condition that it will order and pay for three Filomat machines constructed by Gortec . . .

> The orders have never been made . . . why? This **mystery** is hereafter immediately explained.
>
> **THE HIDDEN AGENDA OF TWC**
>
> In March 2007 EIO [a Belgian distributor for Gortec] telephonically communicated **rumours** to Gortec that the Filomat was being copied by TWC.

---

between a striated, 'legislated' space of channeled flows and a smooth, 'jurisprudential' space of new openings that follows the flow of a singular event (Deleuze & Guattari, 1987).

[48] For an elegant early argument for the non-syllogistic, mutually transformative nature of these legal processes, see Dewey, 1924, p. 567.

Hereafter Gortec received **information** that NV Libra Systems ('Libra' hereafter) had built a copied version of the Filomat for TWC and that this machine was positioned on the site of TWC next to the Filomat supplied by Gortec! Gortec was also able to get **photos** of the machine with which it has confronted TWC by e-mail on 07 April 2007 (see pieces B.II.45, E.1.4, E.3.2). TWC never responded.

The representative of Libra has **acknowledged** TWC request to him for producing a copy of the Filomat (piece B.2.48)

[. . .]

Everything thus **indicates** that TWC has transferred the detailed plans (in AutoCAD format), that it explicitly requested (see piece B.I.19) and received (piece B.I.21) from Gortec, to Libra, with the **purpose of fabricating** one or more **copies** of the Filomat machine (of course at a significantly lower price, since the costs of research and development have already been borne by Gortec. . .)

Allegations of illegitimate copying! The introduction on the stage of a new actor – Libra Systems – and a new object – a copy of the Filomat – in combination with the many stitched references to pieces of evidence, pull the fabric of the case in a different direction. This time the matter of evidence is something quite different from proving mutual cooperation. At stake is a hidden agenda of TWC, namely its intention to use Gortec's designs in order to make copies of the Filomat rather than having to buy them from Gortec. A lot of work is needed to get this hidden agenda out into the open. Over the course of a few phrases some-thing that is first a mystery (TWC has not ordered, contrary to agreement), is first transformed in a rumour (TWC is alleged to have made copies of the Filomat). After being linked to the actions (copying, placing next to) of several actors (Libra Systems, TWC, the Filomat) and being assigned a geographical (TWC's site) and relational (next to Gortec's Filomat) location, it is transformed in a propositional piece of information (Libra Systems have made a copy of the Filomat and placed it at TWC's site next to the original Filomat). The matter of information gains existential value by attaching it to a photo that is claimed to be its representation and by a piece in which a representative of Libra confirms TWC's request for a copy. By stitching together a network of heterogeneous elements like items, actors, actions, places, representations, Gortec becomes able to transform some-thing that is a mystery into a full-fledged matter of proof. This matter of proof is then used to ground an otherwise rather elusive statement: TWC has a hidden agenda that is filled with illegitimate purposes and intentions!

The whole procedure is nothing but a misplaced attempt by TWC to provide her **illegal actions** with an **appearance of legitimacy**. TWC isn't hereby afraid to try to throw dust in the eyes of your Court.

[. . .]

> The **true intentions** of TWC in the context of the present procedure are clear. By means of a complete suspending and **frivolous procedure** TWC wishes to slow down and obstruct the procedure of the European patent application as much as possible.

There is a practical philosophy of appearance and reality (*Schein und Sein*) at work here. The legal process around TWC's claim of joint property of the patent application is merely the apparent goal of the procedure. In reality the true goal of TWC is legitimizing its illegal actions of unauthorized copying of the machine. The attorneys of Gortec try to unmask the real hidden interests of TWC behind the façade of the legal procedure. On the basis of these facts Gortec files a legal counterclaim 'to sentence TWC to the payment of damages [. . .] due to provoking and reckless lawsuit' and abuse of procedure.

We have already mentioned the crucial role interests and preferences play in the process of law. Externalist socio-political criticisms of legal judgments exposing the hidden interests and power relations behind the law and its decisions could be a sign that attorneys and judges have not done their work well enough. When *interests* can be legally recognized as *legitimate* there is nothing hidden about them. They are then overtly made to pass through many procedural nodes of translation. When other interests are found that affect the case in an illegitimate way, it is up to the attorneys to bring these to the fore in the name of the law.

The Matter and Conditions of the Claim

After the work of evidential stitching is done, Gortec's attorneys can now state the matter of their legal (counter) claims and disqualify those of TWC. Apart from grounding TWC's claim 'in fact', it will also have to be grounded 'in law' by making explicit its *conditions of proceeding*. In the previous section we have already encountered an example of one such claim, when Gortec's attorneys cut the constructed threads that qualified TWC as a joint inventor. In this section we will focus on the endeavours of Gortec's attorneys to disqualify TWC's second claim to be imputed the rights of joint property of the European patent application according to article 9 of the Belgian Patent Act.

> To **succeed** in her claim for recovery [of a patent application], TWC is **required** according to article 9 BPA §2 *juncto* §1, to **demonstrate** that two **cumulative conditions** have been **satisfied**:
>
> - First, she **has to prove** that she has effectively developed a part of the invention.

> When there are several people who have contributed to the invention, only those who made a ***substantial contribution* can claim the quality** of inventor (M-C. Janssens, Uitvindingen in dienstverband met bijzondere aandacht voor uitvindingen aan universiteiten, Brussel, Bruylant, 1996, pp. 24–5).
>
> [. . .]
>
> - Second, she **has to prove** that Gortec has unlawfully taken this developed part of the invention.
>
>   This is the case when a third party has appropriated an invention by stealing plans or abusing the trust of the inventor [. . .] a *lack of good faith* **is required (B. Blanchard**, Patent Law, Oxford University Press, 1995, pp. 74–5).

The attorneys of Gortec want to make explicit what a claim like TWC's requires to legally pass. They have inscribed a host of texts from legal doctrine and jurisprudence and have attached them to the legal conditions upon which TWC has grounded its legal claim of recovery. They have even cited a book by B. Blanchard, one of TWC's attorneys, to support their interpretation! If even the attorney of the other party is aligned, how can their proposal fail? Blanchard is driven into a new alliance of sources that authorize Gortec's propositions. Her legal authority is at stake! Gortec's attorneys articulate the conditions that TWC's claim has to satisfy to legally succeed. These two conditions of providing a 'substantial contribution' to the invention and a 'lack of good faith' will be the issue of intense debate. Many other documents will be proposed, attached and disputed to articulate these crucial principles for legal passage. Apart from disputing the *pieces* of proof proposed by TWC, Gortec thus also disputes the 'proof *obligations*' and the *scope* of proof in trying to prescribe what TWC is required to prove and to what extent.

The fact that the work of making explicit the conditions of felicity is such an important integral part of the practical proceedings is definitely a curiosity of legal practice.[49] In scientific practice for instance, these debates arise most clearly in those situations in which scientists are engaged in controversies and conflict, i.e. in periods of crisis and revolutionary science in which the 'normal' practice of scientific activity has broken down (Kuhn, 1996). In law these kinds of situations are at the heart of its ongoing activity because law is a practice that deals with problems, conflicts and breakdowns.

'Condition for proceeding' is a term that bears close resemblance to the conditions necessary for the successful accomplishment of a performative

---

[49] This in addition to the explicit form of legal grammar (code) which is a specific characteristic of legal semiotics (Greimas, 1976, pp. 87–8).

act (Austin, 1976). Several things have to be and go right for someone to succeed in performing such an act. Of special interest here are speech acts that fail due to a breakdown of reference, because the thing the sentence mentions does not exist. In such cases the speech acts performed (like concluding a contract) are null or void, not carried into any effect. This also applies to legal claims. They also fail when reference to the matter of the claim breaks down. Gortec accuses TWC of having failed in this respect.

> ***Refutation of TWC's position***
>
> ***Principally: the claim for recovery is without matter***
>
> - *General principle: the scope of protection of the patent is determined by the contents of the claims within the application for a patent.*
>
> Article 69(1) of the European Patent Convention confirms this general principle: 'the extent of the protection conferred by a European patent or a European patent application shall be *determined* by the *terms of the claims*. Nevertheless, the description and drawings shall be used to interpret the claims' [all italics by Gortec].
>
> From this we can deduce that a person who files a claim for joint property of a patent application is naturally **required to demonstrate** that the **invention,** upon which his action of claim is grounded, is **covered** by the **contents** of the claims.
>
> If this isn't the case his **claim has no (subject) matter**[50] and needs to be declared **inadmissible** due to a lack of interest (or at least be declared **ungrounded**).
> [. . .]
> TWC supports her claim for recovery exclusively on the fact that her alleged inventions – the stapler and the proposed station shift – would be covered by the contents of the European patent application
> [. . .] In this case we have to observe that the claims of the patent application do **not mention a word** about the stapler and station shift concerned.

The matter of the claim is the co-ownership of the invention in the European patent application. According to Gortec the contents of this application – the claims of the patent – make no reference to TWC's alleged inventions. Rather they 'do not mention a word' about TWC's stapler and stage shift. TWC is thus blamed for not satisfying one of the most important legal conditions: providing its claim with existent objects

50 The Dutch term is '*vordering zonder voorwerp*' that can be literally translated as 'claim without (subject) matter'. The term '*voorwerp*' refers in a narrow sense to an 'object' or more broadly to 'purpose' or 'interest'.

of reference. This is a serious accusation! There is nothing in the patent application to ground its immaterial invention upon. No-thing around which to organize a legal process, a *res nulla* that cannot be claimed by anyone (as opposed to a *res nullius* that can be claimed and occupied by anyone). A 'claim without matter' is null and void in its effects and allows no legal action: *nulla res, nulla causa.* When a claim does not even have a matter it does not legally matter. Establishing reference to the matters of the claim, establishing their existence, is thus of utmost importance for the attorneys of TWC.

3.4 STATEMENTS: GROUNDING IMMATERIALITY

After this familiarization with the means and techniques by which a matter of dispute can become articulated or disarticulated in a legal process, we can turn in more depth to the legal objects of the regime of intellectual rights: intellectual creations. We will focus on the processes by which the immaterial nature of patentable inventions becomes grounded. In a new statement of claim, TWC will have to respond to Gortec's challenges and have to prove its inventiveness by showing that elements of know-how in the disputed patent application come from its engineers. In order to do so, the attorneys will articulate an earlier box-filling machine that TWC claims to have co-developed with Gortec. This machine provides the technological setting that occasions the antagonists' struggle for the articulation of the (constitutive elements of the) invention and the assignation of its creators. The etymology of the verb 'to articulate' has a double meaning: 'to separate into joints' and 'to attach by the joints'. This is exactly the task the attorneys have to face. They will have to use their skills to 'open' the machine, differentiate the functional elements,[51] highlight those that are appropriable and stitch them to a host of different events inscribed in several documents like e-mails, letters and contracts. An arthroscopic operation indeed.

When we talk about opening the machine we are not referring to the work an engineer has to do when a machine has broken down in 3-D so to say, and he has to look for the problem in order to fix it. This opening up of machines is a specific operation of attorneys in the field of patent law, which almost entirely takes place on paper. True, these operations do

[51] The functionality of the elements refers both to the function of these elements within the machine and to the function these elements can have for legal claims of appropriation.

involve machines, breakdowns and the work of engineers, but in a different sense and within different mutual relations. We could say that what has broken down is not the way a machine functions reliably for people in practice, but the indisputable way this machine belongs to certain practices in which people know how to construct and use it. It is around this breakdown of the machine's belonging, raised as a cause in patent law, that the constructive work of its engineers becomes an issue. What the attorneys of TWC have to reopen and reconstruct is the network of relations in which the claimed machine came about.[52]

In the summons TWC's attorneys claimed that its know-how was used by Gortec to fundamentally change the patent-pending SPEEDEC machine. Two elements in the machine were singled out: a station shift and a stapler. In their reconstruction TWC's attorneys will have to answer two questions: who invented the ideas and concepts of the machine claimed in the patent application? And, if TWC came up with these concepts, did these concepts make an essential inventive difference and were they illegally taken over by Gortec? For the first question we will focus on the stapler. We will start with the second question focusing on the station shift.

Constructing Identity and Difference

The narration undertaken by TWC's attorneys goes back in time before the European patent application, to the point when the disputed packaging machine only had an abstract existence. At this time the machine was being intensely discussed, drawn and redrawn on paper, and eventually posted on the website of Gortec. No such machine of cogs and wheels could yet be found back on one of the actual sites of Gortec or TWC as would be the case later in the story. The machine was actually still *information*. It has not yet acquired the stability conferred by the format of the patent file and its specific textual techniques and conditions for delineating the invention, which we have encountered in the previous section.[53] The existence of this machine first has to be established and its characteristics articulated.

---

[52] Networks of creation can become closed for several reasons. First, when a machine has become fabricated and taken in use, it will have become a black boxed object that makes invisible all that made possible its coming about (Latour, 1999). Second, a patent can have been authoritatively granted on the machine, which isolates the inventors by cutting them off from the rest of the network of creation (Strathern, 1996).

[53] With regard to this textualized materiality of immaterial inventions, Pottage and Sherman remark that the modern patent document with its single unified form

The attorneys have to prove that TWC's input fundamentally changed and improved the SPEEDEC machine and that these changes were illegally taken over by Gortec. TWC's attorneys come up with a report of a meeting with Gortec on 14 November in Canada. This report contains a list with 34 changes to the SPEEDEC proposed by TWC, which will play an important role in the further unfolding of the dispute. We will focus on one of these points proposed by TWC:

> **THE ORDER HAD TO BE CHANGED**
> [. . .]
> TWC wanted a change in the way the boxes were filled i.e. in the order in which the SPEEDEC machine performed its actions.
>
> [A.] The Order of the Original SPEEDEC
>
> The SPEEDEC has a five stage order [. . .] This order posed several *problems* [. . .] TWC therefore believed that it could not be maintained and proposed a *different* solution.
>
> 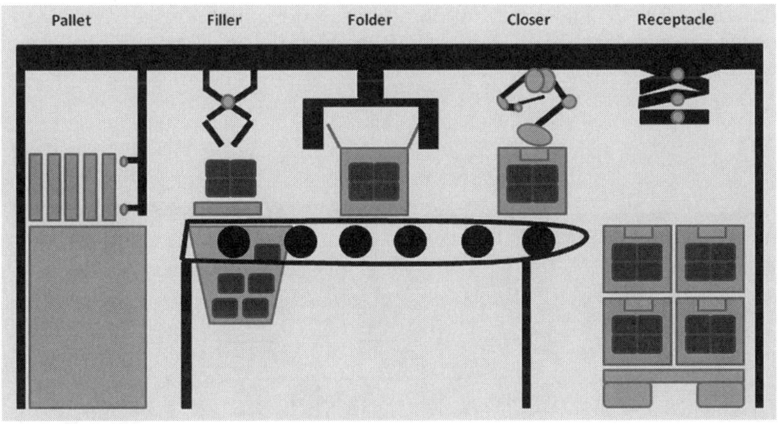
>
>
> [B.] The Order proposed by TWC
> [. . .] This is a *change* of order. Stage 2 becomes stage 3 and stage 3 becomes stage 2:
>
> First SPEEDEC: pallet – filler – folder – closer – receptacle
> Proposal TWC: pallet – folder – filler – closer – receptacle

---

containing patent drawings, patent claims and written description constitutes the invention as a 'textual machine' that can be pried apart semantically (Pottage & Sherman, 2010, Chapter 7).

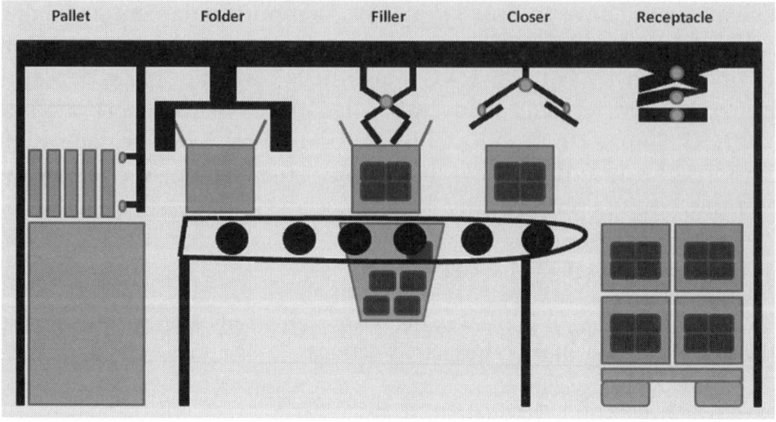

[C.] The Order eventually used in the TWC SPEEDEC

The proposal of TWC, mentioned in a letter of 14 November 2004, will be further developed by Gortec. Gortec will in fact *join* her first design with the design of TWC. The order eventually used does however *correspond* to the order proposed by TWC, since the ***possibility*** to use a box folder here also exists.

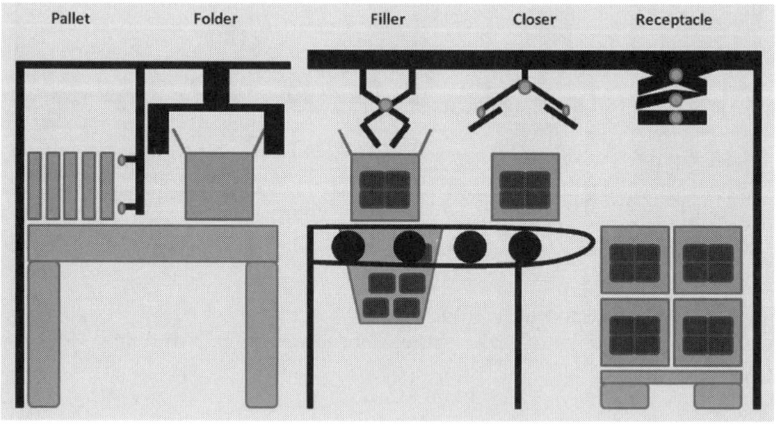

The attorneys of TWC distinguish three different machines. The SPEEDEC is machine A 'originally' invented by Gortec and inscribed in the Canadian patent. Machine B is a TWC proposal that incorporates a change of order of the stations. The TWC-SPEEDEC is machine C inscribed in Gortec's European patent applications and, as such, is the matter of the current dispute. Gortec calls this last machine her 'Filomat'.

The attorneys engage in a kind of *practical philosophy of identity and difference* to establish their invention by performing two operations. First, they endeavour to establish a difference between machines A and B.[54] Second, they endeavour to establish a certain identity or 'correspondence' between machines B and C. The machine proposed by TWC is constructed as a crucial step between the two machines of Gortec. TWC's proposal (B) implied a change of the order of stages of the original SPEEDEC (A) in a way that solves the problems this machine faced. It is a complex change that involves a host of technical details that, regretfully due to confidentiality reasons, cannot all be mentioned here. The attorneys use several techniques of juxtaposition to clarify the nature of this change in an intelligible form for the judges. *Pictures* of each machine are inserted and juxtaposed to make comparison possible at first sight. The first and the third picture are taken from Gortec's two patent applications, the second picture has been dug up from TWC's archives. The functioning order of the machines is further *textually* explicated in different 'stages' or 'phases'. After this description each stage is given a name according to the main operative technical component like 'filler' or 'folder'. The temporal sequence of stages is indicated by connecting the name for each stage to the next by the use of the hyphen ('-'). These techniques permit the order of the machine to be described in a simple and short linear sequence: '*First SPEEDEC: pallet – filler – folder – closer – receptacle*'. This technique is then applied to the machine proposed by TWC rendering the sequence: '*pallet – folder – filler – closer – receptacle*'. The two sequences are juxtaposed under each other in the text. This allows the reader (the judges) to easily notice the differences between the two machines: stages 2 and 3 have swapped places. A complex technical 'change of order' has been represented and 'explained' in the course of just two phrases! We will later come back to the interaction between attorneys and engineers that enables these simplifying representations.

Now, in its statement of defence Gortec did not deny the difference between machines A and B. They denied that the change of order of the machine proposed by TWC was 'essential' for its operation. In the summons TWC had claimed that its innovative concepts improved the

54 In an anthropology of another patent dispute, this play of constructing differences and identities of and between technological productions also turned out to be a pertinent element of the dispute dynamics (Cambrosio, Keating & Mackenzie, 1990).

box-filling capacity of the machine to 1200 boxes per hour. Gortec disputed this statement and claimed that the change of order actually makes the machine less energy efficient!

> **Gortec:** It was thus unthinkable that TWC would actually use this change of order for increasing energy efficiency. This is the reason why Gortec has **never applied this change** in order to the Filomat.

It is unthinkable that TWC would go for a proposal that, instead of improving the effectiveness of the machine that the parties initially set out to achieve, actually increased its energy consumption. Although there might have been differences between the SPEEDEC and TWC's proposal, these do not make a difference in patent terms: they do not inventively solve a technical problem but ameliorate it. The machine proposed by TWC was not an improvement or an 'essential modification' of the original SPEEDEC. It was a dead-end that was never even taken to production. This quote opens up the stage for appropriation by new actors:

> ***The new concept of Mr Tremblay: 3 phases instead of 5***
>
> On 15 January Mr Tremblay sent an e-mail to TWC in which he introduced the outlines of the *new concept*, which was the elaboration of his idea to improve the energy efficiency of the machine. Mr Tremblay's concept was *totally different* from the change of order proposed by TWC [. . .]
>
> – Stages 1 and 2 *no longer exist as such* (in this apparatus the box pallet and folder are *not integrated* in the Filomat itself, but *next* to it)
>
> [. . .]
>
> The same day Mr Graanhof replied with the remark that a five stage order was agreed upon [. . .] 'A first question; where are the boxes folded in this concept? [. . .] In the concept that we have talked about there were five stages. [. . .] Could you explain *your concept*?'
>
> [. . .]
>
> In an e-mail on 17 January 2005 Mr Tremblay corrected the words of Mr Graanhof: '*Our concept* has a five stage order of which three have been *incorporated* in the machine. The first and second station consists of the box pallet and folder next to the machine.'

With the importance of TWC's concept downplayed as an impoverishment, the space is created for Gortec's engineer Tremblay to appear on stage with a brand new concept. Yes, Gortec's attorneys can admit to the difference between machine A (SPEEDEC) and machine B (TWC's proposal). There however also is a 'total difference' between machine B and machine C (which they actually call their 'Filomat' and not the 'TWC SPEEDEC'). They establish this difference by pointing out that the Filomat no longer has a first and second station. It only has three stations. How can a machine with five stages be the same as a machine with three stages? This change is so big that TWC's engineer Graanhof is made to ask where the box folder went. In Graanhof's concept this was an integral part of the machine and in the concept of Tremblay he cannot find it! The authority and expertise of Tremblay is strengthened when he corrects Graanhof's interpretation of his concept. The box folder is no longer part of the machine as a second station, but is externalized and can be put next to the machine as a separate device.

These statements form the backdrop for TWC's new statement of claim. Where Gortec's attorneys had endeavoured to construct a 'total difference' between machines B and C, TWC's attorneys now try to establish an identity. Although, they admit that the box folder is no longer part of the machine, this obstacle however poses no problem for the construction of sameness between the machines. The machine might no longer *embody* the second station, but the '*possibility* to use a box folder' still exists. The apparatus still allows for the function of folding boxes at the same position where the box folder used to be. This is due to the fact that the order of five stages is still the same as the one proposed by TWC! This order permits the insertion of an external device in the slot left open by the absent (first and) second station.

> **TWC:** In contrast to the assertion in their statement of defence, Gortec does ***take over*** TWC's proposal to change the order (but in a **modified form**, since station 1 and 2 have been removed from the machine).

The five *stage* order proposed by TWC is still identical in Gortec's concept: box pallet – box folder – filler – box taper – receptacle. This order however has been put in a 'modified form' by only incorporating three *stations* and externalizing two stations. The attorneys urge a distinction between the conceptual order of stages and their incorporation in technical stations. The stages are conceptual. The question whether all stages have been materially embodied in one machine or whether some of these stages have been delegated to a separate machine is not important, and neither is the question whether these machines have actually ever been produced. Of concern in a patent dispute is the immaterial intellectual concept and its inventor.

Origination and Ownership of Concepts

TWC will first have to demonstrate that this input was actually hers in order to prove the claim that this input changed the SPEEDEC machine in a way that fundamentally improved it. TWC will have to reconstruct the myth of origins in which the invention saw the light of birth through its creator and turn it into a factual history. They start by cutting off short some of Gortec's statements about a meeting between the engineers of TWC and Gortec at the site of TWC.

> **TWC:** Gortec writes the following about this meeting in her statement of defence:
>
> '*Furthermore, TWC's installations were introduced to Gortec. Mr Hesse noticed that the boxes were closed by a stapler. This gave Mr Hesse the* ***idea*** *to implement this stapler in the fourth station of the Filomat in order to possibly shorten production time and enhance the box-filling capacity.*'
>
> This is a *completely false representation of reality*: TWC has shown the engineer of Gortec the stapler of TWC and asked him to implement this stapler in the SPEEDEC. The implementation of the stapler thus was an **idea** of TWC. This is confirmed by the **facts** exposed below.

Gortec claims the implementation of a stapler in the machine was an idea of its engineer Hesse. True, he has gone to the site of TWC and has seen their installations with his own eyes. In one of these installations he noticed a stapler was deployed. The idea to use the stapler *in the Filomat machine* has however been entirely his idea. TWC essentially protests against this position in powerful terms: the idea to implement the stapler has been TWC's and not Mr Hesse's. TWC showed him the stapler and asked him for its implementation in the new machine. To succeed in letting these descriptions pass as matters of fact, they have to be backed up by evidence. But how can an idea or '*having an idea*' be a *matter* of fact? Are ideas not of an intellectual or immaterial nature according to the very theory of intellectual rights? Apparently, in this legal practice the relation of origination of ideas is capable of being proved and turned into a fact. How is this done? Has it left any traces?

TWC tries to reinforce the rough threads attached to some documents in the summons and comes up with several kinds of proof. It's useful to have a closer look at these documents and their respective sources. First, reference is made to an email by Mark Graanhof (TWC) to Martin Hesse (Gortec) about the conditions for buying a machine from Gortec.

> TWC believes it has communicated a sufficient degree of *its know-how* to Gortec to warrant a request for the exclusivity of the *conceptual changes* to the Speedec that were *proposed by us*. These conceptual changes were based on TWC's input and relate to the next properties:
> - The incorporation of a stapler according to the *TWC Concept*
> - The shift of stations in the order of the machine.

This is a document that in so many words states that both the conceptual changes of the stapler and the station shift have been explicitly proposed by TWC and were based on 'its' know-how. They are even called the 'TWC Concept'. The proof of the belonging of the ideas is here effected by pointing at grammatical markers: the Company name 'TWC' is juxtaposed to the 'Concept' of concern as its possessive pronoun. Origination is further demonstrated by pointing out the use of the possessive pronouns 'ours' and verbs like 'proposed by' and 'based on'. TWC here makes a reference to its own e-mailed statements on the matter before the dispute arose. This is interesting: an anterior statement made in the context of business is used as proof for a statement used in the context of a legal conflict. Written documents that originate from a party before a conflict have low evidential value, but once a dispute has started the evidential value of its statements drops to zero. Other sources are needed however. The second piece of proof proposed is an e-mail of 31 October 2004 sent to TWC.

> We have discussed *your* application extensively with our provider, the Gortec company (Mr Martin Hesse), and can inform you of the following: For *your* application Gortec will make a custom-made automatic box filling device *according to your concept*.

This email comes from Mr Raap, a consulting engineer for Gortec, and is supposed to legitimately represent Gortec's views on the matter. In the name of Gortec, Mr Raap announces that the application that Gortec is supposed to develop for TWC will be based on a concept of TWC. The italics in the citation come from the attorneys of TWC. The stress on the possessive pronouns 'your' juxtaposed to a 'mindful' noun (like 'concept' or 'idea') is amplified. We again see that written phrases with possessive grammatical markers are used to prove with whom a concept originated. Mind your words, for they will be mined! In disputes of intellectual rights they will be meticulously queried for appropriable an*noun*cements of mind. Still these phrases are very general, they do not specify which elements of the proposed machine have been concretely joined together by this concept. TWC's attorneys therefore inscribe a third piece of proof already referred to in the summons as the 'TWC Concept Agreement'.

Date: 07/07/2005

The undersigned parties hereby acknowledge that:

- Gortec will not communicate to any third party any information received from TWC concerning the box stapler device (the TWC Concept);
- Gortec will not sell or commercialize the TWC Concept;
- Gortec will guarantee the exclusivity on the TWC Concept until 30 May 2010.

Belgian law is applicable and the court of Brussels has exclusive jurisdiction.

Gortec
Represented by Mr. M. Hesse

TWC
Represented by Mr. M. Graanhof

This signed contract is an important document in which Gortec engages in a binding 'agreement' with TWC about several obligations of exclusivity and non-disclosure of confidential information. The attorneys of TWC are interested in the object of those obligations: the information from TWC. This term can again be taken quite literally here. Of concern are data about a machine that is still in formation. These data are supposed to demonstrate that an engineer of TWC has proposed to cast the machine into the specific inventive shape that is now the matter of debate. The attorneys of TWC want to prove the existence of a relation of origination between TWC and this formative Concept. The fact that Gortec formally declares that they have received information from TWC concerning the stapler and that it calls this the 'TWC Concept' should prove this relation.

3.5 AT THE LAW FIRM: HOW THINGS MAKE ONE SPEAK LEGALLY

It is going to take us a long time to understand precisely what things make us do.
(Latour, 1999, p. 178)

So far we have mostly engaged in textual analysis. Many of the important articulations of the matter of dispute in-deed pass through text: documents, scans, prints and drafts. This might give the impression that law only occurs through text or language. An important part of the case however, is about coming-to-be-textual through the operations of attorneys and for these textual proposals to eventually make their way to the sentences of the judge. Within this task elements of the *con-text* are of concern to the extent that they can be aligned *with* the articulations in the legal documents and thus come to pass into *text*, or to the extent that they allow for these inscriptions or for the organization and change of text.[55]

At first sight the offices of the attorneys at the law firm look pretty ordinary, hosting most of the standard office equipment: a main desk with some additional chairs, filled bookcases, a telephone, a desktop computer, a printer and many many papers, documents, paper folders, clips, pens and fluorescent markers. Sometimes our familiarity with these things however, makes us overlook how each of them works as an enabler for a specific way of organizing the case file and the documents it lodges. Here we will look at the things that allow the attorneys of TWC to write their statements or prepare their pleas: fluorescent markers of change, media for involvement, legal texts and mnemonic and optic devices that support legal speech.

Markers of Change

There has been another round of exchange of documents. Gortec's attorneys have written a new statement of reply. At TWC's law firm the secretary prints out the set of paper sheets and puts a clip around them to keep the document together. The clip herein serves as a 'marker' of enclosure indicating that the sheets together form a statement, similar to the way in which a paper *folder* enfolds several documents and keeps them together as the file of the 'lawsuit'. The secretary takes Gortec's original statement of defence out of this folder and puts it next to the new one on the desk. The documents are compared and the textual parts that have been added or modified in the second statement of defence are highlighted with a yellow fluorescent marker. This fluorescent pen is a 'marker' of change that allows one to see differences. It also indicates what kind of actions are to be performed on these parts. With regard to TWC's own statement of

---

[55] The notion of context has been criticized in social science, since it is all too often used as a term for explaining phenomena, whereas the construction of this context itself has to be explained (Latour, 2005). Here however 'con-text' is not evoked as an explanatory term, but to point attention to all the elements that have been assembled together in the work of constructing a legal text. Furthermore, the proceedings in legal practice do not necessarily all occur in the direction of textualization. In the preparation of the plea, we will see the things that allow an attorney to transform a text into speech in a reliable way.

claim, the digital 'formatting' functions of Microsoft Word allow them to perform more fine-grained marking operations. A whole pallet of colours is employed for these purposes: blue, red, yellow and green. The types of marking include the highlighting of phrases and the **colouring**, underlining and ~~crossing out~~ of letter fonts.

The secretary hands over her marked version of Gortec's statement to the two attorneys. Her yellow highlights quickly allow the attorneys to see what the main efforts of Gortec's attorneys have been. Especially striking are 13 pages entirely highlighted titled 'TWC's alleged "essential contributions"'. Here Gortec's attorneys thoroughly dispute TWC's claim that it was the 'brain' behind the 34 proposals that supposedly essentially changed the Filomat machine:

> **Gortec:** The arguments that TWC tries to derive from this list of points will hereafter be discussed one by one, which will show that each of these points either:
>
> - *was a* **repetition** *of something that already existed in the original Filomat;*
> - ***could* not *be* implemented*;***
> - ***was limited to a certain* specification *for which Gortec had to find a solution (so without any input of TWC that they would be able to claim);***
> - ***or referred to* banal *adjustments commonly requested and agreed to in a relation between a manufacturer/salesperson and a potential customer.***

Gortec's attorneys have worked their way through the whole list of 34 technical points. They seem to have *involved* their engineers extensively in this process and have made their statements rely on their authority. All of TWC's essential contributions have been reduced to 4 categories. Each of these categorical qualifications is a disqualification for patentability in terms of the legal conditions stated in the European Patent Act.[56] Something that is a repetition of something that already exists is part of the 'state of the art' and thus not 'new'.[57] Something that cannot be implemented is not 'susceptible of industrial application'.[58] Someone who merely specifies a modification for a technical problem for which someone

---

[56] 'European patents shall be granted for any inventions which are susceptible of industrial application, which are new and which involve an inventive step' (article 52 EPC).

[57] 'An invention shall be considered to be new if it does not form part of the state of the art' (article 54 EPC).

[58] 'An invention shall be considered as susceptible of industrial application if it can be made or used in any kind of industry, including agriculture' (article 57 EPC).

else is supposed to invent the technical solution is not the 'inventor'.[59] Something that is a mere 'banal' adjustment does not involve an 'inventive step', especially not compared to 'persons skilled in the art' like Gortec's engineers.[60] All of TWC's contributions have been non-essential in patent terms. On the basis of these disqualifications Gortec concludes that 'TWC has not provided a single essential contribution to the modification of the design and development of the machine'. We see here how TWC's practical philosophy of identity and difference is countered by Gortec's practical philosophy of essence and accident.

With these main points of dispute clearly marked, TWC's attorneys can return to their own statement of claim. They are now enabled to localize the parts of their text that have become disqualified and, in turn, start marking them as candidates for change. From now on, in the period of a month, several versions of the statement will be constructed. Different authors will work on these documents all making different contributions. There is a distribution of labour between the two attorneys working on a case. Blanchard writes the legal part of the statement. She does not deal with the facts but 'looks at the case from a distance', checking the text for readability and coherence. Zomers writes the factual part of the statement. He 'is really into the case', is familiar with all the pieces in the inventory, is in contact with TWC's engineer Mark Graanhof about the technical details and writes most of the draft texts.

When we focus on the first written draft that the attorneys have constructed we notice how the formerly sober statement has turned in an extravagant display of colours and lines. The different colours and marks each provide different indications by and for different actors. A legend is needed to understand the whole range of actions performed through these different marking techniques through which firmly stated black statements are turned into the transient coloured fluid (or fluoride) of change. The sections marked in yellow highlights by Blanchard indicate that Zomers is required to change, rewrite or add to this text. Green highlights indicate that the client still needs to have a look at these sections. Red highlights are also addressed to the client, but in a way that requires much more careful attention, because they have been strongly disputed by the other party. The attorneys have also delegated other marking operations to a software subprogram called 'Workshare', which shows the

---

[59] 'The right to a European patent shall belong to the inventor' (article 60 EPC).

[60] 'An invention shall be considered as involving an inventive step if, having regard to the state of the art, it is not obvious to a person skilled in the art' (article 56 EPC).

differences between versions of documents by marking new text sections in blue, underlining the strategically possible options that still have to be explored, and by marking deleted text sections in red, crossing out what is no longer of importance at this point in the dispute dynamics.[61]

Media of Involvement: The Lawyer and the Engineer

The extensive disputation of TWC's alleged 'essential contributions' has become a main concern for the attorneys. The section on this topic in their statement of claim urgently needs to be discussed with TWC's engineer Mr Graanhof. Blanchard and Zomers discuss how to get him involved in this issue. Zomers, who is in charge of the facts and the client, wants to get in his car and drive up to TWC's site, but Blanchard urges him to 'not drive to their site, they are already whining about the costs'. She proposes to first send the statement to TWC by e-mail, request a reply and set up a teleconference.[62] Zomers attaches the multicoloured draft and sends it through (cyber-)space. A bit later he picks up the phone, puts on the teleconference mode and calls Graanhof.

> **Zomers:** *Have you received the statement?*
> **Graanhof:** *Yes, I have it before me.*
> **Zomers:** *I would like to know what Gortec has really contributed. Were all these points already effectively part of the SPEEDEC as they claim? We will have to go through TWC's list of 34 points that demonstrates our know-how. Gortec disputes this list and so* ***we have to respond*** *to this. Although they don't prove their disputations, we have to know the correctness of these statements.*
> *We will have to speak about the parts of the document that are marked in red.* ***Don't worry about*** *the added legal sections. For the section on the facts, the contributions of TWC are* ***important.***
> **Graanhof:** *Our goal was to construct a more efficient device. Gortec has to prove that they have a faster machine. What annoys me are the sections that claim that Mr Graanhof said this and that. Mr Graanhof has nothing to do with this, it's TWC!*
> **Zomers:** *The* ***important*** *section is the one in red.* ***Remember*** *that the goal of the claim is to recover the patent. They have stolen something from us.* ***This we have to prove.*** *We have supplied something that they have used.* ***Read*** *those sections and check whether they are correct in order for us to* ***feel comfortable****. We speak to each other tomorrow.*

---

[61] Workshare also provides quantitative results on document comparison, displaying the amounts of insertions, deletions and movements of text between versions. With these data one can study the movements of change between different drafts and locate the 'sites of change'.

[62] As McLuhan already noted, communication through wheel technologies like cars has become replaced by electronic technologies like telephones (McLuhan, 1994).

This short encounter is important. It is a confrontation between two distinct practitioners – a lawyer and an engineer – whose practices require them to work in their own specific way. The questions they pose, the concepts they use, the interests and concerns they have, the things they work with, make them articulate differently the conflict that gathered them. The engineer has been implicated in the whole process that eventually led to the legal dispute. He was involved in the contacts and contracts with Gortec, the modifications to the SPEEDEC box-filling machine and the conflicts that resulted. Zomers however requires a different involvement of the engineer. As a lawyer he is concerned with the dynamics of this whole process only to the extent that it addresses the legal claim for joint property of a patent on this machine. Successfully resolving the dispute in their advantage requires another mode of thought than the technological one. Zomers has to present himself to the engineer in a way that makes explicit what he requires of him for constructing a firm answer to Gortec's claims. He employs several techniques for directing and diverting attention in order to achieve this goal. First, he asks Graanhof not to be distracted or worried by all the newly added legal talk, since this is the attorney's (or more specifically Blanchard's) business. He should also not be distracted by what annoys him as a representative of TWC. The important sections requiring attention are the ones marked in red. Zomers requests Graanhof to read those sections and contribute his technical know-how. Nevertheless, the engineer's efforts and skills should not address his regular technical obligations. As an engineer involved in the whole disputed process, Graanhof had to make a more *efficient* machine and directed his professional efforts towards this *technical* goal. The ('TWC') concept he came up with was supposed to be the result of addressing these efficiency obligations. As an engineer he is sceptical about the claim that Gortec's modifications have increased the efficiency of the machine and insists that they have to provide proof for this. As an attorney, Zomers however asks the engineer to momentarily suspend these technical goals and to remember the *legal* goal of the patent claim: recovering the invention that was stolen from them. The success of this claim poses different constraints. He needs to translate to the engineer what legal obligations are attached to a successful claim and what they require of the engineer.[63] Such *conditions for proceeding* can often be traced in the attorney's language by the use of grammatical markers like 'we have to', 'we can't'. *Requirements* can in this case be traced by grammatical markers like 'it's

63 For the relation between obligations and requirements (exigencies), see Stengers, 2006.

important' or 'remember'. Zomers knows they 'have to' prove Gortec's theft.[64] He therefore asks Graanhof to specify which exact elements were illegally taken over from his concept in Gortec's patent-pending Filomat. *This* is what 'has to' be proven (not that Gortec has a faster machine as Graanhof states). Furthermore, the attorney knows that the statements of facts proposed by Gortec have to be disputed to prevent the judge from being obliged to consider them as established.[65] Remember that Gortec had reduced many of TWC's essential contributions to mere 'repetitions of something that already existed in the original Filomat', disqualifying them as 'new' patentable inventions. *This* is what they 'have to' respond to. Zomers requires Graanhof to provide facts that falsify the correctness of these statements.

The next day Zomers receives an e-mail from Graanhof with a new draft of the statement attached. Has he fulfilled the attorney's expectations?

> **Zomers:** *Mr Graanhof completely passes over my questions! He is a technician who doesn't understand legal essence.*

The attorneys seemed to have failed in redirecting the engineer's attention. Graanhof's contributions were not led by their legal objectives, but bypassed them, straight back to the achievement of his regular technical goals. Zomers phones the engineer again.

> **Zomers:** *I have* ***incorporated*** *your comments. Let's go through the list of 34 points to see what was already part of the machine, what was not, and what has been implemented.*

Zomers is already constructing a new draft of the statement. He has gotten Graanhof *involved*, but not as an official author. His inscriptions have been anonymously incorporated in the body of the new text. The engineer is now fully *implied* in the statement. Vanished from sight, but relied upon nevertheless. The attorney will again try to make the engineer focus on the legal questions. They will discuss the whole list on an arduous point-by-point basis.

---

64 Remember the first condition of proof: 'Each party has to provide the proof for the facts that it brings forward' (article 870 Ger. W.).

65 An explicit formulation can be found in the Dutch Procedural Code: 'The judge has to consider established the facts stated by one party and not or not sufficiently disputed by the adverse party' (article 149).

[. . .]
Zomers: *What about point 17; the change of the conveyer belt?*
Graanhof: *I have to go way back in memory. It is all* ***ant fucking!***[66]
Zomers: *Yes, but the* ***question*** *is not: haven't they done it, but: have they implemented something off the list.* ***That makes our position stronger****. It might seem like ant fucking, but it* ***demonstrates*** *their use of TWC's* ***input****. That is why it is* ***important.***

The attorney makes the engineer get into the small details of things that seem futile to him. Those parts of the machine in question may be small, but they are legally important. They will both rely on these tiny act-ants to let their input be proved and to make TWC's proposal to be declared 'inventor' legally succeed.[67] The more ants that they can trace as rummaged from TWC's site into Gortec's machine, the stronger the tissue of the factual patchwork becomes in their lawsuit.

[. . .]
Zomers: *And point 32: the motion display?*
Graanhof: *They have placed something different than we asked for. In the end one could say that they have not implemented it.*
Zomers: *Gortec claims they have proposed this.*
Graanhof: *Nonsense! We have asked for it, but they have not done this.* [ironic:] *It sounds like they have proposed everything!!*
It is a very ***difficult*** *discussion. We once discussed all of this in a meeting around the table: questions, remarks and our demands.* ***Who knows*** *who said what? It's someone's* <u>*word*</u> *against somebody else's.* ***It can't be proved.*** *They were* ***conversations****.* ***I can't remember*** *these things.*

The engineer feels undermined by the reconstruction of the course of events by Gortec's attorneys. They move way too fast for an issue that is so complex. How can one possibly make such bold assertions when they are grounded in something as feeble as fleeting memories? There is a practical problem of epistemology here that is hard to tackle. At stake is the question of how to know who is the owner of the 'brain' behind the ideas and proposals, which were alleged to have essentially changed the machine of concern. For these propositions about this intellectual origin to legally proceed, they have to

---

66 This is the literal translation of the Dutch term *mierenneukerij*. The more proverbial translation in English would be 'nit picking'.

67 These 'ants' that act in a certain way are closely related to Latour's (1999) concept of an 'actant' that points attention to how the performance of 'our' actions is distributed over a composite network of humans and non-human things (Latour, 1999). The word 'ANT' is also an abbreviation for Actor-Network Theory that serves to study such hybrid actorship.

have been *constituted* in speech acts like questions, remarks and demands, which, in turn, need to have been fixed in some-thing stable like documents or images that can make them serve as a *piece* of evidence. The conversational acts have however never been *documented*. Nothing enables the epistemological access required. When we do not know who said what, we cannot even begin to *ground* any brain behind anything. It cannot be proved!

> [. . .]
> **Zomers:** *That was the list of 34 points.*
> **Graanhof:** *The most important points are the 2 main components. You remember we discussed the stapler and the stage shift?* ***All the rest is detail*** *and so are the discussions about it.*
> **Zomers:** *We are not in a contractual dispute; it is not a process about delivery. That is* ***not the matter of the claim.***
> **Graanhof:** *There is a* ***difference*** *between my* ***technical side*** *of the story and the talk between Mrs Blanchard and Mr Kirsch about the* ***legal side****.*
> **Zomers:** *We will see.*
> **Graanhof:** *How is our situation?*
> **Zomers:** *Well, we* ***can claim*** *the stapler since it is* ***clearly part*** *of the machine. We have enough evidence to prove this.* ***The judge can hardly get around this point****.*
> *Things will* ***centre*** *on whether TWC has provided the stapler and whether this is a part of the invention. If this is the case,* ***they are stuck and their whole story will collapse****.*
> [. . .]
> **Graanhof:** *I am curious to see the statement.*
> **Zomers:** *I will still make some adjustments.*
> **Graanhof:** *All those* ***details are ant fucking****.*
> **Zomers:** *It's something we want to know to demonstrate the input and cooperation of TWC. Those* ***details didn't drop from the sky****. They are* ***part of a cooperation*** *on all kinds of points.*

Gortec reduced 34 points to 4. TWC's engineer deletes 32 of them! They might be interesting to a legal entomologist, but not for the engineer. He is only interested in the things that clearly incorporate his input. He does not think the other small *corpora* perform any job of importance. Once again the attorney has to advocate the work done by the small act-ants. Ants don't tend to fall from the skies where our (Platonic) ideas are supposed to freely float around. They are rooted in firm ground where their interactions form complex networks through which many actions, both technological and legal, are made possible.[68] We are only enabled to project our ideas in the skies because they can be grounded in such firm networks. In

---

[68] In systems theory such 'trophallaxic' interactions are even proposed as mechanisms for structural coupling between sub-units (individual ants), to achieve

our case this is a network of cooperation that includes actors like TWC and Gortec and a host of detailed technical act-ants that have circulated through many sites and texts. The more TWC can demonstrate its involvement in this heterogeneous network by carefully tracing its many elaborative attachments to these details and stitching them to as many evidential documents, the more they will be enabled to proclaim that the resulting machine has incorporated their inventive ideas.

In order to gain the engineer's attention, the attorney introduces a legal distinction between two different legal forms under which a matter of dispute can be claimed: contract and patent. In a contractual case, the dispute would have mainly been articulated through concepts like 'payment' and 'delivery' and non-performance of contractual obligations like non-disclosure of confidential information. Other conditions would be raised for the proceeding of the claim and other pieces of evidence would have to be stitched into the lawsuit. The attorney would then have required different things from the engineer and these small ants could safely have been ignored. But this is not the case. The attorney and the engineer are jointly bound by their patent claim and what matters is the proof of all inventive parts no matter how small.

The engineer has again become interested in the dispute and the attorney sketches a prospective for its further proceeding. He thinks that all their work on the stapler has been satisfactory. Here they 'have a case'. Through their attachments of the pictures and descriptions in the patent application they will have produced a resistant fact. This fact has an insistent evidential force that will constrain the possibilities the judge will have in determining its evidential value. They will have provided their case with a claimable subject matter and *can* then proceed to centre the main focus upon the conditions for patentability. If they manage to satisfy these conditions they will have also tied up Gortec in a legal straightjacket and decisively cut off their story from legal passage.

The Bookcase: Inscribing and Aligning Legal Authorities

We will not further disturb Mr Zomers in changing the factual part of the statement. We will enter Mrs Blanchard's office and see what is going on here. We find her sitting at her desk which is now filled with huge piles of books, articles and papers, most of them taken from her bookcases. This provides a striking contrast to Zomers' desk which

---

functionalities at the systemic level (colony) (Maturana & Varela, 1998, pp. 184–8).

had been practically empty throughout the teleconference sessions. Blanchard has different exigencies however. She is occupied with revising the legal part of the statement. Zomers was engaged in letting the empirical evidence speak for TWC's propositions through turning the matter of dispute into a matter of fact. Blanchard will have to let the law and its authorities successfully speak for these propositions, by establishing the conditions that they have to satisfy in order to legally succeed.

Blanchard's task is to look at the dispute from a distance that will abstract from the details of its concrete occurrence. But this distance is not something one can just 'take'. Just as there are several media that allowed Zomers to bridge the empirical distance between him and his client's engineers (cars, e-mail, telephone and the other techniques of implication), there are several things that allow one to create legal distance from a case. The bookcases are a reservoir for possible inscriptions of legal authoritative sources in the legal document that is under construction. They are crammed with legislation, doctrine, jurisprudence and handbooks on patents, trademarks, copyright. These texts serve as the main node of entrance for the legislator, the courts and legal theorists in the dispute. Through attaching the claims to parts of these texts, the matter of dispute is made to pass through different legal settings. It will come to traverse some of the legal paths that have once become successfully constructed in past disputes in order to transport their requirements to the present conflict when the lawyers manage to establish sufficient 'reasonances' between them; it will be guided through the preparatory considerations and legal reference checks of the legislative processes leading up to the laws invoked in the dispute; or it will come to pass along the systematic pre-articulations of the webs of authorization for the conditions that govern the proceedings of these kinds of dispute lines proposed in the interpretative writings of legal scholars. In this way, legal authorities become aligned with the claim in a new fabric of alliances.

There is a way however in which Blanchard has been obstructed from easily attaining this legal distance. Remember that the legal authority of Mrs Blanchard was put at stake within this case. Mr Leerbeek, Gortec's attorney, inscribed references to a doctrinal book about patent law she had once written as an academic lawyer. In this way she was made to back up Gortec's legal proposition! Blanchard is thus literally drawn into the dispute in a way that she will have to respond to. Things have to be set straight and her authority needs to be restored.

For TWC's claim for recovery to **succeed**, it suffices to demonstrate that it has contributed to the coming about of the patent (B. Blanchard, Patent Law, Oxford University Press, 1995, 73; Delcore, C., La protection des inventions, Brussel, 1985, 43).

Gortec disputes this point of view by referring to the doctrine inscribed by TWC (**the book by Mrs Blanchard**). Gortec however only refers to those **parts of the doctrine** which are **profitable** for it. The **complete text** is as follows:

'All cases are dealt with by two general hypotheses contained in the law:

1) The patent was asked for an invention that was taken away from one of the inventors or its legal successors: this hypothesis refers to all cases in which a third person has taken away (*soustraite*) the invention by stealing the plans of the inventor or making abuse of his confidential duties.
   Is it necessary to demonstrate that this taking occurred with lack of good faith?
   The answer to this question is **delicate**. In reading the preparatory works of the Patent Act the answer **seems positive**. The preparatory works indeed indicate that 'article 9 treats the recovery of the property of a patent or a patent application. It incorporates the majority of determinations contained in articles 27 and 28 and rule 7 of the Treaty of Luxemburg. *The first paragraph determines that each person affected by deceptive actions can claim the property of the patent or the patent application*'. Article 27 of the Treaty of Luxemburg **however**, to which the Patent Act **refers** and that deals with the hypothesis discussed, **does not contain a single requirement (exigency) of lack of good faith**.
   [. . .] **this idea** expressed in the Treaty of Luxemburg referred to by the preparatory works of our law, **must be adhered to** and a claim for recovery must be permitted each time an invention has been "taken away" from an inventor, i.e., "applied for by a person who was not entitled to do so" [. . .]'
   The doctrine cannot be clearer: the **very establishment** of the fact that the plaintiff for a patent is not the inventor, or not the only inventor, **suffices to grant** a claim for recovery.

In the course of a few paragraphs a whole network of alliances has been displaced and even reversed. Mrs Blanchard has undermined the doctrinal authority of Gortec's attorneys. They are now unmasked as poor academics who engage in practices of selective reference. The attorneys have only cited those parts of the doctrine that are profitable for the position of their client. In this way they have created a very one-sided point of view and taken things out of a context that is far more complex. If Gortec's attorneys would have continued the citation from the very point where they cut off, things would have immediately become more delicate. Blanchard does cite the whole text and hereby manages to cut off one of Gortec's grounding references. Gortec cited parts of the preparatory works of the Patent Act[69] in their statement of defence to back up their proposition that lack of good faith was required as a condition for proceeding. When one just looks at these sections things *seem* positive for Gortec: lack of good faith seems required. However when one continues reading both the preparatory works and Blanchard's text that explicate these works, this apparent answer is suddenly not at all the most obvious! They direct us to an authoritative source in the preparatory works to a Treaty, which the legal articulation of the conditions for wrongful taking must adhere to and which will also govern our case. Within this more elaborate legal fabric of attachments, Gortec's stringent conditions for proceeding find themselves less firmly supported. Instead, the authority of the law is redirected and aligned with the less exigent conditions proposed by TWC.

In the next version of the statement of claim delivered seven days later, this reversal is even further continued. Mrs Blanchard managed to track down an interesting doctrinal article co-authored by one of Gortec's attorneys Mr Leerbeek, which she has inscribed in the statement.

> Gortec unrightfully states that the plaintiff has to demonstrate that taking away the invention occurred with a lack of good faith.
> [. . .]
> the **doctrine underlines** that 'lack of good faith' is not required. **Leerbeek**, De Zeeuw, and Wauters rightfully remark the following: 'according to doctrine proof of a lack of good faith is **not required**' (De Zeeuw, M., Wauters, P., and Leerbeek, G., An Update on the Latest Developments in Patent Law, TIR, 2008/1, 395; in a footnote the authors **refer to** B. Blanchard, Patent Law, Oxford University Press, 1995, 73).

The reversal of the legal fabric has become even more symmetrical. First Blanchard's doctrinal authority has been restored, detached from Gortec and re-aligned in support of the cause of TWC. Second, Leerbeek's doctrinal authority itself has become drawn into the dispute and aligned in support of the propositions of TWC! Lack of good faith is not a condition that is required for a claim for recovery. The circle is closed when Blanchard shows that Leerbeek actually bases this doctrinal position on the very same book of Blanchard that he earlier tried to mobilize in the support of his position in the dispute! Not only has Blanchard's authority been restored and realigned, it has also come to ground and re-align

---

69 The phrase Gortec cited from the preparatory works also occurs in Blanchard's longer citation of the same text. I put this part in italics and will repeat it here: '*The first paragraph determines that each person affected by deceptive actions can claim the property of the patent or the patent application.*'

Leerbeek's authority and force him in an alliance in support of TWC's propositions. Law in action can be a very curious and complicated fabric of cross-references of legal authorities.

Preparing the Plea

Zomers has incorporated Graanhof's contributions in the finalized draft of the statement of claim in which the engineer has now become fully implied. The document is sent to the court and to Gortec. Now the attorneys can prepare themselves for the pleas in court. In this period however, Zomers' own employment ends and he leaves the firm for a position as a partner in another. The attorney most involved in the facts of the case is suddenly gone. Here we have a second reason for distributing the case work over two attorneys. Legal cases last for years. When one attorney becomes unavailable, the know-how will not be totally lost but still partially retained by the other. Mr Peters has agreed to replace Mr Zomers in this case. He and Mrs Blanchard need to start preparing the upcoming pleas. Blanchard has opted for distributing speech over the two attorneys, since 'with long pleas of 90 minutes, listening to the voice of one person, will make the judge fall asleep'. That would definitively not make for a happy performance.

> **Blanchard:** *How do you prepare your plea?*
> **Peters:** *Statements that I have written myself I know by heart. I am <u>not</u> the <u>author</u> here. With a statement that I have not written myself I normally make <u>sheets</u> with bullet points. I also stick little yellow* ***tabs*** *in the document so I can easily find the pictures again.*
> **Blanchard:** *I write <u>plea notes</u> with a summary of the statement. Otherwise I am too much into the structure of the statement. Sometimes I tell the story in the opposite order to <u>confuse</u> the attorneys of the other party.*
> *I have to prepare things on paper, not by heart. When there is an* ***interruption****, I have to be able to find things again. A patent is* ***technical*** *so it has to be* ***prepared well****.*
> **Peters:** *When the* ***pictures*** *are important, we can make a PowerPoint. An image says more than 1000 words.*
> **Blanchard:** *Is that possible?*
> **Peters:** *When we ask for previous permission it is.*
> **Blanchard:** *We can also just make a paper copy. This will clearly make things visible.*

A plea has a threefold structure of satisfaction: *satis-facere, satis-placere, satis-plicare.* An attorney has to do enough (*satis*) work of unfolding and explicating the case, in a way that sufficiently complies with the conditions and convincingly pleases the judges, in order for them to align with the qualification proposed. This is not an easy achievement, since there can be many obstacles. In court the flow of a plea can become interrupted by the adverse party making the attorney lose her points. It is actually a part of the attorney's work to try to punctuate the flow of words of one's opponent by interruptions and reversals. Furthermore, Peters is still being introduced into the firm and into the case and Blanchard will have to plead in the Dutch language and not in French which is her native tongue. The case is also very technical and many facts have become stitched to it. All these factors complicate speech and can make it stutter and stumble. Sufficient preparatory work thus needs to be done for stabilizing the plea. The attorneys employ two techniques for this: mnemonic devices to 'find things again' and optic devices to 'make things visible'. The question here is not merely about how to do things with words. It is rather about how things make us speak legally and how they allow us to say things without words. Speech is supported by a number of paper items that serve to index, trace and retrieve the threads of argumentation. When the attorney loses the aim of her story she can fall back on a paper sheet with bullet-points to retrieve the main ammunition for her plea. Oral speech is substituted by 'speaking' images that serve to visualize the matters of dispute. Sometimes these images tell the story of change more satisfactorily than the attorneys can.

3.6 TO COURT: PLEA AND RE-PLY

It is 26 July 2009, the day of the plenary session in the 'TWC-Gortec case'. We find ourselves in the building of the Court of Commerce in Brussels. The attorneys of both parties have arrived and are gathered outside the courtroom where the plenary session will take place. They seem slightly nervous. Nevertheless, they speak amicably amongst each other, patiently waiting for the judges to appear. While we are all waiting we can indicate how things will proceed. There will be two pleas by both parties and a short round of responses and questions. In the pleas the order of things is tied together differently than in the statements where the complex movements of the dispute have been developed at great length and detail. These statements have become 'corpulent' documents exceeding the mark of hundred pages. In the plea these movements will have to be presented in such a way that the problem, the main points of conflict and the solutions will become clear and evident to the judges. There is a certain contraction at work here. Years of preparations are condensed into a plea of 90 minutes in a way that has to be convincing. Different elements are put to the fore for these purposes.

Plea 1: Of Pilots and Cartoonists

When the judges arrive, all enter the courtroom and install themselves. The actors present at the start of the session are: 3 judges, 1 registrar, 2 attorneys of TWC (Mr Peters and Mrs Blanchard), 2 attorneys of Gortec (Mr Leerbeek and Mr Vetard), 2 employees of Gortec (Mr Hesse and Mr Schmit) and 1 researcher. The registrar writes down the names of all the attorneys and then the word is to the judge presiding.

> **President:** *The session is opened.*
> **Peters:** *Madam president, we represent The Wool Corporation. Today's case is about intellectual property. Our plea will consist of two parts. I will sketch the facts of the dispute. Mrs Blanchard will speak in more detail about the legal grounds.*
> *Some* ***cases*** *can become very* ***corpulent****, whereas the* ***question*** *posed is very* ***simple****. This is such a case. The simple question is: is TWC co-owner of the patent?* ***This is the question which needs to be answered****. The answer however is not so easy to formulate. Both parties therefore have diametrically* ***opposed positions****. On this side the answer is 'Yes', on the other side this will be forcefully denied. It is up to the court to pass verdict about* ***this conflict****. This was my introduction, I will now start my plea.*

The researcher is finally allowed to sit back in the public stand and let the legal actors do the presentation of the legal dispute. After all they can speak much more convincingly. Notice how in the course of a few phrases the proceedings for the case are unfolded: the dispute is situated, the actors are positioned and the plea is organized. First introductory moves are especially important, since they provide the pre-positions for the legal proceedings. 'Madam president . . . today's case is about intellectual property.' The judges are given a first orientation. The case that will be made before them in the succeeding hours has its legal belonging within the regime of intellectual property, patent law to be more precise. Through this territorial situation a whole set of laws and conditions is evoked by which the dispute will have to pass. The judges are hereby addressed in terms of the obligations that will impinge on their work of reaching judgment. This passage to verdict will be full of many proposed sidetracks that might induce appetite (issues like hidden agendas and industrial espionage). The corpus of the case has become quite complicated through all these propositions.[70] The judges are called upon not to be distracted to

---

[70] Similar to the complication of technical projects (Latour, 1996, p. 209), legal patent cases always get more complicated because the attorneys want to reinscribe what threatens to cut off the proceeding of their cause.

follow such tempting deviations and to lose sight of what the dispute is about and what conditions they are bound by. There is a straight passage through the heart of this complex corpus that can be reduced to a short question: 'Is TWC the co-owner of the patent?' The clear territorial situation within patent law allows the location of the positions of the actors with regard to *this* dispute. The claims of both parties must be understood as providing either positive or negative answers to *this* question by which the verdict of the judges must come to pass.

The heart of the case is further fleshed out through the presentation of the mythology about the origin of ideas and the practical philosophy of identity and difference with which we have already become familiar:

> [. . .]
> **Peters:** *I now come to the facts of the case. The contact between TWC and Gortec was about modifying the machine in order to make it work faster. Gortec visited TWC. This visit is very important. Gortec's statement* ***makes it seem*** *as if Mr Hesse had a 'Eureka' experience here. In a cartoon one would draw a shining light bulb above the head of the inventor. Reality however is not a cartoon and this* ***reading of the facts*** *is* ***forcefully disputed****. The statement that the stapler is an invention of Mr Hesse is* ***contradicted*** *by 5 pieces which clearly mark the input of TWC. . .*

Remember that TWC rejected Gortec's claim that its engineer Mr Hesse got the idea to implement the stapler in the Filomat when visiting TWC's site, calling it a 'completely false representation of reality'. Here, Peters tries to further increase the distance between factual reality and Gortec's subjective 'reading'. Gortec's presentation of events is re-presented by Peters within a different context of a Donald Duck cartoon. The narrative about the origination of ideas is hereby transposed. Mr Hesse finds himself transformed in the figure of Gyro Gearloose, the strange inventor-chicken. The origination of the invention is converted into a shining light bulb above the inventor's head. A whole model of invention is simultaneously brought into play and criticized here: the romantic picture of the inventor who gets a brilliant spark of genius that accounts for the whole invention. Both Gortec's presentation and this model of invention are made to pass through Gyro Gearloose's shed and find themselves mutually transformed into a matter of fiction when they come out. These might be nice as amusing bedtime stories, but completely unsuited to describe what has really happened. When Peters shifts us back to the plane of reality, Gortec is suddenly confronted with five pieces of hard evidence that prove TWC's crucial input in the invention. These will demystify Gortec's inventive world and make their spark of brilliance fade away rather quickly . . .

[. . .]
Peters: *Gortec speaks very disparagingly about TWC being the propulsive force against the modifications, but it is the truth. My story will now become very* ***technical****. My apologies for* ***having to pilot the court through this****, but it is* ***very important****.*
[He walks up to the court and shows the pictures of the SPEEDEC; the two attorneys of Gortec also leave their benches to inspect the evidence presented].

'Truth-finding' is an important part of the legal process. We have already expanded on the specific way matters of dispute are progressively turned into matters of fact by the work of evidential stitching. It might sound like a contradiction but legally arriving at the 'real state of affairs' involves a lot of constructive work.[71] This does not necessarily make the attorney a writer of *fiction*.[72] The very moment the adverse party detects that a fictional account has been constructed of what really happened, this account will be forcefully disputed, contradicted, demystified and disqualified. Attorneys have to be good detectives. The narratives they construct must be grounded by gathering many pieces of evidence. These attachments must have been made to resist the cutting operations of the adverse party in a way that the fictional 'just so' story – 'he came, he saw and he had an idea' – can never be.[73] All these stitched attachments, cuts, reattachments and reinforcements can greatly complicate the corpus of the case, especially when it concerns detailed technological descriptions. Belgian judges are generalists in the broad legal field of commerce and not necessarily specialists in the kinds of technical matters that arise within patent law. Speaking the truth, or rather, arriving at the truth *with* the judges is thus no straightforward exercise. Being a good detective and conclusively writing an authoritative body of text within the law firm is one thing, but it offers no necessary guarantees for further proceeding in court. The judges have to be satisfactorily guided through the accumulated specificities and

[71] Remember, truth-finding in law was understood as the fixing of a problem by connecting tubes and screws together.

[72] These narratological fictions have to be distinguished from the legal fictions. As Thomas has elegantly argued, these fictions are specific legal techniques to modify and 'denaturize' the facts for drawing legal consequences (Thomas, 2011, Chapter 6). These *fictio legis* have their own specific *modus operandi* within the practices of law, which are very different from the way fictions operate in literature.

[73] The term 'just so stories' is Kipling's. It was later used as a critique of how evolutionary biologists and psychologists often just invented environmental settings to 'explain' certain features of an organism as an adaptation to such circumstances.

technicalities of the dispute.[74] The attorney is always faced with the risk of losing the judges along the way. In court the attorney has to be a good *pilot* and ensure that the boat that sails the stream of events safely arrives at its proposed destination with all its members still on board.[75] This at least is the meta-theory about pleading and advocacy that Peters proposes.

Peters afterwards proceeds by piloting the judges through all the technicalities involved in grounding immaterial by showing the court the pictures of the machine. In spite of his polite introductory apologies to the court however, he cannot prevent one judge from yawning and another from hiding his face in his hands. The president however is still taking notes. . .

> [. . .]
> **Peters:** *The* ***question which is posed in this factual context*** *is whether TWC has co-ownership? Which* ***rules*** *are* ***applicable*** *here? Mrs Blanchard will answer this question.*

In law one does not just arrive at the truth about a case. A factual context is not a given that provides a straightforward meaning to all the acts of the parties that have taken place within it. It has to be carefully constructed by the attorney's incessant contextualizing work of gathering and attaching documents to the matter of dispute, slowly but steadily turning it into a matter of fact. The prepositions for the case have now been laid out. These provide the factual grounds for posing the main legal proposition: TWC is co-owner of the patent application.

Peters' work is done for the moment. It remains to be seen whether he will have succeeded in letting the court arrive at his factual context. We will now proceed to the legal articulation of the case by Blanchard. The matter of fact must now be transformed into a matter of law by being qualified as a specific legal object: an invention. Notice that this task is not presented as a simple application of the governing legal rules of patent law. The applicability of legal rules is itself put in question: 'Which rules are applicable here?' The application model according to which the attorney's task consists in applying legal rules to cases is an overly simplistic reduction of the process of conflict resolution and does not take seriously the notion of a 'legal dispute'. The dynamics of qualification, disqualification and

---

[74] Although officially in Anglo-Saxon legal systems the judge has a more active role with regard to truth finding and finding out the facts than in Continental legal systems, in practice Belgian judges can also actively intervene and pose questions.

[75] Just as in maritime pilotage, the pilot is an expert advisor and the captain the one who takes the decisions. The judges know however that there will be two navigators on board, or should we say two boats?

counterqualification showed there is no such thing as a straightforward application of the rules. The question of which legal rules and conditions are applicable is part of the very nature of the dispute. Furthermore, each proposition for qualifying the matter of dispute according to a certain legal concept itself requires a lot of work. The conditions that determine applicability itself have to be brought to the fore. Conditions have to be made applicable by tying them together with other legal conditions (the *juncto*), with similar cases of qualification in jurisprudence and with positions in legal doctrine.

> [a guided group of high school students enters the courtroom and sits down]
>
> **Blanchard:** *We are dealing with a claim for recovery according to article 9 of the Belgian Patent Act. Gortec has illegitimately used two* ***inventions*** *of TWC in the patent application in question.* ***As a consequence,*** *TWC* ***is co-owner*** *of this application and* ***thus,*** *according to article 9(2),* ***has the right to file this claim.*** *What are the* ***conditions*** *in this case?*
>
> ***To succeed in the claim for recovery, TWC has to satisfy two conditions:***
>
> *I. TWC* ***has to demonstrate*** *that it is co-owner of the invention as described in the patent application.*
>
> *II. TWC* ***has to demonstrate*** *that the invention has been illegitimately taken from her.*
>
> *I) In order to demonstrate co-ownership, TWC* ***has to prove*** *that she has provided a contribution that has been incorporated in the patent application.* ***No more than that.*** *Gortec will plead that TWC* ***has to prove*** *a substantial contribution. This argument is* ***unconvincing.*** *Nowhere is this condition mentioned in the Patent Act, nor does it occur in jurisprudence or doctrine anywhere. Gortec tries to* ***add an additional condition*** *that is* ***not valid.*** *This is logical, since the* ***quality of co-owner*** *is* ***not dependent*** *on the* ***amount of input*** *according to the general law of co-property. Gortec confuses two separate questions: 1) Am I co-owner? 2) What is my contribution?*

Taking rights seriously means taking conflicts seriously and not just the hard ones. Whether one does or does not have a certain right (of recovery), is the very issue at stake in the dispute. The factual context has been constructed. Does this mean TWC's legal propositions have now been proven satisfactorily? That depends on the theory about the scope of the proof obligations that one holds. The conditions that govern the extent of evidence required in order to prove one's legal propositions are themselves part of the dispute.

In their statement of defence Gortec articulated two conditions that TWC's claim for recovery needs to satisfy according to the law. These conditions specify TWC's 'obligations of proof', i.e. what TWC will have to demonstrate in order for their claim to succeed: co-ownership and wrongful taking. Blanchard does not have an issue with these conditions, she basically repeats them. She does however have an issue with Gortec's construction of the nature of these legal obligations. Here the debate centres on Gortec's assertion that one has to demonstrate a 'substantial' contribution to an invention, in order to be classified as its co-owner. Blanchard tries to cut off the lines that would make such a stringent condition govern the dispute, or rather, she denies that such lines exist at all. The condition of substantiality does not even occur in any legal text of law, doctrine or jurisprudence. Without even so much as a grafting point as a foothold, no attachment can be made and no legal authorities can be mobilized and aligned. Gortec has thus 'added an additional condition that is not valid'. The judges must remain unconvinced, their convictions legally unauthorized, to be moved by Gortec's proposals.

In this specific weft of conditions Blanchard has made TWC's scope of proof shrink and thus raised the chances for evidential success. With these obligations for proving co-ownership established, Blanchard continues by discussing the differences between the machine before and after the Gortec-TWC cooperation and the fact that these differences were due to the input of TWC. She walks up to the judges to show them the paper copies with the images of the different machines.

> **Blanchard:** *How does Gortec respond?*
>
> - *'The stapler is not an invention, but is banal'.*
>   *This is rather unconvincing. The* ***stapler by itself*** *might be* ***banal****, but its* ***use in this machine*** *is* ***inventive****. That is why it has been taken over by Gortec.*
> - *'The* ***claim*** *is* ***without matter*** *because the stapler has not been taken over in the* ***claims*** *of the patent application'.*
>   *The stapler is however depicted in one of the* ***images*** *in the application. In the* ***descriptions*** *of this image it is mentioned as a 'form of construction' of the machine. Article 69 (1) of the European Patent Act states that the claims of the patent application have to be* ***explicated*** *according to the images and descriptions. These are not in the patent for nothing!*

The dispute now centres on the core questions and concepts of patent law. Can TWC's contribution be qualified as 'inventive'? Gortec disputed the essential contributions made by TWC and disqualified them in terms of patentability. Blanchard here makes the discussion about inventiveness proceed by a distinction between a 'stapler by itself' and a 'stapler in relation to'. A stapler as it is by itself might be banal and thus non-inventive. It is an isolated abstraction that has become a rather obvious item to experts skilled in the art of packaging. As such they might find it again in textbooks on engineering. But staplers in practice are barely ever used just by themselves. They are used in more complex technological processing chains in which they have acquired a certain function. Whether the integration of a stapler within such a machine can be qualified as inventive will depend on whether its use enables the machine to solve a specific technical problem that engineers are faced with. Inventiveness does not require a thing to be an isolated object *in and by itself*, it requires a thing to serve a technological function *within* a larger machine *for* engineers or companies.

The second point Blanchard raises relates to Gortec's accusation that TWC had a 'claim without matter', since the claims of the patent application did not mention a word about the stapler and the stage shift, whereas such reference is required according to article 69(1) of the European Patent Act. Blanchard now disputes the restricted way in which Gortec's attorneys have aligned this article with their cause. They have only focused upon and underlined the first phrase of the article ('the extent of the protection conferred by a European patent or a European patent application shall be determined by the terms of the claims'), but they have downplayed its second phrase ('Nevertheless, the descriptions and drawings shall be used to interpret the claims'). This second phrase broadens the conditions of patent coverage. Whereas the scope of protection of a patent may indeed be determined by the text of the claims, these however provide a minimal constitution for the invention. Description and images are therefore inserted in a patent application for further articulating these statements about the machine and fleshing it out in its joints and parts. TWC's inventions might not be articulated in the terms of the claims; they are definitively made present in the terms of the description of the patent application and in its depiction in the drawings. The reference to TWC's inventions is thus re-established and she once again has provided her claim with a matter both in word and image.

> **Blanchard:** *It thus suffices for TWC to demonstrate that the invention in the application originates with her and is filed without her permission. According to article 9(2) TWC* ***can thus*** *file a claim for recovery. She is* ***entitled*** *to a part of the invention. The Court can judge about the* ***size*** *of TWC's part.*
>
> [The group of high school students gets up and walks out of the courtroom]

The plea is wrapped up. The attorneys have worked out the conditions for co-ownership, aligned the legal authorities behind these and established the facts about TWC's contributions and Gortec's taking, which these conditions required them to prove. By having established and satisfied the legal requirements, TWC has acquired the legal quality of co-owner and won the title to file the claim for recovery. Blanchard has endeavoured to make the margin of appreciation for the judges as small as possible on this point and to tie up their 'subjective' preferences. The group of high school children has seen enough and leaves the courtroom, but the judges and the observer have not. . .

Plea 2: Bad Ideas and Facts that Matter

> **Leerbeek:** *Madam president, my client is falsely accused of theft in this case. Let us return to the facts, because in this case* ***the facts tell everything****. One should* ***not plead on the basis of principles****, but* ***look at what happened****. This should occur* ***on the basis of the pieces of evidence that we have deposited in the corpulent file****.*

The case is opened up differently. Gortec's attorney provides a new orientation for the judges. Where Peters started his plea by a preliminary unfolding of what the case was about and how it was to be situated, Leerbeek tries to cut off TWC's discourse by introducing a meta-theory about the foundations of the plea itself. He distinguishes two techniques for pleading: a principled technique that he attributes to the attorneys of TWC and disqualifies in favour of a factual technique. If judges want to 'see what happened' in this case, they will have to turn away from the many abstract legal principles proposed by TWC and return to all the facts that Gortec deposited in the file. Factual grounds before legal grounds. Grounding the case on these pre-positions allows Leerbeek to come up with a different approach on the 'corpulence' of the case. This corpulence is no longer positioned as a negative distraction from the core of the case as in the presentation by Peters. Instead it is presented as a positive result of the laborious accumulation of factual evidence by Gortec! That very empirical corpulence has become the basis for judging the success of the plea itself. Grounding things this way even allows Leerbeek to delegate parts of his speech to the pieces of evidence in the file. These documents will tell the judges everything they need to know about the case. The facts speak for themselves, or rather, the facts are made to speak for themselves by the extensive work of the attorneys.

> **Leerbeek:** *TWC asked Gortec whether it was possible for the machine to be custom made. [. . .] The* ***central point*** *of discussion between TWC and Gortec was the increase in energy efficiency of the machine. [. . .] TWC's engineer Mr Graanhof* <u>*proposed the idea*</u> *to change the stages. This we will certainly* ***not dispute****.*
> *It was an* ***idea of TWC*** *but definitively* ***not a good idea****. It considerably* ***enhanced the energy consumption*** *of the machine. It was a bad idea and, in spite of TWC's intentions, it was* ***never taken over*** *or implemented. When you go through the pieces you will see that the relation between TWC and Gortec has been a* ***relation between customer and provider*** *from beginning to end. It is* ***normal*** *for a client*

> *to propose ideas in such a relation. Ideas or suggestions are* ***by themselves*** *not protectable.* ***Mrs Blanchard*** *will be able to affirm this.* ***An idea is not the object of intellectual property****. The* ***object of a patent*** *is a technical means with a technical effect that is new and inventive with regard to the state of the art.*

There is no dispute with regard to the origin of the idea to change the stages of the machine: the idea originated with TWC's engineer Graanhof. This, Gortec will not dispute. In logic a double negation counts as an affirmation and law is no different in this respect. According to procedural law on evidence, not disputing a factual proposal of the adverse party counts as a 'confession' to this fact. Here the acknowledgement is even confessed explicitly, which is extraordinary in a legal dispute. The judge will now have to take the proposal that the idea to change the stages of the machine is TWC's as proven.[76] This however is not the end of the dispute. This state of affairs might have been turned into a *matter of fact*, but has it been turned into a *fact that matters*? The world is full of facts and only a very small part is of concern for resolving our legal dispute.[77] Leerbeek's efforts are directed to denying just this. We can distinguish four movements according to which the 'idea of TWC' becomes disqualified as a fact that does not matter.

- The idea was 'not good' because it made the machine less energy efficient.
- It was never implemented in the patent application, contrary to TWC's intentions.
- The 'suggestion' of such ideas is 'normal' within a relation between a customer and a producer.
- Ideas are not protectable in patent law.

The first movement is a disqualification according to a technological norm. The idea was 'not good' because it negatively impacted the machine's effectiveness. It does not solve the central technical problem of decreasing the energy consumption of the machine by improving its box-filling efficiency. This is the central point around which Gortec and TWC

---

76 See Laenens et al., 2008, pp. 537–8.

77 The distinction between matters of fact and facts that matter should not be confused with Latour's distinction between matters of fact and matters of concern (Latour, 2005). In contrast to matters of concern, facts that matter have already been fabricated and established as facts. This factual quality of propositions makes a lot of difference for the way they will come to bear upon the convictions and decisions of the judge.

had originally gathered and for which they had become associates. In fact, the new idea aggravates this problem. The idea can thus hardly be called an improvement with regard to the state of the art of existing technologies.

In the second movement the quality of this idea comes to reflect upon its originator. Why would you *want* to incorporate an idea into a machine that augments the main technical problem you *want* to solve? This is an incompatible order of desires and yet TWC is accused of such a contradictory expression of will. In the face of so much technical incompetence Gortec deemed it necessary to not implement the idea in the machine *in spite of TWC's intentions*. The client had to be bypassed for his own sake, i.e. in terms of its higher order objectives! This is an important movement that ends up achieving two things. It dethrones TWC as a co-inventor and shows it to be a company with little technical know-how whose ideas and intentions can easily be swept aside for its own good, even without its consent. It also prepares the later disqualification of TWC's claim as being 'without matter' (no invention of TWC has been taken over in the patent application).

The way is also paved for the third movement: this idea is a normal 'suggestion' of a client to a producer. TWC is no more than a mere client. Someone who merely specifies a modification for a technical problem for which someone else is supposed to invent the technical solution is not the 'inventor' of the resulting product. The link between TWC and Gortec is (dis)qualified as a relation between 'customer' and 'provider', instead of a collaborative relation between 'co-inventor' and 'co-inventor'. This sets up a very different background for the actions that have taken place. Each context provides different standards of normality for what occurs inside it. The act of coming up with ideas is normalized within the context of a relation of commerce that itself is much more common than a relation of co-invention.[78] If something is normal it can hardly be inventive. Within this setting TWC's contributions are a mere 'suggestion' that is 'a usual request from a customer'. As such they can be disqualified as 'banal' or 'standard' which implies that they are not patentable. We see that setting up a context (from Donald Duck cartoons to commercial relations) through which actors and things are then made to pass, can play an important role in the work of legal qualification.

This argument is here followed by a final disqualifying movement. Not only are *ideas in certain relations* (like customer-producer) excluded from patentability, *ideas* are *by themselves* excluded from patentability

---

[78] This is also reflected in the law itself in which patent law is a subspecies of commercial law. Something this Court of Commerce understands all too well.

in all possible relations. In Gortec's final statement of defence this argument was only mentioned fleetingly in a footnote.[79] In their plea however TWC's idea is prominently raised to the status of one of the most basic and general principles of the whole field of intellectual rights: no idea can be the object of intellectual rights.[80] Not only is TWC's patent claim accused of being without matter since reference to any of their inventions is lacking, the claimed matters of dispute themselves – TWC's ideas – are not objects of intellectual property! Only inventions can be the objects of intellectual property, ideas are not appropriable and belong to the public domain open for everyone's use. TWC is again accused of failing to satisfy an important legal condition: providing its claim with an *appropriate* object of intellectual property. Not only are the legal forms of their claim empty of matter, the matter they have initially proposed does not fit in these slots. This is what is called a category mistake. An idea is the wrong thing to ground an immaterial invention upon. It is a *res inappropriata* in the fields of intellectual property. It can be accessed by everyone, but claimed by no one. How can TWC's matter of dispute become a matter of law if it cannot even be qualified as the right legal object? Notice also how once again Leerbeek tries to align Blanchard with TWC's position. '*Ideas or suggestions are by themselves not protectable. Mrs Blanchard will be able to affirm this.*' This affirmation can be traced back to a book she once wrote on the principles of intellectual rights in her capacity as an academic. Blanchard's legal authority is thus again drawn into dispute.

> **Leerbeek:** *After TWC's specifications, Gortec came with a <u>new</u> proposal.* [Mr Vetard shows image to judges.] *You can see that the machine only has three stages, the first and second stage – the pallet and the box folder – have disappeared.* [Mr Vetard shows the judges a movie on a laptop.] *This is a* ***totally different idea and system.*** *It is* ***this system*** *that is* ***described*** *in the European patent application and which TWC claims as their invention.*
> *All technical input originates with Gortec. In the file there is* ***not a single piece*** *that* ***proves*** *that TWC has provided* ***technical knowledge****. They only* ***vaguely plead*** *about TWC providing indications. Generally saying things is not enough, one has to provide demonstrations. Things* ***have to clearly be proven****. Let's not*

---

[79] This footnote stated: 'In any case, the question of *who first had the idea* to use such a stapler is totally *irrelevant* in the context of the present dispute. *Ideas are by themselves not protectable.* Even when Mr Graanhof would have been the first to have this idea – *quod non* – this does *not entail* that TWC would possess *any right* to Gortec's invention.'

[80] This principle has found expression in article 2 of the international WIPO Copyright Treaty: 'Copyright protection extends to expressions and not to ideas, procedures, methods of operation or mathematical concepts as such.'

> *get around it: what they have asked is either: banal, already existent or developed by Gortec.*

TWC tried to establish a certain identity between their idea for a machine and the machine finally inscribed in Gortec's patent application. In terms of this sameness they could claim that their machine had been taken over. Gortec on the other hand, tries to establish a difference between these machines. The difference is again constructed around the apparent disappearance of the first and second stages of the machine. This absence provides the hinge to construct a 'total difference' between the two systems: a machine with only three stages is totally different from a machine with five stages. On the basis of this difference Leerbeek can now claim that no inventive idea has been taken over in Gortec's patent application. TWC's proposal thus shares the same fate as the first and second stage in Gortec's machine: it is characterized by its absence and non-existence. The original birthground of ideas is now again opened up for reclaim: '*All technical input originates with Gortec.*' With TWC's proposed attachments cut off there are no other factual stitches left to bear the weight of its claim. Like an air balloon cut loose, this claim will become as free floating as its immaterial subject matter. TWC's idea is doubly disqualified both as a non-object of intellectual property and as a non-matter of dispute.

Leerbeek re-mobilizes his meta-theory on the conditions of the plea to deal the final blow. Again, TWC's general technique of pleading is disqualified in favour of a concrete factual technique of pleading. Statements have to be grounded on the 'clear' and firm soil of facts and not just in 'vague' and empty words. This firm grounding is all the more required when talking about such ephemeral intellectual (non-)objects as ideas and inventions. Without a single piece of evidence TWC comes out rather empty-handed.

> **Leerbeek:** *This brings me to the legal discussion. **To successfully file a claim** for recovery one has to demonstrate being a co-inventor. Of course it is **not** the case that one can file a claim on basis of just **any input**. According to doctrine this input has to be **substantial**; one has to provide a **creative, inventive** contribution to the invention. This does not mean just **spouting ideas** – ideas are not protectable – but means developing a technical means with a technical effect. It is not the **idea,** but the **technical development** that is the **matter** of the claim for co-invention.*

There is no division of speech labour for Gortec's attorneys. Mr Vetard has limited himself to demonstrating the images and movies to the court. Leerbeek continues performing all the pleading speech acts himself. In his legal discussion, he focuses on the validity of the condition of substantiality for passing as an inventor. A claim of co-ownership cannot merely be grounded on just any contribution; it should be of a certain kind. Leerbeek distinguishes a positive and a negative substantiality. First, the contribution of a co-inventor needs to be 'creative' or 'inventive' to be included in the domain of patent protection. He can also tell us what this creativity or inventiveness should be held to consist in: '*This means developing a technical means with a technical effect.*' Second, the contribution of a co-inventor should not consist in spouting ideas, since ideas are excluded from the domain of patent protection. '*An idea is not the object of intellectual property*'; it is not the *appropriate* kind of thing to ground a patent claim upon. Leerbeek neatly produces his theory of substantiality by joining both criteria in one phrase: '*It is not the idea, but the technical development that is the matter of the claim for co-invention.*'

Re-Ply: The Legal Concept of Ideas

> **Blanchard:** *Madam President, you will understand that* ***we have to reply****. Concerning the stage shift. Gortec states that it has* ***not been taken over in their machine*** *since it was such a bad idea. They might* ***not*** *have* ***applied*** *this* ***idea in practice****, but this is* ***irrelevant****. Their* ***actual application*** *of an invention or what they* ***sell in reality*** *is* ***not important****. We are here dealing with a* ***patent application****. If it was such a bad idea, why have they* ***taken*** *it* ***over*** *in the* ***description*** *of the* ***patent****?*

Considering the contents of Leerbeek's plea, Blanchard is left no other option: she is forced to reply to the accusations. What follows is a thorough discourse on the nature of ideas that is well worth lingering on in detail. In their successive pleas Peters and Leerbeek engaged in practical philosophies of identity and difference especially between two packaging machines: the TWC idea and the idea inscribed in Gortec's patent application. When both machines can be said to be essentially the same, an act of copying can be established. When both machines can be said to totally differ, a new act of creation has taken place and no copying has occurred. Peters claimed the former, Leerbeek the latter. The idea of TWC was a bad idea according to technological norms and was therefore never taken over and put in production, and was thus never incorporated in any concrete existent machine. Blanchard's response brings the defining characteristics of 'intellectual' rights to bear upon the matter of dispute. According to legal theory the objects of intellectual rights are characterized by their immaterial nature. The matter of dispute is not a material machine made of cogs and wheels that has actually been produced by Gortec, but a paper machine inscribed in the documents of the patent application. Through the letters and lines printed on paper, making up descriptions and images, the immaterial form of the invention is legally constituted and further articulated by the specific format of the patent file and textual delineation techniques. TWC claims the co-ownership of the patent on this paper machine folded in a file within the Patent Office, not the co-ownership of any materialized machine installed on any concrete site or sold to any customer.[81] The fact that TWC's idea has 'not been taken over in a machine' is not a problem. Total differences between machines are irrelevant when one of the machines belongs to the domain of 'practice', 'actuality', 'application' or even 'reality'. Such articulators are incapable of transporting the present conflict through the grounds of patent law. The fact that TWC's idea 'has been taken over in the description of the patent' is more appropriate for this legal objective. Essential sameness between two ideal paper machines is the kind of relation that will make them satisfactorily proceed to judgment.

> **Blanchard:** *Concerning the discussion about ideas: this is just a* ***play with words****. Firstly,* ***what is an idea****? What is* ***not susceptible of protection****? Suggestions, general ideas. The use of a stapler however is not an idea. TWC writes to Gortec about 'the stapler you have seen on our site'.* ***One cannot see an idea****! An idea is* ***abstract per definition****. Gortec has* ***seen*** *the stapler and so it is not an idea . . .*
> **Leerbeek:** *Yes, but . . .*
> **Blanchard:** *Don't interrupt me!*
> *Secondly, is the stage shift an* ***'idea' in the sense of patent law or intellectual property law****? Absolutely not. An idea is per definition something* ***vague****. When the functions of a machine are* ***precisely described*** *then it is* ***no longer an idea****, but the* ***elaboration of an idea****. That is why Gortec has three times disputed the fact that those* ***concepts****, the TWC Concepts, were ours.*

What is an Idea? In the very closing statements of the plea the matter of dispute is brought to termination in its being. We have to be careful here however not to be seduced into ontological discourse by the grammatical form of this question of being. Lawyers are not philosophers; they belong to very different practices with different goals, objects, actors, tools and concepts. These make them proceed through distinct *modi operandi* even though some of their central concepts or objects of concern – like 'ideas' might seem the same. According to Deleuze having an idea is an event that is never general, but that is always already devoted to certain practices

[81] The ownership is of course not of this concrete piece of paper either. The patent applies to the form of the invention outlined in the paper documents of the patent application and covers any actual machine of cogs and wheels in which this form can be factually traced back. The specificities of this tracking work can also be empirically studied by observing a patent dispute about the infringement of an existent patent. We will deal with one such dispute in the next chapter.

like philosophy, cinema, theatre, painting, writing, (Deleuze, 1998b) or, in our case, the practices of invention and the legal reconstruction of the processes of invention. Practitioners of both classical metaphysics and intellectual rights can find themselves confronted with the issue of the nature of ideas, although the mode of engagement will obviously be very different in both cases.[82] Within these practices the idea is already engaged in a highly specific way. In metaphysics the question of the Being of Ideas can become an issue for discourse. The question could then be tackled by giving an exposition of the theories of Plato, Descartes, Locke, Leibniz, Berkeley, Hume and Kant about ideas and their relation to ontology.[83] In this sense, the question 'What is an Idea?' seems more at home in this kind of discourse ('What is the Being of Ideas in an ontological or philosophical sense?'). This is not the question that concerns Blanchard as an attorney however,[84] or rather, the question 'What is an Idea?' is already devoted to legal practice. It concerns her in a legal way. This becomes visible in the question which follows: '*What is not susceptible of protection?*' and is later fully formulated as: '*Is X an "idea" in the sense of patent law or intellectual property law?*' 'Being' is evoked in a legal way here, in which it is already engaged in association with many other Xs in other court cases. The details of these other Xs of dispute have served as concrete factual grounds through which ideas have come to be continuously reconstituted. The urge

---

82 Interestingly, in a similar context Pottage and Sherman state 'philosophers recognize that the existence of such things [like ideas as intangible forms] cannot be taken for granted. Patent lawyers, on the other hand, routinely deal with the invention as though the reality of embodied forms was entirely self-evident. Lawyers ask what kinds of ideas should be patentable, but this is usually framed as the question whether an idea has been sufficiently transformed, embodied, or applied as to become something more than a mere scientific principle or product of nature' (Pottage & Sherman, 2010, p. 5).

83 See for example Hight, 2008. The same could be argued for the domain of art theory. In his *Idea*: *A Concept in Art Theory*, Panofsky describes the transformation of the philosophical (and anti-artistic) concept of the idea by Plato, into a concept that has become quite specific to art theory in the sixteenth century (Panofsky, 1968). This account however is also primarily philosophical in nature, instead of addressing the concept of ideas in artistic practices.

84 As far as Deleuze is concerned the same goes for the philosopher, because posing philosophical problems through the question 'What is X' has led to great misunderstandings. This question serves no more than propedeutic aims as an introduction into the region of the problem of concern. Once this has been done and 'it is a question of determining the problem or the Idea as such, once it is a question of setting the dialectic in motion, the question "What is X?" gives way to other questions [. . ..]: "How much, how and in what cases?"' (Deleuze, 2004a, pp. 236–7; Deleuze, 2004b).

for care in our analysis might now become clear. The 'idea' in question is a *legal concept* (*Rechtsbegriff*) that obeys different *laws* from the ones valid in other practices (different for example from the way in which the physicists' use of concepts like 'mass' or 'energy' is 'governed' by the laws of physics). The meaning of this concept can only be understood when looking at all the specificities of the ways in which it is used in practice (Wittgenstein, 2009).

Normally the question 'What is X?' is reserved for the introduction into a subject matter, like in a textbook about intellectual property. In this case it is one of the very closing statements by which the circulating matter of dispute is brought to its legal de-termination. This question is raised because it has become an issue in the dispute: TWC's proposals have been qualified as ideas and thus as non-objects of intellectual property. The question can only be answered now after so much effort has been put in grounding and working out the invention that has become of such central concern. First we are led to pass through a preliminary negative demarcation of what an idea is not. Ideas are not just words written down in an attorney's statement where they can be playfully manipulated at will and costlessly substituted with other words like 'concept'. Ideas legally have a different mode of existence that is not merely nominal. They are characterized by their 'generality', 'abstraction', 'vagueness', 'inelaboration' and their 'invisibility'. With this mode of existence established Blanchard can now determine whether both matters of dispute have their belonging in this domain.

After being drawn into the dispute on this point by Leerbeek, Blanchard is indeed able to affirm that ideas are not objects of intellectual property. Ideas are abstract and not perceptible by any of the senses apart from the mind's eye; only when an idea is given a form that renders it observable by the senses can it be a candidate for protection. The fact that Gortec's engineer Mr Hesse had visited TWC's site and noticed how they made use of staplers in packaging, implies that the (use of a) stapler cannot be an idea, since '*one cannot see an idea!*' Similarly, the stage shift is not an idea either. It is not some vague entity that has only flowed around in the mind of TWC's engineers, but it has solidified as ink on paper. '*When the functions of a machine are precisely described then it is no longer an idea, but the elaboration of an idea.*' Through the efforts of TWC's engineers, the abstract and vague idea of a stage shift has been made visible in paper form by precise descriptions. Hereby, the functionalities of the machine have been worked out to such an extent that it has become constructible, i.e. been rendered capable of materializing in a machine of cogs and wheels on an industrial site. In short, through these elaborations the stage shift has been transformed from the legal mode of existence of ideas into the legal mode of existence of *concepts*, as the inventive 'TWC Concept' that has acquired patent eligibility. Legal inventions are conceptual in nature, not ideal. According to a book she once wrote on this very topic, Mrs Blanchard can definitively affirm that ideas are not protectable, but that concepts are in fact the true object of intellectual property.[85] 'Ideas' and 'concepts' are not just words that can be played with at will. Both have distinct legal meanings and their qualifications make a huge difference in terms of the consequences for legal patent protection.

> **Peters:** *It has been a heated debate, but we thank you for your attention.*
> **Leerbeek:** *It has nothing to do with the good understanding between us.*
> **Blanchard:** *Indeed.*
> **President:** *I hereby close this case.*

The case might have been closed but it has not yet been terminated. We still have to proceed to a decision; we are still to arrive at judgment. The suspense is increased. . .

---

[85] In this book Blanchard states that: 'the demand of formation (*mise-en-forme*) as condition for the quality of the protectable work implies that the thoughts of the author must have left the domain of simple ideas and been structured in the production of a *concept* or a *scheme* [. . .] copyright never protects a simple idea, which is by definition too general and too fluid for having appropriable contours. The second demand of formation implies that the structured thoughts of the author, i.e. the creation, must have a *sensible form*, perceptible by third parties, in such a way that the author can effectively prove the existence and consistence.' (In order to preserve the anonymity of the individuals and entities who feature in the accounts on which this book is based, details of this book are not included in the Bibliography.)

4. Legal pointillism in court: towards the composition of judgment

PRELUDE ~ THE LEGAL PROCESS

'Herald, read the accusation!' said the King.
On this the White Rabbit blew three blasts on the trumpet,
and then unrolled the parchment scroll, and read as follows:-

'The Queen of Hearts, she made some tarts,
All on a summer day:
The Knave of Hearts, he stole those tarts,
And took them quite away!'

'Consider your verdict,' the King said to the jury.
'Not yet, not yet!' the Rabbit hastily interrupted.
'There's a great deal to come before that!'

(Carroll, 1994, pp. 130–31)

'The verdict is not so suddenly arrived at,
the proceedings only gradually merge into the verdict.

(Kafka, 2005, p. 195)

In this chapter we will make a second turn to legal practice when we translocate our studies from the law firm to court. We have already been a while underway in seeking to arrive at judgment in disputes of intellectual rights and we still have to proceed a long way. In this process we will first be confronted with procedures, interim zones, administrative enlistments, admissions, preliminaries and precedings before we get to the legal grounds of judgment. Disputes tend to develop noteworthy, troublesome extensions. Doing justice to these requires not jumping to conclusions that are all too rash. As the two quotes above remind us there is a long process of gradual proceedings that precede arrival at judgment. A practice approach to the grounding of immateriality in disputes within the (in)substantive regime of intellectual rights also brings into focus the different legal regime of *Prozessrecht* or procedural law, relating to the conditions raised in a dispute on its very process of proceeding.[1] Tracing a matter of dispute thus provides an opportunity to study how grounds and process are mixed and become differentiated from within the same dynamics.

Kafka is the great literary philosopher of law as process (*Prozess*). He has provided microscopic analyses of the administrative and legal processes by which cases infinitesimally extend.[2] An approach to legal disputes can take a great deal of inspiration from these analyses of the atmospheres of these proceedings with all their procedures, circulations, visibilities, admittances, devotions, obligations, delusions and convictions. Kafka stages an incessant series of encounters of incompatible 'airs' between the protagonists of the proceedings who insist on (macro-)principles,[3] and the administrative machinations in their inaccessible micro-routines of obtaining behavioural credits. Hereby a rift increasingly opens up between the two, revealing an absence in which no justice is ever dispensed[4] (a void that is filled up with the impending image of the horrors of bureaucracy).[5] We might thus take heed and learn from these lessons by not pushing the envelope of our analysis too far down either of these poles, if we are ever to retain any hopes of arriving at any judgment in matters of intellectual rights. This entails that in this chapter we have to devise a different approach that both tries to steer clear

---

1 I here refer to the legal distinction between 'substantive law' and 'procedural law'. Even immaterial rights constitute substantive law in this qualification.

2 The chapters 'The Mayor' and 'Chapter 24' of *The Castle* are especially lush on 'the endless process of filing' with its descriptions of the circulation of files, lists, numbers, folders, doors, their transportation on trolleys through corridors, offices, departments, bureaus of control, according to proper and improper channels, containing sheets of paper, private letters with official signatures, official communications, appointments and decisions (Kafka, 2009).

3 This is most notably the case with Joseph K. in the course of his many encounters with the court machinations. His flight into principles always makes him stop short in astonished disbelief and obstructs him in getting closer to what is happening.

4 This polar occurrence is even more striking since both do not want the outcomes to which the trial proceeds, not Joseph K. of course, but not the officials either who are often disposed to help him within the margins of manoeuvre allowed by their procedures.

5 In this sense, the writer/lawyer Kafka is the counterpoint on the plane of literature of the thinker/lawyer Leibniz on the plane of philosophy. In his writings Leibniz pushes to their mutual extremes the endless processes of microscopic unfoldings of differentiations and of macroscopic enfoldings of principles of the events in the world (Deleuze, 1993, p. 58). Like Leibniz, Kafka introduces a perspectivism on cases that pushes them to the extremes of an insistence on the sameness of principles and the differences of micro-proceedings. This polar opposition becomes most pronounced when Kafka opposes a 'detached observer' of the court proceedings with someone who knows how the court works (Kafka, 2005, p. 148).

of the doctrinal axiology of intellectual right disputes like the one devised by Troller, but that can also circumscribe the continuous extensions of disputes that we have studied in great detail at the law firm in the previous chapter. Although, such an approach might involve a passage through the oppressive airs inside the court buildings, this should not deter us and make us forego further investigations by resorting to principled assumptions; that is, unless we manage to encounter such assumptions within our investigations.

We will pick up the thread, *the filum*, of our account at the moment when the files have been transferred to the court. After the law firms, the conflicts have become enfolded in cardboard folders and sent or deposited at the registry of the court. We will focus on what happens to the conflict from this moment on, and do so according to different points of attention.[6] We will first observe how an official file is created and circulated throughout the registry according to a series of lists, to make their way to the 'the ivory tower' where the judges reside. We will proceed by following the judges from the tower, down to the courtrooms along an architecture of passages that affords certain relations of accessibility and visibility and thereby mediates legal principles of independence and impartiality. We will listen to the pleas of the attorneys and study the techniques of persuasion they deploy. We will then bite our fingernails in nervous anxiety, when the registrar, judges and files retreat into the chambers of deliberation in which they, regretfully for research purposes, are transformed into hidden nodes in the black box of decision-making, only to come out with a ready-made judgment document.[7]

After mapping the trajectories of enfolded files through these interim zones at the court, we will focus in more detail on the stages at which the files are unfolded and engaged by the legal practitioners. Since these engagements proceed in different ways and are bound by different constraints than in the law firm, we will have to find a mode of presentation that is tailored to the specific manner in which judges arrive at a judgment in disputes of intellectual rights. Conversations with judges provide us with a first outline of the act of judgment as the pointillist art of selective

---

[6] These studies were conducted at two Belgian Courts of Commerce, where several cases were studied. Together with the studies at the law firm, this has provided material for comparison. The account of these legal practices has been further calibrated with the results of ethnographies of legal institutions by other authors, in order to extract the generic elements necessary for understanding how immateriality becomes grounded in legal practices.

[7] It has not been possible to observe the judges throughout their discussions and deliberations, but merely to acquire access to the judgment document that has however undergone a purification of hesitations. For an account of such hesitations in reaching judgment, see Latour, 2010, pp. 141–52.

contractions of intensive points of dispute in a series of operative sentences (linear focus).[8] This offers an alternative, more detailed approach to judgment in place of the rather sweeping conceptualization of the judgment as a macroscopic cut (Derrida, 1992b). Nevertheless, when it comes to the question of how immateriality is legally grounded in the judgment of concrete disputes, these conversations also again break down on the windowless walls of the mental and physical black boxes of deliberation and their circumscriptive regimes of access and visibility.

We will once again be forced to shift the approach and perform thorough analyses of the documents in the case files of different legal disputes and compare these with the judgment documents in order to trace the selective contractions by which the judges transform the matter of dispute into a matter of fact and a legal object of an intellectual right. This is a different situation from the one at the law firm, in which the documents and the case file were still 'under construction'. Now the documents have shed their fluoride colourings for tight black font. The time for reading the documents is also circumscribed by the sheer quantity of conflicts that have to be dealt with in court. This implies an adoption of reading techniques adapted to the circumstances of decision, instead of those of proposition. To convince or to be convinced, that is the question by which much of the legal play oscillates.[9] This study of cases at first makes us proceed from the interim to the preliminaries of judgment. Here, we will become acquainted with the admissibilities and preliminary measures (expertise) of judgment, and with the textual operators, operatives and requisite procession points of its documentation. Afterwards we finally arrive at the grounds of judgment.

With regard to these disputes we find ourselves in a different predicament than at the law firm where we were able to follow the many strands of the unfolding of the corpus of a case. This extensive approach is beyond the bounds for our exercise in this chapter. The access of the judges (and the researcher) to all these sites of occurrences and developments of the matter of dispute is restricted to the presentations of the advocates, experts or witnesses in the case folder. Nevertheless, each of these disputes confronts us with a new extensivity. We will focus our attention on some of the themes that have come to the fore in our account of the proceedings at the law firm, and also encounter the introduction of some new themes. We will see how philosophies of essence and of identity and difference are

---

8 This constitutes a second contraction of the conflict after the contraction in the summons, after which the expansive phase of statements and pleas started.

9 The etymology of *con-vincere* is 'to conquer with', indicating that the attorney has to succeed in deploying the judge along the lines of dispute resolution proposed.

again employed with regard to different matters of dispute. How originality and inventiveness of intellectual rights are conceptualized and are made to depend on a host of (scale) models, signed declarations, drawings, tables of juxtaposition, expert reports, presumptions, legal fictions, grammatical markers, techniques of *Auslegung*, and evocations of legal authorities. We will carefully try to unravel each of these particular features of this heterogeneous web of attachments and see how each co-constitutes the immateriality of a matter of dispute. We will try to trace how attorneys, in deploying this complex web, endeavour to circumscribe the mind of the judge and work upon his or her 'inner convictions'.

The path of law on which we proceed in this chapter is thus a long-winded one, with many deviations or risky dead ends, on which we cannot but travel slowly and where an eventual arrival depends on a mix of persistence and flexibility. Only by patiently tracing these processes along these passages does it gradually become possible to understand the legal constitution of immateriality that we set out to study.

Raising Legal Conditions

Before starting the analysis, the role of legal conditions needs to be considered, especially the ones which pose requirements for the very process of proceeding itself. Many of these conditions have been 'laid down' as articles of legal code in official codices.[10] These conditions become connected to the dispute when the practitioners 'raise' them as the grounds for a certain matter of dispute. This act of grounding as a movement within the dispute will be a main focus in this chapter and will be reflected in the laying-out of our text. The speech acts by which the lawyers ground the dispute will be inscribed in the 'body' text of our account. In order to account for the raising and grounding character of this act, the conditions referred to by the lawyers will be mainly laid down in the footnotes. In this way they quite literally come to figure as the grounds under the body text that inscribes the corpus of the dispute and are projected as its base. This lay-out makes it possible to textually accommodate the (vertical) nature of grounds within an (horizontally) extended account of the dispute dynamics.[11] Both are connected by the (diagonal) acts of grounding.

---

[10] The constraints within legislative practices for the act of laying down such codes constitute a whole topic of separate study. See Abélès, 2000.

[11] They are horizontal both in the textual sense of a linear series of subsequent pages in the medium of this book (McLuhan, 1994), and in the methodological sense of providing 'flat' cartographies when tracing the connections in controversies (Latour, 2005).

Conditions are inscribed when they are raised within the course of the dispute without which they are of no concern or interest (not *inter-esse*, between things), but remain underground as it were. This approach reverses the relation of 'being based on' between dispute and condition. This textual organization also permits us to deal with conditions that are not raised by the legal practitioners. Although such conditions remain unconnected and unincorporated, they are not always without consequences since they might relate to what we will call the 'requisite procession points' of the legal dispute. When these points are not traversed in the dispute proceedings, the felicity of the actions of the practitioners might be put in jeopardy (the attorney filing a claim at the wrong court, the registrar not creating the file in the required way, the court not inscribing the required ingredients in the judgment). When the dispute procession gives rise to mentioning such conditions in this chapter and they are not raised by the legal practitioners, they will be laid down underground in the footnotes where they are separated from the body text of the dispute by the horizontal dividing bar. This bar itself is thus always dynamic and rises and falls in relation to what happens in the dispute. These conditions are thus virtualities, some of which could remain enfolded in unopened books and journals during the whole dispute, others which later could become evoked and unfolded as an explicit point of dispute.

4.1 INTERMEDIARIES: ENFOLDED CIRCULATION

The whole dossier continues to circulate, as the regular official routine demands, passing on to the higher courts, being referred to the lower ones again, and thus swinging backward and forwards with greater or smaller oscillations, longer or shorter delays.

(Kafka, 2005, p. 148)

The registry was an interim zone in which circulating records turned into retired files.

(Vismann, 2008, pp. 97–8)

In this section, we will endeavour to reconstruct the further trajectory of matters of intellectual right dispute, which we have become familiar with at the law firm, throughout the multiple spaces of the courts. In the previous chapter, we have studied the way a dispute *unfolded* through the many mediating actions of a host of different actors, actions, procedures, conditions, documents and instruments. In this way the conflict is gradually made to proceed to judgment. In order to successfully arrive there, the conflict needs to be wrapped up, *enfolded* in the cardboard case folder and transmitted from the law firm to the court where it is deposited at the registry. We will focus on what happens to the conflict from this moment on.

With Vismann, we can call this registry an 'interim zone'. Etymologically *inter-im* means 'in the midst of that', a being between, but between what? We could first say that in a rather eschatological sense, the registry mediates the passage of the life of circulating files either into collective memory or into forgetfulness. We will see how this interim zone has a strong link to mnemonic techniques and techniques of organization and, as the quote of Kafka indicates, to 'regular official routines' by which the court organizes the proceedings of cases and its own memory. We can also take the interim in a different sense as the periods of envelopment of the dispute in the case folder that take place between the periods in which the dispute unfolds. When the cases circulate throughout the registry enveloped in their cardboard folders they have an intermediary existence, an existence as an intermediary between the work of the attorneys at the law firm and of the judges in the ivory tower.[12] For the interim to become the intermediary a lot of administrative work needs to be done and in very specific ways. When this work fails because certain important requisite procession points have been bypassed, and certain proceedings of the dispute have become disorganized and forgotten, the case folder can no longer be called an immutable mobile that transports the dispute without altering it. Rather it will have become a mediating event that will have added something to the dispute: claims of incorrect legal administration which might have all kinds of consequences for the admissibility of the dispute! Or maybe we should say instead that this breakdown of the intermediary also subtracts something from the dispute: its successful arrival at a judgment on its grounds. In any case, it would have transformed the stakes of the dispute.

Registering the File of Legal Administration

The reception of the summons from the attorneys of the plaintiff is the first point of contact of the dispute with the court. From this moment on the dispute will initiate a trajectory of circulation within the building of the court. It will be subjected to a series of steps, many of them legally required by procedural law, which will increasingly come to organize its proceed-

[12] The use of the term 'intermediary' alludes to Latour's distinction between intermediaries and mediators (Latour, 1999, pp. 176–93; Latour, 2005, pp. 37–42) and to his concept of immutable mobiles (Latour, 1986).

ing.[13] At the administrative section of the registry the dispute is first inscribed on the case list called the 'scroll'. This term still derives from the ancient times of Roman law when administrative acts were written on long scrolls of papyrus. This archaic name has still survived even after scrolls were in due historical time subsequently replaced by codices of parchment, books of paper, trays of cards and finally by computer files.[14] The registry is required by the Belgian Code of Procedural Law to keep such a 'general scroll, on which each case is inscribed in the order of arrival' (article 711). The case is inscribed in a computer program (*X-Nest*) by assigning it a national 'serial number', which fixes the position of a dispute in the series of cases that continuously enter the court. This number has installed the case within the order of organization and functions as the point of grasp for administrative operations and to keep track of the case along its further voyages.

Next, for each case that is inscribed on the scroll, the registry is required to create a '*dossier van de rechtspleging*'.[15] This term *rechtspleging* is important. It can either be translated as judicial 'procedure' and 'process' or, more literally, as 'administration' of law. In this last sense the term deals with 'the makeup of the legal enterprise' (Brenninkmeijer, 1995). If we thus want to know how law is administered we would do well to follow this newly created file and take a look at the way it is organized. *Lists* play an important part in this process. We have already encountered the scroll, or 'case list' that organizes and serializes the different cases.[16] The file itself however, is itself also guided by all kinds of lists. Files are at their core governed by lists, which 'govern the inside of the file world, from their initial compilation to their final storage' (Vismann, 2008, p. 7).

The summons is first put in a yellow cardboard folder. The colours here also function as a marker. Unlike the documents at the law firm however, the colours do not mark the author who is writing – in the world of files the author is less relevant – but what kind of procedure is involved: how the files are to be processed. Next, the cover of the file is stickered with a printed-out label that contains the data that were inserted

---

[13] Latour has given a thorough account of how files are transformed by their circulation over several stages through the French Council of State and how they increasingly become 'ripe' for use (Latour, 2010, Chapter 2).

[14] For this material evolution of the media of law, see Vismann, 2008.

[15] Article 720 of the Belgian Code of Procedural Law.

[16] This scroll can be called a 'file plan', which already has a close connection to law. 'Much like laws, file plans require an abstract form capable of anticipating as yet unknown specific cases. Administering files, then, is raised to the status of a quasi-juridical endeavor' (Vismann, 2008, p. 142).

in the computer just before. The cardboard file itself hereby also becomes inscribed within the order of the scroll. Apart from the summons we find two other documents within the folder, which are both also lists. First, there is a document called the 'Minutes of the Public Hearings'. Like the folder it also has an empty square for the scroll label and is further organized in two columns of blocks. In each block the left column serves for the inscription of the specific Chamber of the Court, the date of the hearing, and the official actors (president, judges, registrar, prosecutor) present at the hearing (who will leave their stamps on the document). In the block in the right column the names of the attorneys present at the hearing will be inscribed. This list will thus come to organize the actorial and spatiotemporal trajectory according to which the dispute proceeds through the series of legal hearings. Second, the folder also contains a document called 'Inventory'. This is the inventory of pieces of evidence that have become stitched to the dispute. This document is also printed with an empty square where the scroll label will be stickered. It is further organized in many rows and three columns for the 'number of the pieces', 'nature of the pieces' and 'date of deposition'. The pieces will be numbered in the order in which they are received at the registry. This list will come to organize and keep track of the several pieces of evidence accumulated in the course of the dispute. In this function it will stabilize the possibility of reference to these pieces and thus facilitate the possibility of retrieval. When the attorneys deposit their statements and pieces of evidence at the registry, these documents will be stamped with the date of deposition, their metadata will be inserted into the computer file and they will also be put within the cardboard folder. Case lists, inventory lists, minute lists, the inscriptions in such lists enable the progress of case files and allow them to move throughout the court in a stable, ordered and retraceable manner.[17]

Once created, the folder is transferred from the desk to a filing cabinet in which it is inserted in a circular system of rotating rows. This filing cabinet contains the current pool of files, or, as we could say more literally, the files that are in *circulation* in the court. Seven days before a hearing, a secretary takes the files out of the cabinet and brings them from the secretariat to the office of the registrar of the chamber in which the case is pending. The spatial shift of the files is significant; we will quite literally cross a regime threshold. Whereas anyone can have access

---

[17] For an anthropological history of the materiality of script, the instruments of information retrieval, and the cognitive procedures of listing as parts of the intellectual technology of writing, see Goody, 2000.

to the secretariat of the registry, for instance members of the public or attorneys to deposit files, this is not the case for the place where the judges and registrars reside: the 'ivory tower' as one of the secretaries called it. Only certain authorized people (people at the registry, judges and interns) have credentials to pass into this 'non-public' zone. *Un passe-partout, mais pas pour tous!* The architecture of this brand new court building requires the passenger to be in possession of a magnetic card that, when held in front of a small device at the end of the hallway, will open the solid door that gives access to the tower. The former role of the 'gatekeeper' of the secretariat has thus been delegated to this gateway technology that divides the reception, the secretariat and organizational offices of the registry, and the coffee kitchen on the one hand, from the library, the chamber of closed session, and the offices of the judges and registrars. This technological apparatus thereby subjects its passengers along the binary axes of the private/public and authorized/unauthorized distinctions in general, and, as we will see, mediates the legal values of due process in specific.

Monadic Passages and Visibilities in Court

The first moment the file is brought in contact with a judge is when she comes and picks it up at the office of the registrar. Depending on the judge, this will either be for some preparatory reading, or on the day of the hearing itself when s/he takes them to the relevant courtroom where their chamber presides. The architecture of the court building again intervenes on this path in important ways. A detailed look at the little blueprints of the court on the wall of each floor shows us that 'the tower' has its own self-enclosed interiority within the court building. The great rectangular building is roughly divided in two blocks: a block with offices and registries and a block with court rooms. There are two parallel pathways connecting both blocks throughout the length of the building, one at the front and one at the back. The one at the front is directly connected to the public entrance and both gives access to, and connects the public part of the registry offices with the public entrance to the court rooms for the attorneys, parties, journalists, students and others (Figure 4.1). It is called the 'public axis' that is part of the 'public zone' of the building. The other pathway at the back of the building connects the private offices of the judges and registrars with an entrance to the court rooms, which directly allows the judges to take their place behind their table. This entire passage; from their offices, through a whole internal series of hallways, stairs, elevators and doors, is hermetically closed off from every public part of the building through the same kinds of technological gatekeepers

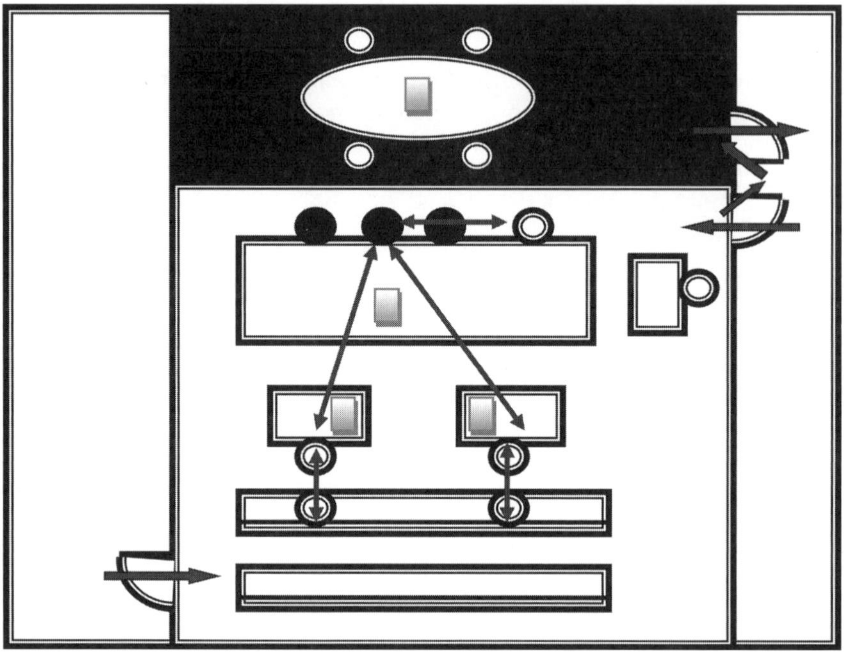

Figure 4.1 A spatiotemporal slice of the proceeding and interactions of a dispute within the setting of the monadic court architecture

just encountered. This is part of the 'non-public zone' of the building.[18] The courtroom and the registry are called the 'semi-public zones' of the court situated 'between the transparent corridors and the secured office zone. Here public, magistracy and personal encounter one another'. The building is designed in such a way that perpendicular from the public axis there is 'a decreasing degree of public character'.[19] In these ways the court building has become the place-keeper for the symbolic legal values of due process: impartiality and independence. Through its architecture attorneys are physically unable to get in contact with the judges before and after the court hearings to exert any unwarranted influence on them.[20]

---

[18] There are architectural variations between different courts in this regard. In older court buildings a strict division between public and private passages is not always enforced. There can for instance be only one common entrance to the courtroom for all actors, public and judges.

[19] Publicity Folder: *Nieuw Gerechtsgebouw,* Regie der Gebouwen.

[20] These legal principles have found a different 'matter of expression': instead of being articulated in legal codices, they are now articulated in the architecture

In the courtroom the network of people and things involved in the proceeding of the dispute for the first time finds itself gathered in such spatial proximity staged around the case files. This is the same courtroom in which the pleas in the TWC-Gortec dispute were performed. That time however, we came from the law firm and entered the court room through the public entrance (down left in Figure 4.1). Now we have come from the tower through the passages and entered through the private entrance (upper right in Figure 4.1). Accordingly, the people and things in the courtroom are already differentiated according to their path of entrance into the courtroom. The private corridor from the tower is not accessible to everyone. Only the judges, registrar and interns are granted passage through here. Attorneys, clients, witnesses, press and the public (like school classes) enter through the public passages. A similar thing can be said about the files; they are also differentiated according to how they have arrived in the courtroom. The judges bring the file that has circulated throughout the court's registry in which it gained a coloured folder, stickers, and filled out lists, which, upon its arrival in the courtroom, mark it as the 'official' file of the dispute. This file thus differentiates itself from the files that the attorneys bring along to the court. Whereas the attorneys might have been closely involved in the process in which the file came about, it has now passed into a different register of proceeding governed by lists, procedures and conditions. From here, the file has now returned to the attorneys as the official file in relation to which their very own folders have become mere versions. Sometimes these versions do not always contain the same contents due to last minute additions of pieces for demonstration in court or as candidates for inclusion in the official file.

The interior of the courtroom further distributes a variety of positions which can be assumed by people and things and thereby further differentiates them.[21] The three judges and registrar sit down next to each other behind the bench on which they place the official file. The attorneys take a stance behind the two lecterns on which they place their case folders. The judges and the two attorneys hereby assume a primary triad of oppositions. The clients or witnesses take a seat behind the attorneys on the first

---

of the court building (Latour, 1999). This Code of Law has now been coded in architecture (Lessig, 2006). In these cases we are however no longer dealing with conditions in legal processes, but rather with scripts or programmes of action within technological and organizational projects which have to satisfy very different requirements (De Vries & van Dijk, 2013).

[21] Scheffer calls the courtroom a 'discourse automat arranging the staging of cases' which 'resembles an order of relational discourse-positions' (Scheffer, 2004, p. 371).

row of pew benches of the public gallery. They hereby assume a back-up position for the attorney in question. Public and press take a seat on the other pew benches in the public gallery.[22] A bailiff (or an intern when no bailiff is present) will sit down behind the bailiff table (right of the bench). The triadic positioning of the two lecterns in respect to the court bench provides the setting for the spectacle of demonstration during the hearing. As we will see later, the attorneys have adjusted their pieces of conviction in regard to these visibility relations. Furthermore, when the case folders are opened on the tables and the voices of the judges and attorneys resound against the glass walls, the courtroom also comes to stage the verbal and textual modes in which the dispute is unfolded. As such it can be added to the history of procession of the matter of dispute.

This distribution of positions through the layout of the courtroom, in combination with the surrounding architectural setting of the court, like the deliberation room and corridors linking to the tower and registry, enables certain relations of visibility and obscurity. This assemblage of visibility relations distributes what will remain opaque about the dispute and what can be seen and by whom.[23] Somebody who passes through the public corridor might catch a glimpse of the hearing through the transparent glass walls. The press and gathered public only get to see a very small part of the proceedings of the dispute from their positions in the back of the courtroom. The attorneys and parties can survey the courtroom from their positions in front of the court and can look inside 'their' case folder or 'look back' at the processes in which they came about. The further circulation of the official file through the court, including the acts of deliberation of the judges, remains opaque to them however. Interns (and researchers) can 'look around' in court into the case folders, along the circulation of files and in the courtroom, but for them the processes of deliberation in the deliberation rooms are invisible. Judges and registrars cannot see how the files have come about before they were deposited at the court (including the important and relevant occurrences which eventually have not been included in the file). It might be clear that this assemblage of visibility relations is not limited to the court alone but extends along the

---

[22] In British criminal law there are additional enforced or marked divisions in the courtroom, like the bar (between working area and public area) or the well (between bench and council).

[23] Visibility must here be taken in a larger sense than what can be seen; rather it is that which is disclosed or enclosed within a certain setting, a setting which is legally overcoded with sets of permissions. In this sense each setting is similar to Sloterdijk's bubbles in affording an own mix of circumspection (*Umsicht*) and blindness and an own 'lighting of impenetrabilities' (Sloterdijk, 2004, p. 63).

proceeding of the dispute. Some of these relations are explicitly inserted by statements of procedural law (the public courtroom, the private chamber of deliberation)[24] of which some are delegated to the court architecture (the exclusive *passe-partout*, the transparent courtroom, the opaque chamber of deliberation),[25] others are inserted by contractual agreements (the non-disclosure clause between client-attorney or researcher[26]).[27]

When the hearing has finished the judges and registrar retreat into the deliberation room situated next to the courtroom (see Figure 4.1). This chamber offers a very different arrangement of visibility. The courtroom with its transparent glass walls was open for many persons, each differentiated according to a distribution of positions. To the contrary, the chamber is an opaque room without windows and walls, impenetrable to the outside gaze. In this sense the bicameral image in Figure 4.1 also reveals the existence of an abstract diagram of 'a pure architectural and optical system' (Foucault, 1991, p. 205) operative within these legal practices. This system is not Panoptic but *Monadic* in combining an open *camera lucida* of public hearing and a closed *camera obscura* of private deliberation, which become connected by the passage of fold(er)s.[28] It cross-cuts legal practices

---

[24] Article 148 of the Belgian Constitution states that 'the hearings of the courts are public, except when . . .' and the 'discussion of the case in the chamber of deliberation during deliberation is secret' (Laenens et al., 2008, p. 465).

[25] Even the choice of materials for building the court has been of considerable architectural concern in its design phase. 'The more a zone was accessible to the public the more use was made of glass in the build-up of the facade. In this way the public axis as a public zone was completely executed in glass, while in the zone of offices the accent shifts to the use of natural stone.' (Publicity Folder: *Nieuw Gerechtsgebouw*, Regie der Gebouwen).

[26] The researcher 'will have access to and acquire information which for legal or deontological and ethical considerations cannot be made public' (excerpt from a 'Contract of Confidentiality').

[27] These are rare moments of what Deleuze and Guattari call a 'point of intervention or insertion' between the power relations of an assemblage of visibility and a regime of statements (Deleuze & Guattari, 1987, pp. 86–8). Foucault has for instance analyzed the articulations between the statements of penal law and the visibilities of the prison (Foucault, 1991). In our case, it further turns out that statements can have their own visibility and that visibilities have their own statements. The architectural (in)visibilities of the court incorporate legal statements of procedural law. Later in this chapter, we will see how the visibility of a scale model of an invention materializes legal statements of patent law and how a judge describes the role of the attorney's plea statements in terms of techniques of lighting and visualization of the dispute.

[28] 'Monadic' is here used in the sense developed by Leibniz and further architected by Deleuze. Leibniz called the monad a room 'without windows through which anything could come in or go out [. . .] from the outside', which

in several ways, since this model is not limited to the design of the building settings, but also extends to the mind of the judge as we will see.

The private cell of deliberation is furnished with four chairs and a table on which the file is placed and opened . . . after which the door is closed and the scene vanishes from sight. Later we will discuss how to deal with this black box of deliberation. Here we will stick to following the files. When the judges are done deliberating they leave the chamber and return to their offices in the tower through the private passages. One judge has described the way back from the hearing in the court room to the offices as a return to 'monastic life'.[29] Here, in isolation, the president of the chamber will work out the basic decision reached in deliberation. S/he will provide the grounds for the judgment and the concrete sentence. S/he then circulates a preliminary version of the judgment to the other judges who either accept it as it is, or suggest changes. When these are incorporated the final version of the judgment is reached.

After a dispute has been judged on its grounds, the file goes back to the filing cabinet in the registry. There it remains active for a period of three years, after which it can be cancelled from the scroll. The case then becomes inactive and can only be activated again by a new payment of the registry charges. After a period of eight to nine years the folders are removed from the filing cabinet and moved to the archive in the basement of the court building. This transfer happens for practical reasons: this is the time interval in which a row in the cabinet becomes filled and the transfer is thus instigated by the material constraints of the storage medium. The files remain in the basement until 30 years after the moment of their creation. They are then transferred to the State Archive, a federal scientific institution that profiles itself as a centre for historical knowledge and as a governmental archive. Here the most important cases are filtered out on the basis of pre-established selection lists, packed in box folders and stored on the shelves amongst the 250 kilometres of other files, where they can later be consulted. The remaining unselected files face a less appealing destiny: paper files will be burned or shredded, and digital files

---

he opposed to the body that has 'parts constantly coming into them and going out' (Leibniz, 2010, §§ 7, 71). Deleuze has extrapolated this monadism into an architectural system of two rooms of a Baroque house in which the lower public room is commonly visible and has a coming and going, whereas the upper room is a 'closed private room' which is a *camera obscura*. The combination of the two constitutes a 'new regime of light and color' and of 'legibility' (Deleuze, 1993, Chapters 1, 3).

[29] '[J]udges are like monks without the unifying bonds of a common faith' (Wald, 1992, p. 179).

will be destroyed by demagnetization of hard disks. Their only remaining trace will be the formal registration of the documents which were destroyed and a certificate of the act of their destruction. Once again the life path of files is governed by a list, but now this list even governs their very existential fate. In this sense we can concur in Vismann's description of the registry as the 'interim zone'. The selection office of the State Archive becomes the purgatory gateway either for the future historical redemption of files into our 'collective memory',[30] or for their doom in the oblivion of the flames. We could also even invert the argument in order to come up with a bolder hypothesis. The very religious image of access to the gates of Heaven mediated on the basis of lists of souls to be damned or saved, so well depicted in Michelangelo's *Last Judgment*,[31] is itself modelled upon administrative practices operating on the basis of files and lists.

INTERLUDE 1 ~ OPENING THE CASE FOLDER: FROM ADMINISTRATIVE ENVELOPES TO LEGAL DEVELOPMENT

In her book *Files* Vismann rightfully observes that 'legal studies lack any reflection on their tools' and that this constitutes a 'blind spot of jurisprudence' (Vismann, 2008, p. 11). The role of files in law as a medium of legal transmission has never been properly investigated. Files are interesting due to their intermediary position between the written laws and the oral utterances in court and the fact that they bear a close proximity to the events, since they allow access to 'the struggles that preceded decisions' (*ibid.*, p. 9). In this way they do indeed provide a great opportunity to study decision making in-process.[32] The important question however is how to study the relation between law and files. What status can files be assigned within an approach to law as a practice in action in which the lawyers

---

[30] See the brochure *Het Rijksarchief Belgie. Ons Collectief Geheugen!* and its motto of 'selecting, organizing and storing'.

[31] Below the Christ figure which passes the judgment there is a cloud with angels. Archangel Michael on the left reads from the book of the souls that are to be saved. Another angel on the right reads from the larger book that contains a list of the damned that are destined for hell (see the image at the beginning of this chapter). The scene of judgment is governed by files.

[32] Files programme which acts come next and document what has come to be enacted (Vismann, 2008, pp. 7–8). Scheffer calls this the 'continuation' of files (Scheffer, 2004, p. 378).

are engaged by the event of a certain dispute? In her media-technological studies of law, Vismann explicitly excludes the 'content' of files, focusing exclusively on their 'external characteristics' like their materiality, mediality and their function as recording devices.[33] In this way she sets out to 'ground the law in files and records' and even calls files the 'variables in the universe of law' (*ibid.*, pp. 39, xi). But how are we to understand the relation of files to the antagonistic events when the file remains closed? In such a pure processual approach the event of the dispute is with hindsight reduced to the linearities of legal process.[34] A file can only be logistically transported within or between places as long as its contents remain enclosed in paper folders. It can thus only be the unit of administrative circulation at the expense of black boxing all the documents of the very *conflicts* that clients, attorneys and judges occupy themselves with and that make up the body of the case file. What does the case file consist of? Which documents and pieces of evidence are in these folders? And what are those documents *about*?[35] By focusing mainly on *how* enfolded files logistically circulate throughout the institution, we miss out on an important part of *what* the legal process is about. We will have lost all the intricate ways in which a dispute *unfolds* when lawyers gradually make it proceed to judgment.[36] Files are not *just* purely functional, procedural entities. They have to be opened because otherwise we will miss the whole dimension of concern: the dispute events that occupy the lawyers in the course of their work.

We have followed the trajectory of the 'official' files from their creation, enlistment and circulation in the registry (or at the law firm if we go further back to the previous chapter), their passage to the private tower onto the desks in the judge's private offices or the library, their transportation

[33] 'When files or records are referred to in the plural, their content rarely seems to matter; it is buried underneath their materiality. And even when files are opened to reveal their contents, they are not simply read. Files are *processed*, just like stones and other such matter.' (Vismann, 2008, p. xi). This exclusion of content is a typical imperative of media theory.

[34] For the relation between process and event in legal approaches, see Scheffer, 2007.

[35] Kozin approximates this differentiation when he distinguishes the collecting materiality of the file as a folder document from the different kind of materiality of the case, which is closely related to the former but cannot be reduced to it (Kozin, 2007).

[36] Latour rejects assigning too much explanatory power to such technological devices, but instead claims that they are useful to the extent that they help an actor to solve an agonistic situation by aligning and convincing new allies for his or her solution (Latour, 1986). In his studies of law he asserted that there is something more to law than this dimension, something he calls the legal regime of enunciation. For a critical discussion see van Dijk, 2011; van Dijk 2015.

through the private corridors onto the bench into the courtroom and later into the adjoining chamber of deliberation, their return to the tower for decision, their descent into the archive in the cellar of the court, and their eventual passage to the State Archive for storage or destruction. Along this trajectory we can distinguish two important movements of the case file: its enfolding for administration and transportation and its unfolding for engagement with the dispute. This chapter has until now been predominantly focused on the former, but will now turn to the movements of the unfolding of the file and the legal developments of the dispute. We will start by addressing the processes of deliberation by the judges.

Reasoning and Judgment

How are we to deal with this black box of deliberation? Which aids are we to mobilize to understand what is happening here? The Belgian Code of Procedural Law does not help us much in approaching the processes of deliberation. It merely tells us that the chairman divides the different cases that have taken place that day amongst the judges in order to write their opinion[37] and that after the discussion amongst the judges in the chamber the judges give their opinion or 'vote', starting with the judge most recently appointed in the court and ending with the chairman.[38] We will thus have to look elsewhere for answers and turn towards some observations of judges on processes of deliberation (see box on next page).

Although very illuminating, it needs to be emphasized that these observations are made by judges in the US[39] and that we should hesitate to transport them too easily into our present analysis.[40] We will therefore

---

[37] Article 777 (CPL) 'The cases taken into deliberation or cases of written procedure are divided amongst the judges by the chairman.'

[38] Article 778 (CPL) 'After the discussion the chairman questions by turn, starting with the most recently appointed judge and thus rising to the longest serving appointed judge. The chairman gives his opinion last. When opinions are divided, a new vote is cast.'

[39] The US system in which judges can write dissenting opinions has an advantage over the Continental system of 'unanimous' decision. The problem with the latter is that this total locking up of the processes of deliberation makes invisible the hesitations that are essential for the making of law. This veil allows the judges to defensively hide behind presentations of their work in terms of purifying notions like legal certainty, impartiality and unanimity. In this way, it does not allow those approaching legal practices to address the judges in terms of what makes them do their work well in judging a dispute.

[40] Ethnographic studies of the French Council of State for instance show intense discussion between the judges (Latour, 2010). Whereas such studies teach us a great deal about processes of legal reasoning in the preliminary *séances*

The Black Box of Legal Deliberation

In his book *How Judges Think*, US Justice Posner says the following on deliberation:

> 'The difficulty outsiders have in understanding judicial behaviour is due partly to the fact that judges deliberate in secret, though it would be more accurate to say that the fact that they do not deliberate (by which I mean deliberate *collectively*) very much is the real secret. Judicial deliberation is overrated' (Posner, 2008, p. 2).

This statement seems to be confirmed by the observations of two other US Justices on the processes of deliberation. In an article titled *Some Real-Life Observations About Judging*, Justice Wald states:

> 'After the arguments each day, the judges confer. When I first came on the court, I imagined that conferences would be reflective, refining, analytical, dynamic. Ordinarily they are none of these. We go around the table and each judge, from junior to senior, states his or her bottom line and maybe a brief explanation. Even if the panel is divided, the discussion is exceedingly crisp. The conference changes few minds. Assignments are made, life goes on' (Wald, 1992, p. 181).

Former Chief Justice Rehnquist of the US Supreme Court concludes that:

> 'My years on the Court have convinced me that the true purpose of the conference discussion of argued cases is not to persuade one's colleagues through impassioned advocacy to alter their views, but instead by hearing each justice express his own views, to determine therefrom the view of the majority of the Court. This is not to say that minds are never changed in conference; they certainly are. But it is very much exception and not the rule' (Rehnquist cited in (Posner, 2008, pp. 303–4)).

Posner adds that this 'bespeaks a voting model, not a deliberative model'.

turn to self-reflexive observations by three Belgian judges at the court described above, which deal with the status of the statements, the pieces of evidence, case law, the plea, the interactive debate, with the perceived role of the attorney and its relation to the judge, with the reasoning involved in constructing legal argument and the movements of the judge's inner convictions.

Judging is not complicated, reasoning is complicated.

This is the first thing the judge mentions when he introduces the act of arriving at judgment. This short phrase provides a formula that we will try

---

d'instruction of the Administrative and Litigation Sections, they do not deal with the inaccessible processes of deliberation. Unfortunately, the humble Trial Court of Commerce does not even host such *séances*.

to understand in this chapter. We will see that the whole process of arriving at judgment by constructing lines of reasoning is long and winding and involves many different steps that have to become aligned. The judgment is already implicated in these lines of reasoning, but has to be extracted from them separately in a way that responds to the claim and contracts the dispute into verdictive sentences.[41]

> **Judge A**: *A* ***plea*** *of 90 minutes is totally senseless. A judge cannot stay concentrated that long.* ***In a plea one has to be concise and only situate the case.*** *That is enough. I once told an attorney that with New Year I had assumed the intention to only read 16 pages per case. This was a* <u>*rhetorical move*</u>*. Attorneys have to be effective and be to the point.* ***The statements have to be more limited*** *and without stupid arguments. One does not understand this at the big law firms. How can a judge read such long statements? He does* ***not have any time*** *for this. Besides, way* ***too many pieces are added*** *to the file. Are all these pieces relevant?* ***Are they pieces of conviction: pieces to convince me****? 90 % of the pieces are not relevant, i.e., do not offer a* ***sufficient basis for judging a case****. They are rather* ***meant to confuse*** *the judge, so that he will* ***start to doubt himself****.*
> *With regard to the* ***legal arguments****: when you do not restrain yourself, you will overshoot your goal. The judge will not see the wood for the trees. He will be* ***led astray*** *by being* ***overloaded with data which are*** <u>*unnecessary*</u>*.*

The judge is confronted with a problem that is well familiar to practitioners in the fields of data mining who continuously face data overloads. The important question is how to get the relevant information from an avalanche of data in the light of considerable limitations of time. Furthermore, the search of the judge is complicated by the fact that this avalanche has deliberately been set in motion by the attorneys to obfuscate the weak points in their case so that the judge might get lost. The meta-theory on pleading in which the attorney has to be a good pilot, proposed by attorney Peters in the previous chapter, does not seem too far off here. A case can become quite corpulent due to a flood of legal arguments and to the many attachments, cuts and reattachments of pieces of evidence to the dispute by the attorneys. These can complicate the passage to judgment by opening up many sidetracks that obscure the dispute. The judge might hereby be 'led astray' from the grounds of judgment since it does 'not offer a sufficient basis for judging a case'. The judge links the relevance of the endeavours of the attorney to the degree in which they support the act of judgment. On this basis he provides a

[41] Dewey argued that the legal operations of reasoning and judgment are guided by the quite different logics of exposition and of search and inquiry (Dewey, 1924, p. 568).

different account of the dispute dynamics that reshuffles the role of the attorney's actions and productions within the dispute. These productions have to be limited and made more concise, which entails fewer silly arguments and unnecessary pieces of evidence. With regard to the latter the judge provides an interesting conception of relevance. Are the pieces gathered in the file 'pieces of conviction', are they 'pieces to convince the judge'?

In the previous chapter we have already become acquainted with the peculiarities of the legal concept of evidence. This concept is closely linked to other legal concepts of presumption and conviction. What transmits to certain pieces a certain value of evidence that works upon the inner convictions of the mind of the judge? We can here make a small diversion to an excerpt of the proceedings of a patent dispute in this court, which offers a glimpse of the relation between pieces of evidence and inner convictions as typical legal concepts in the dispute dynamics. The next phrases are extracted from an interactive debate after the two pleas of the attorneys at the end of a hearing:

> **President:** *Can you provide me the piece of evidence? I do not like to make a judgment that is not based on all pieces, but one that is as close to reality as possible and rests on evidence which is as complete as possible. Do I have to assign a conclusion to the fact that you have not provided the evidence? I will now retreat with my colleagues to think about this.*
> [. . .]
> **Attorney:** *You are not required to only look at the individual pieces. When you take all the pieces together, it is your* ***inner conviction*** *that counts. Then you will see that the publication is part of the existing state of the art.*

The judges deem a certain piece of evidence important for judging a claim of patent infringement, since it might contain proof that the main matter of dispute was already state of the art. This piece is missing from the plaintiff's bundle, because it has been very difficult to obtain (it would require calling up an unwilling elderly person from France and forcing her to testify). According to the judges this constitutes a hole in the grounds that would convincingly support the judgment, since it needs to 'rest on evidence which is as complete as possible'. Whereas a judge might not be obliged to respond to all the propositions of the attorneys, she states that the ones which do get implied in judgment preferably need to be 'based on all pieces'. The attorney replies by proposing a different theory on the relation between pieces of evidence and the judge's conviction. He replaces the judge's atomic theory of (ideal) complete proof with a holistic theory of sufficient proof, by basing himself on the legal requirements for the concept of the 'inner conviction'.[42] This conviction does not require an exhaustive proof based on pieces of evidence that would all be individually necessary. It is satisfactorily moved by sufficient grounding, which requires the pieces of evidence to be taken together in a holistic impression, instead of them being taken individually. This downscales the degree of certainty required, from an approximation of an ideal of completeness to one of probability ('beyond reasonable doubt').[43] We could say that on this view conviction is reached not along a chain of reasoning which would break when one link is defective, but along a path of stepping stones which could probably still be passed when one stone is missing. We see here that even the nature of the conviction of the judge has itself been drawn within thc dispute as a topic of debate!

> **Judge A:** *I believe in an* ***interactive debate****. In complex cases lawyers have to shortly* ***extract the core in their plea. By asking questions you can take them out of their argument and expose the weak points that they have tried to conceal.*** *[. . .] Schematically, it should all fit on one paper leaf. This way you can* ***see the gaps much quicker****. The* ***attorney often does not know the weak points in his case, he proceeds much too rashly****. The methodology is wrong.* ***Between attorney and judge there is a relation of mutual distrust.***
> *A* ***plea*** *about legal points is rather senseless; a plea about the facts is not.* ***The task of the attorney is to enable the judge to return to his office and do his job. He has to indicate the important points. The function of the plea is to highlight certain topics that are decisive for the judgment of the judge. The art is to provide the judge with the right stepping stones for a legal argument, to put the right stepping stones in the right place.***
>
> **Judge B:** *The* ***plea is civilized theatre****.*
>
> **Judge A:** *When emotion enters in a case through the attorneys, I intervene.* ***Emotions perturb the course of events and make the decision more difficult.*** *In the end* ***I am a technician****.*

The requirements of the attorneys to convince differ from the requirements of the judge to be convinced. Whereas attorneys often get to work

---

[42] In French (criminal) law this is an explicit legal concept. Article 427 of the French *Code de procédure pénale* states that 'Except where otherwise provided by law, the offences may be established by any mode of proof and the judge decides according to his inner conviction'.

[43] The Belgian Court of Cassation once judged that 'a judge assesses the guilt of a suspect according to his *inner conviction*. He condemns him when he has the *human certainty* that the suspect is guilty of the facts he is charged with'. (Cassation 10 November 1992, A.C. 1991–92, nr. 726, my italics). This was a case of criminal law however and not of civil law.

on a case for extensive periods of time, the judges cannot indulge in such 'luxury'. Not only is the time they have for dealing with cases limited by their workload, it is also, to an important degree, circumscribed by conditions of procedural law (disputes have to be judged within a reasonable time[44]). When attorneys have proceeded too rashly in extensive constructions of their case through their statements and pieces, it is up to the judge to slow things down. Judges have to contract the conflict by selecting the points of the dispute that will permit them to do so.

Such a point of dispute can be of two kinds. It could be a gap enveloped or 'concealed' in some other extension of the dispute. These are 'weak points' that cannot bear the weight of a legal argument or might even destabilize and implode the whole legal proposition (the gap as a black hole). The judge deploys two rhetorical techniques to make the attorney get 'to the point'. First, by requesting that the attorney curtail his exposition of the case in the plea or statements, the judge tries to induce a schematization of the dispute in which the empty gaps, the absences, become more striking. Second, by intervening in the plea, the attorney is made to lose track of an extensive argument that might have enveloped a weak point and which might become thus exposed. No wonder there is a 'relation of mutual distrust' between advocates and judges!

The point at stake could also be a 'strong point' that includes an intensity that could support legal arguments and thus serve as 'a sufficient basis for judging the case'. The judge casts the role of good advocacy as an art of stagecraft in constructing and lighting the way to arrive at judgment. We could say that in the statements the attorney has to assume the role of the stage builder who needs to construct the sets of the dispute, whereas in the plea s/he becomes a lighting technician who has to light the way in this 'civilized theatre'.[45] In the plea the attorney has to first *en*lighten the scene to the judge by 'situating the case'. Within this situation s/he has to direct the judge's focus by *high*lighting the 'topics that are decisive for the judgment'. These *topoi* or places are the zones that indicate 'the important points' in the dispute; the strong intensive points of the attorney's case.

---

[44] This is one of the conditions of fair trial of article 6 of the European Convention on Human Rights.

[45] Pursuing these theatrical dramatizations of disputes, we could say that the attorneys further perform the role of the playwrights of the (two) scripts, the choreographers of the movement sequences and the casting directors choosing the actors to introduce on stage. The judge performs the role of the film editor in cutting scenes, selecting sequences and arranging them in a final line of movement (the movie). Lastly, the registrars would fulfill the part of the production managers, logistic crew and the camera operators.

Simultaneously the attorney will necessarily shade the *topoi* or zones which are 'irrelevant' in this respect. The judge concludes that a convincing performance of this scenographic task is summarized in the following formula: 'to put the right stepping stones for legal argument in the right place'. This is what enables the judge to go back to his office and do his job as a 'technician' in the art of judgment. The attorney has to select and align the intensive points of the dispute and highlight them as a solid path to arrive at judgment and not digress and drown in irrelevant specificities and technicalities that have accumulated in the dispute. In this sense the judge wants theatrical realism not emotional melodrama, since such 'emotions perturb the course of events and make the decision more difficult'.

Once this is done well, the whole exercise of reaching an opinion boils down to the judge having to assume a point of view on the dispute, or rather an alignment of points of view, cleared from within the dispute dynamics. This happens when reasoning strikes a line that selects and connects points of intensity from the dispute dynamics and includes these into a unity of a 'linear focus' from which the cases of the attorneys can be arranged into an opinion (judgment).[46] Once this linear focus is assumed, the selected points can be projected as its reasons which together are sufficient for grounding judgment (reasoning). These grounds are thus unfolded and raised from within the interiority of the dispute. Such a line of reasoning is like a strike of lightning that bifurcates downwards in a tentative series of points of embranchments until one of them arrives at the ground and the charge reinforces itself as the running line of those bifurcations that constituted this passage.[47]

---

[46] Deleuze extracts this notion of a linear focus from Leibniz' *Monadology* as a 'power of arranging cases' in a certain area. 'In all these areas Leibniz constructs the "table" of cases that refers to point of view as *jurisprudence* or the *art of judgment*' (Deleuze, 1993, pp. 19–21, my italics). This art of judgment of extensive cases is connected to the two conditions of 'selection' and 'closure' for creating a clear monadic point of view on and from the infinity of minute obscure perceptions (pp. 90–91, 131–7). It is also important to add that such a point of view 'does not mean a dependence in respect to a pre-given or defined subject or mind; to the contrary, a subject will be what comes to the point of view, or rather what remains in the point of view' (Deleuze, 1993, p. 19). With Whitehead we could call such a point of view a '*locus standi*' for such a subject or mind, which is always tied to a 'foothold' in an 'event here' (Whitehead, 2004, p. 107). Here, this event is the dispute that allows certain loci to be assumed as points of view.

[47] Although these grounds might be projections on something darker and deeper that withdraws itself in this very act of grounding, what Deleuze, 2004a, calls *Ungrund* or groundless, such a projection is sufficient for legal purposes. He later relates this ground to the singularity of an encounter according to the 'principle of contingent reason' (Deleuze & Guattari, 1994).

Judge A: *The attorneys from the firms in Brussels sometimes first look who the judge is. As if the* ***person of the judge*** *matters!* ***I have no personal case law, but judge differently each time.*** *Of course there are cases which have to be judged in a standard way. Normally, the actuation is different in every case however.*

Many attorneys refer to cassation case law and ***extract general criteria*** *from it. Cassation judgment is often not important however.* ***One has to concretely know which case it was and what the circumstances were. Then it becomes clear that referring to such a sentence in a certain case is totally not relevant.*** *Furthermore, it is said that the court of cassation only enacts legal judgments, very often however they do decide on the facts of the case.*

In Belgium there is no [common-law] case law based on precedents like in the UK and US. We thus do not always follow the court of cassation. ***Sometimes some judgments are just plainly wrong.*** *Too often people base a kind of morality on case law. When you would have to adopt all this, one could just as well put a computer in the place of the judge which bases itself on a database in which a short legal rule is extracted from each judgment.* ***When one refers to a case, one has to re-explicate the case and indicate why it is relevant in the present dispute.*** *This does not necessarily need to be very extensive.*

After the status of the statement, pieces, plea and reply we now turn to that of case law. The judge states that the discourse on the role of the person of the judge in judgment has contributed to the mutual distrust between the attorneys and the judges. This might be unsurprising when some judges have themselves uttered such statements as 'law is a prophesy of what the courts will do'[48] or 'judgment is what the judge had for breakfast'.[49] This judge is more concerned with talking well about the constraints he encounters in arriving at judgment, in a way that is not mobilized too rashly by such extra-legal reductions to psychology, statistics or gastronomy. It is interesting to see that the judge does not try to steer clear of such a charge of subjectivity by resorting to the safe classical legal self-representation in which the judge enacts judgments that are legally objective by subordinating cases to abstract rules and criteria.[50] According to the judge, such a

[48] Holmes, 2009, p. 9. See the discussion in Chapter 6.

[49] This infamous statement is attributed to US Justice Jerome Frank and has become a maxim for the movement of Legal Realism. In an article entitled *What I Ate for Breakfast and Other Mysteries of Judicial Decision Making*, US Justice Alex Kozinski phrases this view (which he criticizes) as follows: 'If the judge has a good breakfast and a good night's sleep, he might feel lenient and jolly, and sympathize with the downtrodden. If he had indigestion or a bad night's sleep, he might be a grouch and take it out on the litigants' (Kozinski, 1992–93, p. 993).

[50] Latour provides an interesting alternative account of legal objectivity in which the circulation of certain legal means throughout the fabric of legal texts

solution would be part of the problem. Through a strange circle, the standardized way in which a specific judge would apply these objective criteria, would render a (statistical) regularity about his or her judging behaviour that would constitute his 'personal case law'. This information could then once again be mobilized by an attorney to determine 'who the judge is' and address him accordingly.[51] By running from legal subjectivity to this opposite of legal objectivity, the judge would have been transformed from a person into a kind of person, from psychology to data science, which renders a personalization which might even have more far-reaching consequences.[52]

How to break out of this tedious circle? The judge here introduces an interesting differentiation between a standard but abnormal way of judging and a normal unstandardized way of judging. Standardized judgment would render an author of case law who would regularly judge in the same way. In normal practice however, the person of the judge vanishes in an 'actuation' of judgment that is addressed by the matter of dispute at stake. Each matter of dispute implicates its own requirements and sufficiencies. It forces itself upon the people it has gathered as a stubborn problem, an objecticity, which, from within this common interiority, requires a course of legal action that is tailored to its singularity, and will therefore often be different in different disputes.

This approach has consequences for the status of case law in disputes. According to the judge many attorneys use judgments in past disputes as a kind of standing reserve for the extraction of general legal rules that can be mobilized in other disputes. Since many are derived from judgments by the Court of Cassation, these abstract rules are framed as a source of law imbued with the authority of a normative imperative that should be applied in other disputes. On this view disputes form parts of a database of case law in which each dispute becomes a first case of the general rule of law isolated from it and by which it is summarized. This is quite literally the case with legal internet databases like http://jure.juridat.just.fgov.be, but is also facilitated by certain legal journals which only present short

---

and precedents continuously raises objections on the path of judgment and resists any quick pre-meditated solution by forcing judges to modify their preferences and prejudices (Latour, 2010, Chapter 4).

[51] Compare Llewellyn, 2008, p. 6. See the discussion in Chapter 6.

[52] We could think here of the rise of the discipline of 'legal informatics' (Schmidt, 1986). Within the growing field of artificial intelligence and the law, machine learning techniques are already used to identify 'the main schemes of legal argument' (Prakken, 2006). This could be a step in such predictions of human judgment by computer reasoning.

abstracts of judgments.[53] The judge likens this approach to a kind of autonomic data mining in which the pluriverse of disputes is substituted by a database with extracted rules, and the judge by a computer which subsumes new disputes as cases under these rules. It now becomes clear why this metaphor breaks down here.[54] According to the judge the abstraction of legal criteria from one dispute and their mobilization in another is often unconvincing, since it does not take into account the concrete traits and circumstances of the dispute in terms of which the judgment has been reached and which provide their existential cause. These imperative rules are based on the presumption of the *similarity of cases* that the judge opposes with the *difference of disputes*, which often makes the norm extracted in one dispute 'irrelevant' for another. In this sense these rules shortcut the typical jurisprudential work of establishing what we can call successful '*reasonances*' between the different disputes. This work is far from automatic or self-evident but proceeds by a careful attunement to the evoked dispute, a re-explication of what it is about, and an indication 'why it is relevant in the present dispute'. Only when sufficient reasonance has been reached can a dispute come to figure as a *jurisprudential character* for the reasoning in another dispute and only then can arguments shift between the two.

How do judges attune to a particular dispute however? What makes them become convinced in reaching their judgment?

> **Judge C**: ***You cannot look inside my head!*** *We provide you with the files and judgments.* ***You are a lawyer and are supposed to form your own judgment about these.*** *We form our judgment on the basis of the documents and pieces. When we are wrong we will be corrected by a court of appeal.* ***We are not obliged to respond to all arguments.*** *We have a lot of cases and a lot of arguments are often raised in one case. It would be impossible to address all of them.*

---

[53] Legal textbooks or handbooks can also have purifying effects on disputes. Short quotations from the judgments inscribed in a section on the 'state of the art' or doctrine of a certain legal regime are all that remains of the dispute. In science, Kuhn has described how textbooks only provide accounts of the winners of scientific conflicts (Kuhn, 1996), and legal textbooks have a comparable effect. Forgotten are the singularities of the dispute, the risky propositions of the lawyers (especially the losing ones) and most of the compositional activities of the judges.

[54] In this context Latour has stated that law 'is the least technical of all forms of enunciation [. . .] one cannot calculate law by summing it up by the mediation of some mechanical device – like a calculator replacing mental calculation' (Latour, 2010, p. 272). To which Stengers adds: 'Thus no application or blind practice (*dura lex sed lex*) where one could replace the jurist by a deciding machine, a machine for making the law [. . .] that would not be the law that we know' (Stengers, 2007).

Judge B: *Judges want to* ***address the arguments of the unsuccessful party as much as possible****, so that they might not appeal too readily. No judge wants his or her case to be corrected.*

After a judgment in a particular dispute on patent law, the researcher laboriously attempted to pose different kinds of roundabout questions to the judge concerning the judgment, the role of the pieces and the arguments of the attorneys. As can be seen, this was to no avail. The judge who, until this moment, could be heard on the act of reaching judgment suddenly retreats into unavailability. We can however draw valuable lessons from this failed attempt, since the response of the judge provides a glimpse of the co-articulation between the visibilities, statements and conditions of deliberation. The mind of the judge turns out to also function as a kind of mobile black box which one 'cannot look inside'. It is an enclosed 'chamber of deliberation' similar to the monadic *camera obscura* situated next to the courtroom (this is why the three judges in Figure 4.1 are depicted as black dots). It also has no windows which would make its inside visible for outsiders, but may merely be moved by its inner convictions that are in turn circumscribed by the legal texture. This is not so much a black box of behaviourist psychology in which the processes of deliberation going on inside would be methodologically circumvented by the researcher, but rather a legal black box that is inscribed in the prescripts of procedural law and which circumscribe the mind of the judge within a regime of invisibility.

The judges do provide two clues as to the requirements that constrain the processes of reasoning offered to support a judgment. Reasoning is an obligation for the judges, one which is even constitutionally recognized: article 149 of the Belgian Constitution states that 'for each judgment reasons are given'. Formally this requires that each judgment contains all the factual and legal elements on which the decision has been based.[55] This allows the parties involved in the dispute to know the grounds of judgment and to determine whether they want to appeal against it. On the basis of the whole corpus of propositions, pieces of evidence and arguments of the dispute, we might expect this exercise to be quite extensive. The judge however states that she is 'not obliged to respond to all arguments'. The legal obligation of reasoning does not imply an exhaustive reply. It might be a desirable requirement, but it is checked by requirements ensuing from the judge's other legal obligations, like judging all her disputes within a reasonable time. Since judges have to decide several (five to six) disputes

---

[55] Laenens et al., 2008, p. 470.

per week, they have to be selective. Moreover, as we have seen in the previous chapter, commercial law has a regime of free valuation of evidence, which grants the judge a lot of room for manoeuvre in dealing with the attorneys' pieces of evidence in order to become convinced. This contrasts with civil law with its evidential force and its valuation hierarchy of evidential means. This regime of forces and values circumscribes the field of the judge's movements of conviction in a dispute within much more narrow bounds.[56] If the judges are not obliged to respond to all arguments, which arguments do make them reply? Here the second judge provides a different requirement that weighs on his reasoning. A judge does not want his legal authority to be diminished when his judgment will itself be judged and overturned by a court of appeal. This requires a judge to mostly focus on the arguments of the unsuccessful party (so that they may lose all hope for appealing the decision). Although the judges might not explicitly respond to the arguments and pieces proposed by the successful party, we will nevertheless see that these do often become implicated in the judgment.

INTERLUDE 2 (REPRISE) ~ UNFOLDINGS: TURNING TO MATTERS OF DISPUTE

> *[F]inding out what the judges say is but the beginning of your task. You will have to take what they say and compare it to what they do.*
> (Llewellyn, 2008, p. 7)

For the rest the discourse with the judges breaks down at the point where we tried to get most close to the processes by which immateriality becomes legally grounded in judgment. Our observational gaze is not allowed to penetrate any further inside their heads in this manner. In resonance with Llewellyn's adage we will make use of this point of thwarted access, to turn away from what the judges say about what they are doing *about* disputes and towards what they are doing *in* disputes, or, more precisely, look at what they say during what they are doing and what they hereby do by saying it. We will thus once again turn to disputes in action, through a study of several cases as they proceed in court. In each case we will perform detailed (document) analyses of the summons, statements, pieces and pleas of various disputes of intellectual rights that three chambers in

---

[56] This again shows that this 'conviction' of the judge is a legal concept rather than a psychological one. Civil law would provide an interesting site to study how the mind of the judge is circumscribed in a legal regime of conviction.

two courts have been engaged with, and compare these to the judgment documents. In this way we hope to follow which propositions have jumped over the gap between the documents where the black box of deliberation is situated, and in what way they have done so, whether and how they have been selected, transformed, implicated, explicated, cut off, postponed or abandoned altogether. This approach hopefully allows us to extend our textual account in a way that enables arriving at judgments that ground the dispute. It does not however assure such an arrival. Each legal dispute always carries the risk of an imminent breakdown or an indefinite postponement halfway in its process, so that it remains in its preliminaries.

The term 'judgment' comes from *iudicem* with the etymological connotation of 'speaking legally'. In order to approach the way judges manage to legally speak well about disputes, we have to take into account several of its constraints.[57] This implies that the ways of reading all the relevant documents will also be adapted to the temporal constraints, the mediated access to the happenings, and the requirements of sufficient conviction. Furthermore, we will have to invent a way of writing that takes into account the requirements of the legal processes of proceeding.[58] Moreover, this textual account has to itself also perform several pre-selections. These pre-selections have a twofold orientation, both prospective and retrospective, on a judgmental contraction. First, they are prospective to the extent that they will trace some of the propositions the attorneys introduced to convince the judge and that could lead to a judgment. Here the focus will be on the introduction of new figures, things and techniques that mediate the grounding of immateriality of the matter of dispute, and how they endeavour to circumscribe the 'inner convictions' of the judges in this regard. Second, they are retrospective to the extent that we will present the arguments that the court has actually selectively contracted in a judgment. Here we will select the argumentative points, pieces of evidence and legal texts offered by the attorneys, which have either become cut off as unconvincing assertions or have been implicated in an authoritative linear focus as convincing grounds.[59]

---

[57] I refer here to Stengers' concept of 'speaking well' about a certain practice, which is about characterizing the mode of action of its practitioners without insulting them (Stengers, 2006, pp. 24–9).

[58] See also the section 'Raising Legal Conditions' in the Prelude to this chapter.

[59] These selections cannot replace the extensions of disputes that we have encountered in the law firm. The lawsuit only becomes closely tailored to the matter of dispute when attorneys spend a lot of work on it. When less energy is invested, one often observes shortcuts that repeat the same general themes, whereas only in the extensions can one really see how the immateriality of the

These considerations relate to the textual account that we will have to give per dispute. We will however be confronted with a plurality of (five) different disputes, each with its own singularity. Of interest in this book are the legal acts of grounding immateriality, especially those of judgment. This focus can also move us *inter-esse* – between things – by taking our observation from *res* to *res*, from legal dispute to legal dispute. Each dispute allows the (reasonant) extraction of a certain theme or 'movement' of immateriality, which can provide ways for extending each dispute in such a way that it passes over into another. The dispute frequently becomes transposed in different situations or along third characters, authorities or tools, which are continuously introduced to achieve a stable point of view. Each immateriality theme will itself vary when moving between disputes according to its specific reflections or anticipations on previous or upcoming disputes. It will be modulated according to the manner in which it connects disputes according to their legal regime, and evokes legal authorities, protagonists, figures, techniques, tools or situations.

4.2 PRELIMINARIES: PASSING THE THRESHOLD

Before the Law stands a doorkeeper. To this doorkeeper there comes a man from the country and prays for admittance to the Law. But the doorkeeper says that he cannot grant admittance at the moment. The man thinks it over and then asks if he will be allowed in later. 'It is possible,' says the doorkeeper, 'but not at the moment.'

(Kafka, 2005, p. 197)

Along the paths by which we have proceeded so far there has been an important relation between law and admittance, which the quote from Kafka reflects well. We have already become acquainted with the regimes of accessibility within the court building. This (in)accessibility of the law is an issue for an approach to law as a practice. It can however also be raised as an issue within the disputes that we seek to approach. These issues are called the preliminaries of judgment. Etymologically *pre-limen* means 'before the threshold'. In court proceedings it relates to the points of dispute that are dealt with before passing the threshold of a judgment on the legal grounds of a dispute, or, in our case, 'before the law' of intellectual rights. In this section we are interested in this threshold, i.e. in Kafka's door that opens the way for a matter of dispute to gain admittance to the grounds of its immateriality. This image of the door is of course a metaphor and a rather static one. These preliminaries do not relate to the kind

---

matter of dispute becomes grounded in the network of act-ants. This is why the lessons of the previous chapter should be kept in mind throughout their treatment.

of closed doors and windowless walls of chambers of deliberation. Instead they are more dynamic relating to legal forces at work in the dispute that make judges raise the inadmissibility of a claim by their own motion.

We have to be careful in the kind of lesson that we draw from Kafka's parable. According to Derrida it is a story about the 'essentially inaccessible character of the law' (Derrida, 1992a, p. 196). This conclusion is only obtained because the law is interpreted after Kant's and Freud's writings on a moral law that has already been elevated to a transcendental level as 'the law of laws'.[60] Law is not essentially transcendental, it lies low, the law has been 'laid down', underground as it were. It is not what is already raised, but what always has to be raised. It does not trans-cend disputes or stories, jumping over from case to case in an unaltered form, imperatively categorizing each one, but it jumps in a case from a below within. It is not essentially inaccessible, but has many practical gradients of (in)accessibility, never granting a *passe-partout* or panoptic visibilities, but always monadic visibilities and authorized passages.[61] This implies that if we want to encounter Vismann's 'variables in the universe of law', we cannot allow our approach to remain trapped before the law, indefinitely circulating through the interim zones of the registries where we can only ground the law on administrative envelopes.

We can here turn to an interpretation that Kafka himself provides after inserting this parable in his novel *The Trial*. The character of the priest there states that someone who keeps to the door is deluded since 'he does not know the Law from the inside, he knows only the way that leads to it, where he patrols up and down' (Kafka, 2005, p. 201). On this approach we are required to move along the path *to* law and not stop at the first threshold, but, in Holmes' expression, to persist and continue to proceed along the path *of* law until we arrive at the grounds of judgment. Before we are able to do this however, we first have to study the operations of these preliminary thresholds themselves. We will now turn towards the first dispute.

***

60 These reflections highlight 'the juridical features' within philosophical thought itself (Deleuze & Guattari, 1994, p. 72), in this case of the 'laws of the subject' to which we will return in Chapter 6.

61 This also applies to the research approach itself. In order to gain empirical access to the legal processes described here, a chain of authorizations had to be obtained starting from the president of the highest Belgian Court of Cassation, downwards to the presidents of the Courts of Commerce.

~ 1ST MOVEMENT ~

Theme A. Intellectual Formation

Can the form of the matter of dispute be attributed to the intellect of the designer? In order to answer this question the protagonists set out to delimit a design space by introducing forced moves, rooms to manoeuvre and barred places. This delimitation occurs in more dimensions than merely along the brief axial idea – form(/concept) figure in the [TWC-Gortec] dispute in the previous chapter. Two additional axes are introduced here to delimit this space: the function-form axis and the fact-form axis. Once the boundaries of design space are drawn, the stage is set for a play of identities and differences.

Theme E. Identity and Difference

What is the immaterial form of one's designs in relation to those of the opponent's models? The matters of dispute find themselves opposed in an antagonistic dance of comparison on their lines, contours, colours, shape, texture, materials and ornamentation. Here they meet the fictive character of the informed user, appear as specimen models in the libraries and offices, or reappear inscribed in tables of juxtaposition in an expert report that itself becomes entangled with several legal authorities and raised as a figure on a fictive plane.

***

Models of Expertise (Case 1: Oil Spout Designs)

We find ourselves in the private library of the court in front of a pile of case folders, which have just been picked up at the office of the registrar of the 8th Chamber that deals with cases of intellectual rights. We will engage with the documents enclosed in these folders. In the previous chapter we saw that the introduction of the matter of dispute is a precarious activity, since disputes characteristically have the tendency to draw all speech acts about them, including constatives, introductives, and summatives within its antagonistic dynamics. In this chapter we will opt for a different mode of presentation that will oscillate between the attorney's propositional and the judge's decisive modes of proceeding. From the summons we get the following orientation onto the dispute. Plaintiff A is designer and producer of two kinds of spouts for bottles of olive oil. The model 'Summer' has the form of an olive tree; the model 'Autumn' has the form of an olive (see the images on page

152). The two models are deposited trademarks both in title and drawing at the Trade Marks and Designs Registration Office of the European Union. Defendant D has later introduced its products on the market. According to A these products are identical to A's original products but bear a different name and were offered without any permission. A thus stakes the claim:

> To hear legally declared that the designs sold by defendant are an infringement of plaintiff's designs 'Summer' and 'Autumn'.

Here we have our matters of dispute: the intellectual rights on two models of olive oil spouts. The intellectual rights implicated in the case are copyright, trademarks and community designs. On plaintiff A's request the court has ordered a 'descriptive seizure' by expert E. Defendant D later appointed expert F with the assignment to do a counter-expertise. In this case we will focus on the dispute around the existence of infringement and on the expert reports as a mode of evidence. We will start with D's defence against these accusations. In his investigation expert F compares the two alleged counterfeited objects of D to the two olive oil spouts of A. With regard to the model 'Summer' the expert states the following:

> I have found that the **form** of the components 'cork' and 'spout' of the bottle spout of D are **determined by their function**. Also, the component 'trunk' is **no copyright infringement**, but a **copy of a trunk of an olive tree present in nature . . .**

A lot is condensed in these two sentences. Let us start with the introductory presentation through the performative phrase 'I have found that'. In speech act theory it is listed as a verdictive utterance that delivers a finding upon evidence and hereby establishes it as a fact.[62] Austin calls such an utterance a 'judicial act' even though it is here performed by a scientific expert. This goes to show that the role of the scientific expert in legal proceedings is already a hybrid one.[63] The expert is appointed by the court in the context of a 'descriptive seizure', i.e. an investigation measure

---

[62] Austin, 1976, p. 153.

[63] Latour remarks that the situation in which scientists give evidence before the courts in a matter within their area of expertise, bears the imprint of law rather than of science itself (Latour, 2010, p. 206). Jasanoff states that the 'borderline between value decisions that should be the prerogative of judges and factual matters that are properly reserved for experts is itself a construct, negotiated anew from expert to expert and from case to case' (Jasanoff, 1997, p. 48). For a focus on the interactions of law and science with regard to legal expertise in patent disputes, see Cambrosio et al., 1990 and Smith & Wynne, 1989.

of 'expert evidence', one of the important branches of legal evidence.[64] We will try to understand this hybrid character when looking at the status of the expert reports as a means of evidence. Here, we will follow how one can come to 'find' that there is no infringement of intellectual rights. What allows one to arrive at such a finding?

The expert has pried the olive oil spouts apart in several components – cork, spout, trunk and canopy – and has subsequently investigated each in the light of the claim of counterfeit. Each of the findings presents us with different arguments and evidential techniques. With regard to the cork and spout we are presented a functional finding of a technical nature. In order to understand this point we have to first go back to a relevant legal condition. D's attorney here cites article 8, §1 of Regulation 6/2002 (EC) as the applicable law on community designs. 'A Community design shall not subsist in features of appearance of a product which are solely dictated by its technical function.' The 'form' or 'appearance' of a product cannot be attributed to the intellect of its designer when this form is 'dictated' or 'determined' by its technical functions. It would then not qualify as 'individual', which is the condition of intellectuality within this Regulation, since these technical functions would have curtailed the 'degree of freedom of the designer in developing the design'.[65] The function of the cork is to close the bottle. Since the size and shape of the openings of olive oil bottles is more or less standardized, the designer has to adapt the form of the cork to this specification. In order to find a solution to a general design problem, the designer thus has a limited freedom of choice and he has to make 'a forced move in design space'.[66] A similar finding is presented with regard to the straight cylindrical form of the spout. The function of the spout is twofold: it allows and modulates the passage of olive oil from the bottle through the cork so that it may be poured in a moderate fashion; and the spout in turn functions as a new receptacle on which the ornamented tree-shaped cap is placed (hence its straight form).

---

64 On the basis of article 1369bis/1, §1 (CPL) the court can, in the case of alleged infringement of intellectual rights and on request of the plaintiff, appoint an expert who gives a 'description of all objects, elements, documents or ways of working which are of the nature to demonstrate the alleged infringement as well as its origin, destination and scope'.

65 Article 6 of this Regulation states that: '1. A design shall be considered to have individual character if the overall impression it produces on the informed user differs from the overall impression produced on such a user by any design which has been made available to the public [. . .] 2. In assessing individual character, the *degree of freedom of the designer in developing the design* shall be taken into consideration.'

66 I am here borrowing Dennett's expression (Dennett, 1996).

These observations lead the expert to 'find' that not enough space is left for attributing the form of the spout to the human intellect, but that it is instead 'determined' by these two technical functions. Both the forms of the cork and the spout are 'necessary for the functionality' of the product.

Next in the delineation of the design space is the form of the trunk component of the oil spout and the form or idea of an olive tree or an olive itself.

> **D's Attorney:** We are dealing with intellectual rights. An **idea by itself is not protected**. The idea to use oil spouts is not protectable, the idea to use an olive or an olive tree on a spout neither. The idea to use a smurf on a bottle spout would enjoy protection.

The expert finds that the 'Summer' model is 'a copy of a trunk of an olive tree present in nature' and is thus not protectable by intellectual rights. Here we arrive again at the crucial ontological compartmentalization operative in intellectual rights between the human intellect and the realm of nature. The form of an olive tree or an olive is the result of natural processes. When a designer makes a bottle spout that incorporates the shape of any of these, the form of this product can thus not be attributed to his or her intellectual activities, but must be considered a copy of the shape of the olive trees or olives we find in nature. D's attorney contrasts these natural forms with a typical Belgian example. The figure of the smurfs is evoked, since they do not exist in nature (at least not in nature out there), but are rather an intellectual creation by their author Pierre Culliford (Peyo). If the smurf idea had been used for the bottle spout, it could thus have constituted a community design.[67]

Now that the boundaries are drawn and the negative space of non-protectable design is delineated, D's attorney can proceed to outlining

---

[67] This is a sweeping statement. Since these arguments will not be addressed in the court's judgment, they need to be qualified. Following the divisions proposed, we could also say that Van Gogh's painting of *Olive Trees with Yellow Sun and Sky*, (or basically any artistic representation of nature) constitutes a copy of the natural form of an olive tree and would thus not merit intellectual right protection. One might start to feel that something is not quite right here. It is this feeling that we will have to cultivate for understanding intellectual rights judgments. Furthermore, when the judge would follow the expert 'findings' it seems he would merely confirm a given distinction between the pre-existing realms of intellect and nature (here represented as a warehouse of all kinds of forms). It has become the argument of this book however, that instead of a confirmation, this judgment rather re-constitutes this distinction through the practical particularities of this dispute. The two models that are the matters of dispute have mediated the boundaries between different realms of belonging. Nature would have been authoritatively re-assembled and so would the reach of the intellect.

what can be protected. He here evokes article 3 of the Regulation 6/2002 EC, which defines a design as 'the appearance of the whole or a part of a product resulting from the features of, in particular, the lines, contours, *colours*, *shape*, texture and/or materials of the product itself and/or its *ornamentation*' (attorney's italics). All these elements are relevant for judging similarity or difference between the products of A and D. Here he once again turns to the expert report of Mr F in which the expert finds that

> . . . the **differences** between the bottle spouts of A and D are clearly noticeable.

What makes these differences between the two bottle spouts so clearly noticeable? And what makes them clearly noticeable in a way that convinces the judge? Several techniques are used for these purposes. First, we see that a *table* is deployed as a technique of presentation and arrangement, which allows two pictures of the models to be closely juxtaposed in a way that facilitates comparison, like a game of 'finding the differences'. The similarities and differences that are 'found' in this way can be subsequently inscribed in slots in the rows straight under the pictures in a way that feeds back into the comparative juxtaposition. This technique of the

Bottle spout of D	Bottle spout of A
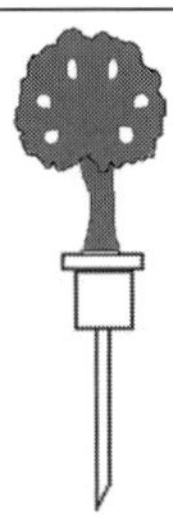	
All components have the same colour tone.	The leaves in the canopy have a different colour than the other two components (trunk and spout). Use is made of contrasting colours.
A stylized tree with an equalized form and 6 similar standardized windows on the outside of the canopy.	A stylized tree with an asymmetrical form of 5 differently shaped branches, all with a very deep cut into the tree trunk.
The windows in the canopy have a tear-shaped form.	The form of the branches and leaves in the canopy is organic.
The width of the tree is 5.1 cm.	The width of the tree is 6.9 cm.

Bottle spout of D	Bottle spout of A

The olive component has 1 colour.	The olive component has different colours and ornamentation.
Thickness 1.5 mm.	Thickness 2.5 mm.

table is very close to the operation of lists that we have seen at the beginning of this chapter. Here, it mediates observation and what can count as a finding and hereby serves to articulate the practical philosophies of identity and difference that pervade disputes of intellectual rights. Second, *specimens* of the bottle spouts here depicted have been added as evidence within the folder with the pieces.[68] These objects enable the constitution of the identity of a work or design through the comparative differentiation of specimens, since they allow the judges to go from the table to the specimens and back in order to 'see for themselves' whether the stipulated differences can indeed convincingly be found. The attorney concludes by selecting those aspects that can be qualified according to the criteria of article 3 of the Community Design Regulation. Big differences can be observed between the two models: a contrast of different *colours* vs. a uniformity of colour; an equalized standardized *shape* vs. an asymmetrical organic shape (in the case of the tree); the absence vs. the presence of *ornamentation* (on the olive).

A's attorney disagrees. Olive oil spouts 'Summer' and 'Autumn' do not just have a functional goal, but are wholly original design objects, so the decorative aspects are just as important. The functional aspects of the cork and the spout neither require that the upper part of the model – the cap on the spout – be a decoration in the form of an olive tree or olive, nor that this decoration extensively sticks out from the bottle when it is closed. The form of the spout is thus sufficiently original, to be protected by copyright.

[68] Later in this chapter, we will discuss the use of scale models of machines as pieces of evidence in patent law to make visible the modus operandi of an invention.

Furthermore, the attorney states that the olive oil spouts offered by D are identical to the olive oil spouts 'Summer' and 'Autumn', except that the former are mono-coloured and the latter bi-coloured. He here cites a legal case stating that 'copyright infringement is rather judged on its similarities than on its differences, which are rather destined to conceal the fraud' (Burg Hoei, 28 mrt 1994, JLMB, p. 938). This is an interesting citation. Intellectual rights on community designs and copyrighted works are infringed when they are illegitimately reproduced, which requires that the alleged copy must be sufficiently similar. Finding similarities thus provides the focus of the investigation. Differences between the products are simultaneously recast as masks to conceal the infringement. Something akin to a legal presumption is introduced here, which shifts the burden in the identity-difference ratio. Finally, strengthened by the finding of expert E that 'in its folder (p. 11) D offers almost similar bottle spouts with the same form and measures', the attorney concludes that since the 'global visual aspect' of the models is identical, these models are thus copies of the registered trademarks of A.

Now, expert E was appointed by the court, so his findings could well provide a certain inconvenience for the defence. The attorneys of D will dispute this report, which provides us with an interesting example of the relations between experts and lawyers. Is the expert not brought in to put an end to the debate and at last shortcut it with a factual account of what actually happened? How is a lawyer then in the position to dispute what an expert says at all? Here we get on the terrain of legal expertise. Jasanoff has described how expert claims can become contested throughout the adversarial process in court, during 'orgies of deconstruction' (Jasanoff, 1997, p. 53).[69] We want to understand the typical legal techniques and procedures that enable the lawyers to deal with reports of expertise. We have to apologize to the reader for the somewhat 'technical' character here (and this pertains to the legal passages not the ones by the expert!).

> Expert E has not taken into account the contestability that is required by law (article 973.1 of Code of Procedural Law). This is an **essential aspect** for its **validity**.
> Article 1369bis/10 (CPL) determines that in the case of legal expertise in copyright infringement **a certain number of articles of legal expertise is not applicable**. Article 976 however, about the communication of the report to both parties afterwards and responding to their questions, **does remain applicable**.

[69] Expert reports are also mobilized for the normative agendas of the parties within the adversarial process in order to expose holes in the evidence of the other party and undercut their credibility (Jasanoff, 1997).

> In case law consensus has grown about the fact that the sanction for not honouring contestability is not nullity but non-opposability (Lyssen & Naudts, Bestendig Handboek Deskundigenonderzoek, TBBR, 1995, p. 156). The report of expert E is thus non-opposable to D.

The propositional argument of D's attorney is fourfold: proposing and grounding the condition of (non) validity for an expert report, its exclusion from exceptions, the kind of infelicity that follows from non-compliance, and imputing this infelicity to the expert report of Mr E. The reasons stated have nothing to do with the truth or falsity of the report, but with its validity *as* an expert report. We are here dealing with a *legal* expertise which has to satisfy its own particular set of constraints, in which the expert has to operate. When s/he fails to do so the report might suffer from certain kinds of infelicity.[70] In this case, the condition raised by D as 'essential' for the valid proceeding of the expert report is that of its contestability. Article 973§ 1 (CPL) determines that 'the judge who ordered the expert report [. . .] sees to it that the deadlines are met and contestability is observed'. Although the expert is not required to let parties contest his descriptions at the moment of the seizure, this does not apply to his (pre-) report about this seizure. D's attorney states that 'the principle of equality would be violated when a party in defence against a claim of infringement of copyright could not make remarks on the findings of experts in trial'. Here we see how a small action, or rather a lack of action of not allowing the defendant to make comments to a pre-report of the descriptive seizure, can provide the occasion for evoking grand principles of equality and fair trial.

In the next step of the argument, this proposition is steered clear of some exceptions which might strand it. We are dealing with an expertise in the context of an infringement of intellectual rights. In the Code of Procedural Law this kind of expertise is partly exempted from the general regime of constraints that an expert report has to satisfy in order to be valid. Article 1369bis/10 states that several articles governing legal expertise do not apply to this infringement procedure: 'The articles 962 till 965, *973, §1* and 3, 978 and 985 are not applicable to a procedure for seizure for infringement' of intellectual rights. We see that article 973, §1 that inscribes the condition

---

[70] In Austinian speech act parlance this would be a case of 'misexecutions' of a conventional procedure (either correctly or completely), which invalidates the purported act (Austin, 1976). He again resorts to law and legal examples as paradigms for the infelicities that can befall this type of speech act: 'examples are more easily seen in the law; they are naturally not so definite in ordinary life, where allowances have to be made' (Austin, 1976, p. 36).

of contestability, which was raised earlier by D, is included in the list of exceptions and would thus not be applicable here. D's attorney however, points to another article, article 976 §1, which requires the expert to send the finished report to both parties and respond to their questions.[71] This article is not excluded for intellectual right infringement cases and *this* condition of contestability thus remains applicable to the expertise. The legal tissue can be full with exceptions. It requires detailed work of legal expertise in aligning and disaligning legal authorities, to steer one's propositions past these sandbanks of exceptions, in order to successfully invalidate other kinds of expertise.

Now, what about the consequences of all of this? What infelicity ensues from the supposed misexecution of the expertise by not providing contestability of the pre-report? D's attorney mobilizes a supposedly arisen 'consensus' in case law and aligns it with a legal handbook and the judgment of another court, to authorize the position that the sanction for not satisfying the condition of contestability is not that an expert report is null, but that it is non-opposable. The report of Mr E could thus not be opposed to D within the present legal proceedings. Now, when we turn to A's statement of claim, this supposed 'consensus' is short-lived and turns out to be nothing more than a transient iceberg of solidity which once again is made to melt into the stream of dispute.

> D unjustifiably states that the expert report of expert E is not valid and not opposable. Since the law of 3-8-1982 there are two grounds of nullity for the expert report. The Court of Cassation has judged that violation of the principle of adversary debate does not imply the nullity of the report.
> Concerning the opposability: 'in contrast to the **classical expertise** the **expert who is appointed in the context of a legal proceedings on infringement of intellectual rights** will not give technical advice, but shall limit himself to provide a description of the matters which violate the intellectual right of the plaintiff. The expertise will be one-sided and be **non-contestable**.' (Mignolet, O., L'expertise judiciaire, in Rep. Not., Larcier, 2009, p.53). [. . .] D tries to **raise confusion** by **mixing classical expertise** with **expertise in infringement of intellectual rights**.

Both parties might be in consensus about the consequence of not satisfying the condition of contestability in the expertise: the report will at least not be null. With regard to the sanction of opposability however, the attorney aligns a doctrinal text to authorize an important differentiation between

---

[71] Article 976, §1 'After his work the expert sends his findings, to which he adds a provisional advice, to be read to the court, the parties and their lawyers. [. . .] The expert receives the comments of the parties and their technical advisers before the expiration' of the deadline.

two *different legal regimes of expertise*: 'classic expertise' and 'expertise in infringement of intellectual rights'. In the non-classical regime, contestability does not hold as a condition of validity: the expertise will be one-sided and non-contestable. In this sense, A's attorney accuses D's attorney of trying to muddle the differentiation between these two regimes of expertise in presenting them in a singular fashion. We find the main statement of classical expertise in article 962 (CPL): 'for the resolution of a dispute brought before him [. . .], the judge can order experts to make determinations or give technical advice.' Through this intervention of the expert, who is supposed to provide impartial and independent advice, the judge is enabled to gain a better insight in the technical aspects of a dispute.[72] Now, in expertise in infringement of intellectual rights the expert is to limit him or herself to a mere description of 'the matters which violate the intellectual rights of the plaintiff', instead of providing technical advice to the judge. It is on this very point that the report of expert F is criticized.

> Moreover, expert E has not **exceeded the limits of his assignment**, in contrast to Expert F who was appointed by D. Expert E has only pronounced himself about the characteristics of the products on the basis of the gathered information. Expert F has **judged** the infringement, which is a **competence which would not be given to him, should he be assigned by the court**.

Apparently not only D's attorney, but also his expert F has muddled the differentiation between the two regimes of competences. Expert E, who was appointed by court, has limited himself to a mere gathering of information and description of the characteristics of the encountered products. Within his course of work, he has thus remained within 'the limits of the assignment' set out by the legal regime of expertise in infringement of intellectual rights. Expert F however, who was appointed by D in order to provide a counter-expertise, has exceeded these limits of mere description. By providing a judgment ('D offers quite different oil spouts with the different colours, lines and forms') he has committed a twofold transgression of competence. First, the expert has committed the unforgiveable sin of *hubris*, assuming the power that transcends those of one's own regime: the powers of judgment. The expert can never provide advice about the groundedness (merits) of the claim.[73] This follows from the prohibition against judges transferring their *juris-diction*, their capacity to speak the law, to judge; a prohibition which is anchored in the Belgian constitution

[72] On this point, see Laenens et al., 2008, p. 579.

[73] An alternative, more modest interpretation is that the expert has provided technical advice instead of sticking to description.

(article 11, §1).[74] A judge is a judge, an expert is an expert, and an expert is not allowed to take the place of the judge.[75]

The attorney further states that this is 'a competence which would not be given to him, should he be assigned by the court'. This is an interesting phrase that nicely brings out the contrafacticity of certain legal operations. In this case we are dealing with a positive legal fiction. This fiction sets up a counterfactual reality (that in which expert F would have been appointed by the court in an infringement procedure) in which certain conditions hold as a default (the expert can only describe, not give advice or judge), projects a certain act on this plane (the supposed judgment) and draws the legal consequences within this projected reality (the nullity or non-opposability of the report or the relevant parts of it).[76] The statutory articles of legal expertise refer only to experts appointed by the courts. Mr F has in fact been appointed by D and is thus, strictly speaking, not bound by these articles. Nevertheless, the deployment of this legal technique of fiction repairs this factual obstacle in showing the requirements that such a report would have had to satisfy in a procedure like the present one. This nicely demonstrates the proper legal techniques that lawyers have at their disposal to contest the reports of experts and maintain their independence from science. Now we can proceed to judgment to see whether they have done so convincingly (see judgment box on opposite page).

What just happened?!? Alice's damn rabbit was right; a lot has to indeed occur 'before judging the claim'. We are confronted with a preliminary judgment. The attorneys might have pried apart the Belgian Code of Procedural Law and Regulation 6/2002 EC on the infringement of community designs and the validity of expert reports, but in both legal sources they have overlooked the important preceding conditions of competence of the court![77] According to the set of articles linked together in this judgment, it turns out the Court of Brussels and not the one of Leuven is granted the competence to hear a claim of infringement of community designs. Access to the ears of the judge is carefully circumscribed. If the judges are not competent to receive the claim, they would have to declare it inadmissible. The attempt to make judgment shift to the grounds or merits of the disputed claim has hereby failed. For the moment, admittance is not granted and the dispute is sent back into its process of circulation.

---

74 Laenens et al., 2008, p. 580.

75 See footnote 162 in this chapter.

76 For a detailed account of the legal fiction as a technique for the passage of law, see Thomas, 2011, Chapter 6.

77 Article 8 (CPL) defines competence as 'the power of the court to hear a claim brought for him'.

JUDGMENT

3.1
Article 574 of the Code of Procedural Law determines:
'The Court of Commerce will, even when parties are not traders, hear:
[. . .]
14 ° the claims under Article 81 of Regulation (EC). 6 / 2002 of the Council of 12 December 2001 on community designs.

Article 633quinquies determines that:
§ 1. Only the Commercial Court of Brussels has the competence to hear the claims of intellectual property rights referred to in article 574, 11 °, **14** ° and 19 °.

3.2
Plaintiff bases himself on the provisions of Regulation 6/2002 EC of 12 December 2001 on community designs and argues that defendant has infringed his deposited community designs.

According to the provisions cited above (3.1), only the Court of Commerce of Brussels has the competence to hear legal claims about community design infringements.

Since the rule of judicial organization – the rule of the competence of this court – **touches upon public order**, the Court believes that it **needs to doubt** its competence **of its own motion** [/*ex officio*] and raises the objection of competence. According to article 774 § 2 (CPL) the debates need to be reopened *ex officio* to allow parties to assume their position with regard to this raised objection.

FOR THESE REASONS
THE COURT

Before judging the claim

REOPENS THE DEBATES OF ITS OWN MOTION.

None of the parties evoked this objection of competence during the process, but the court 'raises the objection of its own motion'.[78] How is this possible? What is this immanent motion proper to the court and how is it activated?[79] The judges have checked whether the conditions of

[78] The Dutch term here is *ambstshalve*, sometimes also translated in Latin as *ex officio*.

[79] The principle of 'party autonomy' in civil law implies that litigating parties determine the shape of the dispute through their propositions and that the judge is held to passivity. The judge however 'does not merely need to judge and resolve the dispute (*geschil*); he also has to control the proceedings (*geding*) to an important extent' (Laenens et al., 2008, p. 56). The passivity of the judge is thus limited to the scope of the dispute presented to him, but s/he has more room for motion with regard to its conditions of proceeding.

competence were satisfied for the infringement claim and found this was not the case. Something interesting happens at this point. Through raising this condition to the surface of the dispute, the dispute has come to touch upon something other than its own procession to judgment; something beyond the antagonistic bounds of the claims of the parties involved. It suddenly threatens to disturb the very organization of the judiciary and thus the orderly administration of justice. In this way this condition of competence has let the dispute 'touch' upon a larger fold in which it will become temporarily enveloped.[80] By the act of raising this condition, public order is projected outwards beyond the confines of the present dispute as an attractor that requires the court to act out of its own motion. It makes the court 'need to doubt' its own competence and makes it reopen the debates at a later date.

The Belgian Court of Cassation once judged that 'acting out of its own motion', acting *ex officio*, means that a judge can take a decision 'without being required to do so'.[81] It is an act that immanently belongs to the office of the judge and which is not incited by the external causes advocated in the claims of the parties. Instead it is properly raised from its own depths, a kind of Leibnizian court monadology.

***

These *ex officio* doubts by the court of its own competence 'before judging the claim' bring us to the preliminaries of judgment: the points of a dispute dealt with before passing the threshold of a judgment on its legal grounds. Another such 'threshold' example was encountered in a different case on copyright infringement at our court, to which we will briefly turn. In its judgment a seemingly marginal piece of evidence – an Arab document signed by the two parties – suddenly took centre stage and postponed the termination of the dispute proceedings.[82]

We here again encounter a false ending. Why can we not write with confidence that at the end of the dispute is this deed of judgment? Is it just as difficult to begin at the beginning of a dispute and not go further back, than it is to stop at its end and not stop short of it or pass beyond? How can we come to the end of the legal dispute and then stop? In the previous chapter

---

[80] The Belgium Court of Cassation judged that conditions of material competence (*ratione materiae*) touch upon public order (Cass. 2 April 2001, Soc. Kron., 324).

[81] Cass. 27 April 1989, A.C. 1988–89 1004.

[82] This case could not be included in this book, but can be consulted elsewhere (van Dijk, 2013).

JUDGMENT

Alkari and Durbik are diametrically opposed with regard to the sworn Dutch translations of the document written in Arabic dated Sept. 1996 and signed by Mr Alkari and Mr Durbik. Taking into account the contradictions between the translations of this document presented by both parties in the context of the present procedure, the court judges that **expert advice**, to be determined hereafter, **previously imposes itself**.

FOR THESE REASONS
THE COURT

Before pronouncing judgment on the grounds,
Appoints as an expert translator: Mr E.
[. . .]

Sends the case to the special scroll of the 8th Chamber for further settlement.

our treatment of the legal dispute 'started' with an enacted piece of code by the Belgian legislator that prescribed its formal initiation. To conserve symmetry I will also inscribe the enactment that authorizes me to state by which deed the incessant proceeding of a dispute is formally brought to a halt (*arrêt*). Article 19 of the Code of Procedural Law states that:

> The judgment is a **final** judgment in so far as the jurisdiction of the court on a **point of dispute** is hereby exhausted, apart from the legal remedies provided by law.
> (**Prior to doing justice**, the court may, at any stage of the legal administration, order a **preliminary measure** in order to investigate the claim, to rule an intermediary dispute with regard to such a measure, or to provisionally rule the state of the parties . . .)

It is interesting to see that what has been brought to an end, the unit of finalization, is not dispute itself but a 'point of dispute'. This confirms our impression of a *legal pointillism* of disputes (points of dispute, weak points, strong points, bullet points, points of view, points of reference, appointments) in which lawyers continuously endeavour to contract zones in the extensive dispute dynamics into discrete points. When this is done in the performative sentences of judgment, the enunciating court hereby unauthorizes its capacity to speak legally about this point of dispute any further.[83] In our case a judgment is indeed reached, but not one

[83] In Austinian terms we can call this the perlocutionary effect of the act of pronouncing judgment: *by* this enunciation the court finalizes its jurisdiction.

which finalizes this *iuris-dictio*. Apparently, the contradictions between the two different translations offered by both parties constituted such a contentious issue that the appointment of an expert translator 'previously imposes itself' on the judges 'before pronouncing judgment on the grounds' of the case.[84] What a remarkable turn of phrase! Certain kinds of contradiction between pieces of evidence can preclude a judge from reaching a final conviction. Within the interiority of the dispute they have the force to raise a legal figure from the depths – legal expertise – and impose it upon the mind of the judge. Apparently this is possible 'at any stage of the legal administration' of the dispute. We are here faced with what is called a *preliminary* judgment or measure that is reached 'prior to doing justice'. Our false beginning might serve to heed the White Rabbit's interruption in not jumping to the finality of judgment all too hastily, since there is still a fair deal to come before that. It does actually provide us with an opportunity to observe the textual articulations of judgment without distracting us too much from following a dispute. Let us have a look at the way the legal speech of the judges is organized within these judgment documents.[85]

The Operations of Judgment

> [T]o utter the sentence (in, of course, the appropriate circumstances) is not to describe my doing of what I should be said in so uttering to be doing or to state that I am doing it: it is to do it. [. . .] What are we to call a sentence or an utterance of this type? I propose to call it a performative sentence or a performative utterance, or, for short, 'a performative'. [. . .] A number of other terms may suggest themselves, each of which would suitably cover this or that wider or narrower class of performatives: for example, many performatives are *contractual* ('I bet') or *declaratory* ('I declare war') utterances. But no term in current use that I know of is nearly wide enough to cover them all. One technical term that comes nearest to what we need is perhaps '***operative***', as it is *used strictly by lawyers* in referring to that *part*, i.e. those clauses, of an instrument which serves to *effect the transaction* (conveyance or what not) which is its main object, whereas the rest of the document merely 'recites' the circumstances in which the transaction is to be effected.
>
> (Austin, 1976, pp. 6–7, my italics)

This document introduces several preliminary degrees of judgment. Its heading is aligned with the enlistments of the 'Minutes of the Public

---

84 The Dutch expression is *beslissing ten gronde* that is translated as 'judgment on merits' but is more literally translation as 'decision on grounds'.

85 The document depicted below is assembled from the features of different judgments of different chambers at different courts encountered throughout the duration of the observational study.

Public Hearing of [*date*]
[*number*] Chamber

Scroll Nr. [. . .] Repertory Nr. [. . .]

The Court of Commerce of [*City name*], [*number*] Chamber, has passed the following judgment in the case of:

[*Proper Name*]
Applicant, represented by LLM [*Proper Name*] advocate

Against:

[*Proper Name*]
Defendant, represented by LLM [*Proper Name*] advocate

[***]

I. PROCEEDINGS
[. . .]

II. ADMISSIBILITY OF THE CLAIM
[. . .]

III. THE MATTER OF THE CLAIM
[. . .]

IV. THE FACTS AND PRECEDINGS
[. . .]

V. JUDGMENT
[. . .]

FOR THESE REASONS **[/ 6. THE OPERATIVE PART]**
THE COURT

Judging after trial

Rejecting all more-encompassing or contradictory conclusions as non-relevant

Joins [. . .]
Declares admissible and grounded [. . .]
Legally declares [. . .]
Declares void [. . .]
Sentences [. . .]
Orders [. . .]
Grants [. . .]
Denies [. . .]
Prohibits [. . .]
Appoints [. . .]
Ensures responsibility for [. . .]
Says [. . .]

Judgment thus given by the court of commerce of [*City name*], [*number*] Chamber

Pronounced at the ordinary and public hearing by [*Proper Name*], judge at the court, president, [*Proper Name*] and [*Proper Name*], judges in commerce, assisted in judgment by [*Proper Name*], registrar

On [*stamp with the date*]

[*signature*] [*Proper Name*]	[*signature*] [*Proper Name*]	[*signature*] [*Proper Name*]	[*signature*] [*Proper Name*]

Hearings' document in the official case folder. This header has grammatical slots for the inscription of the date of the public hearing and the number of the specific Court Chamber dealing with the dispute, thus registering the spatiotemporal trajectory of the dispute in court. This is followed by grammatical slots for the inscription of the scroll number and the repertory number of the dispute. These are situated between two horizontally drawn lines that create a separate textual space in the margin of the document. Such lines were known as *praescripta* in late Latin: pre-drawn lines that separate the text that comes before (the administrative pre-script) and a certain execution of the text that follows.[86] The numbers inscribed in this row function as *operators* that both link this judgment document to the case file (or actually turn it into a file) and install it within the order of administration as the point of grasp for further execution operations (the Rabbit's scroll).

The margin of the document is prolonged by a textual series of actorial enlistments, initiated by the sentence: 'The Court of Commerce of Leuven, 8th Chamber, has passed the following judgment in the case of'. This sentence performs several announcements (the Rabbit's trumpet): it announces that the enunciator of judgment in this dispute is the Court of Commerce of Leuven; it announces that the pronouncement of this judgment will follow later in this document; and it announces the names of the enunciatees to whom this judgment is addressed (the plaintiff, the defendant and the attorneys). This list organizes the actorial dimension in the enunciation of judgment. Now, these actorial enlistments respond to a set of requirements for the legal administration of the text of judgment.[87] The speech act of passing judgment has its own conditions for successful proceeding, some of which organize the 'contents' of its documentation and are explicitly inscribed in article 780 of the Belgian Code of Procedural Law:

[86] See Vismann's discussion on this point (Vismann, 2008, p. 23).
[87] This distinguishes them from the inscriptions of the scroll and registry numbers on the judgment document that might be organizationally but not legally required.

> The **sentence contains**, under penalty of being **null and void**, apart from the **grounds and the operative part**:
> 1. A mention of the judge or **court** which has passed it; the **names of the magistrates** which have judged the case [. . .] and the **registrar** who was present at the pronouncement;
> 2. The **name, first name and residence** that the **parties** have mentioned at their appearance and statements;
> 3. The **subject matter of the claim** and the **response to the statements and means** of the parties.
> 4. A mention of the advice of the public prosecution [not relevant here].
> 5. A mention of the **date** of the **pronouncement** in a public hearing.
> 6. The indication of the **names of the attorneys**.

The act of judgment of the court is itself also subject to infelicities, not just the attorney's claim. A failure by the court in its requirements of documentary containment will expose the judgment to the risk of being declared null and void by another court. We can call these the 'requisite procession points' of judgment.[88] These are the points that the court's judgment 'has to pass' if it wants to avoid such an infelicity. They are distributed throughout the document in a way that seems to blur the borders between its margins and body text, but rather mix both into a 'margin/body content'. Apart from these spatiotemporal and actorial enlistments, the inscription of the matter of claim and the grounds and acts of its judgment are also requisite procession points.

(I) The document does not directly proceed to the matter of dispute. There is an intermediary passage along considerations of interim 'Proceedings' and preliminary 'Admissibility'. It contains sentences like 'Taking into consideration the introductory summons', 'Taking into consideration the pieces and statements deposited by parties', 'Having heard the parties at the public session'. All the dynamics of the proceedings of the dispute and the circulation of the case file, which we have so extensively followed until now, are here condensed into a mere few procedural sentences. Their performative inscription ('taking into consideration') transforms these movements into

---

[88] This term adapts Callon's concept of 'obligatory passage point' (Callon, 1986) to our legal context. The term 'requirements' links to the constraints that legal practitioners are bound by in their concerned dealings with practical problems (Stengers, 2006). It differs from the term 'obligation' by the fact that the latter is never general but always circumstantial in making the practitioners hesitate about what a matter of concern obliges them to do next. The term 'procession' links to the legal processes by which matters of dispute come to proceed. The term 'point' links to the legal pointillism that we have become acquainted with in this chapter.

vectors of consideration in the field of forces that will impinge on the minds of the judges during the processes of deliberation.[89]

(II) The treatment of the admissibility of the claim is often totally absent from the document. We have seen how certain contradictions in a dispute that can make a preliminary measure 'previously impose itself' before judgment, or can make a court raise an objection of competence 'of its own motion', are important ways in which the issue of admissibility can emerge in the preliminary considerations of judgment.

(III) In the section titled 'the matter of the claim' the court repeats the attorney's first contractions of the dispute into its most condensed states of the stick-like claims. This matter of the claim however might show variations between the attorneys' documents. In order to stabilize these fluctuations the court refers to the latest unaltered claim: 'The claim of plaintiff, as was last formulated in its [document] deposited on [date], states that [. . .]'. These constitute the points of dispute with regard to which the court will have to exert its *iurisdictio*. In the operative part of the judgment hereafter the court will perform a second differential contraction of the dispute. Between these two 'little deaths' of the dispute[90] unfold the 'preceding' passages of fact and reasoning.

(IV) The section 'Facts and Precedings' is comparable to the sections of 'in fact' in the statements of the attorneys, introducing the parties and stating the facts that provided the occasion for the dispute. These facts relate to applications and grants of patents, inscriptions of trademarks or community designs in a registry, signing of contracts, letters of formal notice (of infraction), letters of reservation of title, requests for seizure, expert reports and lodging of applications. All these factual acts are either formally mentioned or these documents are inscribed in great detail within this section. These factual passages show a certain overlap with the procedural passages, the difference being that the latter are called 'proceedings' whereas the former are called 'precedings'. This change of denomination signals that we have passed into the proximity of judgment. We are no longer dealing with acts of the attorneys that merely procedurally proceed and which are only heard or taken into consideration. The acts of the parties in question have now been drawn into the preparation of judgment as its significant factual precedings.

---

[89] And this only applies to the summons, statements and pieces, since the judges are not legally obliged to take the pleas of the attorney into consideration (Laenens et al., 2008, pp. 427–8). They merely constitute a 'hearing'.

[90] See footnote 26 in Chapter 3.

Furthermore, in comparison with the statement of the attorneys the absence of a section 'in law' in the judgment document is striking. According to the principle of *ius curia novit* the court is supposed to know the law and to determine how the case will be legally judged. If the judges do not know the law or have doubts about it with regard to a specific point of dispute, they are required to conduct their own investigations for which the library in the tower provides ample sources. Whereas the judge cannot pass beyond the attorney's factual stitches, s/he is not legally obliged by their legal alignments in the same way. Attorneys are not even required to state or prove the law at all. In practice however they extensively do so as we have seen in the previous chapter. The evocation of certain legal authorities and their connection to the matter of dispute address the judges in terms of the legal passage points by which they might feel obliged in the course of their work.[91]

(V) After all these proceedings, interims, preliminaries and precedings we finally seem to arrive at judgment. But do we? And finally? Have we not rather arrived at something far more complicated than judging? Between the headers of 'Judgment' and 'The Operative Part' we find the reasoning passages, which we will still study closely. The fact that reasoning is placed under the header of judgment is significant. It confirms that reasoning also already implies the operations of judgment. In comparison to other requisite procession points, those related to the processes of reasoning are much less circumscriptive and thus allow for a much greater degree of variation. The sentence is required to contain the 'grounds' of judgment and 'the response to the statements and means of the parties', i.e. all the factual grounds and legal grounds on which the judgment is based.

The organization of the judgment document so far discussed might have given the impression that the act of judgment is inscribed within a format of predetermined textual structures. This view has to be disputed. The textual proceeding of the dispute in the document is influenced by a variety of organizational factors which should not be confused with such textual structuralism. We have seen that the requirements of administration pre-scribe a certain organization of the margins of the document. Furthermore, many requisite procession points of judgment require certain spatiotemporal and actorial enlistments spread throughout the document:

[91] Crommelin, 2007 states that legal elaborations of the dispute play such an important role in contemporary disputes that they often cannot be missed.

the date, place, enunciators and enunciatees of judgment and the matter of the claim. Although these points are rather minimal they also quite strictly circumscribe the proceedings, leading to a rather stable manner of textual documentation with room for little variation. In contrast, although procedure, admissibility, facts, precedings, grounds and replies have been ascribed to such passage points to a certain degree, these do not require the same rigid passages. To the contrary, these passages exhibit considerable variation between different disputes from non-existent to very extensive. Certain developments within these disputes can make such points emerge or 'impose themselves' in which case they become distributed throughout the document. These organizational variations must thus also be understood according to the singularity of the matter of dispute at stake.

FOR THESE REASONS
THE COURT

Towards the end of the judgment section we find this bold and capitalized phrase which divides the text into two parts that it simultaneously relates. The phrase 'for these reasons' is a conjunctive grammatical marker that indicates an important transition from the acts of reasoning to the enactment of judgment. In other courts the text which follows is separately organized under the header 'The Operative Part'.[92] This section inscribes the *dictum*: the thing said legally; the judgment considered in its narrow sense. The connective is followed by an inscription of the enunciator of judgment: 'the court'. The court enacts the judgment by pronouncing a range of utterances, each of which performs a specific operation, indicated by the verb that initiates the utterance ('declares', 'sentences', 'orders', 'grants', 'denies', 'prohibits', etc.). These *operatives* of judgment are performative acts that carry a preceding cause or *causa* (contracted in the sentences) into its instantaneous consequents (legal effects). In these operatives the dispute finds its second intense contraction after the contraction in the attorney's claims in the summons, selectively bringing together many of its heterogeneous elements in these few singular formulas. These two 'little deaths' of the dispute formally compose the rhythmical interval of the life of the conflict as a matter of legal dispute.

Before we analyze these concrete performative acts, attention has to first be pointed at the deep link between these legal 'operatives' and the notion of the performative itself. In the quote that opens this section, Austin states that he discovered a particular kind of linguistic utterance in

---

[92] The Dutch term is '*beschikkend gedeelte*' which is also called '*dictum*' or '*dispositief*'. It can be translated as 'the operative part' or 'the enacting provisions'.

which the speaking of a certain sentence is the performance of an action. The term that is most closely related in naming this kind of utterance is the technical term 'operative'

> as it is used strictly by lawyers in referring to that part, i.e. those clauses, of an instrument which serves to effect the transaction (conveyance or what not) which is its main object, whereas the rest of the document merely 'recites' the circumstances in which the transaction is to be effected (Austin, 1976, p .7).

Austin eventually calls this kind of utterance a 'performative', which will become the cornerstone of speech act theory. It is interesting to note that these performatives take the kind of legal operatives analyzed here as the very paradigm upon which they are modeled.[93]

In the judgment document these legal operatives constitute different vectors in a performative force field. First, the court starts its enactment of judgment by the inscription of an utterance in which it literally does what it says: the court 'judges after trial'.[94] The court proceeds by 'rejecting all more-encompassing or contradictory statements as non-relevant'. This is an interesting and rather sweeping move by which all the arguments of the unsuccessful party that have not explicitly been addressed in the reasoning part are here still retroactively rejected in one short phrase. Next, the court either 'declares the claim admissible and grounded' or it declares it inadmissible or ungrounded. In the former case it pronounces itself competent to receive and judge this claim and pronounce it to be sufficiently backed up by factual and legal grounds. In this case the court proceeds to a legal declaration of *what* the claim proposed. It will for instance 'legally *declare*' a party to be qualified as a co-inventor, a matter of dispute to be qualified as an invention, or it will 'declare void' a certain trademark or patent registration. These utterances are 'declaratory judgments' (or 'verdictives' in speech act theory) that declare what is factually and legally the case in a dispute. Such declarations often carry legal effects in that they can give rise to further pronunciative operatives by which the court '*sentences* to pay damages', '*orders* a cancellation', '*grants* a measure', '*prohibits* a continued use of certain intellectual rights', '*appoints* an expert', or '*ensures responsibility for* legal expense'. These utterances are 'condemnatory judgments' (or 'exercitives' in speech act theory): as official acts these

---

93 Ducrot has stated that the illocutionary, the kind of linguistic activity or 'force' that gives birth to performatives, is itself defined as an intrinsically juridical act. 'The illocutionary appears now as a particular case of a juridical act: a juridical act accomplished by speech' (Ducrot, 1991, p. 78).

94 The Dutch term is '*rechtdoende*', which is more literally translated as 'doing law'.

rulings also make law and they condemn the execution of a certain course of action.[95]

From this perspective it is significant that most of the court's verdictive utterances with verbs like 'find', 'understand', 'interpret as', 'hold', 'read it as', 'take it' do not actually occur in the operative part, but are rather deployed in the reasoning passages of the judgment document. This again confirms that the verdict is already implied in the reasoning. Moreover, the Belgian Court of Cassation has judged that any decision by a judge inscribed in the reasoning section of the judgment still constitutes an operative judgment 'considering that each decision of a judge on a point of dispute is an operative part regardless of its place in the text of the judgment and regardless of the form in which it is posed'.[96] Form and textual location within the documents' order of organization are not decisive, but such decisiveness is itself measured in terms of a *legal operability with regard to concrete points of dispute*. In our subsequent 'case studies' we will try to focus on this legal *modus operandus.*

Although we have finally arrived at judgment, this judgment turns out to have been long immanent in the legal processes in which we have been involved. This is most clearly the case for the passages of reasoning, but it also extends further back to admissibility and in a certain sense throughout the whole document and even throughout the 'whole' network of proceedings of the matter of dispute up until this point. In this sense we can speak of the *distributed* nature of *judgment*.[97]

Judgment thus given by the Court of Commerce of Leuven, 8th Chamber

Pronounced at the ordinary and public hearing by Abelard Bernardus, judge at the court, president, Celia Doyle and Ephraim Fernandez, judges in commerce, assisted in judgment by Geraldine Hoei, registrar

On **08-09-2010**

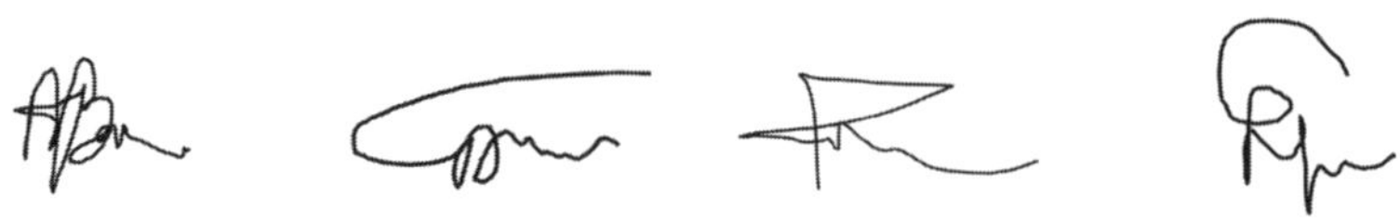

Abelard Bernardus   Celia Doyle   Ephraim Fernandez   Geraldine Hoei

---

95 Austin, 1976, pp. 153–7.

96 Court of Cassation, Belgium, 28/04/1994, C930245F.

97 Obviously, there are similarities here with the field of distributed cognition (Hutchins, 1995).

These textual passages by which the document ends constitute a particularly rich node of intersection in which several different strands mutually intervene on one another:

- the coordination of the oral pronouncement (presence) and the written documentation (repetition) of judgment,
- the typing of the spatiotemporal localization of the enunciation of judgment,
- the typing of the actorial identification of the enunciators of judgment,
- the establishment of their binding reference within the judgment document through a series of signed and stamped inscriptions,
- the passage from body text towards the margins of the judgment document (from the operatives to the operators of judgment),
- the legal code which raises requisite procession points for the finalization of the act of judgment in a concrete dispute.

The initiation of the operative part of judgment was performatively marked by the phrase 'the court takes the following decision'. It is finalized by the marking phrase 'judgment thus given by the court'. Hereby the *operatives* of judgment enacted just before are wrapped up and the judgment then passes towards certain *operators* in its margins by which these operatives become precisely assigned to their spatiotemporal coordinates and their actorial enunciators. This is achieved by a series of phrases with prepositional markers that indicate that the judgment was orally pronounced *at* the public hearing *of* the 8th Chamber *of* the Court of Commerce *of* Leuven, *on* date 08-09-2010, *by* president of the court Abelard Bernardus, judge in commerce Celia Doyle and judge in commerce Ephraim Fernandez, assisted by registrar Geraldine Hoei.

This pronunciation of judgment is also linked to a series of requisite procession points, many of them explicitly inscribed in different phrases of legal code. A failure in this mode of passage once again exposes the judgment to the risk of being declared null and void by another court. Article 149 of the Belgian Constitution states that each judgment 'is pronounced in a public hearing' hereby linking the act of passing judgment to an oral pronouncement, staged in a courtroom and within a regime of public accessibility. Judgment is thus first of all required to be a *speech* act, which is verbally uttered by its present authoritative enunciators. The primacy of orality over writing in this act is reflected in the fact that, although prscribed in civil law, the written judgment document is not even a condition for the validity of the judgment![98]

---

98 Stein & Rueb, 2002, p.178, n. 50.

Interestingly, this hierarchy becomes strangely inverted by a series of practices and conditions that turn judgment into an act of writing and in which oral pronouncement is inscribed as a legal fiction. First, the Belgian Court of Cassation has judged that for a judgment to qualify as pronounced in a public hearing, it does not actually have to be (orally) pronounced by the court and in practice in most of the cases it is not! Nevertheless, the judgment can pass as pronounced when it is inscribed by the registrar on the sheet of the hearing session for that court day.[99] On this sheet the registrar is required to inscribe: the case treated, its scroll number, the names of the parties and their attorneys, the date and hour of the treatment of the case, the names of the judges present at the hearing; the legally prescribed and executed procedural acts; all findings necessary for controlling whether the substantial formalities and formalities prescribed under penalty of nullity were complied with.[100] These minutes are signed by the president and the registrar. This written document is hereby authorized to replace the oral pronouncement of judgment by the court. This fixation of the temporal co-ordinates of the act of (pronouncing) judgment is further achieved through the manual impression of a stamp with the date of the public hearing. This stamp establishes more authoritative reference between the document of judgment and the discrete temporal series of hearings (of a certain chamber) at the court. Furthermore, the enunciators of judgment, the judges who pass it, are not even all required to be present at this fictive occurrence of the pronouncement. Article 782bis (CPL) states that 'the judgment is *pronounced* by the president of the chamber which has passed it, even in *absence* of the other judges' (my italics). We are thus faced with a fictive presence of an enunciator at the fictive occurrence of a verbal utterance![101] Just like the orality of its pronouncement, the presence of its enunciators is replaced by acts of writing. Article 782 (CPL) states that '*Before its pronouncement* the judgment is *signed* by the judges who have passed it and by the registrar' (my italics). The presence of the judges at the passing of judgment is legally guaranteed by an inscription of their nominal place-holders – their names – which authoritatively come to re-present them through the subscription of their signatures at the edge of the document.[102]

---

[99] The Court of Cassation judged that 'the public character of the hearing can be demonstrated by a certified copy of the session sheet' (5 April 1984, Arr. Cass 1983–84, 1042).

[100] Article 783 CPL requires the registrar to write all these metadata in the minutes of the hearing.

[101] This is another occurrence of a positive legal fiction as described by Thomas, 2011.

[102] Derrida describes how the inscription of this sign has the singular effect of marking the writer as having been present in a past now, and maintaining

This singular node of intra-textual intersections between legal codes, typed documents (the judgment document and the session sheet), stamped dates, and inscribed signatures is supposed to put in operation the legal fiction of a verbal utterance of judgment, pronounced by its enunciators who are present to this utterance, which is required for the passage of a successful act of judgment. Through this forward detour to its being fictionally 'pronounced at the public and ordinary hearing', the 'judgment thus given', written and signed 'before its pronouncement' in this hearing, can come to refer back to the operatives of judgment within the organization of the judgment document.

4.3 GROUNDS: PATHWAYS FROM BELOW

In all grounding and getting to the bottom
we already walk on the path to a ground
(Heidegger, 1997, p. 3)[103]

The ground of things is not death or life
The ground is something else
Which sometimes comes ashore.
(Juarróz, 1958, p. 12)[104]

We have been a long while underway on our criss-cross travels through wide fields of issues. Within the passage of disputes encountered, each dispute forced the researcher to take different routes, sometimes paths to law and sometimes paths of law. In this section we will try to move beyond the preliminaries towards a 'judgment on the grounds' of a dispute of intellectual rights, without being previously being cut off short. In this way we can focus on how the acts of judgment perform a grounding of the immateriality of the matters of dispute. Such grounding, however, always already moves on a 'path to a ground'. The phrase from Heidegger highlights not so much the ground, the grounded or the grounder, but the *act of grounding* which has the character of being underway, of proceeding, of seeking to arrive. These acts of grounding are indeed closely related

---

[*maintenant*] him in a present or future now (Derrida, 1988, pp. 19–20). He calls this the '*juridic signature*'. This signature is never completely inside nor outside the text but always on the edge at the margins of the text (p. 32).

103 The German text is: *Bei allem Begründen und Ergründen laufen wir schon auf dem Weg zu einem Grund.*

104 The Spanish text is: *El fondo de las cosas no es la muerte o la vida. El fondo es otra cosa. Que alguna vez sale a la orilla.* The last phrase can also be translated as: "which sometimes rises to the surface".

to a judgment in which the ground will bring something – the matter of judgment – to a stand (*zum-stehen brengen*) as an object (*Gegenstand*) when it will have provided a sufficient (*vollstandig*) account of it.[105] In a legal dispute this is quite an achievement. We have seen this in the twofold of ap-plication in which the proceeding matter of dispute is gradually halted by being transformed into a matter of fact and a legal object of a certain intellectual right (invention, work, trademark).

These grounds themselves however, have to be distinguished from this life of the matter of dispute and the little deaths of the dispute in the operatives of judgment (and in the claim in the summons) that formally enclose its legal life. 'The ground of things is not life or death', although it is closely related to these. As Juarróz indicates, grounds do sometimes rise to the surface of things, they make their ingression in a dispute from a below within. The raised grounds (|) are different from the horizontal extensions of the dispute (-) and the diagonal acts of grounding (/) and judgment with its striking linear focus (\). A ground only makes its ingression in the dispute when it is raised within the practice of its proceedings through an act of grounding.[106,107]

***

---

[105] Heidegger here specifically refers to the philosophical connections between judgment and ground as first established by Leibniz and later systematized by Kant (Heidegger, 1997, pp. 104–7, 173–5). With Heidegger the ground is transformed from principle, ratio or causing instance, to a supportive instance which is always linked to a 'while', 'during' or 'as long as', and not to a 'because' or 'since'. For a contemporary philosophical exploration of the plurality of ground functions, see Bakker, 2011.

[106] There is a link to the Deleuzian principle of contingent reason in which the rising of the ground is always related to the singularity of a contingent and problematic encounter that transforms it (Deleuze, 2004a, p. 344–5; Deleuze & Guattari, 1994, p. 93). Prolonging Juarróz' theme, Deleuze and Guattari say that 'a mountain had to rise here or a river to flow by there again recently for the ground, now dry and flat, to have a particular appearance and texture. It is true that very old strata can rise to the surface again, can cut a path through the formations that covered them and surface directly on the current stratum to which they impart a new curvature' (Deleuze & Guattari, 1994, pp. 58–9).

[107] In 'grounded theory' in social science, practices are often themselves conceived as the ground of things. We cannot content ourselves with this view. We have to study how grounds themselves operate *within* practice, how they become raised, mobilized, enforced, cut off, instead of positing practice itself *as* a ground. How can one take serious law as a practice in which grounds play an important role, when the researcher already knows in advance what counts as a ground? For a criticism of the misplaced notion of ground in grounded theory, see Thomas & James, 2006.

~ 2ND MOVEMENT ~

A helpful way to cross over from the preliminaries to the grounds of judgment is the DEQU case. This case will further take up the identity/difference theme played out throughout the [Oil Spout] case.

Theme E: Identity and Difference

What is the immaterial form of a mark in relation to an opponent's sign? The disputed signs find themselves in a semiotic lab opposed in an antagonistic play of comparison on their auditory, visual and semantic dimensions and about what herein belongs either to their immaterial identity or to their material representation. Afterwards, they are transposed to the shop where they are staged for different rival publics. On the one hand they are viewed from the points of view of the fictive characters of the average consumer and the specialized public, which each have their own presumptions, levels of attention, memories and mental confusions about their similarities and differences. There is an interesting perspectival variation here with the fictive character of the informed user in the [Oil Spout] case. On the other hand the signs are viewed through statistical consumer profiles of market research, and the tables of juxtaposition that we also encountered in the [Oil spout] case. Each perspective from which the sign is approached itself becomes drawn in the dispute by each transposition and becomes linked to legal authorities.

J. *The court invents a threefold scaling process along which it stabilizes the shifts between situations. Each scale is assigned a different technique according to which the trademark is to be approached: desktop semiotics of the trademark, shop presumptions about consumer observation, and market research of the quantities of usage. In this way the ratios of the importance of the dimensions – sound, word, image – of the trademark are determined on each scale.*

***

Correspondence of Signs: Semiotics, Markets & Minds of the Public (Case 2: DEQU Mark)

Notwithstanding the empire of the imagination,
there is a secret tie or union among particular ideas,
which causes the mind to conjoin them more frequently together,
and makes the one, upon its appearance, introduce the other.

(Hume, 2000, pp. 416–17)

This is a dispute in trademark law.[108] A accuses D of having infringed its 'DQ' trademarks on power tools by inscribing the trademark 'DEQU' for power tools on its own name at the Benelux Office of Intellectual Property (BOIP). The infringed trademarks concerned are both the word mark 'DQ' and an image mark (depicted on page 179). In this context A claims the nullity of D's inscription, since it will likely lead to confusion amongst consumers with its own trademark. In this dispute we will focus on this alleged correspondence between the two brands and on the confusion it raises amongst the consuming public. We will start with A's claim that there is a correspondence between the signs DQ and DEQU.

- The challenged trade mark inscription DEQU contains the *same* letters D and Q
- Letter D is taken as Dé
- Letter Q is taken as Qu
- *Same* number of syllables

> Even when the graphical elements have to be compared there still is a *certain measure of correspondence*. Both trademarks are characterized by an object placed on the head: a plug and a crystal.
>
> The colour used by D is *irrelevant* since plaintiff has a word mark which can be the matter of many different graphic representations. Plaintiff can thus use her trade marks in different colours, which has happened: DQ was depicted in black (piece 6) and nowadays in blue and red (pieces 7.1−7.8).

We here encounter a threefold gradient of correspondence. The first and strongest measure of correspondence ('sameness') is established through a peculiar semiotic exercise. The *semes*, the DEQU and DQ signs, are first pried apart into their smallest constitutive elements: graphemes (the alphabetic letters 'D' and 'Q'), phonemes (the phonetic units of speech 'Dé' and 'Qu') and syllables (the units of articulation of phonemes 'De' and 'Qu'). They are then related to each other in terms of these basic units and a semiotic equivalence is found between these elements. This atomistic equivalence allows the attorney to claim a semiotic correspondence between the two signs. This correspondence is brought forward as in itself sufficient to ground the infringement of the trademark. In order to provide an extra secondary anchor, a second correspondence is established through a graphical exercise. On the one hand this correspondence

---

[108] Trademarks deal with exclusive rights on signs. According to WIPO, trademarks are also 'creations of the mind' and as such classified as intellectual property (see: http://www.wipo.int/about-ip/en/).

is not as strong as the semiotic one, but holds 'to a certain measure'. On the other hand it is not deemed totally necessary either ('even when the graphical elements have to be compared'), but is considered to be of an auxiliary nature. In the comparative exercise the trademarks are taken as images and analyzed in terms of their visual elements. Apart from the body or head of the trademark (the word image), both trademarks also have an object that is placed on top and constitutes its 'headgear'. The DQ trademark has a crystal on top, the DEQU trademark has three plugs on top (see the depiction below). This comparison establishes a certain measure of similar graphic 'characterization' between the trademarks.

After having established the elemental form of the trademark by isolating its semiotic and visual units, A's attorney can now raise it to the level of the immaterial in order to disqualify D's subsequent graphical argument that 'in judging the visual correspondence a comparison of used colours is very important'. Although there is a difference of colour between the trademarks, this does not affect the correspondences established, since colour is a legally irrelevant element. As an immaterial thing a trademark can supposedly 'be the matter of many different graphic representations'. A's attorney assigns elements of colour to this accidental level of 'representation' thereby demarcating it from the immaterial 'matter of representation'. In this way this trademark is supposed to be incorporable in representations of many colours without thereby itself changing in the least.

We will now turn to the contestations of D's attorney on these points.

> The correspondence between the trademarks needs to be judged according to the visual, auditory and conceptual similarities.
>
> Concerning the phonetic correspondence, D does not contest that the word elements show a **certain degree of correspondence**. That this phonetic correspondence between the trademarks is **not as evident** as the plaintiff wants it to appear however, is demonstrated in a sample made by the bailiff on commission of D on 25-06-2007 and trialled with 100 customers of the department store chain Brico in Hasselt. This research shows that only 9% (9/100) of the customers knew the trademark. A significant part did **not even recognize the letters** 'D' and 'Q' and thus, **consequently, did not pronounce** the trademark as deequ. Only 30 out of the 100 (30%) recognized the letters. 35 of the 100 (35%) thought it should be pronounced as D and Q. The answers of the remaining respondents (35) are very diverse [. . .]

The threefold correspondence is plied differently here and an extra kind is added as a requirement: conceptual correspondence between trademarks. We will get to this later. First we will have a look at how D's attorney tackles the phonetic correspondence established by A's attorney as a relation of semiotic sameness. Although the existence of a relation of correspondence is not denied, this relation is downgraded from a measure of 'sameness' to a measure of 'a certain degree'. The '=' relation is not backed up by sufficient evidence to support such a strong link. The downgrading is achieved not by letting the two trademarks pass through a rival semiotic analysis, but by percentages obtained through market research. We have to dig deeper into trademark law to understand why this move could be convincing. A trademark serves to distinguish the goods of an enterprise from the goods of another enterprise.[109] The conditions evoked in this case are those stated in article 2.20 of the Benelux Convention on Intellectual Property, which governs the protective scope of the trademark holder.

> A registered trademark shall provide its owner with an exclusive right [. . .] to prevent any third party, without its consent, from:
> (a) using in business a **sign** that is **identical** to the **trademark** for goods or services that are identical to those for which the trademark is registered;
> (b) using in business a sign in respect of which, because it is **identical or similar** to the trademark and because the goods or services covered by the trademark and the sign are identical or similar, there is a **risk of confusion in the mind of the public** which includes the risk of **association** between the sign and the trademark.

We can indeed find two measures of correspondence within this article: identity (correspondence as sameness) and similarity (a certain degree of correspondence) between the trademark and the sign. Now, notice that when one, quite literally, downgrades the first relation of correspondence stated in the first member to the second relation of correspondence stated in the second member, the conditions of proceeding also change. Whereas in the case of identity where *no observer position* is specified, the relation of similarity is correlated with '*the mind of the public*'. Apparently not only do traders battle for the mind of the public, but so do their trademark lawyers, although in a quite different way. This perception of the trademark in the mind of the public emphasizes the status of this sign as an intellectual object. It provides an important site for the constitution of immateriality in discussions about the mental confusion through the association of signs, the level of attention of the average consumer and the consumer's holistic memory of the dominant components of the trademarks.

What kind of public are we talking about here? How can the judge know what the public thinks? Kabel has distinguished three different approaches to this mind of the public: facts (obtained by market research), fiction ('the average consumer') and experience (rules of thumb, facts of general experience and presumptions about the observation of consumers), which are all

---

[109] See article 2.1 of the Benelux Law on Trademarks.

operative within a legal framework (Kabel, 2006). We will later see how A's attorney seems to take the fictional approach. D's attorney has clearly taken the factual approach, which achieves a displacement of the way we access trademarks and the way they are compared. By approaching the trademark through market research in which consumers are *shown* the trademark, the auditory elements of a trademark become mediated through its visual and conceptual elements. The 'recognition' of the visual letters of the trademark is a first necessary condition for its 'consequent pronunciation'. Since a 'significant part' of the respondent public did not recognize the visual letters 'D' and 'Q' when seeing the trademark, the auditory identification with the trademark 'DQ' could not conclusively be demonstrated. Furthermore:

> The auditory similarities are neutralized by the visual and conceptual differences.

Defendant	Plaintiff
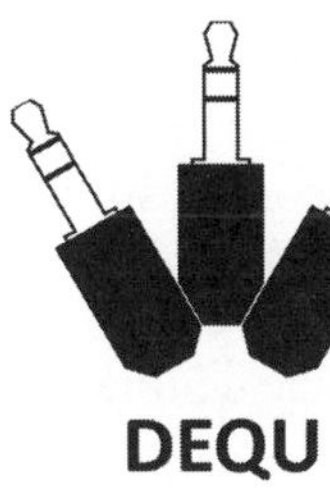	
DEQU	DQ

Here we have a graphical depiction of the image marks (logo) and word marks. They are also inscribed in a table in order to juxtapose them and bring out their visual and conceptual similarities and differences. In this way, it becomes 'striking' to observe that the logos 'clearly' contain different visual elements: the trademark of D contains a words in standardized letters and three plugs; the trademark of A contains strongly stylized letters and a crystal. Furthermore, D's attorney states that when judging visual correspondence, a comparison of colour is very important. The trademark of the plaintiff is black whereas the defendant uses a blue trademark [not depicted here]. Secondly,

> There is no conceptual correspondence since the **word elements** of both trademarks have no **meaning**. The **images** indisputably have a **different semantic**

> **content** (crystal vs. plug), so that there cannot be any confusion. The plug has an **'electric' connotation**, whereas the crystal has a pronounced **resonance of quality and durability**.

'Meaning', 'semantic content' and 'connotation' – within a few phrases different strands of linguistics are mobilized. After the phonetic and graphical analysis, the discussion about *correspondence* is here transposed onto the plane of semantics. We are first told that the word elements of the two trademarks have no meaning. We seem to be faced here with what in philosophy of language is called 'extensional semantics' according to which the meaning of a word is determined by the existence of an object to which it refers. Since in our case the words 'DQ' and 'DEQU' do not correspond to an existing object, they have no semantic extension beyond themselves that would give them their meaning; they are trapped in their mere nominal existence so to say. Therefore, both words do not even have a stable common starting point of reference for conceptual correspondence. Things are different with the image elements of the trademarks, which are both said to have semantic contents [*begripsinhoud*]. Here, the mobilized theory of meaning changes into an intentional semantics in which the interiority of a concept, or here an image, implies its own meanings without necessary reference to an external object. The image '' contains the meaning of a crystal, whereas the image '' contains the meaning of plugs. Neither stylized image seems to refer to any concretely existing crystal or plug however. Furthermore, beyond the meaning that each image denotes, it also implies a set of connotations. Connotation etymologically derives from *co-notare*: to mark along with; to mark one thing in addition to another, to implicate it.[110] Each of the image elements of the trademarks marks its primary meaning and, in addition, marks those further properties that are commonly associated with it. The plugs connote electricity, the crystal has a 'resonance' of quality and durability.[111] The extensive, intensive and connotative meanings of the two trademarks show no conceptual similarities. An intriguing exercise. In which other circumstances can one actually find such a practical linguistic philosophy in action?

Summarizing the point of D's attorney, the correspondence between

[110] In J.S. Mill's classical definition: 'A connotative term is one which denotes a subject, and implies an attribute. By a subject is here meant anything which possesses attributes' (Mill, 1981, p. 32). Denotation relates to a possession and connotation relates to an implication of attributes.

[111] Trademarks are considered to be both denotative signs that indicate a certain product or a producer, and connotative symbols that suggest further more abstract meanings and values (Drescher, 1992, p. 328).

the trademarks has been judged according to the visual, auditory and conceptual similarities. Although there was a certain degree of correspondence with regard to the phonetic correspondence, this correspondence has been downgraded from sameness to similarity by passing through the researched mind of a public which was not co-responsive. Moreover, the visual and conceptual differences between the trademarks 'found' in the analyses above, enable D's attorney to 'neutralize' whatever was left of this certain degree of similarity.

A's attorney contests these arguments in his plea during the hearing. He takes a quite different approach to the issue of correspondence:

> *There is a correspondence between similar products when the consumer connects the two products and the thought of the trademark is evoked in him. The* ***method*** *that my colleague has shown you [he lifts a large cardboard sheet on which the two trademarks are juxtaposed] is* ***not correct****. The criteria in jurisprudence are clear: the consumer does not have the possibility to juxtapose products.*

The existence of a 'similarity' between trademarks was one part of the conditions of proceeding for an infringement claim. We have seen that the law related this similarity to the observer position of a public in whose mind it creates confusion. We followed the factual approach that D's attorney took through conducting market research and will now focus on the approach that A's attorney takes to the mind of the public.

. . . and a very Humean mind it turns out to be. When a consumer observes a power tool with a DEQU sign (in a shop or in a brochure), due to their mutual similarity the impression of this product is associatively connected in his mind with the memory of the impression he has had on some other occasion of the power tool produced by A. Consequently, the thought which is evoked by the perception of this product is that of DQ. The mind of the consuming public is thus sent off on a trail of associations that leads to confusion. When we substitute the word 'signs' for 'ideas' in the words of Hume at the beginning of this section, we could thus say that 'there is a *secret tie* or union among particular signs, which causes the mind to conjoin them more frequently together, and makes the one, upon its appearance, introduce the other'. This is a rather adequate description of confusion that A's attorney attributes to the mind of the public. We could say that this attorney sets out to expose this Humean 'secret tie' that entails such a 'risk of association between the sign and the trademark'[112] in order to finally let it be cut by judgment. In this sense he assumes the position of the Kantian lawyer-philosopher who, confronted with this

112 Article 2.20 of the Benelux Convention on Intellectual Property.

empiricist geography of the human mind, stakes a rightful claim before the tribunal, in accordance with the laws, to pry apart what is confused in the human mind.[113]

Most efforts of D's attorney were aimed at the isolation of the auditory, graphic and conceptual identities of the trademarks through semiotic and visual analyses, in order to demonstrate that the two trademarks were not similar. In his plea A's attorney points out that the similarity between trademarks is not something that is to be appraised by itself in clear and neat isolation, but (according to article 2.20) is a 'business' of the consuming 'public'. The attorney thus transposes the discussion by shifting its locus from the desk to the shop. This move enables him to unauthorize the technique for the determination of similarity that his adversary deployed earlier: the comparative table of juxtaposition that we have seen above. The attorney manages to present this method within the hearing in the courtroom by showing a large cardboard sheet to the court on which the two trademarks are depicted side by side as in the comparative table. This method of visualizing the signs at stake is immediately disqualified in the course of the same statement,[114] since a 'consumer does not have the possibility to juxtapose products'. The table is a luxury of analytics that the consumer cannot indulge in. Since this tool is not available to the mind of the public, and since this is the point of reference for judging the claim, it is also not allowed to enter the mind of the judge in order to convince her.

At this point D's attorney interrupts the plea of his adversary however, by stating that 'But in the Brico folder the products are juxtaposed!' to which A's attorney hastily replies that this answer is 'purely for the sake of argument [*pour besoin de la cause*] and is irrelevant here'. We must remember that the possibility of comparison referred to is a 'criterion in jurisprudence' that establishes a certain legal presumption about the observational processes of consumers and that does not necessarily refer to the actual presence-at-hand for a consumer of a means of comparison. In this sense the brochure is legally irrelevant.

> *The danger of confusion between the trademarks* ***should not be viewed from*** *their different details. As a consumer one* ***retains only a general imperfect image*** *of a trademark, one* ***does not remember the details****.*

---

113 Kant, 1998, A XI.

114 This is a rare 'point of intervention' between the relations of force of an assemblage of visibility and a regime of statements (Deleuze & Guattari, 1987, pp. 86–8). A technique of visualization of two signs is mobilized in the middle of a statement on these two signs. The visibility is punctuated by a twist in the statement that disqualifies its status and dislocates its repeatability.

> *There has to be visual, auditory and conceptual correspondence, but there only has to be correspondence on one of these aspects. [. . .] The most* ***dominant component*** *is the word not the image. When you view these products [the attorney shows his breakfast: an empty plastic bottle and an empty carton] you might notice 'Campina' [a Dutch dairy brand] and 'Mulino Bianco' [an Italian nutrition brand], but not the images of the brand. The consumer has a vague memory.*

Two subsequent legal presumptions are introduced here about the mind of the consuming public and the ways its memory and observation work.[115] First, this memory is represented as a holistic and rather imperfect process that is infused with forgetfulness, in which the visual impressions that are received in perception are only 'vaguely' retained. What is preserved is the general form or outline of the thing perceived, a template in which the details have disappeared. Second, it is thus important to distinguish the details from the dominant aspects of the trademark, since the former will have fallen back in oblivion and only the latter are retained. These two presumptions about the memory of the public have a further legal effect on the mind of the judge as vector of convictions. They provide a certain default point of view ('should be viewed from') on the comparison of trademarks, from which the danger of confusion between trademarks and which of its elements can be allowed as more or less convincing will have to be judged. In this case the word element of the trademark – DEQU – is brought forward as the dominant component, whereas the image is relegated to the details. This qualification is achieved in a way that makes full use of the scenery of the court room. From behind his pleading table the attorney shows the judges the packages of milk and sandwiches which are left over from his breakfast when travelling to the court. Through this action the layout of the courtroom depicted earlier becomes enrolled as a stage for a demonstrative spectacle. By casually showing these products to the judges, within the constellation of presumptions previously laid out, the attorney endeavours to enact and establish a fact of common experience about the observation of trademarks: in observing trademarks on

---

115 Kabel has made a small cartography of the different presumptions about consumer observation that are operative in trademark law. The judge has to *judge the danger of confusion in a global way* with regard to the circumstances of the case. In this judgment, he has to *presuppose an average consumer of the kind of products at stake who is reasonably well informed and reasonably observant and circumspect.* In this global judgment, the judge has to presume that the consumer normally *observes a trademark as a whole and does not pay notice to the different details.* In this total impression, one has to *look at the dominant or distinctive components of both trademarks.* He also has to presume that the *level of attention of the consumer can vary according to the kind of products* concerned (Kabel, 2006, pp. 10–11).

products, one generally only remembers the brand names, not the visual elements of the trademarks. We could say that this 'rule' gives a further articulation of the term 'dominant component'. This might even be seen as a proposition for the introduction of a further legal presumption about the mind of the public, which co-intentionally proposes a new default point from which the trademark is to be observed by the judges.

> **A's Attorney:** The **relevant public for the present products** is the **average consumer with a low attention span**. The products are not destined for a **specialized public**, but for everyone. The public to be taken into consideration is thus the normal average consumer. The products DQ and DEQU thus **do not require an extra heightened attention**. We are not dealing with the purchase of medicine or a car or house, the arranging of an insurance or a financial product, which are not everyday activities for most people.

We set out to find out what kind of public we were talking about in our trademark dispute. We have already seen the introduction of several presumptions that mapped out the cognitive maxims according to which its Humean mind was stipulated to operate. Here the issue of the nature of the public at stake is confronted in its most direct way. The attorney endeavours to specify 'the relevant public for the present products' which are power tools. Each product has its own public for which it has relevance. A public in the legal sense is thus always tailored to the products that are in dispute. The attorney introduces a distinction between two different types of products on the basis of the amount of mental attention that they require from a consumer when s/he purchases them. Products like our power tools that require a low level of attention are established as the normal case. Once this baseline is installed the deviating cases can be determined when the consumer needs to invest a 'heightened attention' for special products. On the basis of this distinction between the two types of products the relevant kind of public for each type can now be determined. Consumer goods like our power tools that require a low level of attention are destined for 'everyone'. They are part of the normal case in which the public finds itself in its 'everyday activities' of consumption. The relevant public for these products is the 'average consumer'. Deviating special products that require the consumer to spend a high level of attention have a 'specialized public'. D's attorney contests this point:

> **D's Attorney:** The **relevant public** in this case is not the average consumer with a low level of attention. It is not understood why this consumer should be taken as **point of reference**. Jurisprudence shows that for **rarely or infrequently bought products (like the goods which are the matter of the contested trademark registrations)** it **needs to be presumed** that a consumer will only purchase after

> **particularly careful examination**, so that the **danger of confusion** of trademarks on such goods is **less**.

Each product might have its own public, but which public belongs to which product is a matter of debate. In this case, D's attorney does not so much contest the distinction between the two types of products and publics that A's attorney made, but rather his assumption about which type of public would purchase power tools. He contests the relevant 'point of reference' from which the baseline for the public of power tools is to be drawn. Average products might have an average consumer as their normal public, but power tools are no average products since consumers do not buy them frequently. Within jurisprudence legal consequences have been attached to this behavioural fact. Products which are bought infrequently have been implicated with the legal presumption that the consumer will only buy them after careful examination. In other words: the normal public for special products like power tools is a specialized public with a heightened level of attention.[116] In turn, this has direct consequences for the danger of confusion in the mind of the public between the trademarks DEQU and DQ. When consumers are more observant and circumspect when they buy these products, they are less likely to confuse these trademarks. The mental connection has been dissociated, the secret tie of association severed, and the lurking danger of confusion has been thwarted . . . at least temporarily. We will now return to the plea of A's attorney to see how he reinvigorates this danger by laying out a categorical space in which the associative connection is reestablished.

> **A's Attorney:** It is not contested that the regularity with which tools, equipment and utensils are bought is different than, for example, food. This does not mean that these products would fall in a **different category** and could not be considered **consumption goods (in the sense of the international Nice classification)**. The purchase **cannot be equated** with the purchase behaviour of the relevant public of a car or mortgage. In those cases the averagely informed consumer will have to show a **high level of attention**, which is not the case here.

The attorney turns the two types of products that he distinguished earlier, into full-fledged legal categories by linking them to a legal document: the International (Nice) Classification of Goods and Services for the purposes of the registration of trade marks. A product that requires a low level of attention is transformed into a 'consumption good' in

[116] This is a rather Wittgensteinian position in which mental states are attributed to people based on their observable behaviour within practices that provide the rules for such attributions.

the sense of this classification. These products can receive trademark protection. Simultaneously, the deviating products that require an extra heightened level of attention are assembled into its negative rest category of 'non-consumption goods' that cannot be trademarked. Both categories are constructed around certain paradigmatic products that form the points from which the baseline of each category can be drawn. The exemplars of consumption goods are food products. The baseline of this category is an equilibrium at a low level of attention. The exemplars of non-consumption goods are cars, houses, medicine, mortgages and other financial products. The central line of this category is an equilibrium at a high level of attention. In the linkage to the Nice classification something like a threshold of attention is set up between both equilibria that establishes a categorical ceiling. When the attention for a product is heightened from the baseline onwards beyond this ceiling, this product will have migrated beyond the category of consumption goods that can be protected by trademarks, towards the baseline of the category of non-consumption goods. This is a clever move, since it creates a categorical space between the baseline and the threshold of consumption goods in which a 'heightening' of attention does not automatically entail category migration. Now, in relation to the paradigm of food, power tools might require somewhat more attention from consumers when they go shopping, since these products are not bought that frequently. Nevertheless, this raised attention does not cross the categorical threshold and make it more closely related with cars or mortgages and thus 'equated' with a non-consumption good. As the attorney will later state in his plea 'one can buy tools in a supermarket without receiving information from an employee. You just take them from the shelves and put them in the cart'. The power tools remain within the relational space of the trademarkable category.

Earlier, we have studied the *factual* approach by D's attorney to the mind of the consuming public by conducting market research in order to determine the 'average' consumer statistically. A's attorney takes a different approach. The nature of this approach comes out most clearly in a comparison with the law on community designs we saw in the last section on the olive oil spout case. For these purposes it is instructive to shift back to what the attorney of the defendant stated there when explicating article 10 of Regulation 6/2002 (EC) on community designs.

> The protection provided by a community design includes every model that does not leave a different general impression on the informed user. This article introduces the notion of the 'informed user'. This is not the same **fictive person** as the '**average consumer**' from trademark law. The former has **more knowledge** than the latter and is **more alert** to the look of a design as a design.

In order to approach the mind of the public with regard to the DEQU and DQ trademarks, A's attorney introduces the 'average consumer' as a *fictive person*. This fictive person has its proper belonging within trademark law and can be contrasted with that of the 'informed user' that belongs to the law of community designs. Both fictive persons install different baselines of attention and knowledge. In jurisprudence the former has been most elaborately articulated as the 'average consumer who is reasonably well informed and reasonably observant and circumspect'.[117] We have seen that such 'reasonable' observance and circumspection was established at a rather low equilibrium of attention. The baseline of the informed user is installed at a rather higher state of equilibrium. This person is credited with 'more knowledge' and more attention than can be reasonably expected from the average consumer. Both figures constitute different views on the nature of the mind of the public that perceives the relevant products. We could say with Wittgenstein that this fictive person is where the legal presumptions about this mind can find a 'foothold' on the legal plane. Within the regime of trademark law the average consumer constitutes the 'point of grasp' for the implication of all the cognitive maxims about the operations of its memory, attention and observation.[118]

This fictive person of the average consuming public is an intriguing figure that can be compared to phantom publics, legal fictions and conceptual persona. Although this public definitively has some gathering force within trademark law, since it was evoked as a legal authorization in several arguments in the process, it is not at all a kind of active social agent.[119] The average consumer and especially the informed user are rather passive abstractions, which we might call *phantom publics* in the way Lippmann has coined the term (Lippmann, 2009).[120] Lippmann argued that the idea that people are informed on all the things by which they are affected is a fiction and calls this public a phantom. The term 'phantom'

---

[117] *Case C-210/96 Gut Springenheide and Tusky, ECR I-4657, 1998, §31.*

[118] See Wittgenstein, 2009, §284, §617.

[119] For an active conception of the public in which people gather around an issue that affects them and organize themselves in order to deal with this problem, see Dewey, 1957.

[120] Kabel has commented on this passive aspect in trademark law. Trademark law is not primary about the interests of the public. It is a subjective right and an exclusive right of the trademark holder, which is mainly about the distance that trade competitors should respect with regard to one another. The interests of the consumer are, at most, what he calls: an *erfreuliches Nebeneffekt* (Kabel, 2006, pp. 23–4). In this sense it is comparable to the notion of the public in the regime of copyright, which is also economical (tied to acts of exploitation) rather than anything else (Depreeuw, 2011). We could speak here of the 'exploitable' public.

or 'fiction' is here used in a derogatory way to denounce a certain theoretic image of an informed public used in government theory.[121] Many critical thinkers, like deconstructivists and psychoanalysts, have also used such terms to denounce and disqualify law itself.[122] We must however understand that in law calling the publics of average consumers and informed users 'fictions', does not disqualify them in any negative way. To the contrary, as Thomas has so elegantly demonstrated, it affirms them as positivities that have their belonging amongst the very techniques of qualification that are operative within a certain legal regime.[123]

On closer sight however, these fictive persons cannot properly be called legal fictions in the sense in which Thomas has discussed them. The average consumer does not set up a *counter*factual plane that necessarily transgresses the facts in order to allow a legal operation (like the expert in our previous olive oil spout case). It can well run in line with the facts and this alignment could strengthen its operations. This figure itself belongs more to the legal techniques of *presumption* than fiction. It is linked to legal evidence in providing conjectures in situations of uncertain knowledge about complex phenomena like the mind of the public, in order to arrive at judgment in a reasonable period of time (Thomas, 2011, Chapter 6).

Lastly, although quite distinct, the fictive person bears a certain relation with what Deleuze and Guattari call a 'conceptual personae'. In philosophy a conceptual personae is a figure that produces movements of thought by its intermediary role between concepts and a pre-conceptual plane.[124] Like such a conceptual personae, the fictive person encountered here *constitutes a point of view* and certain conditions of belonging together. Nevertheless, the perspective that it offers is quite different. The 'average' fictive person lacks the figural singularity proper to a conceptual persona, but constitutes a point of view that is closer to a 'psycho-social type' on the territorial plane of everyday life (Deleuze & Guattari, 1994). Nevertheless, on the legal plane there does exist a figure that operates more properly

---

[121] Interestingly, Lippmann stated that 'we *must assume* as a theoretically fixed premise of popular government that *normally* men as members of a public will *not* be *well informed*' (Lippmann, 2009, p. 54, my italics). He thus also introduces a presumption about the level of knowledge of members of the public.

[122] One merely needs to visit the annual *Critical Legal Conference* to verify that this disqualification of law as a fiction is still reiterated.

[123] For an elegant case study of the positive generative power of the technique of legal fictions, precisely due to the fact that they do not conform to (market) realities, see Riles, 2011.

[124] Exemplars are Plato's Socrates and Nietzsche's Dionysus and Zarathustra.

as the counterpoint of the philosophical conceptual persona. This is the singular figure of the *jurisprudential character*, with which we will become acquainted hereafter.

Judgment: The nullity of the trademark inscriptions in the name of D
[. . .]
3. The danger of confusion between deposited trademarks

3.1 Article 2.20 of the Benelux Convention on Intellectual Property governs the protective scope of the trade mark holder.
[. . .]

3.3 Apart from the question whether the trademarks of plaintiff have to be qualified as a 'known trademark', it certainly has to be checked whether the trademarks **correspond as signs**.

It is not disputed that the trademarks of parties are used for the same or similar kinds of products in economic traffic.

It also needs to be checked whether the **use within this economic forum** can provoke **confusion in the mind of the public**, including the danger of association. In judging these dangers it is important to **take account of the degree in which** the distinctive trademarks are well known. The question needs to be posed whether the confrontation of the public with the one trademark or the other is such, that an **averagely informed, observant, circumspect and normal consumer establishes any connection** between one trademark and the other (see Cassation 3 November 2006, T.B.H. 2007/6, p. 565 with a note of L. De Gryse on 'known' trademarks and 'relevant circumstances').
3.4 The application of the mentioned criteria is not different for the three trademarks registered by the defendant.

Following the treatment of the case and considering the numerous pieces of conviction, it **cannot be denied** that the **most important component** in the distinctive *trademarks* is the auditory element that sounds as DQ/DEQU. The way of writing and depiction is of less importance. Account is also taken of the fact that the trademarks refer to all *kinds of tools* which, qua form, show great similarity. **It is assumed** that the everyday consumer interested in the purchase of mentioned products, has **more ear for** the auditory mark DQ/DEQU than for the word mark or image mark. Furthermore, **the deposited pieces demonstrate** that within the *commercial world* in which the mentioned products are traded, the word mark DQ is **more explicitly used** than the image marks [logos].

Thus, there is **sufficient correspondence and similarity** between the contested trademarks. Plaintiff has legitimately claimed the protection of article 20.2 [sic] BVIE
[. . .]

ON THESE GROUNDS
THE COURT,

Declares the claim of A admissible and largely grounded.

> Declares null the trademark inscriptions on the name of D, known under the numbers 38361 and 38362.
>
> Orders the cancellation of these trademark inscriptions for all goods for which these marks were deposited.
>
> Imposes on B the prohibition to still use mentioned trademarks in whatever way, directly or indirectly.

We have finally arrived at judgment and a lot has indeed happened before. In the previous chapter we have seen how the body of a dispute can acquire large extensions and we followed how the attorneys tried to navigate the judges through this complexity. Here we will focus on how the court contracts this complicated body into a decision: what it inscribes and what it leaves out, which connecting lines it reinforces, cuts or ignores, which positions it assigns weight and which ones it marginalizes. We could say that following how courts arrive at judgment might well have something in common with the practice of political commentators who specialize in interpreting every word in the speech of politicians in order to find the traces that might indicate a change in political direction or weight assigned to certain matters.

Under the header of judgment, the court starts by explicating the conditions for the proceeding of A's claim for declaring D's trademark inscriptions null. It states that the claim is supported by three such conditions of which we will only treat the third: the danger of confusion between the trademarks. The court starts (in 3.1) by citing article 2.20 BCIP, since it 'governs the protective scope of the trademark holder'. Subsequently (in 3.3), three conditions of proceeding are extracted from this article: there has to be correspondence between the trademarks as signs, the trademarks are used for the same or similar kinds of products in economical traffic, this use provokes confusion in the mind of the public through danger of association. These conditions for proceeding are here reformulated as obligations that the court raises for itself in the act of arriving at judgment. So far so good. Through the alignment of the legal authority of an earlier judgment of the Court of Cassation and an annotation, the court has articulated this condition of danger of confusion between trademarks, highlighting the reputation (well-known) and relevant circumstances of the trademark. In judging this danger, the court is required to take into account: the economic forum in which the products are used, the degree to which the trademark is well known and whether the averagely informed, observant, circumspect and normal consumer establishes any connection between the trademarks. Especially this last criterion is interesting. The 'point of reference' for the relevant public of power tools has been determined: it is the average consumer and not the specialized public.[125]

In section 3.4 the court applies the raised conditions to the pieces of conviction in the folders of evidence.[126] A careful reading of section 3.4 teaches us that the application consists of a twofold of three-tier strands. Firstly there is a scaling strand that subsequently focuses on: the trademarks themselves, the relevant products for which the trademarks are registered and the larger economical fora in which the trademarked products are used. Secondly, each scale is pervaded by a dimensional strand that reiterates the phonetic, graphematic and pictographic sides of the several trademarks (*semes*): their auditory component, their way of writing or word mark, and their depiction or image mark. Each scale is also assigned its own approach on the trademark.

> Following the treatment of the case and considering the numerous pieces of conviction, it cannot be denied that the most important component in the distinctive **trademarks** is the auditory element that sounds as DQ/DEQU. The way of writing and depiction is of less importance.

First the trademarks are judged by themselves, isolated from their larger circumstances. The court here subscribes to the presumption of the dominant component, which it determines on the basis of 'the treatment of the case' and 'numerous pieces of conviction'.[127] Their force of conviction is such that the dominance of the auditory element in the trademarks (the registered image mark) 'cannot be denied'. The way of writing and depiction are less important. On the scale of the trademark the phonetic dimension of the trademark is thus qualified as the 'dominant component', whereas the graphematic and pictographic dimensions are (dis)qualified as 'details'.

---

[125] It is not clear how the court arrived at this decision. Does the economic forum imply the relevant circumstances for the evocation of this fictive person?

[126] The linear presentation of the text in two separate sections separated by a blank line might appear like a subsumption exercise. When we read section 3.3 together with 3.4 in the light of all the prepositions that the attorneys proposed however, it becomes clear that the explication of conditions has already occurred in the light of the study of the facts and vice versa. This is in line with the concept of ap-plication as mutual folding of the factual patchwork and legal weft of the case.

[127] This is a large black box and we are left to guess which grounds are raised. The treatment of the case could imply the small spectacle of demonstration the attorney performed during the hearing or his semiotic analysis in the written statement of claim. It could also be that the court has gone through the thick folders with the pieces of evidence in order to convince itself.

> Account is also taken of the fact that the trademarks refer to all **kinds of tools** which, qua form, show great similarity. It is **assumed** that the everyday consumer interested in the purchase of mentioned products, has more ear for the auditory mark DQ/DEQU than for the word mark or image mark.

Here the judgment shifts from an explicit present-at-hand examination of the trademarks by themselves, to an analysis of the relevant products to which the trademarks refer in the more ready-to-hand situation of the consumer's everyday purchasing behaviour within the shop. Preceding this shift, the court first judges that the power tools produced by A and D have a similar form, which was one of the three conditions of proceeding the court extracted from article 2.20b (BCIP). The satisfaction of this requirement was not that difficult since it was not disputed by D so it counted as a fact. Next, on the scale of the 'relevant circumstances' of the shop, the court also judges that the phonetic dimension is the distinctive component when compared to the graphematic word mark and the pictographic image mark. Here we seem to encounter a variant of the presumption that A's attorney proposed. Whereas above, the court's judgment of the trademarks by themselves seemed to rule out such an acceptance as a general presumption, on the product/shop scale this seems to be different. Notice how the court already implicates the distinctiveness of the phonetic element in the framing of the way the public observes. It 'assumes' that the consumer observes the trademark by ear rather than by eye. Here, the attorney's proposition that the average consumer only remembers the brand name and not the visual elements related to the image mark seems to be accepted, but in a more specified manner. The court seems to further pry this brand name apart in its graphematic element – the word mark – and its phonetic dimension which it even raises to the status of a full-fledged 'auditory mark'. Only this auditory mark is distinctively observed by the consumer.

> Furthermore, the deposited pieces demonstrate that within the **commercial world** in which the mentioned products are traded, the word mark DQ is more explicitly used than the image marks [logos].

The products and trademarks are now positioned within the larger circumstances of the relevant economic forum in which the trademarked products are used. The approach to the trademark changes on this scale. This trademark is no longer observed by the (semiotic) analyst from his desk, or by the mind of the consumer in the shop. On the scale of the commercial world in which the trademarked products are traded, observation of the trademark no longer plays a role. More important are the times the trademark numerically occurs in each of its different dimensions: the word marks are here used more frequently than the image marks. The phonetic dimension is not mentioned but the graphematic dimension is judged to be more distinctive than the pictographic dimension.[128]

The court concludes by stating that there is 'sufficient correspondence and similarity between the contested trademarks'.[129] The plaintiff has legitimately claimed the protection of article 2.20 BCIP and the trademark inscriptions on the name of D are declared null. By this judgment the DEQU trademark has now itself become a *jurisprudential character* on the legal plane, which can now be raised as an authoritative figure in future cases (granting sufficient reasonance is established between the disputes).

***

~ 3RD MOVEMENT ~

In this dispute we will continue our journey through trademark law. Whereas in the previous case we focused on identity and similarity in the mind of the public, here we will dig deeper into misleading and well-known brands.

Theme F: The Real and the Virtual

What is the reputation of the mark amongst the public? What is the nature of the good to which the mark refers? These questions lead into two separate exercises in which the real and the virtual become differentiated. This dispute is all about marking borders: borders between goods, borders between legal regimes, and borders between virtual and real worlds.

We will encounter the most extraordinary stagings of the Duff beer logo in the fictive world of the Simpsons and in the real world of the market. The mobilization of a mythical status (akin to ambrosia) fades the borders between these two worlds and between copyright and trademark law and opens the path for turning trademarks into a device for incorporating virtual universes as properties of the franchise. The mobilization of differ-

---

128 This is the sort of fact that could be demonstrated by the type of market research that was used to measure whether a trademark is 'well-known'.

129 The court has done quite a lot of work on the qualification that the auditory dimension is the distinctive component of the trademark on the scales of the trademark and the products, and that the graphematic dimension is the distinctive component on the scale of the commercial world. It has however not indicated how these components of the marks of A and D correspond, but simply speaks about 'the auditory mark DQ/DEQU', thus already implying that they are the same.

entiations between specific legal regimes, fiction and market and the kind of different publics we just encountered in the [DEQU] case, redraw the borders against such wholesale appropriation.

J. *When the court's voice intervenes it relates the virtual and the real in two different ways. With regard to the reputation of the trademark the virtual and real are kept apart. The court will select some of the de-mythological differentiations and draw a distinction between two publics for a mark: as the name of a (mythical) virtual product for a specific public, and as the trademark for a public of a real product on the market. This public can be compared to the scale of the economic forum drawn in the [DEQU] case. With regard to the reference of the trademark to the nature of its product, the virtual will be granted full legal reality. The court here mobilizes and compares two conceptions of references of a mark: its fixed reference to categories of products it is registered for, and its reference to the products that these words are commonly used for in specific (virtual) situations. These two conceptions only have limited co-extensions with the semantic conceptions mobilized in the [DEQU] case.*

***

Marks of Trade and Real Virtuality (Case 3: Duff Beer Mark)[130]

The virtual *is fully* real *in so far as it is virtual.*
(Deleuze, 2004a, p. 260)

20th Century Fox is the producer of the well-known animation TV series 'The Simpsons' in which the character Homer Simpson has an obsession with Duff beer. Duff beer has a characteristic design and name both with regard to the logo and the beer label. A whole line of products has been developed around Duff beer on which 20th Century Fox possesses all the trademarks. The occasion for the present dispute is the production of Duff beer by the Belgian Haacht brewery and distribution on the market without previous permission. 20th Century Fox claims this constitutes an infraction of the trademark in the sense of article 9.1 of the **Regulation of the European Council on the Community Trademark,** and of the copyright on the denomination 'Duff beer', the Duff beer logo and the Duff beer label.[131]

---

130 The judgment in this case has been published in BMM Bulletin 2011, 1, 49.

131 This dispute took place in a different court than the previous two cases. The researcher only had access to the pleas during the hearing and the judgment. Since these are public, no anonymization was necessary, which has the advantage

> **Haacht:** *It is up to the suing party to choose its juridical arguments and they have chosen for trademark and copyright law. They choose the* **stick** *with which they want to beat us. We are allowed to question this stick.*
> *[. . .]*
> *Trademarks are not monopoly rights, but the right of resistance against certain uses of a trademark. There are three conditions or sticks for this:*
> *[. . .]*
> *c. It has to be a* **known** *trademark within a community and there has to be loss of reputation due to the infraction. Relevant here is the reputation of the trademark of the beer as a* ***good within economical traffic****. It is not about the reputation of the series or the brand* ***Duff beer in the series****. Duff is a* ***virtual brand in a virtual world, not in the real world****. It is* ***not a sign to distinguish trademarks and to take part in the market. Trademark law is a legal figure for real trademarks and not for virtual products****.*

The *agon* in the dispute is brought to the fore in the beating with sticks. In the previous chapter we have seen that the dispute found its most contracted form in the stick-like claim that evokes a certain legal regime. Fox has contracted the dispute in two such sticks. It claims that the production of Duff beer by Haacht brewery constitutes an infraction of its trademark and of its copyright. The trademark claim turns out to be itself made of three (sub)sticks. In this sense it is more like the infamous birch rod or 'judicial birch', a bundle of sticks historically used for corporal punishment in British courts. This gives a whole different meaning to the bundle of rights approach in Anglo-Saxon legal theory for understanding the complexities of property ownerships.[132] Haacht's attorney will try to both disable Fox's melee weapons and construct a different stick for himself through a claim of misleading trademark. He sets out to carefully disassemble each stick in the trademark bundle of his opponent. In the DEQU case we have dealt with claims a and b – the identity and similarity of trademarks and the products. Here we will deal with claim c, taken from article 9(1)c of the Regulation: is the trademark well-known and does the infraction lead to a loss of reputation of the trademark?[133]

---

that other sources like websites and trademark registrations can be inscribed that would have otherwise led to de-anonymization.

132 This conception is attributed to Hohfeld, 1913 and sometimes to Honoré, 1961. See Chapter 6.

133 'The proprietor shall be entitled to prevent all third parties not having his consent from using in the course of trade: [. . .] any sign which is identical with or similar to the Community trademark in relation to goods or services which are not similar to those for which the Community trademark is registered, where the latter has a reputation in the Community and where use of that sign without due cause takes unfair advantage of, or is detrimental to, the distinctive character or the reputation of the Community trademark' (article 9(1)).

Reputation is a tricky concept. Determining the relevant public for a certain kind of good was already quite a matter of debate. Things become even more complex when this kind of good is itself drawn into the dispute: what is the relevant good to which the trademark refers? This question leads us into a fascinating differentiation of real worlds and virtual worlds. Although this distinction might provoke several theoretical and philosophical explorations, these would lead us astray from the dispute at stake.[134] It is thus best to first follow how the legal practitioners themselves articulate these notions within the antagonistic dynamics of this trademark dispute. We will then be led into a discourse with its own character in which different 'theories' about this distinction are worked out through the legal term of 'reputation'.

Here, it quickly becomes clear that the 'real world' referred to is very material indeed: it is the economic reality of the actual marketplace.[135] The relevant good in terms of which the reputation of a trademark is to be calibrated is the beer 'as a good within economical traffic'. This product is contrasted with the beer as a 'virtual product' as it figures within the Simpson series. The Duff beer mark has quite a reputation within the Simpson series. As Fox's attorney stated, Duff beer 'has gotten a life of its own in the series: there is a Duff man, a Duff stadium, etc.'[136] The mark might also serve to distinguish certain products within the virtual world of the Simpsons (for instance to distinguish Duff beer from other beverages which are branded as 'Buzz Cola', 'Squishee' or 'Blue Bronco Energy Drink').[137] These facts are legally irrelevant however. A trademark is a legal figure that only serves to distinguish products in the world of the market that gives the beer its reality. The real world and the virtual world are legally pried apart. We can call this the *dual theory* of reputation and

---

[134] We could for instance inquire whether the real and the virtual can be opposed in this way, or whether, in line with the quote of Deleuze at the beginning of this section, the virtual is itself fully real (and not fictional).

[135] For another example of this legal use of the concept of 'real world' for the context of the market, see the description of a patent dispute by Cambrosio et al., 1990, p. 280.

[136] *Within* The Simpsons series, the Duff brand is itself portrayed as a full-fledged trademark with a long historical period of investment in its reputation. In the 'Duffless' episode within the Duff brewery we get a short historical tour of past TV ads from the 1950s and 1960s, billboards, stadium ads, bar ads, zeppelin ads, Duff Gummi Beers, and the brands Duff, Duff Lite, Duff Dry, Duff Raspberry, Duff Lady, Duff Dark and Duff Out of Control. See: http://www.watchcartoononline.com/the-simpsons-episode-416-duffless.

[137] For a summary of the brands figuring in The Simpsons, see: http://simpsons.wikia.com/wiki/Category:Brands_parodies.

of the relation between the virtual and the real, in which the reputation of the trademark is established in the actual market.

> **President:** *How known is Duff beer? How often is it used within The Simpsons? What are the statistics? You* ***have to prove*** *that the trademark is known and not just state it.*
> ***Fox:*** *Even the defendants call it known. Gleeson [one of the other defendants] states that 'one could say that everyone knows this product' and talks about the 'famous bottle of Duff beer'. Duff beer has a* ***mythical 'cult status'*** *equal to Bert & Ernie and is always marketed with a legendary, mythical standing. There is a large (sub) audience that experiences this brand as known. Due to this known character so many beers have been sold. Fox has built up the name of the beer by producing the TV series for 20 years. Haacht is using this success for free. The* ***difference between virtual and real is thrown overboard here****.*

After the two pleas the presiding judge reminds Fox's attorney about the condition of reputation that needs to be satisfied for a successful trademark claim. She suggests several possible ways in which this reputation might be proved. The attorney replies by rearticulating the difference between the real and the virtual in terms of the existence of a specific audience. Like many other long-running television series, such as Star Trek, Game of Thrones or Sesame Street, The Simpsons have gathered a considerable fan base of devoted followers. Amongst this audience, frequently returning products (like Duff beer) or characters (like Bert and Ernie) have attained a 'mythical cult status'. In the franchise business this is no easy feat and the attorney claims that Fox has needed 20 years of continuously producing episodes of The Simpsons on television to carefully build up this status of Duff beer. Now, every time Fox markets products like T-shirts, caps, can coolers, tank tops, ceramic mugs, greeting cards, mouse pads or swim wear with the Duff beer trademark, it connects to this cult status in order to also confer on these products a legendary or mythical standing. In this connection the reputation is thus transferred from the virtual product within the TV series to the 'real' merchandise products in the economical world. The reputation of the virtual brand has become realized through this transfer and the 'difference between virtual and real is thrown overboard'. Haacht taps in on the cult reputation of Duff Beer in the same way by producing and distributing Duff Beer on the market. Since they have done nothing to contribute to the creation of this status, this gives them an unfair advantage (in the sense of article 9(1)c). We can call this a *franchise theory* of reputation and the relation between the virtual and the real, based on market potential for the mythical 'value' of the trademark.[138] On this view the

---

[138] This evocation of mythical status perfectly fits within the evolution of trademarks from a mere sign that refers to a concrete product, to an all-encompassing myth, through techniques of advertising and 'brand extensions' (Drescher, 1992).

reputation of fictional characters or products extends beyond the virtual bounds of the original work in which they are conceived, to the whole franchise in order to protect the whole range of marketing processes in which they are realized.

> **Haacht:** *Is the trademark known? The question is whether Duff beer is a known and distinctive trademark? Is Hogwarts a known name for a school in Harry Potter? But is it a known name for a trademark? And* ***Muffin [Schanulleke] in Spike & Suzy [Suske & Wiske] or Thomson and Thompson in Tintin? No, we are in the virtual here.***
> **President:** ***But there is an author***.
> **Haacht:** *But I am now in the trademark chapter.*
> **[. . .]**
> **Haacht:** *The fact that one is the* ***right holder of a TV series*** *does not mean that one is the* ***right holder of the logo Duff beer within that series****. They are the right holder of audiovisual* ***works*** *not of all the* ***elements within***.

In order to strengthen his dual position on reputation, Haacht's attorney subsequently shifts away from Duff beer in The Simpsons towards a school, a doll and detective twins within the known franchises of Harry Potter, Spike & Suzy and Tintin. Through these transpositions he is able to demonstrate that all these might be well-known as fictional figures in virtual worlds, but not as trademarks with an established reputation in the actual market. Curiously, the presiding judge at this point evokes the author function. The two birching bundles of copyright and trademark here become mixed together. The figure of the author of creative works like books and comics has its belonging in the regime of copyright. Trademark law instead stages the legal figure of the trademark holder of a known sign for specific products. The Duff beer logo however is the matter of both a copyright and a trademark claim in which it is sent off in different directions.

The judge is not alone in this mixture. It has been pointed out that claims of entertainment franchises are gradually transforming the protection provided by intellectual rights and are leading to a new intellectual property at a higher level of immateriality. 'The primary property at stake has become the immaterial entertainment concept: an aspiration to own a fictional universe coupled with the promise of its materialization in a bottomless array of consumer relationships with fans – exchanges that hopefully endure across the decades. Often this is in relation to an identity such as Pixar or J.K. Rowling' (Bowrey, 2011, pp. 193–4). The judge here indeed links the reputation among fans of Duff beer or Hogwarts to the identities of its authors like Matt Groening and J.K. Rowling, thereby mixing the two legal regimes. Haacht's attorney tries to keep them apart by discussing them one at a time. With regard to the copyright bundle, he tries to block Fox's proposed *passe-partout* that would permit ownership of all the elements within the fictional universe of The Simpsons. He tries to restrict the scope for the successful passage of the copyright claim to the concrete works of authorship that constitute the TV series. These audiovisual works are the object of the intellectual right, not all their elementary ideas and characters.[139] Has the expansion of the author function been temporarily brought to a halt?

All the birching bundles of Fox are disassembled and its sticks are broken. Haacht proceeds by arming itself with a judicial birch of its own in order to strike back. It has filed a counter-claim to declare the trademark of Fox null for all the goods for which it was inscribed, according to article 52 *juncto* article 7g of the Regulation. On the basis of this article a trademark can be declared null when it can mislead the public with regard to the nature, quality or geographic origin of the goods.[140] Haacht's attorney points out that the trademark 'Duff beer' is actually not registered for beer, but rather for products like sodas, powders, etc. He even refers to a quote of Matt Groening on Wikipedia who stated that he would not license the Duff trademark for the production of real beer since it would encourage children to drink![141]

> **JUDGMENT**
> **[. . .]**
> **On the alleged trademark infraction**
> [. . .]
> The court finds that the trademarks evoked in this case can indeed mislead the public to the extent that they **refer to beer**, since the **word 'Beer'** is part of the sign that is the matter of the trademark registration concerned, **without** them being **inscribed** or used **for beer**. They were inscribed for class 28 (puzzles, toys, board games, Christmas tree decorations, flying saucers) and class 32 products (sodas with and without carbohydrates, ginger ale, fruit juices, . . .).

---

[139] 'It is entertainment concepts, characters and fictional worlds that are the foundation of the global entertainment franchise. Concepts, characters and creative ideas are not supposed to be capable of protection under copyright or trademark law' (Bowrey, 2011, p. 189).

[140] Article 51(1) 'A Community trademark shall be declared invalid on application to the Office or on the basis of a counterclaim in infringement proceedings, (a) where the Community trademark has been registered in breach of the provisions of Article 5 or of Article 7.'

Article 7(1) 'The following shall not be registered: [. . .] (g) trademarks which are of such a nature as to deceive the public, for instance as to the nature, quality or geographical origin of the goods or service.'

[141] https://en.wikipedia.org/wiki/Duff_Beer.

> The public which is confronted with plaintiff's trademark in which the word 'beer' is used, or any of plaintiff's drinks or any other **product to which it refers**, could hereby **think that a product is intended that contains alcohol and which has fermented like beer**, whereas plaintiff's trademarks are only inscribed for several sorts of drinks, without mentioning any alcoholic drink.

The judgment of the claim that Duff beer is a misleading trademark leads to a whole discourse on reference. In what way can a trademark be misleading? When there is a mismatch between word and thing (or image and thing), or, more accurately, between two referential relations. A trademark is misleading when there is a mismatch of the relation between the trademark and the product category for which it is inscribed in a registry, and the relation between the trademark and that to which it commonly refers. Community trademarks are filed at the Office for Harmonization in the Internal Market (OHIM). A registration consists of an inscription in a public registry that includes the applicant's name and address, its signature, a representation of the trade mark, and a list that indicates the nature of the goods and services for which the trademark is registered. This list 'allows each item to be classified – preferably in only one class of the Nice Classification'.[142] Another file and another list! We could call this relation between the trademark and the product 'enlisted reference' that has both a teleological and categorical character. The list in the file indicates *for* which *kind* of product the trademark is registered. This document in the register would, as such, by itself already be worth the study of the organization of its inscriptions: its lists, images, certifications, numbers, dates, types, categorizations and addresses.[143] When we look at this document, we see that the Duff trademark is enlisted for: knapsacks and backpacks; wallets; all-purpose sports bags, tote bags, book bags, beach bags; fanny packs (categorized by the Office as class 18 of the Nice classification); jigsaw and manipulative puzzles; toy figures; board games; Christmas tree ornaments; flying discs (categorized as class 28); carbonated and non-carbonated soft drinks, ginger beer, fruit drinks, fruit juices, mineral and aerated water, syrups and powders for making soft drinks and other beverages (categorized as class 32). This is a whole range of different things, but, as the court observes, the crucial inscription for beer is missing. This absence is all the more striking since class 32 of the Nice classification is even entitled '*Beers*; mineral and aerated waters and other non-alcoholic drinks; fruit drinks and fruit juices; syrups and other

---

[142] http://oami.europa.eu/ows/rw/pages/CTM/regProcess/classifications.en.do.

[143] See the file (nr. 001341130) on http://oami.europa.eu/eSearch/.

preparations for making beverages'.[144] We could say that the inscription of an image of the trademark and its product list in the registry authoritatively *fixes a reference* of the sign, which will serve as a line of comparison for the other referential relations.[145]

The second notion of reference is about the relation between a word or image element contained in the trademark and that to which it commonly refers. We can call the second relation between the trademark and the thing 'common reference'. But how do we exactly know or determine what a word in a trademark commonly refers to? Again a wildly different array of semantic theories is mobilized. The court's judgment seems to employ three conceptions of reference: direct, descriptive and use. First, the court states that the word 'beer' in the name 'Duff beer' refers to beer. Reference does not come any more direct than this.[146] The meaning of the word is the product to which it refers. This is an extensional semantics of direct reference somewhat similar to what we have seen in the DEQU case.

This conception however, is complexified and supplemented in the next paragraph, where the court transposes the trademark to a setting in which a public is confronted with one of Fox's products on which the Duff beer trademark is put. We could again think of a shop here. Now, within this confrontation the meaning of the word 'beer' in the trademark consists of what the public takes the producer to intend when he puts it on one of his products. A trademark refers to the product on which it is put. The word 'beer' in 'Duff beer' thus refers to the contents of the bottle on which it is put. Nevertheless, normally, somebody who uses the word 'beer', for instance by putting it on a bottle, could be taken to intend to communicate that it contains 'a product that contains alcohol and which has fermented like beer'. Alcohol and fermentation are thus important properties in the

---

[144] http://web2.wipo.int/nicepub/edition-20130101/taxonomy/class-32/ (my italics).

[145] This term 'fixing a reference' is inspired by the linguistic philosopher Saul Kripke (1980), but is used in a very different sense here. Kripke stated that the reference of a term like 'light', 'heat', or 'water' can be directly, and unmediated, fixed to a thing when a scientific discovery has been made about the essential properties of these phenomena. This is an unrealistic presentation of how reference is established within scientific practices where reference circulates throughout long chains of mediation, which will eventually allow a word to refer to a thing (Latour, 1999). Furthermore, it is an overly monopolistic attribution of the powers to determine meaning to just one practice (science) within the 'ecology of practices' to the exclusion of all others (Stengers, 2006). In our case, we encounter another very different technique to fix reference belonging to legal practice, which can be included in the assessment of the meaning of words.

[146] We could call this the Kripkean conception of reference.

description of what is intended by the use of the word 'beer'. The court attributes to the mind of the public a grasp of an intention (by 'beer' I mean a certain kind of fermented alcoholic drink) that the public attributes to a third party (the producer of consumer products) on the basis of a certain linguistic act (putting the word 'beer' on a bottle). The meaning of beer here consists in a description of this intention, which would be an intentional descriptive conception of semantics.[147]

The court calibrates both the extensional and the intentional semantics of the word 'beer' in the trademark with its enlisted reference that was fixed in the registry. It turns out that there is a mismatch between the two. The list in the registry contains inscriptions of many different drinks. It however neither contains an inscription of 'beer', nor an inscription of an alcoholic product or a product which has fermented like beer. The trademark is thus misleading with regard to the nature of the product it refers to.

> Plaintiff finally argues that the words 'beer' and 'ale' are also used for non-alcoholic drinks. This argument **does not convince** because in those cases the word is used in combination with a vegetable or herb. In plaintiff's trademarks the word 'beer' is only used in combination with 'duff'. This **refers to real beer**, although it is **virtually real beer as Homer Simpson drinks it in the series**.

> From the preceding it follows that the trademark inscriptions 1289842 and 1341130 have to be declared null on basis of article 52 *juncto* 7g.

This is a conception of reference that ties the meaning of the word 'beer' in the trademark to its use. On the two former semantic conceptions of the Duff beer trademark, the court judged that the word 'beer' referred to beer and, when someone put it on a product, s/he could be understood to mean an alcoholic product. Fox has argued however that the words 'beer' and 'ale' are sometimes also used for non-alcoholic drinks. This argument could be problematic for the court's judgment, since it would weaken the strength of the referential tie between the trademark and alcoholic products. The court however judges that this argument 'does not convince'. We will follow how it thwarts this convictive force. First, it limits the occurrences in which the word 'beer' is used to refer to non-alcoholic drinks to cases in which it is juxtaposed to words which refer to vegetables or herbs like 'ginger' or 'root'. We could think here of denominations like 'ginger ale', 'ginger beer' or 'root beer'. In this way a limited number of word pairs is created in which the word 'beer' can successfully establish a reference to

[147] We could call this the Searlean conception of reference.

non-alcoholic drinks. This is a limitation of reference by addition. Next, the court observes that no one of these combinations is present in our case. In Fox's trademark the word 'beer' occurs together with the word 'Duff' forming the 'Duff beer' pair. 'Duff' does not refer to any vegetable or herb, but rather means 'worthless', 'spurious', 'counterfeit' or 'poor quality'.

After thwarting a reference to non-alcoholic drinks, the court proceeds by establishing a positive reference and arrives at an intriguing result. The word 'beer' in Duff beer 'refers to real beer, although it is *virtually real beer* as Homer Simpson drinks it in the series'. The world in which the Simpsons live might be a virtual world and the beer in this world might be virtual, but, in so far as it is virtual, it is no less fully real. Within this world Duff beer also contains alcohol and is thus not drunk as a non-alcoholic drink like ginger beer. In the 'Duffless' episode, Homer Simpson tests positively for driving under influence in a police control with a breathalyzer after visiting the Duff brewery, and has to attend meetings of Alcoholics Anonymous.[148] Duff beer is thus virtually real beer in the way that Homer Simpson drinks it in the virtual environments of Moe's bar, the Duff brewery and at home. The logo is put on bottles and cans that contain beer or other products that refer to beer. The meaning of the words in the trademark is here determined by the way this trademark and the products to which it refers are used in circumstances of the real virtual world.[149] There is thus also a mismatch between this pragmatic conception of reference and the fixed reference in the registry.

In the calibration of the fixed reference with all three other analyses of reference, the trademark is found to be misleading with regard to the nature of the product it refers to. On the basis of all these 'preceding' considerations it 'follows' that the court will 'have to declare' Fox trademark inscriptions null. The force of conviction that has come to pass through the specific alignment of references, grounds, arguments, fixations, classifications and qualifications has made the court arrive at this judgment.

The Court next proceeds by judging Fox's claim of trademark infringement due to illegitimate use of its reputation. Interestingly, in terms of this legal concept we will see a different articulation of the relations between the virtual and the real.

> Article 9.1c of the Trademark Regulation states: 'A Community trade mark shall confer on the proprietor exclusive rights therein. The proprietor shall be

---

[148] http://www.watchcartoononline.com/the-simpsons-episode-416-duffless.

[149] We could call this the Wittgensteinian conception of reference.

> entitled to prevent all third parties not having his consent from using in the course of trade any sign which is identical with or similar to the Community trade mark in relation to goods or services which are not similar to those for which the Community trade mark is registered, where the latter has a **reputation** in the Community and where use of that sign without due cause takes unfair advantage of, or is detrimental to, the distinctive character or the reputation of the Community trade mark.'
> [. . .]
> Plaintiff does not demonstrate that its trademarks are known by an important part of the **general public in the Community**, and thus fails in its burden of proof for the applicability of article 9.1c of the Trademark Regulation. If plaintiff had effectively created a **market** in the Community for the products falling under the evoked Community trademarks, she could have easily demonstrated this by referring to sales numbers. She does not do so.
> [. . .]
> 'Duff beer' can be **known** with a **certain public** in the Community **as the name of a virtual beer** that figures in the Simpson TV series. This denomination is however **not known** in the Community **as a trademark for the goods for which the trademark is inscribed**.

With hindsight the question of the president during the hearing to Fox's attorney had been prescient. The attorney has failed to prove that the trademark is known, not offering any sales numbers, 'statistics' or market research like the attorneys in the DEQU case. The Court has not been convinced by the franchise argument and has rather followed the dual approach to reputation. Duff beer might indeed have a cult status under a specific public within the European Community 'as the name of a virtual beer that figures in the Simpson TV series'. The court however cuts off the connection that would have let the reputation of this sign for virtual beer in a virtual world pass to the world of the markets of consumer goods. We have seen that Fox registered Duff beer for many different kinds of products but not for beer. For these kinds of products the sign is not really well-known. Whereas with regard to reference of the trademark to the nature of its product the virtual was granted full legal reality – Duff beer referred to real virtual beer. With regard to the reputation of the trademark the distinction between virtual and real is not thrown overboard, but firmly reinstated and no *passe-partout* is granted to the Fox franchise. There is thus an important difference between the legal immateriality of the objects of trademark rights and the fictive virtuality of objects in virtual worlds and these have to be strictly kept apart.

***

~ 4TH MOVEMENT ~

We will leave the regime of trademark law and return to the grounds of invention already tentatively explored in the previous chapter. What is the invention? This question leads to a quest for the characteristics and the working principle of the invention. Before the question can be answered the protagonists first need to establish how to locate the invention's whereabouts, by constructing and authorizing an indexing map of the domain of the patent file. Simultaneously visual, written and numeral approaches are mobilized in order to articulate the patent matter into its distinctive elements. After these fore-articulations of the internal space of the patent file, the quest proceeds in two different directions.

Theme C: Essence and Addition

The search for the essential features of the patent matter leads to a different terrain than the list of 34 essential contributions encountered in the [TWC-Gortec] dispute. There the theme of essence and accident was evoked along the lines of co-ownership of a patent according to concepts like idea, concept, contribution and inventor. In this dispute this theme appears along the lines of a claim of infringement of a patent, which brings it into proximity with the [Oil Spout and DEQU]. Accordingly there is a movement from the demarcation of the essential and accidental contributions in the process of origination of an invention, to the demarcation of the very essence of the invention itself. In the [TWC-Gortec] dispute this theme was still evoked hesitantly in the margin of other themes like identity/difference. Here it emerges fully developed in its own right saturating the dispute dynamics, whereas the identity/difference theme merely appears in minor chords.

Once the patent matter is located its essential features need to be separated from its additional features. This is achieved through several textual techniques. The nature and permissions of approaching the invention are first discussed through the mobilization of conditions and protocols of interpretation. These can be compared to the set permissions for how to approach the DEQU trademark. In the ensuing antagonistic dance the patent matter is alternatively textually laid-out and cut up in its elementary features, or staged before the interpretative figure of the expert for a holistic approach. This figure is another interesting variation on the fictive characters of the informed user and the average consumer in the [Olive Spout and DEQU] disputes. The expert figure is set up to access the inventive solution the inventor had in mind when solving a technical problem.

Theme D: Mode of Operation and Realization

The search for the functional working principle of the invention is no longer confined to the envelope of the patent file but also alternates with that of the grant file of the patent. The figure of the expert is here both evoked as a character who actually was involved in this granting process and as a fictive character able to extract the intangible mode of operation of the invention from its tangible means of realization. We have seen a comparable alternation between actual and fictive figures of the expert in the [Oil Spout] dispute. There the dispute matters also appeared as specimens in the libraries and offices of the court. Here the invention will appear through working scale models, which enables the judges to observe its function in action.

J. *The court intensifies the alternating movements in the inter-filing space. Similar to what we have seen in the [TWC-Gortec] dispute, the invention is cast into its history of origination by passing through a series of written communications, this time between the inventor and an expert of the patent office. Hereby a delimited historical position on the invention is set up on which the inventor is fixated in the present dispute. Next, the rival machine is also transformed into a text on the basis of drawings and models. This sets the stage for a play of identity and difference between the two textual devices with regard to their features and functions.*

***

Models and Layout of Invention (Case 4: Tarpaulin Patent)

Defendant D is the right holder of European patent no. 1405804 for a 'covering element for container or the like' (Figure 4.2).[150] In this case, plaintiff A does not claim co-ownership and recovery of D's patent, as in the previous chapter, but a legal declaration that it does not infringe this patent by producing, keeping in stock, importing, exporting, offering or marketing of its tarpaulins (covering canvases) (Figure 4.3).[151]

The attorneys will articulate each tarpaulin device by distinguishing its essential features and by extracting the valence of its mode of operation.

---

[150] https://register.epo.org/espacenet/application?number=EP03356145.

[151] This case has been practically impossible to anonymize convincingly. Most of the text and images on the disputed machine have therefore been taken from publicly available sources like the patent file, the judgment of the court and the pleas in court. The presentation has been limited as much as possible to legal arguments, discussions and interpretations.

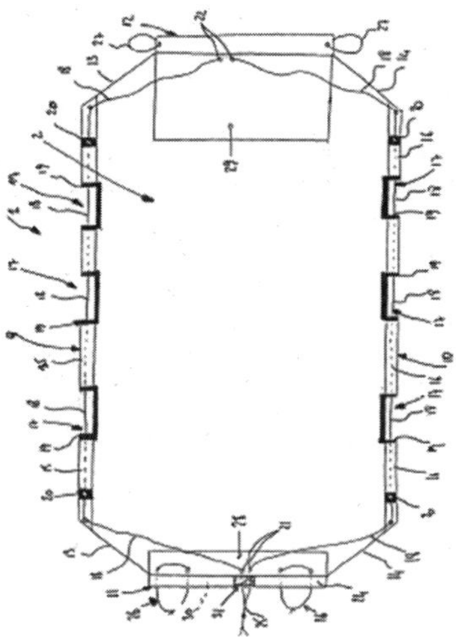

Figure 4.2 *Tarpaulin of D as depicted in drawing 3 of its patent application*

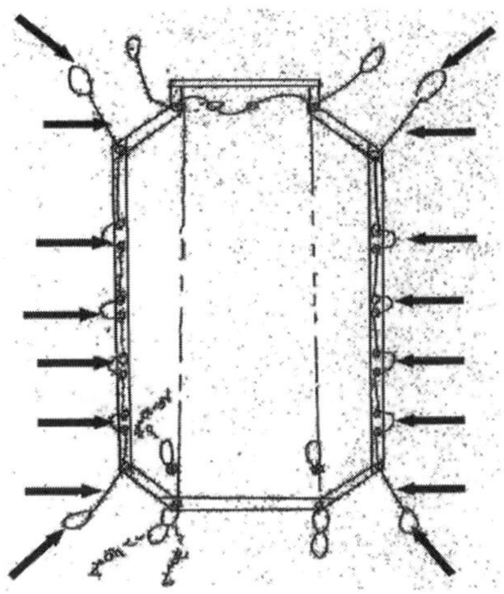

Figure 4.3 *Tarpaulin produced by A (taken from the court's judgment)*

This is done by connecting each device to a variety of scale models, drawings, legal texts, doctrine, expert findings and patent applications. The articulation of D's tarpaulin is then compared to the articulation of A's tarpaulin for establishing the existence of copies and equivalences. An important feature highlighted in these devices is the number and trajectory of elastic ties that run through the edges of the tarpaulin. In the summons A states that:

> The tarpaulin of A has **no single elastic tie** that **stretches out onto the end edges**. It has **three unconnected elastics**.
>
> 'Plaintiff's tarpaulin **does not allow the automatic folding** of the longitudinal edges of the covering element over the container **through the operation of the elastic wires**.'
>
> According to the patent application this automatic folding is an **essential feature** of the patent. Since this **characteristic** is **missing** there can be **no infringement**.

This dispute is all about lines and folds: automatic folding and assisted folding, patent folders, grant folders, implications and explications. In a nutshell, these phrases introduce the matter of dispute and foreclose its further proceeding. The tarpaulin of D includes one single elastic tie that runs through and connects all four edges (the side and end edges). This enables the side edges of the tarpaulin to automatically fold over the container to cover it. According to D's patent application this automatic folding would be an essential feature of the patent matter, also called a 'characteristic' of the invention. In contrast, the tarpaulin of A includes three unconnected elastic ties: two which run through the longitudinal side edges and one which runs through the top end edge, whereas the bottom end edge contains no elastic tie. These elastic ties do not connect all the edges and thus the device lacks the essential feature of automatic folding and does not constitute an infringement of D's patent.

Later, a further differentiation between two kinds of infringements is formulated: direct infringement and infringement by equivalent. We will start with the first.

> There is **direct infringement** when all the **essential features** of the patent claims can be found in the alleged counterfeit. There is no infringement when 1 essential feature is not present in the alleged counterfeit (Blanchard, Patent Law).

A's attorney raises a condition of proceeding for its non-infringement claim: D's patent is infringed by A's tarpaulin when all its essential features could be recognized in it. This proposition implies that when A's attorney is able to find one characteristic of D's invention that cannot be found in A's tarpaulin, there will be no patent infringement. But what is all this talk about essential features? Again there is a mobilization of a practical philosophy of essence and accident, now concerning the demarcation of the very essence of the invention itself. In order to recognize something in something else, we first have to know what this something is. It turns out that the immaterial identity of the tarpaulin invention is not at all something pre-given but has to first be established through several techniques of demarcation like textual *Auslegung* and the inscription of legal conditions.

According to the title of the patent, D's invention is a 'covering element for container or the like'. This indication is too broad so we will have to open the patent file in order to draw more narrow boundaries. When we look at the patent however, we see a host of numbers, dates, names, addresses, references, descriptions, claims and drawings. How do we know where in all of this text we can find the essence of the invention? The attorneys engage in a series of demarcations to achieve this. Just as we have seen in the TWC-Gortec dispute, the attorney firstly demarcates the invention through 'indexation' by connecting it to article 69(1) of the European Patent Convention. Hereby he raises the legal condition that the scope of protection of a patent is primarily determined by the *claims* in the patent and that the descriptions and drawings serve to explicate these claims.[152] The focus in D's patent text is thus put on the 'claims' section. This section contains nine claims in which the 'covering element' is articulated. Which differential weight are we to assign to each of these claims? In the discussions between the attorneys, the first claim of the patent ('claim 1') is often referred to as the '*main*' claim. This 'main' claim, also called the 'independent' claim, is distinguished from the other eight claims of the patent that all 'depend' on this main claim. Here we have a second demarcation of the invention according to whether it is articulated in a main or an additional claim.[153] Claims 2–9 all start with the phrase 'Covering element *according to claim* [number]'. Each of these claims refers back to an earlier claim in its description of the invention and further articulates a specific element of that earlier claim (pulling tube, flexible connection, longitudinal edges, sheaths, etc.). In contrast, claim 1 states the following:

> Covering element made from a protective tarpaulin or net or fabric (2) which is placed over an open vehicle body or a container or a trailer (3) transportable on or by a towing vehicle, said covering element comprising longitudinal edges (9, 10) and end edges (11, 12), said longitudinal edges (9, 10) of longer length being passed through by an elastic tie (18) making it possible to fold said edges onto one of the faces of the covering element (1), **characterized in that** the elastic tie (18) passes through the end edges (11, 12) near the longitudinal central axis of the covering element (1), at least one end edge (11, 12) interacting with a pulling tube (23, 30) for folding the longitudinal edges (9, 10) onto one of the faces of the covering element (1) and the covering element comprises attachment means (26, 27) for fastening the end edges (11, 12) to the open body or container (3).

This claim does not describe a covering element according to another claim, but provides an independent description of the invention. The title 'covering element for container or the like' does here not suffice anymore. The claim *articulates* what material the invention is made from, on which other devices it is to be placed (not the vague 'container or the like' but the more explicit 'open vehicle body or a container or a trailer'), what elements it comprises, how these elements interact and what operations

[152] '[T]he extent of the protection conferred by a European patent or a European patent application shall be determined by the claims. Nevertheless, the description and drawings shall be used to interpret the claims' (Article 69(1) EPC).

[153] According to doctrine, the dependent claims mention 'additional' or 'optional' measures (http://www.iusmentis.com/octrooien/spoedcursus/procedure/).

Figure 4.4 Fragment of tarpaulin of D

these enable. The matter of the patent is here separated into several articulations according to linguistic sequences of the sentence of the claim.[154] Furthermore, in this text of the European patent file a number is inserted after each of the distinguished elements of the invention:

Example: 'elastic tie (18)' or 'longitudinal edges (9, 10)'

These numbers perform two actions: they establish a numerical differentiation of the constitutive *elements* of the invention within the text of the claim, and they establish referential links between the claims and the drawings within the patent file. In Figure 4.4 we can see how the same numbers are inscribed in the drawing of the invention. Through the addition of connecting lines or arrows, these numbers come to point at sections of the graphically outlined invention.

Through the mutual envelopment of the claims and the drawings within the confines of the same patent folder, the numbers in claim 1 come to pictographically *point out* the elements of the invention which has been (linguistically) articulated. Internal reference is thus established. In this way the drawings thus serve to '*ex-plicate*' the claims as we have seen in the previous chapter. All these precedings might provide an answer to where in the patent we have to search for the invention and how this matter of the patent is articulated into its distinctive elements. We still do not have an answer to the question of which of these articulations are essential and which ones are additional. A's attorney provides a further demarcation on this point through hermeneutical techniques of textual interpretation. Amongst the pieces of conviction that he has deposited is a plasticized, A3-sized sheet of paper on which patent claim 1 is visually presented as follows:

---

154 See McLuhan, 1994 about the lineal or sequential structuring effects of alphabetic writing and how it breaks things up in discrete elements. On the latter point see also Goody & Watt, 1963.

Patent Claim 1

(a) Covering element made from a protective tarpaulin or net or fabric which is placed over an open vehicle body or a container or a trailer transportable on or by a towing vehicle, **(b)** said covering element comprising longitudinal edges and end edges, **(c)** said longitudinal edges of longer length being passed through by an elastic tie making it possible to fold said edges onto one of the faces of the covering element, **characterized in that:**

(d) the elastic tie passes through the end edges near the longitudinal central axis of the covering element, **AND**

(e) at least one end edge interacts with a pulling tube for folding the longitudinal edges onto one of the faces of the covering element **AND**

(f) the covering element comprises attachment means for fastening the end edges to the open body or container.

The Germans have a suitable word for interpretation in this context – *Auslegung* – which can be more literally rendered as 'laying out'. This is exactly what A's attorney has done in interpreting the patent claim: the A3 sheet provides a different layout of the invention than the text within the European patent file. In the latter the text of claim 1 consisted of one continuous compound sentence in which the invention was numerically differentiated into its 18 constitutive *elements*, each of which was inscribed as a noun in the sentence. On the A3 sheet there is a different articulation through an interesting linguistic arthroscopy. First of all, the numbers are removed from the sentences so that the hermeneutical scalpel no longer cuts out the nouns as elements of the invention. The removal of the numbers also cuts the reference of the claim to the drawings, and thus cuts the graphical ex-plication of the invention that was more circular (or hexagonal) than the linear articulation through the sentence of the claim. Instead, A's attorney has cut the compound sentence at its syntactical joints, mostly indicated by commas, and has divided it into six clauses lettered from 'a' to 'f', each of which contains the matter of the patent: the 'covering element'. The invention hereby receives a sixfold layout in which it is not articulated according to the elements out of which it is made, but according to its *features* or *traits*. The word 'feature' comes from the Old French root *faiture* which means 'doing', 'action', 'performing', 'forming', 'shaping' which in turn comes from the Latin root *facture* meaning 'a working', a 'formation'. Each clause articulates a way in which the covering element relates to several elements in specific interactions, often indicated by a verb, which form a distinctive trait of the patent matter.[155] This indicates what the covering element 'is made from', 'comprises' or by what it is 'passed through', what it is 'placed on'.

When we compare the text on the plasticized A3 sheet with the text in the patent file, we can further observe that additional punctuation marks and formatting changes have been inserted. The phrase '**characterized in that**' has been underlined and after it a colon [:] has been placed. This is followed by an indent in the layout of the subsequent clauses lettered 'd, e, f' and their isolation in separate paragraphs. At the end of paragraph 'd' a coordinating conjunction is added that is put in capital bold letters [**AND**], and the same treatment is given to the 'and' that connects the clauses 'e' and 'f'. Why invest this effort in providing a separate linguistic layout on all these points? Why is this relevant for the dispute?

> **The essential features (where the invention is inscribed** and which **start with the words 'with the characteristic that**') are three:

After the differentiation of the matter of the patent in six features, the attorney proceeds with the demarcation of those features that are essential. He assigns the underlined phrase '**characterized in that**' the status of a grammatical initiating marker that performs the characterization of the invention. The phrase indicates the position in the order of the sentence in which the essential features of the matter of the patent can be found, i.e. it indicates the grammatical place 'where the invention is inscribed'. In this sense the claim is literally punctuated by the insertion in the middle of the colon [:] and thereby divided in two sections. The clauses before the marker contain non-characterizing aspects of the invention and are therefore not essential. The clauses after the marker contain the three characteristics of the invention.

> It therefore **follows** from the text of the claim that feature (d) of the characteristics is **essential** to the invention, namely that there is an elastic tie in the cover element that runs through the end edges near the longitudinal centre of the cover element.

The attorney has deployed several techniques of hermeneutical layout to articulate and demarcate the essence of the matter of D's patent, which can now be used to ground his proposition on direct infringement. The feature

[155] The term 'trait' is etymologically derived from *trahere* as 'drawing a line' or 'pulling'. In the case of our tarpaulin, we can take such a trait quite literally in the sense of a 'drawn line that pulls'.

that an elastic tie runs through the end edges of the cover element near the longitudinal centre of the cover element is inscribed in the characterizing part of the claim. This feature is therefore essential for D's invention and constitutes one of its characteristics. It permits the automatically folding of the longitudinal edges of the covering element over the container. Since A's tarpaulin does not contain this feature, it does not constitute a direct infringement of D's patent.

D's attorney will dispute A's demarcation of the invention by raising different conditions for how an exercise of hermeneutical layout of a patent can proceed. He starts by also raising the condition in article 69 of the European Patent Convention, that the scope of the patent is determined by the claims and that the drawings and descriptions serve as explication. He however connects this condition to the '*protocol of interpretation*' for article 69 of the Convention.[156] Interpretation of patents is not just a legal technique to articulate the matter of the patent and demarcate the invention; 'interpretation' is itself inscribed within the law as a legal concept that will have to be interpreted.[157] The way a patent is to be interpreted and the requirements that this interpretation has to satisfy can thus themselves become a topic of legal contention. Through the alignment of the protocol of interpretation D's attorney can raise what article 69 EPC 'should not be understood as meaning' and what 'it is to be interpreted as'.[158]

> **D's Attorney:** The scope of patent protection is **neither defined by the literal text** of the claim, **nor** is this text to be taken as a **mere guideline**. [. . .]
>
> Each **invention needs to be understood** in the light of the **objective technical problem** that it aims to solve and in which the **expert** will understand the patent. [. . .]

---

156 http://www.epo.org/law-practice/legal-texts/html/epc/2010/e/ma2a.html.

157 For some of the problems involved in this process, see Sherman, 1991.

158 Article 1 of the protocol states that 'Article 69 *should not be interpreted as meaning* that the extent of the protection conferred by a European patent is to be understood as that defined by the strict, literal meaning of the wording used in the claims, the description and drawings being employed only for the purpose of resolving an ambiguity found in the claims. *Nor should it be taken to mean* that the claims serve only as a guideline and that the actual protection conferred may extend to what, from a consideration of the description and drawings by a person skilled in the art, the patent proprietor has contemplated. On the contrary, *it is to be interpreted as* defining a position between these extremes which combines a fair protection for the patent proprietor with a reasonable degree of legal certainty for third parties' (my italics), http://www.epo.org/law-practice/legal-texts/html/epc/2010/e/ma2a.html.

> Each claim **must be considered in its totality** to **judge the whole of the claimed apparatus**. [. . .] A wrongly concentrates attention on 1 of the characteristics of claim 1 and gives this characteristic a totally limited interpretation. [. . .] **A splits claim 1 up into 6 features to make us forget that the claim forms one whole** and that the features mentioned **have necessarily to be understood in terms of each other**. The **features co-operate** to form an easy universally usable cover element **as the patent holder had in mind. The expert will not** engage in such cutting up. The **numerical cut up** cannot make one forget that the claim **has to be read as a whole**.

> According to a judgment by a British court the patent has to be given a **purposive** and **not a direct interpretation. A patent is actually aimed at the expert, since it is from his point of view that one has to analyze things**.

The invention as the inventor had in mind is a prototypical example of the intellectual nature of the legal object of patent law, but also the most enigmatic and elusive. As Robinson already stated in 1890, '[t]he actual operations which have taken place in the mind of the inventor are not open to inquiry. Concerning these he alone has any personal knowledge, and even his impressions are often vague and unreliable. The invention must, therefore, speak for itself' (Robinson cited in Pottage, 2011, p. 629). No invention speaks for itself by itself however, but has to be made to speak for itself through the deployment of a plethora of techniques. In this context D's attorney engages in an intricate hermeneutical exercise of the matter of the patent inscribed in the claim. A's attorney articulated D's patent claim in six separate clauses, each inscribing a feature of the matter of the patent, and demarcated the essential elements of D's patent matter focusing on one characteristic that was missing in A's device. Instead, D's attorney (dis)qualifies these hermeneutical efforts as 'direct' interpretation in which the scope of the patent is defined by the literal text of the claim. He unauthorizes this mode of interpretation by linking it to the protocol of interpretation. Article 69 EPC 'should not be understood as meaning' this. Instead, the attorney proposes a different mode of interpretation of the invention, which he calls 'purposive'. 'Each invention needs to be understood in the light of the objective technical problem that it aims to solve.' We could call this a 'teleology of inventions', which will articulate the patent matter along a different orientation to the claim and along different figures. First, the claim is not approached in an atomistic manner in which its matter would be 'numerically cut up' along the linguistic joints of its literal text in order to arrive at its separate *elementary operations*. It is rather approached in a holistic manner in which the claim 'forms one whole' that 'must be considered in its totality'. When one wants to understand how a certain device solves a certain technical problem that exists in the field of transportation, one has to look at 'the whole of the claimed apparatus' in order to judge what kind of solution it provides to this problem. Within this whole of the apparatus, all features that one might want to distinguish in the device actually engage in *holistic co-operations* in order to achieve the required solution. They thus 'have to necessarily be understood in terms of each other'.

The attorney reinforces this mode of articulation by establishing an observer position from which the matter of the claim is to be approached: it is from the *expert's 'point of view* that one has to analyze things'. This point of view does not necessarily belong to this-or-that expert who has actually made such-and-such an analysis of an apparatus, but is rather a proposal for assuming a default orientation along which one has to legally understand and judge this apparatus. In this sense the expert is a fictive person not unlike that of the (mind of) the public that we encountered in the DEQU case on trademark infringement. Notice how a second point of view is implicated by this fictive person. The expert will understand the invention in the same way 'as the patent holder had in mind' when inventing the invention. This is a quite different articulation of the invention that eventually even involves the *mind of the inventor*. This is not about what the inventor actually had in mind while inventing however, but what he can be attributed to have had in mind when one manages to make the invention speak through the expert. The expert will know that the inventor was confronting a certain technical problem and will thus understand that the matter of the claim as a whole was aimed at solving this problem. Therefore s/he will not engage in the artificial kind of numerical cut-up that A's attorney has performed. The expert is the figure who understands this purpose of the patent matter and in this sense the patent itself 'is actually aimed at the expert'. For these reasons D's attorney later states that in order to understand the invention, one not only 'has to pay attention' to the text of the claim, but also to the 'descriptions' section in the patent since 'usually the patent holder there describes the existing techniques and their disadvantages for which he wants to provide a solution'. These descriptions 'allow understanding the disadvantage' that the inventor was confronted with – problems in the unwinding and winding of the canvas – and that he tried to solve.[159]

[159] Description [0009] of the patent states that: 'The covering device described above has some disadvantages, more particularly concerning the *difficulties faced by individuals to unfold and fold the sheet*, because of its position on the arm with hooks attached to the towing vehicle, and it does not allow protection to the container on the trailer' (my italics).

> **A's Attorney**: There also is **no infringement by equivalent**. Belgium has the doctrine of equivalence in which one has to analyze which **technical functionality** the concrete essential element offers. There is equivalence when the concrete **substituting element** (the technical factor) has the **same technical function** – **working principle** – and the **same technical effect**.
>
> The **functional difference** between the characteristics of the two tarpaulins is that according to the patent the side edges are **automatically folded** due to the position, trajectory and tension of the elastic tie.

Apart from the whole discussion on direct infringement, there is also the question whether A's tarpaulin infringes D's patent by equivalent.[160] The question here is not whether an essential element can be recognized in the allegedly infringing device, but whether an essential element is substituted by another element that has the same technical function and through which the same technical effect is achieved as in the patented device. The constitution of the invention thus changes from a demarcation of its essential elements and traits, to a demarcation of its essential functions and effects. The attorneys will have to extract the '*working principle*' of D's patent matter. In order to judge whether A's covering device is functionally equivalent to D's patent matter, the functional valences of both devices needs to first be determined. But, how does one know what the function of an invention is?

This analysis involves a host of patent specification, descriptions, expert communications and scale models. According to A, its tarpaulin does not include one single elastic tie that stretches out onto the end edges, but contains three unconnected elastics, two of which run through the longitudinal side edges and one which runs through the top-end edge. The bottom-end edge contains no elastic tie. In D's patent on the other hand, the tarpaulin includes one single elastic tie that connects all four edges (see Figures 4.2 and 4.3). The combination of this 'trajectory' of the tie that runs through the 'positions' at all the edges, combined with a certain elastic 'tension', grants the tarpaulin a certain technical functionality. According to A this 'operation' of the elastic tie enables the side edges of D's tarpaulin to be automatically folded over the container. In A's tarpaulin, the elastic tie does not connect all the edges and thus lacks this essential functionality. There is thus a clear 'functional difference' between the working principles of the two devices. Their modes of operation have a different valence and

---

160 'For the purpose of determining the extent of protection conferred by a European patent, due account shall be taken of any element which is *equivalent* to an element specified in the claims', Article 2 EPC Protocol of Interpretation.

therefore A's tarpaulin does not constitute an infringement of D's patent by functional equivalence.[161] What allows the attorney to make all these statements? How is he able to extract the automatic folding as the functional essence of the invention?

> The word 'automatic' does not occur in the claim. The **claim only describes the characteristics of the invention, not its function**. Thus this function has to **necessarily be sought in the descriptions and drawings.**

Just like with the essential features of the matter of the patent, the attorney first asks the question 'how' it 'occurs' and 'where' we are supposed to find it, before answering the question 'what' the function of D's invention is. Above we have seen how A's attorney demarcated the characteristics of the invention through a hermeneutical layout of claim 1 of the patent. With regard to the function, he proposes a different hermeneutical indexing through an exhaustive interpretation of the claims. A claim only describes the characteristics of the invention, which we might use to ground claims about direct infringement. The function of the invention is not implicated in the claim and thus 'has to necessarily be sought in the descriptions and drawings'. The attorney finds this function in descriptions 60, 61 and 64 of the patent file, which describe how the elastic tie 'permits' the edges of the cover element to 'fold automatically' on itself.[162] Grammatical markers of affordance like 'permit', 'enable', 'allow', 'make possible' or 'thanks to' often indicate the inscription of such functionality.[163]

> In his communications an investigator of the EPO states that it is **indispensable for this function** that the tie runs through the end edges. [. . .] 'The fact that the tie extends through the end edges near the longitudinal centre, does seem an **essential feature for the realization of the pressing down** as drawing 4 demonstrates. In

---

[161] We can use the way the term 'valency' is used in chemistry as the measure of the number of bonds formed by an atom of a given element to understand the mode of operation of the two tarpaulins. The valence of each side edge can then be taken to consist in the number of bonds it has with other edges (including itself). Both tarpaulins have four edges. A's tarpaulin thus has the valency of [1, 1, 1, 0] (three edges are only connected to themselves and one edge has no connections), D's tarpaulin has the valency of [4, 4, 4, 4] (each edge is connected to all the others, including itself). These valencies enable the specific folding functions – manual or automatic – of each tarpaulin device.

[162] Description [0060] of the patent states that 'The position, trajectory and tension of elastic tie 18 in the length of the covering element 1 permits edges 9, 10 to fold automatically in the direction of the inside of the said element 1.'

[163] This notion of grammatical markers of affordance indicating the things that enable a certain function is inspired by Norman, 1988.

> the entire application no other version is shown, nor described'. [. . .] This **function is not realized** when the tie only runs through the side edges. The tarpaulin of A thus does **not have the same technical function or the same technical effect.** One has to fold over the edges **manually**. This is only possible when the canvas is on the floor. Manual folding has occurred for centuries and can thus never be an invention of D.

A's attorney affixes 'this function' to the communications between D and an expert of the European Patent Office involved in the granting procedure of the patent. In this preliminary granting process, the demarcation of the matter of the patent is also an important matter of concern. The expert establishes a close connection between the demarcation of the essential features of the matter of the patent and the extraction of the function of the invention, based on the way this function is 'realized' and what is 'essential' for its realization. The claimed characteristic of the invention (previously called feature 'd') that an elastic tie runs through the end edges near the longitudinal centre of the cover element, is not only an essential feature that gives shape to the patent matter itself. Based on a drawing in the patent, the expert states the operation of this feature is also 'indispensable' 'for the realization' of the invention's function of automatically folding onto itself. This essential trait of the patent matter articulated in the claim thus constitutes a line of realization for the function of the invention. A's tarpaulin did not contain the essential feature of the elastic tie running through the end edges. The tie only ran through the side edges. This implies that the line which permits the automatic folding is missing and that the 'function is not realized' in this device. Instead the tarpaulin has to first be put on the floor and be manually folded onto itself. There is thus no equivalence of functions.

Of special interest among the pieces of evidence deposited by A's attorney are two *scale models* of A's tarpaulin and D's tarpaulin. Due to a scale of these models that is much smaller than a real-sized tarpaulin, the models can both be put next to each other on a table in the court library or in the judge's office. This allows the judges to observe the two represented devices from different angles, to touch, turn and manipulate them and to compare them. It also allows the party who constructs these models to foreground certain features and remove or background certain others, all in order to ground its positions in the dispute. In this context, Pottage has called scale models the 'essential medium of courtroom rhetoric' in the sense that these models materialized the arguments of parties in patent infringement cases (Pottage, 2011). Now, the models enable the judges to check the differences and similarities between both devices – either the ones proposed by the attorneys or the ones they observe by themselves – in a way that would have been inaccessible on the basis of the drawings, descriptions or claims in the patent file alone. It thus provides a position upon the invention beyond the immanence of the file. The models allow the judges to 'find' the essential features of both devices in order to affirm or reject the claim of direct infringement. More importantly and relevant here, they allow the judges to extract the function of the devices. The models enable the judges to repeatedly pull different elastic ties and on each occasion observe what kind of folding takes place. In this way they can extract and compare the working principle of each device and determine whether there is functional equivalence between both devices. The materiality of the model thus also comes to ground the immateriality of the invention.

> **D's Attorney**: There has been an **infringement by equivalent** for the sake of the **whole configuration**.
> [. . .]
> Case law shows the importance of the **expert who, behind all the concrete means known from the patent, recognizes the functions that are relevant to realize the invention, and dedicates himself to judge the function, mode and result, not literally but 'in essence'**.

D's attorney again stages the figure of the expert as the point of view from which to analyze the apparatus.[164] The expert has to 'judge' the functional essence of the invention (thereby strangely endowing him or her with typical legal features). Through the introduction of this figure the attorney manages to move beyond the textual materiality of the patent file itself, with all its literal claims and descriptions that inscribe a variety of concrete means. The whole is more than the sum of its parts. In an invention the means are not just assembled and juxtaposed in textual descriptions, but they are configured in a certain way to produce a certain effect. This function exists 'for the sake of the whole configuration' of these material means and herein 'realizes' the immaterial essence of the invention. This might seem quite complex, but that seems to be exactly the attorney's point. A lay person (or attorney) who will look at the invention in the patent might be confronted with a complexity of many material parts mixed together beyond which s/he cannot reach. In order to deal with the technology this layperson will therefore reduce this complexity by isolating the invention into separate means. To the contrary, the expert is able

164 I hesitate in also calling this figure of the expert a 'fictive person' in this case. This figure seems tailored for actual experts assessing the function of an invention, like the expert above who was involved in the granting procedure of the patent.

to assess how all parts are *com-plicated* together in a whole configuration. This expert can extract the abstract intangible mode of operation of the invention 'behind' all the concrete tangible means.[165] The introduction of this figure thus plays an important role in the constitution of the immateriality of D's invention.

> **D's Attorney:** According to a French judgment the description serves to explicate the claims and **give these a full meaning** when they are unclear. It is **not permitted** to add a characteristic through this interpretation which the claim does not provide. **Interpreting is not adding**. [. . .]
>
> The **term automatic** does not occur in the claim. The word 'automatic' in the explication of the example (par 60 & 61) refers to the position and trajectory of the tie, namely that the tie runs in the direction of the interior cover element. In this sense 'automatic' is **to be understood not in the limited technical meaning** of the intervention of an internal or external motorized element (like an automatic door), **but in the usual meaning of the word**, namely 'by itself' and 'easy'.

Both parties agree about the fact that the word 'automatic' does not occur in the claim. They disagree about the question whether it belongs to the essence of the folding function of D's invention and how to establish what belongs to this function. A's attorney proposed that the claim was exhausted by its inscription of the characteristics of the invention. Its function had to therefore be necessarily sought elsewhere in the descriptions and drawings in the patent. D's attorney contests this layout by mobilizing and authorizing a different theory about the nature of patent interpretation and the permissions that follow from this nature. He argues that the division of the patent in descriptions and claims does not imply a separation of the places where the characteristics and function of the invention can be found. Descriptions and claims are not mutually exclusive. The claim already implicates the function of the invention, but its meaning might not always be totally clear. Descriptions 'fill up' this gap. They serve to explicate this implicated function of the claims and 'give them their full meaning'. This coincides with the nature of interpretation that D's attorney inscribes: 'interpreting is not adding' but rather unfolding. An interpretation of the descriptions unfolds what was already contained in the claim but was not fully clear. From this view it follows that inter-

---

[165] On the difference between the complexity (as an unstable chaos of many equal parts mixed up together) and complication (as a stabilized technological folding together of many simple means for achieving a certain functional goal in which the part is inferior to the whole) of technological devices, see Latour, 1996, pp. 219–20.

pretation cannot add something extrinsic which the claims themselves did not already provide. This 'is not permitted'. Now, since the term 'automatic' does not occur in the claim it should not be interpreted in a way that would add an extra characteristic to what is already inscribed in the claim. This would be the case when the term is understood in its 'limited technical meaning' in which a motorized element is added to the device, which would 'intervene' by determining the way it functions. The attorney states that the term 'automatic' rather needs to be understood in a more common everyday sense when a cover element 'once put in movement, [...] functions by itself'. The operator of the cover element has to initiate the movement and the longitudinal edge subsequently folds up by itself, due to its position in the trajectory and the tension of the tie over the length of the covering element.

> In this case the use of **two ties** is an infringement by **equivalent** since they fulfill the same **function** as the **one tie**, namely being able to press down or fold up the longitudinal edge. These ties **allow the edges to be folded on the side of the covering element by normal traction or by the driver taking hold of them**.

> The **manner is the same**: the folding happens by itself by means of traction. The **result** is also the same. **Legally no single perfect identity is required**, nor of the manner, nor of the result, in which case the doctrine of equivalence would be robbed of any real scope. They thus fulfill the same function as described in the first claim of the patent. So there is infringement.

The attorney now demarcates the functional essence of D's invention. Now that the automatism has been eliminated from this essence, the function is broadened to include all acts of 'folding up of the longitudinal edge'. *In this sense*, A's tarpaulin and D's tarpaulin have the same manner of operation and are thus functionally equivalent. With this elimination, the point of initiation of the act of folding becomes irrelevant. It does not matter whether the operator has to manually fold the cover element by pulling the elastic ties or whether the cover element folds by itself through the traction of an elastic tie. Both accomplish the same folding function. Furthermore, the number of elements by which the function is realized is also irrelevant: it does not matter whether the folding is accomplished by one or two elastic ties. In a strict mathematical sense it might be obvious that a tarpaulin with 2 or 3 ties is not identical to a tarpaulin with 1 tie ($1 \neq 2 \neq 3$). *Legally* however 'no single perfect identity is required'. In terms of its function a tarpaulin with 1 tie can operate in the same manner as a tarpaulin with 2 or 3 ties ($1=2=3$). A function is abstracted from its elements and would lose all its independent sense when reduced to these elements.

Judgment

The judgment of the court in this case is quite extensive, which seems to be typical for patent disputes with their highly 'technical' character. The 'judgment' section is divided into several subsections. Section 3.3.1 raises the legal conditions for this dispute from article 69 EPC and the protocol of interpretation. Section 3.3.2 is about the granting file of the European Patent Office and the history of how D's patent came about. Section 3.4.1 is about the question of direct infringement and judges the essential features of the matter of D's patent. Section 3.4.2 judges the features of A's tarpaulin and whether it qualifies as a direct infringement of D's patent. Section 3.4.3 is about the question of infringement by equivalent of A's tarpaulin on D's patent.

We will start with section 3.3.2 in which the court tackles the question about the nature of D's invention by determining which documents are relevant for the interpretation of the scope of protection provided by D's patent. For this purpose, the court turns to the granting file of D's patent application. The European Patent Office keeps a file that documents the history of granting the patent application, which includes the correspondence between the patent applicant and (experts of) the Office.[166] The court reconstructs some of this history in its judgment, by inscribing parts of the documents from this file, like the original patent application and D's correspondence with the EPC's expert. 'The granting file shows that in the original patent application EP 1405804 A1, the main claim 1 of the patent' states that the elastic tie that runs through the longitudinal edges of the cover element is a characteristic of the claimed invention.[167] Notice that the court from the outset has already qualified claim 1 as a 'main claim' thereby reiterating a differentiation of the patent claims into main claims and dependent claims. When researchers of the Patent Office investigated 'the prior art relevant for this invention' filed by D however, they encountered a German document that already revealed a cover element with an elastic tie that extends throughout the longer side edges of the cover element (feature 2).[168] According to the researcher this feature was thus already known as part of the relevant prior art.

---

166 For an account of the work of patent examiners at the patent office and the relations between law and science and technology involved in their work, see Kang, 2013.

167 The term 'original' here refers to the text that the Patent Office first received for D's patent application.

168 D's patent file contains a document titled 'application with search report' (https://data.epo.org/publication-server/pdf-document?pn=1405804&ki=A1&cc=EP). It includes an annex that 'lists the family of patents relating to docu-

In his letter of June 30 2005, the EPO researcher has invited D to propose a new patent claim, in which **feature 2 was moved to the non-characterizing section of this claim (called the 'preamble')**, not only in order to satisfy the requirement of clarity of art. 84 EPC requirements, but also because the characterizing section must indicate how the relevant invention would be novel and inventive. The EPO researcher stated more concretely:

> 'Claim 1 that would have been amended in this way would also **define a new and inventive object of patent** in light of the documents cited, and would be **correctly delimited** (rule 29 (1) EPC) with regard to what is revealed in document DE – U – 298 15 603 (D1) that reveals a cover element in which an elastic cord 60 extends throughout the longitudinal edges and the end edge of the cover element.'

In this reconstruction by the court, the link that the EPO researcher established with the German document created two obstacles for D's original patent application. First, since the feature in question already occurred in the German document it cannot be 'new' anymore with regard to the prior art (in the sense of article 54(1) EPC), which is one of the requirements of patentability. Second, we could say that the claimed invention in D's original patent application is hybrid in mixing characteristics of another invention together with its own characteristics. Therefore 'the matter for which protection is sought' is not 'clear' (in the sense of article 84 EPC) in its demarcation.[169] In order to overcome these obstacles D's invention has to be 'correctly delimited' in relation to the invention claimed in the German document. For these purposes 'a new and inventive object of patent' has to be constructed, which incorporates the limits posed by these earlier inventions identified as relevant prior art. In his proposal for achieving this change, the patent researcher makes a cut in the claim – a *sectio* – dividing it into two distinct performative sections: the 'preamble' that constitutes the non-characterizing section of the claim and the characterizing section that inscribes the invention. The researcher proposes to textually move the phrase that inscribes the relevant feature (cover element that '*includes edges with a larger length throughout which an elastic tie extends which enables these edges to be pressed down [folded] on one of the sides of the covering element*') from the latter to the former. In this

ments cited in the European search report referred to above', amongst which we encounter a reference to the document that inscribes the German invention: http://worldwide.espacenet.com/publicationDetails/biblio?CC=DE&NR=29815603U&KC=&FT=E&locale=en_EP).

[169] Article 84 EPC states that 'the claims shall define the matter for which protection is sought. They shall be clear and concise and be supported by the description'.

way a correct limit would be drawn between the German patent in which this feature was a new and inventive part of the invention, and D's patent application in which this feature would not constitute a new characteristic of the invention, but would be part of what came before it (*pre-ambulare*); its prior art.[170] The matter of D's patent would no longer be a hybrid, but clearly demarcated.

> Furthermore, in this same letter of June 30 2005 the EPO researcher stated that: 'Lines 8 and 9 are **not clear**, since the presence of a tie that runs along and through each of the longitudinal edges, does **not allow an explanation of how this enables folding** over the edges on one of the sides of the cover element. **This folding can only occur by the extension of the tie through the end edges near the longitudinal centre of the cover element**'.
> [. . .]
> D (through its patent attorney) wrote on February 2 2006 to the EPO Researcher: 'In response to your notification of January 16 2006, you hereby find a new set of claims of which the main claim was **changed according to your comments**'.

Perhaps a more important obstacle than the unclarity that results from being a hybrid object, is the fact that it is 'not clear' how feature 2 can technically realize the claimed function of folding the cover element. The researcher concludes that this function can only be realized when the elastic tie does not merely run through the longitudinal edges, but also extends through the end edges of the cover element. In its first response to the letter of the EPO researcher, D still sticks to its position that this characteristic is not essential for folding the cover element. Nevertheless, in a next communication the researcher replies that the 'objection of unclarity' is retained. 'The fact that the tie extends through the end edges near the longitudinal centre, does seem an essential characteristic for the realization of the pressing down, as drawing 4 demonstrates.' In the end, D gives in to these objections and delimits the matter of the patent. Claim 1 is changed along the lines of his comments. Feature 2 is moved to the non-characterizing section and in the characterizing section D has added '*that the elastic tie passes through the end edges near the longitudinal central axis of the covering element*'. We have now arrived at the eventual patent text that was inscribed at the beginning of this section.

> **In the opinion of the court, these elements from the grant file, in particular the position assumed by patentee D, are relevant in determining the scope of EP '804, in particular its main claim.**

---

[170] As Vismann states 'preambles pave the hermeneutical access to legal texts' (Vismann, 2008, p. 21).

> While in its original patent application **D claimed** a cover element which was characterized by the fact that it had an elastic tie through the longer side edges, it has **afterwards changed this and has agreed to add the feature** that the elastic tie runs through the end edge near the longitudinal centre **as an essential feature of the invention**.
>
> **Hereby, the scope of protection of claim 1 of EP '804 was limited and in the context of this proceeding D cannot argue** that the feature that the elastic tie runs through the end edge near the longitudinal centre would **not be an essential feature**.

There is a different engagement with hermeneutical permissions here. In section 3.3.1 the Court raised the conditions for the weight of the different parts of the patent file (claims, drawings, descriptions) for determining the scope of protection of D's patent and which interpretations of these were and were not permitted (according the protocol of interpretation). These elements were intrinsic to the patent file. These conditions will serve as the prepositions for the judgments, which will follow in sections 3.3.3 and 3.3.4 on the infringement questions. In section 3.3.2 something different happens. The court constructs another line along which the hermeneutical permissions are extended beyond the interior bounds of the patent file, when it judges that all the 'extrinsic' elements from the granting file are also relevant for determining the scope of protection of the patent and especially its main claim.[171] Now it becomes clear why the court has taken the pains to reconstruct this little history of how D's patent came about. The court attaches particular importance to 'the position assumed by patentee D'. The granting file 'demonstrates' that D had aligned with the comments of the researcher that feature 2 (elastic through side edges) was not essential and also added an extra characteristic (elastic through end edges) of the invention. This alignment was registered in its correspondence in the grant file and became implicated in the changed claim 1. The conclusions by the EPO researcher had set up a position on the patent that D was eventually led to assume. The scope of protection covered by the patent was hereby significantly limited. Once the court has judged that the grant file is relevant for determining the scope of the patent, it is able take this *position* that D assumed when the patent came about and *fix* it for the present dispute. This fixation of a position is no meagre achievement. In the legal geometries of disputes no point is ever pre-given, but has to be painstakingly

---

[171] In legal doctrine, the granting file is called an 'extrinsic element' with regard to the patent file. See De Preter & Roox, 2008.

established as a post-given beyond dispute in the dynamics of the legal fabric.[172] Positions have to be extracted from the extensions of the conflictual dynamics that constantly threaten to destabilize and engulf them. This work of extraction requires prudential acts of stitching pieces of evidence and legal documents to the matter of dispute in a way that establishes a foothold on its incessant proceeding and ground a position in relation to it. This is by itself no different than the work in which the attorneys continuously engage. The fixation of the position only occurs however when the court brings the proceeding of the matter of dispute to a (temporary) halt (*arrêt*) in terms of this carefully extracted position and freeze it in that specific relational state (*D agrees that: the elastic tie running through the end edges is an essential feature of its invention*). In this case this freeze will allow the court to mobilize this agreement and transpose it from its situation between D and the EPO researcher in the process of granting the patent, to the relation between D and A in the present dispute. This entails important consequences. Once this position is fixed, D 'cannot argue' anymore that feature 2 is not an essential feature of the invention 'in the context of this proceeding'. By fixating the position of a party on a certain *point of dispute*, it is transformed into a *point beyond dispute* for the linear focus of judgment.

The two attorneys have drawn two maps of the dispute and as a result different navigational courses that will have to be sailed to arrive at judgment. The court in the end will have to draw up its own map on which it can fix positions.

> **3.4.1.** There is a **direct infringement** of a patent if all essential features of the patent claim involved can be found in the alleged infringing product.
>
> As expounded above, the essential features of the cover element, the matter of EP '804, are the following:
>
> 1. The elastic tie extends throughout the end edges near the longitudinal centre of the cover element,
> And
>
> 2. At least one end edge cooperates with a draft tube that enables the pressing down [folding] of the longitudinal edges [side edges] on one of the sides of the cover element, And

[172] There is a similarity here with Whitehead's writings on the relations between points and positions and the fixation of time-systems and events (Whitehead, 2004).

> 3. The cover element comprises fasteners that enable fixation of the end edges on the open tank or container.
> [. . .]
>
> **Both on the basis of the patent claims and the grant file the court found** that the **fourth feature**, and the precise positioning of the elastic tie extending from the end edges near the longitudinal centre of the cover element, is an **essential feature** of EP ‘804.

We have now arrived at the judgment of direct infringement. In doctrine it is sometimes said that the process of determining this infringement involves ‘reading’ a claim onto the allegedly infringing technology or process at stake.[173] If all the essential elements of the claim are found in the relevant technology, the claim can be considered to ‘read on’ the technology. If an essential element of the claim is missing in the technology, the claim does not directly ‘read on’ the technology and does not constitute a direct infringement of the patent. Before this reading can take place the essential features of D’s patent matter first need to be determined. Notice that the way the court proceeds with this determination seems to reiterate the textual layout that A’s attorney provided. The characterizing section of the first patent claim is articulated in three linguistic clauses that all inscribe a separate essential feature of the patent matter. The non-characterizing section is not inscribed. The court’s approach seems to discard D’s articulation of the patent in which all the claim cannot be isolated in separate elements but has to be read as a whole in which all elements co-operate as a solution to a technical problem. But remember that on the basis of the grant file the court managed to fix D’s position in the dispute to the extent that it could no longer argue that the fourth feature was not essential (the first one in the court’s numeration). Drawing all previous lines of argument together the court is able to judge that the feature that an elastic tie runs through the end edges of the cover element is a characteristic of D’s invention. It grounds this demarcation of the invention ‘on the basis of the patent claims and the grant file’.

> **3.4.2.** In the cover element developed by A there is **no elastic tie that extends through the end edges near the longitudinal centre of the cover element**.
>
> **As the drawing above (and the other pieces at hand) demonstrate:**
> – the cover element of A **does not contain one elastic tie, but two elastic ties,**
> – these elastic ties are nowhere connected to each other,

---

[173] Blenko Jr., 1990.

- these two elastic ties run through the side / longitudinal edges of the cover element as (cf. the elements expounded above from the grant file) **already existed in the prior art** (and are not claimed as invention in the header of the patent claim),
- **no elastic tie runs through** the beginning or **end edges** of the cover element,
- the **elastic ties in no way traverse** the beginning or end edges element of the cover element near the **longitudinal centre** thereof.

> **Since an essential characteristic of the main claim of the EP '804 patent is missing, it needs already to be decided that A commits no direct infringement of D's patent No. EP 1405804.**

Until now the dispute has concentrated mainly on the demarcation of D's invention. Infringement questions however, are clearly relational questions between two devices. After extracting the essential features of D's patent matter from the main patent claim, this claim will have to be read on A's tarpaulin device in order to determine whether all these essential features can be found. How can a patent be read on a technology however? This is only possible when the supposedly infringing technology is also transformed into a text. But how is this done? The court provides two indications: based on the 'drawing above' (Figure 4.3) and based on 'the other pieces at hand'. It is not unlikely that amongst these other pieces the scale model of A's device has played an important role, considering the fact that there are barely any other pieces in the bundles that provide evidential grounds that 'demonstrate' what this device 'contains'. The drawing and the model serve as the media through which A's tarpaulin device can be translated into an articulated text and inscribed in the judgment. Maybe we should speak of 'enlistment' rather than 'inscription' in the judgment, since the device is already textually laid out in a highly detailed list of separate features. What made the court arrive at this specific list? At the beginning of the paragraph the court provides the orienting preposition for its reading of A's device. There it inscribes the feature 4 that it distinguished in D's patent matter.

> the elastic tie – extends throughout the end edges – near the longitudinal centre of the cover element.

I have added hyphens between the phrases of the sentence in order to foreground the grammatical joints that the court will 'read' on A's device. We could say that each phrase of this sentence works as an articulator that translates (the drawing and model of) A's device into a separate textual feature. When we also formulate the resulting list of features as a sentence (but retain the '-' bullets), A's tarpaulin contains:

> not one but two elastic ties – that are unconnected – and do not extend throughout the end edges – and do not extend near the longitudinal centre of the cover element.

Each feature of the list constitutes a cut ('not', 'un') of identity with feature 4 of D's patent matter. D's patent claim thus does not read on A's tarpaulin with regard to one of the characteristics of its invention and does not constitute a direct infringement.

> **3.4.3.** Contrary to what D asserts, in the opinion of the court there can also be **no infringement by equivalent**.
>
> The claims, description and drawings, as well as the grant file of EP '804 show that the function of the elastic tie that runs through the end edges near the longitudinal end edges, is that the side edges are **automatically** folded thanks to the position, trajectory and tension of the elastic tie along the length of the cover element.
>
> Thus the description of the EP '804 patent [0060] and [0061] mentions that:
> [0060] The position, trajectory and tension of elastic tie 18 in the length of the covering element 1 **permits** edges 9, 10 to **fold automatically** in the direction of the inside of the said element 1.
> [. . .]
>
> The grant file shows that in his communications of 16 Jan. 2006, the EPO researcher stated that:
> 'The fact that the tie extends through the end edges near the longitudinal centre, does seem an essential characteristic for the **realization** of the pressing down like drawing 4 demonstrates.'
> [. . .]
> In the **opinion** of the court file the **pieces at hand show** that the **function** of the elastic tie of turning the side edges as described in EP '804 (and grant file thereof) is **only realized** by the tie running through the end edges near the longitudinal edges centre and **will not be realized if** the tie only runs through the side edges, because in that case the edges **cannot be automatically folded** over as described in the patent.

The court passes judgment on the claim of infringement by equivalent straight away. D's statements and pleadings are reduced to mere assertions that have not been convincing in the opinion of the court. The court starts by demarcating what the function of D's invention 'is' and then proceeds to work out how it is 'realized' in D's tarpaulin. It then works out whether an equivalent function is realized by A's tarpaulin: the automatic folding of the side edges of the cover element. 'Automatic' is thus clearly affirmed as a part of the functional essence of the invention. The court grounds its judgment on the claims, description and drawings of the patent file as on the grant file. This is a rather large and indefinite reservoir, but when we follow the line of argumentation we see that the court has specifically singled out two documents: the descriptions of the patent and the communications of the EPO researcher. It is noteworthy that the court grounds its judgment on the same two pieces of evidence that A's attorney stitched to the patent matter. This is a remarkable selection considering that none is intrinsic to the patent claim. The first is ex-plicative of the claim and the second is ex-trinsic to the whole patent file. The patent claim is itself not separately inscribed here. By this judgment the court implicates the proposition advanced by A's attorney that the function of automatic folding of D's invention has to also be sought in the patent descriptions, since the term 'automatic' occurs nowhere else.

Apart from the extraction of the function from the patent file and the grant file, the court also deals with how this function is realized. It affirms A's proposition that the operation of the elastic tie that runs through the end edges of the cover element, constitutes a line of realization for the function of automatically folding. It also enforces this position by inversing the argument and stating that the function of D's invention 'is not realized' where the elastic tie only runs through the side edges; this hypothetical case is of course already anticipating A's tarpaulin.[174]

> As expounded above, the cover element / **tarpaulin of A** contains elastic ties that are located in each of the side edges of the cover element and do not extend until near the longitudinal centre of the end edge. As the EPO researcher pointed out, **this version does not allow turning the edges in the direction of the interior of the tarpaulin**.
> [. . .]
>
> Through the use – in the product of A – of two separate elastic ties, which are arranged in different ways in the cover element, it is **impossible that the cover element '*folds towards the middle by itself through traction*'.**
>
> At removal the cover element of A must be completely detached from the container, put on the ground and subsequently **folded manually**, in which the side edges are turned upwards.
> [. . .]

---

174 The court bases this 'opinion' on 'the pieces at hand'. The only piece of evidence explicitly mentioned is the communication of the EPO expert from the grant file. Nevertheless, the scale model can also not be excluded here. When I was first introduced to the dispute one of the judges demonstrated to me how the different devices worked by pulling the different elastic ties of the models in order to observe what kind of folding took place in each device.

> **It must therefore be concluded that the cover elements/tarpaulins of A do not realize the function of the invention of D thus do not necessarily offer the same technical function nor the same technical effect** and cannot constitute an infringement by equivalent.
>
> The patent EP 1405804 B1, as granted to D, is clear and **cannot be interpreted in the sense that a scope of protection is given to it that was not intended**.
>
> **3.5.1.** In these circumstances, A's claim of the legal declaration of non-infringement of the European patent with number EP 1405804 B1 in the territory of Belgium, has to be declared **grounded**.

The court started by extracting the functional being of D's patent matter from the patent and grant file. In this way it grounded the immaterial invention. It then proceeded by determining how this immaterial function was realized by the material configuration of features of D's tarpaulin. Here the court will judge whether this same function is also realized by A's tarpaulin. The court starts its analysis by using their textual translation of A's tarpaulin into a list of features as a basis for extracting the functional valence of this device. It is interesting to see that the court uses the analysis of the EPO researcher, which was written in the process of granting D's patent, for the (negative) extraction of the function of A's tarpaulin. Above we have seen how this researcher stated that the function of D's invention would not be permitted where the elastic tie only runs through the side edges of the cover element. Well, this case has now arrived. A's tarpaulin contains two separate elastic ties that only extend through the side edges. 'This version does not allow' the cover element to fold 'by itself' through the traction of the elastic tie. Such automatic folding is in fact 'impossible'. The cover element has to be folded manually. The court cuts off the proposition offered by D's attorney in which the point of initiation of the act of folding and the number of involved elastic elements would become irrelevant. The patent 'cannot be interpreted' in this way, since this would give it a too broad scope that was 'not intended'. On the basis of its own analysis of the texts of the patent file the court is thus able to understand what the patent intended to protect more authoritatively than the very patent holder who applied for it![175] Once a patent application is

---

[175] This could be called a Schleiermacherian position on hermeneutics in which the interpreter is able to know better than the author what was intended by the text. This 'better' however has to here be substituted by 'more authoritatively' which sends the (permissions of) interpretation off towards a more properly legal hermeneutics. This intention also has nothing to do with Schleiermacherian psychology, it is rather a *filed and conditioned intention*.

filed at the EPO, its files and the documents they contain will become the foothold or point of grasp for the attribution of the intention behind an invention, which has the authoritative power to substitute the intentional account by the author/inventor him or herself. According to the court the patent is 'clear' on what it intends and on the functional being of D's immaterial invention. On the basis of the preceding the court arrives at the judgment that the material configuration of elements in A's tarpaulin does 'not realize the function of the invention of D'. The two elastic ties do not constitute lines of realization for the function of automatic folding. There is no functional equivalence between the two tarpaulin devices and therefore A's claim that there is no infringement is declared grounded.

***

The Legal Concept of Ideas (Reprise: Box-Filling Machine Patent)

. . . So what happened to the case that started our turn to legal practice at the law firm? Has it finally also arrived at judgment? Well, as it turns out the whole process of the dispute has in our absence been extensively prolonged. Preliminary judgments on additional expertise have been pronounced, expert reports have been written, a new round of statements has taken place and a new hearing has been conducted. Years after the start of our study, a judgment on the grounds of the dispute was finally passed. In an exemplary way these proceedings show the ravages of legal disputes and some of the difficulties involved in approaching them in empirical research. As a closure to this chapter we will turn to this judgment. To shortly recapitulate the stakes: TWC claimed to be the co-inventor of a patent application filed by Gortec on the basis of contributing to the improvement of the Filomat machine for automatically filling boxes by providing the inventive input of a stapler and a change of the order of the stations of the machine. The court arrives at the following judgment on these propositions.

> **JUDGMENT OF THE CLAIMS OF TWC**
>
> [. . .]
> In the judgment of the court TWC does not prove that these elements are her own invention or that she has provided any creative and inventive contribution.
>
> ***Concerning the stapler:**
>
> The use of a stapler claimed by TWC can **by itself** not constitute an invention. A stapler – and its use **together with another machine** – has long been **state of the art**.

> Thus the use of a stapler cannot possibly be the **matter of a patent application** and at most constitutes an **embodiment variant** of the invention of Gortec and this use of the stapler is by itself neither **new nor inventive.** [. . .] The stapler is **not claimed** in any claim of European patent application no. YE672573.

TWC's proposition of being the co-owner of the patent application filed by Gortec was based on the claim that the inscribed invention incorporates the use of a stapler and a station order change, which constitute TWC's input. With regard to the use of the stapler, the court in a twofold way finds TWC's legal proposition empty of any matter and does not grant it legal passage. First, since the stapler does not occur in the words of the claims of Gortec's patent document, the court considers it not to be a *matter of the actual patent application*. This implies that TWC's proposition is a claim without matter, which is one of the greatest infelicities that can befall a legal performative. The legal speech act of claiming does not succeed due to a breakdown of reference, because the object that TWC's proposition mentions does not exist, that is, it does not exist in the sentences of the patent claims. It is a *res nulla* that is unable to ground the proposed invention. TWC has thus not succeeded in providing an object that co-responds to its claimed proposition and as such this proposition is devoid of the capacity to carry any further legal effects.[176]

Second, the court further states that the use of the stapler can also not be the *matter of any possible patent application*, not now and not in the future. The lawyers of Gortec have in the meantime successfully involved a patent attorney who has conducted research on existing inventions that use staplers and has come up with two previous patent documents that claim the use of a stapler. On the basis of these facts the court disqualifies both the use of the 'stapler by itself' and of the 'stapler in relation to' Gortec's machine in which it has a certain technical function as 'not new', but rather as belonging to the 'state of the art'. As such a matter of fact, this matter of dispute cannot constitute an 'invention' and is disqualified as a legal object of patent law.

> The **facts** show that the **idea** to use a stapler in the fourth station of the Filomat **emanated from** Gortec – Mr Hesse – during the first visit at TWC on 15 October 2004 and that the **carrying out of this idea** has been exclusively **elaborated and developed by** Gortec.

---

[176] One could still ask here about the occurrence of the stapler in the images and descriptions of the patent application. Unfortunately, the court does not provide a motivation for this bypass (apart perhaps from setting up the category of 'embodiment variant').

> The facts and the communications between parties show that Mr Graanhof of TWC has explicitly asked for explication about the development of the **concept** (see e-mail of Mr Graanhof on 18 January 2005 and the reply by Gortec on 22 January 2005).

In the previous chapter, we have studied the ways in which both TWC and Gortec tried to transform the question of who had the idea to use the stapler in the Filomat machine into a matter of fact. They did so by the attachment of several pieces of evidence like communications and contracts and by grammatically marking possessive pronouns in these documents, all in order to ground the relation between the creator and the idea and to claim its ownership. The court arrives at its judgment by unfolding an argument in two steps about the legal concept of the 'idea' and its relation to the concept of the 'concept'. First, it authoritatively turns the myth of origins of ideas into a factual history of origination. 'The facts show that the idea to use a stapler' was Gortec's. The idea 'emanated' from Gortec's engineer Mr Hesse during the hotly disputed meeting at the site of TWC in which he saw the stapler in use in one of TWC's machines. It is not entirely clear why the court considers this emanation to be demonstrated as a fact and on the basis of which pieces of evidence. The point might actually be that this whole question does not even legally matter all that much. In the subsequent judgment on the station order change, we will see that the court raises the legal condition according to which ideas are not the appropriate legal object of patent law. Instead the court distinguishes this simple idea from an idea which is 'elaborated and developed'. Borrowing from the e-mail correspondences between TWC and Gortec, it uses the term 'concept' for such a (technical) development of an idea (remember the 'TWC Concept'). The court thus qualifies the use of the stapler as an idea, as something simple that is not worked out but that emanates from its originator, and as a concept as something more complex that has to be elaborated and developed by its inventor. Interestingly, through such elaboration and development the idea becomes '*carried out*' (*uitvoeren*) and we can interpret this in different senses. By the labour of 'developing' the idea, it is carried out from the public domain of unprotectable ideas into the regime of patent protection for concepts; in this way the idea becomes 'exported' from the property domain of TWC and carried into that of Gortec.[177] Furthermore, the court later argues that due

---

[177] We still need to understand why the court finds that the use of the stapler in the Filomat machine is a concept of Gortec. Why does it prefer the possessive pronouns in Gortec's pieces of evidence to those by TWC? It seems the court does not affix the stapler concept to a piece of possessive evidence to prove the relation

to '*the permission granted by TWC for the machine to be* ***viewed*** *by several potential clients of Gortec (in May 2005 and March 2006) [. . .] TWC hereby also* ***eliminates any possibility to file a patent application****, since her "invention" could not have been considered* ***new*** *in these circumstances.*' This gives a third meaning to the notion of carrying out. Mrs Blanchard had argued that the fact Gortec's engineer Mr Hesse had visited TWC's site and noticed how TWC made use of staplers in machines, implied that the use of a stapler could not qualify as an idea, since 'one cannot see an idea!' The court apparently not only not follows this proposed concept of the idea as an abstract imperceptible entity, but assigns legal consequences to the fact that TWC has let it be viewed by Gortec and third parties: it has hereby 'eliminated any possibility to file a patent application'! By opening up its private site of ideas and concepts to external visitors, TWC has also allowed these to be carried out from its 'secret know-how' into 'public' knowledge. As such they qualify as not-new in terms of patent vocabulary.

> ***Concerning the station order change**
>
> The station order change proposed by TWC also cannot be an **invention** susceptible for patent protection, but is **merely an idea that is not susceptible for (patent) protection** and of which the **realization was merely an embodiment variant** of the Filomat machine invented by Mr Tremblay for Gortec in 2004.

The court continues with an elaboration of the concept of the idea with regard to TWC's proposition of the station order change. In its judgment it seems to pursue a line of argument that passes over the stepping stones that Gortec's attorney Mr Leerbeek had put into place in his plea. Whereas, above, the question of who had the idea of using the stapler was disputed (attested by the court's phrase 'the use of a stapler *claimed* by TWC'), the originator of the idea of using the station order change is accepted by the court as a matter of fact ('the station order change *proposed* by TWC'). It is however not a fact that matters. The idea becomes disqualified by a series of norms: ideal, technical and real.

First, the station order change is disqualified as an idea in the sense of patent law. The court states that the station order change 'is merely an idea that is not susceptible for (patent) protection' and thus cannot qualify as an invention. The station order change is not the appropriate object for patent protection, but a *res inappropriata* in the regime of intellectual rights that can be used by everyone but not claimed by anyone. This

of origination ('our concept', the 'TWC Concept'), but rather mobilizes a piece of confessive evidence to cut this relation for TWC ('your concept').

qualification enables the court to take a crucial next step within a strange axiology of immaterial gravitation at work here. Both TWC and Gortec have tried to propose and install different centres of incorporeal gravity with a certain identity – the TWC Concept and the SPEEDEC invention respectively – in relation to which the technical proposal of their opponent would constitute a mere corporeal variation. Since the court qualifies TWC's concept as an idea that is unprotected, it makes this centre of immaterial gravity implode and thus opens up different avenues in which this idea might itself become 'realized'. This makes it possible to assimilate this idea as an 'embodiment variant' of Gortec's original invention. This is the second time that the court mobilizes this category. The court follows Gortec's proposition and totally reverses TWC's argument. Instead of Gortec's Filomat machine constituting a '*modified form*' of the station order change proposed by TWC, this station order change is actually itself an '*embodiment variant*' of Gortec's earlier patented invention. The court here allows a quite ample space in which Gortec's invention can expand and assimilate other ideas. These ideas will not come to constitute the essence of the invention, but will become a variable part of it as a direction in which the invention is allowed to be realized.[178]

> The station order change proposed by TWC, consisting of exchanging stations 2 and 3 of the machine compared to the original order, could not **possibly have improved the energy efficiency** [. . .]
>
> TWC in no way demonstrates that the station order change requested by her – but not applied by Gortec – forms an '**inventive** input' and that TWC has thus provided any creative contribution.

Second, the station order change is disqualified as a bad idea according to a technological norm with important legal consequences. The stage shift 'could not possibly have improved the energy efficiency'. This improvement of the energy efficiency was one of the main technical problems for which the creation of a new Filomat machine was to be a solution and constitutes an important legal requirement for the patentability condition of 'inventive step'. Since TWC's proposal does not decrease the energy

---

[178] Unfortunately, the court again does not provide reasons for selecting Gortec's stepping-stones. It merely selects them (and does not so much 'address the arguments of the unsuccessful party'), but does not indicate why the station order change is an idea in the sense of intellectual rights (why is it not sufficiently elaborated?) and why this idea is an embodiment variant of Gortec's original patented SPEEDEC invention.

consumption of the machine by improving its box-filling efficiency, it does not offer the court a stepping stone for qualifying the station order change as inventive.

> Moreover, Gortec has **never applied** the station order change requested by TWC in the Filomat, neither for TWC, nor for any other customer. After all, the present order of the Filomat **essentially merely consists of three instead of five phases**. This order thus does **not correspond** in any way with the proposal by TWC but is the result of Gortec's own development.

Third, the station order change is disqualified according to the facts of reality. During her plea in court Mrs Blanchard objected to Mr Leerbeek's point that 'If it was such a bad idea, why have they taken it over in the description of the patent?' Now it seems that this is what the court denies. It states that Gortec 'has never applied' the station order change. It is crucial to understand what the court here means by 'application'. It takes two steps that can be viewed as answers to the questions: '*In what* has the station order change never been applied?' and '*As what* has the station order change never been applied?' We will start with the former question. Remember that Mrs Blanchard argued that it is irrelevant whether Gortec actually applied this idea in practice. At stake was not some actual machine of cogs and wheels located on a site or 'sold in reality', but the paper machine inscribed in Gortec's patent application. Now, the court states that Gortec never applied the station order change for TWC or any customers. The court here however refers to 'real' machines that were actually sold by Gortec. The court also speaks about the 'present order of the Filomat'. 'Filomat' is the commercial name of the box-filling machine as it is sold on Gortec's website, not a name for the machine as inscribed in its patent application and which is the matter of dispute. Now, just like with the stapler, the court again does not respond to Mrs Blanchard's statement that the station order change is part of the descriptions of the patent application. To the contrary, later in the judgment the court will even state that '***not a trace can be found*** *of the alleged "secret know-how" of TWC in the international and European patent applications of Gortec.*' No trace of TWC's input can be found in Gortec's patent application! Not even the slightest starting point on which to begin grafting an iteration of a possible copy.

We will now turn to the question '*As what* has the station order change never been applied?' leading the court into the theme of identity and difference. Remember that TWC endeavoured to construct an identity between the machine according to the 'TWC Concept' and Gortec's 'Filomat' machine, based on the conceptual order of stages (regardless of how many machines actually embodied these stages). Gortec tried to construct a 'total difference' between these machines based on the different number of stages incorporated in the Filomat (and the fact that two stages were externalized in another machine). The court selects Gortec's argument when it states that 'the Filomat essentially merely consists of three instead of five phases'. The court thus constructs the essence of the Filomat machine to consist in its number of phases (3) rather than its conceptual order. With this identity demarcated it can now identify a numerical difference with TWC's concept: $3 \neq 5$. It thus finds that there is no correspondence with TWC's proposal.

There is also another sense in which we can conceive of this notion of *correspondence* evoked by the court, by turning to the radical empiricist sense in which it was used by William James (James, 2003). In James, correspondence would not consist in a great jump over some vertical transcendental gap between the incorporeal idea of TWC's station order change and the corporeal object of Gortec's machine. Instead this correspondence would rather consist of a long horizontal series of intra-empirical steps of the extensive legal process from its initiating proposition in the summons to its legal termination in the operatives of judgment. Only when all the carefully riveted links in this chain manage to eventually hold convincingly can some-thing first become retroactively constituted as the original idea or concept in the mind of the inventor and something else as its copy. In our case, the machine inscribed in the judgment could then be said to legally correspond to the idea claimed by TWC, and the court could be said to *co-respond* to TWC's *proposition*. This is however not the case in this judgment. TWC's idea and Gortec's machine do not successfully arrive together at the same *position* originally *pro*posed by TWC, they do not arrive 'con-terminously' in James' words, and the co-respondence fails. TWC's cause is not performatively carried into its proposed legal effects.

To the contrary, things get much worse for TWC. The counter strand proposed by Gortec's lawyers on TWC's hidden agenda has become a full-blown pathway. TWC was accused of abusing the whole legal process, since its claim of joint property of the patent application only served as an appearance and had to legitimize its unauthorized acts of reproducing Gortec's invention. During the absence of the researcher this hidden agenda has been researched by an expert appointed by the court, who has written an extensive report about these allegedly copied machines located at two different sites. After these preliminary prolongations the court passes its judgment:

ON THESE GROUNDS, THE COURT

Judging after trial,

[. . .]
Declares the claim of TWC against Gortec admissible but rejects it as ungrounded in all its parts.

Declares the counter claim by Gortec against TWC admissible and grounded as follows:

Legally declares that Gortec alone is entitled to the European patent application no. YE672573.

[. . .]
Sentences TWC to the provisional payment to Gortec of **FIVEHUNDREDTHIRTYTHOUSANDANDTWO euro (530,002 EUR).**

[. . .]
Charges TWC, represented by its delegated director or directors, to take a proceedings decisive oath [*gedingbeslissende eed*] in the presence of Gortec, with regard to the number of machines made by NV Libra Systems commissioned by TWC in order to estimate the damages for Gortec.

The legal dispute finds its termination in these operatives of judgment. The matter of TWC's proposition has not survived its proceeding on the grounds of judgment and is declared ungrounded. Its lawyers have not managed to fix all the holes in the extensive grid of connected tubes that has been constructed and the legal fluids finally seep away. To the contrary, Gortec's lawyers turn out to have done good detective work by investigating and assembling the whole network of dispersed factual elements from many different sources and places in which they eventually encountered two crime scenes with the two *machinae delicti.* The accounts produced about these have convinced the judges and made them correspond to Gortec's propositions. The court contracts the dispute along several of the operatives Gortec proposed and judgment is hereby enacted. Gortec is declared the sole heir to the title of owner of the patent application on the box-filling machine. TWC is consequently sentenced to pay huge sums of money for the infringement of this patent by commissioning the unauthorized construction of two copies of this invention by NV Libra Systems. Furthermore, the directors of TWC are even summoned to appear in court in order to take an oath in the presence of Gortec.

Whereas the researcher's empirical job is for now done with the termination of the matter of legal dispute in this judgment, Mrs Blanchard has immediately selected the unconvincing points in the document and lodged a claim in appeal against this judgment at the Court of Appeal. These two subsequent legal contractions of the dispute are so close to each other in its life-time, one constituting its little death and the other its resurrection and rebirth. A whole new proceeding is reinitiated through this appeal, with whole new lines of work to be done and whole new corpulent extensions to be unfolded into a future once again indeterminate . . .

5. Conclusion: immaterial performances in the life of the legal dispute

What is the relation of [. . .] 'the facts' to the brute raw events which happened long before? What is left in men's minds as to those raw events has been canvassed, more or less skillfully, by two lawyers. But canvassed through the screen of what they consider ***legally*** *relevant, and of what each considered legally relevant to win the case. It has been screened again in the trial court through the rules of about what evidence can be admitted. [. . .] Finally, with the decision made, the judge has sifted through these 'facts' again, and picked a few which he puts forward as essential – and whose legal bearing he then proceeds to pronounce.*

(Llewellyn, 2008, p. 34)

We can now draw the different lines of investigation in this book together to address how immateriality is legally constituted in intellectual rights (the first research question). The first chapter tried to understand how immateriality of intellectual rights was grounded by the theories of immaterial goods. We saw how the incorporeal and its distinction from the corporeal were merely postulated *a priori* as legal axiology for disputes, or to the contrary, how concepts like 'idea', 'creation' or 'work' used in legal discourse, were considered sufficiently explained by recourse to informational, political, economic or even romantic processes. Rather we set out to understand them as legal concepts and to study the practices of intellectual rights in which they became deployed. This 'turn' of approach has yielded its results. These concepts are tightly interwoven with practical happenings and crucially related to the dimension of the problematic that is at the heart of legal practice. Legal practices of intellectual rights are the site of the conflictive encounter that will eventually lead to the constitution of immateriality. We can here speak of the *res* or 'thing' as a primordial gathering in conflictive relations that are productive of a becoming and are a 'cause' for the action of practitioners. This is not an external object for a legal subject, but, before anything else, the matter of dispute that gathers its protagonists within the same common interiority. These concepts of a *res* and a *causa* bring things back to their legal belongings and can be

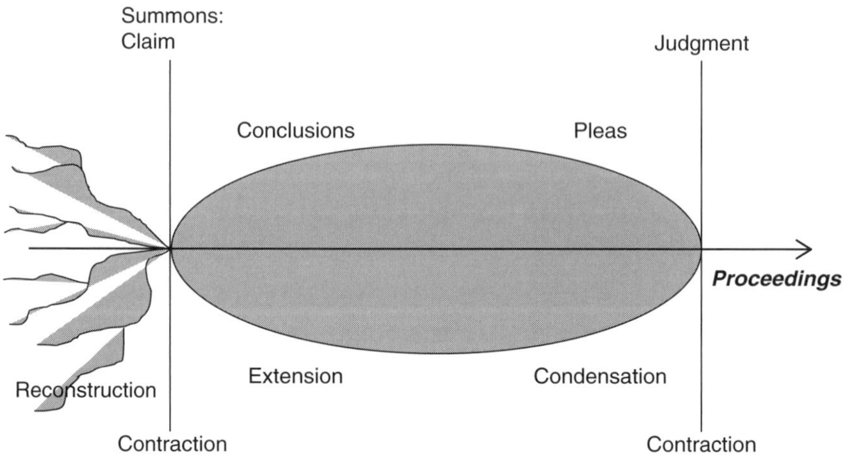

Figure 5.1 Life of the legal dispute

integrated into the core of our concept of legal practice. We can speak here of a conflict-based approach to legal issues (van Dijk, 2011). The proceeding of this *res iuris* is a singular event that has the power to transform and constitute both the legal objects and the legal subjects involved.

Approaching the practices of law in the nearness of their peculiarities is not a straightforward matter. There is a certain implicative traction to the approach to disputes in legal practices. Disputes are events that tend to draw all accounts and meta-theories on what they are about into their very dynamics. These impede the researcher in simply assuming an impartial stance as a fly on the wall and writing a neutral account of things. Furthermore, the approach of the researcher can itself become constrained by the same conditions (disclosure, access and monadic visibilities) that constrain the dispute protagonists studied. The researcher will have to take account of these constraints that a matter of dispute poses for legal practitioners and of what enables them to legally succeed in constituting the immaterial in the practices of intellectual rights.

The previous two chapters have mapped the proceedings of the matter of dispute and its two little deaths that constitute the rhythm of its legal life (see Figure 5.1).[1] This life is characterized by double parallel dynamics: the dynamics of contraction and extension of the lawsuit on the level of the event

[1] For a more thorough extraction of the contours of 'the life and deaths of a dispute', see van Dijk, 2015.

of the proceeding dispute, and the dynamics of enfolding and unfolding on the intersecting level of the process of the circulating case folder.

At first, the dispute has to be retraced and reassembled by the attorneys of the claimant from the institutional network of memories and documents throughout which it has become dispersed and is contracted into the points of dispute that will come to determine its aboutness. This contraction of the many heterogeneous elements of the dispute finds its most intense form in the performative claims proposed in the summons document. Through the typical legal act of qualification the matter of the claim is translated according to the conceptual vocabulary of a certain legal regime like copyright, patent or trademark law, which assigns the matter of dispute a belonging and orientation. In the antagonist dynamics that ensue, the matter of dispute can become disqualified or counterqualified by the attorneys of the other party. From here on, things complexify rapidly through the legal work of animation, detection and plumbing, mediated by a host of things, procedures, techniques and architectures that enable the organization and circulation of the file in law firms and courts, and that enable the jurists to speak legally about the dispute. The lawsuit readily extends in a series of ap-plications throughout the 'statement' documents, in which the matter of dispute becomes mutually stitched to or cut from pieces of evidence, and aligned with or disconnected from conditions of proceeding and legal authorities. After this the dispute becomes condensed throughout the pleas in court, which provide certain piloting directions for passing through the assembled corpus of the case. Eventually the dispute will find a second differential contraction through the pointillist acts of judgment according to a linear focus. Judgment can achieve such a contraction through its own *modus operandi* that consist of aligning a succession of operators, operations and operatives. First the judgment becomes organized according to a series of operators (e.g. scroll number, repertory number, etc.) that both link the judgment document to the case file and install it within the order of administration as the point of grasp for further acts of organization. The dispute subsequently becomes further compacted through a series of operations preceding judgment, which transform the dynamics of proceedings of the dispute into vectors of consideration, admission and conviction that will impinge on the minds of the judges during the processes of deliberation. Many of these operations will have to pass certain 'requisite procession points' that condition the felicity of the act of judgment itself (e.g. the contents that the verdict has to inscribe to avoid being declared null or void itself). Finally, the dispute becomes contracted by a series of operatives that enact the judgment through a series of performative acts that carry a preceding cause or *causa* into its legal effects.

When the work of enfolding and organization is done well and the preliminary thresholds have been crossed successfully, the dispute can gradually undergo a spatio-temporal and actorial shift from the level of legal process to the level of the grounds of creation. To put it in dramatic terms, this is a change in focus from the work of executive production management by the secretaries and registrars, the mutually divergent work of script writing, stage building, highlighting, casting and choreography by the two attorneys and the work of editing by the judges, to the acts of the protagonists who have been drawn into the antagonistic dance of the dispute. Through this work the dispute will be moved away from the organizational and procedural spaces like the filing construction sites at the law firm, the spaces of enlistment at the registry and the monadic visibilities of the court and is made to proceed throughout a variety of different situations through which it gradually gains qualities.

The appearance of the matter of dispute becomes more and more *evident* by being shifted in and out of: the desk, the shop, the market and even virtual worlds in cases of trademarks; the indexical spaces within patent files and the machine rooms and meeting rooms at techno-industrial sites in cases of patents; and the axial space of free, forced and barred creative moves for events of origination in the cases of copyright and community designs. The matter of dispute becomes more and more *conditioned* through its passage along the paths of judgment reached in other past disputes (jurisprudential characters); the preparatory considerations and legal reference checks of legislative processes, and the pre-articulated webs of authorization proposed in legal doctrine. Within these situations the matter of dispute is staged in relation to a plethora of actors, figures and things in ways that allow the protagonists to assume certain (op)positions on it. In each legal regime different fictive persona can be introduced that install certain presupposed *observation positions* on the intellectual nature of these disputed matters. As such we encountered the informed user of community designs, the (mind of the) average consumer of trademarks and the expert person skilled in the arts of patents. The jurists endeavour to fix and stabilize points of view on the dispute by a series of tools and techniques like juxtaposition and depiction, or more regime-specific ones like indexation, interpretation and scaling in patents; reference, presumption and market research in trademarks; and sampling and declaration in copyright and community designs.

In the whole *antagonistic dance of forms* that ensues, the immateriality of the matter of dispute becomes hereby gradually composed along certain themes as intellectual formation, identity and difference, essence and accident, and function and realization. The matter of dispute is finally slowed down and positioned as an *immaterial object* of intellectual rights on the selected legal path of strong intensive points. Furthermore, throughout these series of performations the protagonists drawn into this conflict gradually become *legally subjectified*, by being affixed, disaffixed or re-affixed to its disputed matter along themes of origination. On this basis they can retroactively be appointed or disappointed as its author or inventor. Within this specific *theatre of legal operations* crucial conceptual questions like 'What is an idea?', 'What is a work?', 'What is an invention?' and 'What is a sign?', which philosophy once considered as its own, can become posed, dramatized as disputed stakes and answered through these dynamic *immaterial performances* with their peculiar effects. As legal concepts, they are operationalized and grounded on the erected stages of immateriality of these intellectual rights regimes.[2] What ideas, works inventions and signs essentially are as immaterial entities is thus dependent on these constitutive trajectories within legal practices. As we have seen, these trajectories are quite different for each of the regimes of intellectual rights – copyright, patent, trademark, community designs – due to the deployment of different concepts, techniques and figures.

All these observations have to be related back to the theoretical positions on intellectual rights analyzed in the first chapter. This book started by sketching the role of intellectual rights in the context of emerging technologies in the information society, their convergence in a single paradigm of engineering of abstract intangible information in different material media, and the docking of this frame with the discourse on intellectual property in which the immaterial objects eventually became informational goods, easily communicated and transferred to other material media. This study has tried to show that no-thing can legally be designated as a material embodiment of an immaterial object *without a problem*. It is this dimension of the problematic at the heart of legal practice that provides the site where these distinctions can first be made and where the material and immaterial are first mutually constituted.

In the first chapter, we saw how Troller framed the whole 'legal game

---

[2] Where Deleuze argued that 'What is?' definitions do not produce interesting philosophy and that philosophy rather needs dramatization, legal processes actually manage to dramatize such 'What is?' questions. The dynamics of legal practices of intellectual rights especially resonate with Deleuze's 'method of dramatization' of ideas, in which an idea is only positively determinable by a casuistry of spatiotemporal dynamisms, which: 1) create particular spaces and times, 2) provide specification rules for concepts, 3) determine qualitative and quantitative differentiations through internal 'qualification' and external 'organization', 4) entail or designate a subject, 5) constitute a special theatre that enables the determination of each concept, 6) express ideas through this dramatization of concepts (Deleuze, 2004b).

of rights and claims' in disputes, extensively studied in Chapter 3, in terms of fixed points on the doctrinal axiology of legal objectivity and subjectivity. This framing is a secondary imposition and a purification of the conflict dynamics. The turn to the practices within the law firm and the court has shown the importance of following the legal proceeding of the matter of dispute in conflicts of intellectual rights. Here the fabric of the lawsuit grows from the middle along tentative lines of proposition towards its edges. Only on the basis of these lines of movement does it become possible to assign co-ordinates to the so-called 'fixed points' of legal theory. Something similar can be said with regard to the distinction according to the axis of corporeality and incorporeality. We have seen how a turn to legal practices revealed a complex heterogeneous quilting to the matter of dispute in the legal constitution of the immaterial. In the law firm, we have tracked how extralegal matters of dispute slowly became legally constituted as ideas, concepts, inventions, works and signs through ceaseless operations and procedures of proof, qualification, authorization and ap-plication, mediated by a range of different instruments like office tools, computers, media of communication, books and documents. Additionally, in court we saw how the identity or essence of the eventual intellectual object was further demarcated: by a whole range of tools like (scale) models, specimen models, drawings, tables of juxtaposition, declarations, market research, grammatical markers and other semiotic and hermeneutic techniques; by a plethora of fictive, virtual and real characters that constituted points of view on the dispute like (the minds of) the public, the expert, the creator and the witness; and by the evocations and alignment of legal sources authorizing certain approaches and interpretations.

Primordially however, within these complex processes the matter of dispute is not a corporeal object, nor an immaterial entity, but a gathering in conflict of a complex web of relations that make these secondary determinations possible in the first place. The immaterialities in intellectual rights are *com-positions*: they can only be stated when posed together with many aligned points that come to provide the grounded positions in a certain dispute. Only then can something be first constituted as an immaterial object or 'its' material embodiment. In this sense, we could provide the following answer to our first research question: the immaterial is a compositional result, not a fixed starting point.

Troller further stated that the intellectual nature of immaterial goods – their independence from corporeal fixation and use – assures these goods a 'particular power' of unlimited proliferation. The same identical immaterial good can be embodied or represented in many corporeal media at different places and moments according to the authoritative rules for their production.[3] As such they can be indefinitely repeated and communicated. Since they are spatio-tempo-materially independent this process of communication does not affect them and they remain identical throughout. The corporeal thing is a mere medium for the transmission of the self-identical immaterial good. A specific conception of power can be detected in this theoretical framing. This power is not so much 'particular' but actually so 'ubiquitous' that it has become of the most general kind, potentially recognized everywhere and in every-thing, at least in every corporeal object. We have skipped here into a mode of operation that, with Foucault, we can call the 'governmentality' of goods, a position we could not have arrived at through legal tools and concepts. When we instead turn to conflictive legal practices, we will see that the immateriality of a certain thing is not something global, free-floating and pre-given, but the constitution of which is a local achievement of abstraction, always firmly grounded and rooted in *medias res*. This achievement of grounding immateriality does not by itself legitimate a general governmental power over many 'material' settings. Even when the resulting immaterial invention or work is later redistributed to different sites of industrial production, publishing houses, record companies, or merchandise enterprises, this transportation and reproduction can never be taken for granted but has to itself be seen as a part of complex organizational chains that manage to maintain the matter of concern in existence. This shows that there might be a confusion here between immateriality and the 'immutable mobile' character of inscriptions into a stable (paper) format, in which something can be transported without alteration.[4] In this sense, the so-called power and proliferation of immaterial goods Troller alludes to might well be an effect of the great distributional chains of these immutable mobiles.[5]

---

[3] This dimension of power comes out clearly in the WIPO's statements on intellectual property: 'Intellectual property relates to items of information or knowledge, which can be incorporated in tangible objects at the same time in an unlimited number of copies at different locations anywhere in the world. The property is not in those copies but in the information or knowledge reflected in them.' At: http://www.wipo.int/export/sites/www/freepublications/en/intproperty/909/wipo_pub_909.pdf.

[4] Eisenstein described how the printing press and its typographical fixity allowed for reproduction and distribution of quasi-identical texts, mediating the difference between original and copy. The spread of this technology in different European countries further led to the issues (battle of booksellers) on the basis of which the distinctions of material and immaterial were framed in the birth processes of intellectual property.

[5] Although, the invention or work is the result of a whole process instead of its starting point, once constituted there is a certain retro-activity at work in legal

Finally, in following what happens between the moment a particular conflict is first brought into contact with attorneys and the moment it is decided by the judges, the conflict-based approach has also made visible all the things that precede and make possible legal judgment in the first place and which normally remains invisible behind limited images of law in which the act of judgment is conceived as a kind of macroscopic cut with the sword of justice,[6] or in which judged cases are treated as a database of extracted general rules under which future disputes can become subsumed. From this perspective, we have observed how the case file itself comes to be assembled and how these antagonistic processes, initiated and sustained by the constructive micro-actions of attorneys and mediated by a host of things, render the case legally decidable.

judgment according to which the matter of dispute is declared to have always been the immaterial invention or work of the party now declared author or inventor.

6 See Derrida, 1992b and, in a very different way, also Dworkin, 1998 as we will see in Chapter 6.

6. Coda ~ philosophy and law: a conflictive encounter

We have arrived at the point where the transversal movement of legal thought, which was set in motion in this book, diverted in turn and slowed down in the middle, can now be tentatively turned back on to itself. This final part of the book will seek different ways to reengage with the results of the empirical studies in the previous chapters in the light of the practice approach to legal phenomena explored in Chapter 2. By traversing these accounts again from different orientations, it will extract and bring together several movements of thought in a series of philosophical themes raised for separate exploration. These themes are first, the possibilities for the legal becoming of philosophy and the juridical features of thought that might thwart these, and second, its relations to existing philosophies of law in the practice of legal theory and the theories of legal practice. They will constitute a set of codas that will bring this book to a close.

The studies in the previous chapters have been equally concerned with intellectual rights issues and with creating a setting in which a new philosophical approach to law could become possible, which was reflected in the second research question of this book. Both strands were two sides of the same coin. One cannot dissociate an investigation of the nature of fundamental concepts and distinctions of intellectual rights from the specific legal practices in which they are deployed and from the way these practices and concepts are approached by the researcher. The approach matters. In order to understand the way these legal concepts and distinctions come to refer, operate, and produce their effects, we could not limit ourselves to approaches that on the one hand situate themselves so close that they no longer see anything else than pure law, and, in absence of any other constraints, merely chase the discovery of their own dualistic dreams (legal positivism),[1] or, on the other hand, to 'approaches' that assume such a distance that what is specific about law has vanished from sight,

[1] Chapter 1 described how positivistic legal doctrine was caught on its axiological grids of binary oppositions between incorporeal – corporeal, idea – concept, legal subject (author and inventor) – legal object (work and invention).

reduced to remote extra-legal causes like justice and morality (natural law, ethics), the social (sociology of law), finance (law and economics), politics, class, the unconscious (critical legal studies). The former sees no external constraints, whereas the latter can only see external constraints. Instead our investigations have tried to take a turn away from much of this existing legal theory and traversed the middle ground across legal practices in which law is approached through the dispute in which practitioners are prudently engaged and which draws them into its dynamics.

In this way, these investigations have provided what we could call the prolegomena for a different philosophical approach to legal phenomena. In what way however, is this approach philosophical? And how is it related to classical legal theory? These are questions we can no longer postpone. In the introduction to this book, this approach was called an experiment with positions and movements in a philosophical thinking addressed by the legal regime of intellectual rights. Does this approach constitute a philosophy of law? The answer depends on what we mean by the possessive preposition 'of' in 'philosophy *of* law'. Does philosophy take law as an object according to her own mode of proceeding? In such an exercise, philosophy of law becomes a branch of philosophy and the philosopher endeavours to lay down the foundations of law, often in a larger philosophical system. Or is the arrow of possession rather inverted and can lawyers lay claim to a discipline and intellectual territory of their own? Has this philosophy genitivally become theirs?

In the way the term has been used in this book, 'philosophy' does not refer to a disciplinary demarcation of an intellectual territory, but to the movements of thought performed throughout and between the chapters. In this sense it is not so much a philosophy *of* law or a philosophy of intellectual property, as if these were *single objects* of analysis. Instead, it deals with *singular things* (*res*) and tries to envisage the trajectories between different laws and rights; a thinking that has come to pass through legal histories, doctrines and practices in order to raise or take down concepts and explore the legal plane from different directions and orientations. In this sense the orienting question for the investigations is not so much 'What is law?' – the classical question addressed by legal theory – but the question 'How does some-thing become legal?' This question moves us away from statements like 'everything is legal' or 'law is everywhere', pointing instead to the ways in which concrete things (maybe even every-thing) can be transformed into the matter of a legal conflict in which it becomes juridified. This is not a question of a stable or pre-given identity, nor necessarily of the things that have already become legal, but of a becoming in which both the legal and the thing can mutually change.

The same pertains to the relation between philosophy and law.

Throughout their mutual encounter a path of co-becoming might open up, with regard to both the different ways of *becoming-legal of philosophy* and to the ways in which law (or rather legal practice) creatively deploys its own operations and practical theories on questions of philosophical interest (like the nature of ideas and concepts, identity and difference, real and virtual, essence and accident). The relation between these two movements can be illustrated by what Rancière remarked about Deleuzian philosophy with regard to cinema:

> Philosophy is always a discourse between something and something. [. . .] I do not, for example, think that Deleuze has a philosophy of film. He makes a theory of the movement-image and a theory of the time-image. He proposes a metaphysics that passes through the film. [. . .] In speaking of films, Deleuze finds his own concepts [. . .] The images serve him to develop an ontology, a material phenomenology of elements (Rancière, 2005, 142–3, my translation).

Legal practices can inspire philosophical discourse in comparable ways to films.[2] We have seen how disputes in intellectual rights can come to constitute practical exercises on the themes of origination and intellectual formation and on the relationships between identity and difference, essence and accident and function and realization. Furthermore several of the research findings on legal disputes can have interesting effects for other fields. Some philosophical concepts are closely linked to legal practice, like those of 'thing' (res), 'cause', 'performative', 'evidence' and 'process'. Where better to study their mode of deployment than in these legal settings? In this sense it can provide new insights for speech act theory and the study of performatives, for the new 'object-oriented philosophy',[3] and for studies of the judicial features on the plane of science.[4]

The approach sketched here moves between Deleuze's concept of

---

[2] See the hesitation in De Sutter, 2009 on applying these remarks to the legal situation.

[3] See Harman's https://speculativeheresy.wordpress.com/2009/01/06/object-oriented-philosophy/.

[4] Zilsel pointed out how the concept of physical *law* originated in a juridical metaphor (Zilsel, 1942). Shapin and Schaffer showed how Robert Boyle only considered experimental scientific knowledge legitimate when it was observed by several reliable *witnesses*. Poovey and Shapiro more broadly analyzed the legal features in the modern concept of the *fact* (Poovey, 1998; Shapiro, 2000). Francis Bacon modelled many aspects of the *scientific method* on the features of legal procedures (Bacon, 2000) thus affecting the nature of *knowledge* (Foucault, 1991). This interesting topic merits more detailed exploration.

'jurisprudence'[5] and his conception of philosophy as the creation of concepts (Deleuze & Guattari, 1994; Deleuze, 1995).[6] In the second chapter we already signalled a move from (practice) theory that endows its object with a certain identity like Law, towards an approach to law (*ius*) focused on the prudence (*phronesis*) of concernful action (*praxis*) with and among things (*pragmata*) with regard to matters of dispute (*res*). We could use the term 'jurisprudence' for this approach, but we then have to abstain from the way in which the term is often equated with 'legal theory' providing the first principles or general elements of legal systems. Deleuze has stated that 'jurisprudence is the philosophy of law, and deals with singularities, it advances by prolonging singularities' (Deleuze, 1995, p. 153). This legal philosophy is related to the singular event of the dispute before it. It is a position close to case law,[7] but not of databases with general extracted legal rules that can be mobilized in similar cases, but a case law in which the difference of disputes could only be overcome by the prudential work of establishing reasonances attuned to the specific singularity of each. Legal philosophy in turn operates by prolonging and iterating such singularities, but in different directions through the extraction of figures and concepts.

Here, a comparison can also be made with Deleuze and Guattari's conception of philosophy as the creation of concepts on the plane of immanence, but with some important variations. Firstly, the primary creations on the legal plane are not concepts,[8] but what we can call *appointives* and *performations*.[9] Within legal practices the proceeding matter of dispute undergoes a series of performations by which it is gradually carried into

---

[5] For extrapolations of this concept of jurisprudence opposed to that of law in Deleuze, see Lefebvre, 2008; De Sutter, 2009.

[6] What we cannot keep from Deleuzian legal philosophy is his theory of judgment. According to Deleuze, judgment presupposes criteria that pre-exist it for all time, so it can never apprehend what is new in an existing thing. We therefore need 'to have done with judgment' (Deleuze, 1998a, pp. 134–5). A different view opens up when law is approached along its own creativity register, in creating linkages, qualifications, persuasions, and imputations in the composition of judgment. A distinction needs to thus be made between generalized judgment about others *tout court* and a judgment that can make judges hesitate (Stengers, 2006, p. 189).

[7] On this relation of the Deleuzian concept of jurisprudence with case law, see Lefebvre, 2008, pp. 53–9.

[8] Continental civil law is not so much oriented towards the creation of new concepts, but towards the reconstitution of existent concepts (the judge is constrained by legislative concepts and is not at liberty to reinvent these). Such concepts have to be reactivated in each case according to its particular problem. Components extracted from the dispute are here added to these concepts, which make them change on each occasion while often remaining nominally the same.

[9] See the section *The Proposition of Legal Effects* in Chapter 3.2.

its legal effects. This is achieved through several appointives that make a dispute come to a point by contracting its corpus, halting its proceedings (*arrêt*), bringing it to a stand as a legal object and directing it into its consequences.[10] This legal plane itself can be called the *plane of grounding*, which becomes gradually laid out through the incessant work of contraction and aligning of qualifications, pieces, conditions, requisite procession points, operators and operatives into these appointives and performations.[11] This plane and these performations are mediated by the mobilization of different *jurisprudential characters* and *fictive persona* that constitute and fix points of view on the causes at stake. Second, in a philosophy that moves across legal practices, the concepts at stake are often not so much created but rather raised, or transposed, from law to the plane of its own discourse.[12] Other concepts were created or borrowed from philosophy in order to point attention to, or think about particular aspects of legal practices. In this way philosophy continuously intersects law like a wave that describes a to-and-fro movement of approximation and distantiation and from which the legal plane can come to be explored in a piecemeal fashion.[13]

Several elements can be singled out for such an account of law (van Dijk, 2015), which can be horizontally situated along the life-time of the legal dispute depicted in Figure 5.1:

- *matter of dispute* (thing, antagonism)
- *qualification* (claim, translation, legal concept)
- *performation* (cause of action, legal effect)

---

[10] The term 'appointive' is based on the old French verb *apointer*, with its etymological sense of coming to a point (*à point*) about some matter and thereby settling it.

[11] Similar to the way the philosopher condenses several components until they coalesce indivisibly in a new concept. We can add this plane of grounding of law to the plane of reference of science, the plane of composition of art, the plane of immanence of philosophy, the plane of transcendence of religion and the plane of territory of the Socius that these authors distinguish (Deleuze & Guattari, 1994).

[12] This has been the case with concepts like 'matter of dispute', 'claim', 'proceeding', '(file of) legal process', 'evidence', 'condition', 'ground', 'operative', 'own movement', 'judgment', 'point of dispute' (and with figures like the detective, the plumber, the pilot, the public and the expert).

[13] The movement of shifting out to philosophy when writing an account of the legal dispute is guided by questions ('*How does immateriality become grounded in legal practices of intellectual rights?*', '*How can philosophy approach legal practice?*') that are different from the ones that address the lawyers in writing their accounts of this dispute ('*Is the plaintiff the co-inventor of the disputed machine?*'). These orientations provide important differentiations in the directions of proceeding and dispute engagement.

- *proceedings* (process and procedure)
- *evidence* (facts, conviction)
- *conditions* (authorization, legal sources)
- *ap-plication* (affixation, extensive development, mutual folding)
- *jurisprudential character* (reasonance, points of view)
- *fictive persona* (presumption, points of view)
- *monadic visibility* (bicameral public hearing / private deliberation)
- *grounding* (reasoning, bringing-to-a-halt, fixing position)
- *pointillism* (contraction, points of dispute, appointment)
- *judgment / ius dicem* (linear focus, operativity)

An important open question that does resound from Deleuze and Guattari's '*What is Philosophy?*' is whether law, like science, art and philosophy, can also be called a 'Chaoid': a mode of thought and creation that confronts chaos. Or should law rather be of a different dimensional order and, like religion, exclude itself from a confrontation with chaos by a mode of flight on the plane of transcendence? This seems to be the case when law is 'approached' as the law of laws, the very being of lawhood independently of any concrete laws, be they moral, legal or physical, but already elevated to the transcendental level (Derrida, 1992a). Does law not also confront chaos in the passage of disputes with its own internal register of proceeding, thrown in a virtual world amongst a pluriformity of concrete laws and conditions? The attorney confronts the extensive chaos of the conflict that has to become contracted. The judge confronts the legal chaos that sieves through the fabric of law with its many virtual figures and conditions that might become activated or spark legal actions into motion, the chaos of occurrences that sieves through the factual extensions enfolded in the bundle of pieces, and the chaos condensed in the claims by the attorneys. Is law not also a form of thought and creation? Or does it rather think and create through forms? Law seems to have a curious position between the two. Legal grounds might always seem on their way to transcendence, but they never reach it because of the curious way law always closes in upon itself. Law is a diagonal field, so to say, through the acts of grounding.

Philosophy has already had its legal becomings on many occasions in the past. In order for a chaos-oriented modulation of law to become possible, in which law and philosophy are each granted the power to mutually change each other, we will have to take account of the different ways in which the 'terms and conditions' of interaction might have become prefixed. This could prevent an eventual encounter on the path of thinking under the authority of certain judicial features and figures of thought or certain exclusionary alliances. A double analysis will therefore have to be undertaken, first of the juridical features in the constitution of philosophical thought, and second of the creations of paths and concepts for the approach of law (philosophy of law, legal theory).

6.1 JURIDICAL FEATURES OF THOUGHT

In this section we will deal with some of the juridical features that have been incorporated on the plane of philosophy itself and have come to function as some of the guiding presuppositions of thought,[14] especially the ones along which legal phenomena become installed on a plane of transcendence (instead of the plane of grounding). When such a thinking uncritically sets out and turns to legal practices, it essentially risks becoming auto-recognitive of itself at the outset. It risks recognizing the features and figures that it will itself have taken along for the investigation. In this context it becomes the task of thought to unravel or dissolve some of these conceptual and pre-conceptual amalgams of such judicial features. Some of them will have to be downplayed and relocated within philosophical thinking in order to create an openness for encounters with the event of a dispute in which new features, figures and concepts can become raised or older ones can become relocated. This exercise would by itself be food for a whole separate investigation. Here we will merely limit ourselves to a sketch of two of the judicial features that are operative in philosophical thought: those of the trial (of ideas) and of laws (of the subject).[15]

Ideas on Trial

In the *Phaedo* Plato mobilizes the jury trial as the arena for thought in which the concept of the idea or form is developed as a standard for judging sensible objects. Plato introduces the persona of Socrates who tries to defend his propositions against the 'charges' of his visiting opponents 'as if in a court of law'.[16] These visitors are staged as his 'jury' who will have to be 'persuaded' of his claims. During this interrogation the concept of the idea is gradually developed over a series of different

---

[14] Deleuze and Guattari distinguish a few of the juridical features that thought lays claim to by right, mobilized in certain conceptual persona (Deleuze & Guattari, 1994, p. 72).

[15] Other interesting examples for studying certain judicial features of thought might be Cicero's philosopher as persuasive orator about 'things' conceived not as objects but as disputes to be debated, and Leibniz' philosopher as lawyer defending the cause of God.

[16] Plato, 1999, pp. 8–9 [63].

arguments: where it is first introduced as a mere proposition of common knowledge, the idea gradually gains in priority and characteristics and is finally posited as a full-fledged independent criterion for judging properties of people or objects.[17]

With empiricism there is a very different mobilization of the figure of the legal trial. Francis Bacon introduces it not as the arena for thought, but rather as the procedural model for the construction of philosophical and scientific investigation.[18] In order to shape the new empirical method of science Bacon, who as Attorney General was also the main legal adviser to the British Crown, enlists many legal concepts, devices and maxims, like trial, examination, judgment, verdict, law, right, rule, procedure and evidence.[19] He sets out to 'put on trial' older philosophies and arts for the ways and procedures by which they approach natural things and condemns some of them for making false accusations against nature.[20] Instead the production of all valid knowledge has to be tied to a certain method and procedures of experimentation and induction 'so that the mind may exercise its rights over nature'.[21] He describes this procedure in the following juridical terms:

> What the sciences need is a form of induction which *takes experience apart and analyses it*, and forms necessary conclusions on the basis of appropriate exclusions and rejections [. . .] we place the foundations of the sciences deeper and lay them lower, and set our starting points further back than men have ever done before, subjecting them to *examination* [. . .] not one of the things which the intellect has accumulated by itself escapes our suspicion, and *we do not confirm them without submitting them to a new trial and a verdict given in accordance with it*. Furthermore, we have many *ways of scrutinizing* the information of the senses themselves. For the senses often deceive, but they also give *evidence* of their own errors (Bacon, 2000, p. 17, my italics).

The trials of which Bacon speaks are empirical experiments, which are set up with a double function. First, by granting natural things an active role in the experiment, they become authorized to set bounds to the activities

---

17 Deleuze called this ground a test for determining to what extent different claimants participate in the idea (Deleuze, 2004a, pp. 71–7).

18 Foucault controversially claimed that the old Inquisition procedure of legal truth-finding hereby becomes extended to the formation of knowledge and the constitution of empirical sciences (Foucault, 1991, pp. 224–8).

19 Coquillette has analyzed the link between Bacon's inductive method for science and the procedures of the law-courts in which Bacon practiced throughout his professional life (Coquillette, 1992).

20 Bacon, 2000, pp. 13, 39, 73.

21 This is a phrase taken from the title of the preface.

of the intellect in a certain investigation.[22] The older notions of the intellect will be examined and judged in the context of these new experimental trials. Second, within such a trial, the evidence provided by the senses will now also have to be duly examined according to certain procedures. The senses are no longer authorized as the judge of the things in nature, but they 'judge only of the experiment, the experiment judges of the thing' (p. 18).[23] In these ways Bacon sets out to provide a new foundation for philosophy itself. Plato's philosophy was founded on the investigation, discovery and explanation of the Forms as the abstract natural 'law and its clauses' in accordance with which all individual bodies act, as if it was a statute law with its many clauses.[24] The new empirical philosophy was to investigate 'those laws and limitations of pure act which organize and constitute a simple nature', dealing rather with 'the common and ordinary course of nature' as if it was a case of common law jurisprudence in which a ruling had to be reached for the concrete cause of action that was under experimental trial (pp. 128, 109).[25] Bacon's use of the concept of a 'law' of nature, governing the actions of things not people, is one of the first historical instances in which the concept of a 'physical law' was used in a modern scientific context.[26]

---

[22] Bacon, 2000, p. 103.

[23] Galileo made a similar authorization move. His invention and use of an experimental set-up in order to find and explain the reasons of things, constituted 'the invention of the power to confer to things the power to confer to the experimenter the power to speak in their name' (Stengers, 2006, Chapter 4).

[24] See also the translator's note on this point (Bacon, 2000, p. 103, n. 2).

[25] After these demarcations, Bacon sets out to design the procedure by which these investigations will have to proceed in which several legal devices and maxims are also enlisted. His investigation begins with a presentation (*comparentia*) of all known individual instances into tables of existence and presence, divergence and absence, and degree and comparison. A *comparentia* is the presentation of defendants and documents in court and the tables of inscription are not unlike the 'Minutes' and 'Inventory' lists of legal administration (Chapter 4). Afterwards, he interprets the things of nature according to the often neglected 'privileged instances', which are akin to the typically legal evidentiary presumptions, values and forces.

[26] Zilsel has argued that the genesis of the concept of physical law originated in a juridical metaphor, first fully created by Descartes in combining the Biblical idea of God's legislation for nature and the idea from physics of using empirical rules and quantitative terms to capture physical regularities (Zilsel, 1942). Nevertheless, Zilsel's dismissal of Bacon's concept of physical law formulated 17 years earlier is too rapid. Bacon's concept is especially interesting since it does not directly rely on the theological idea of law, but is more properly ingrained with concrete juridical features taken from the legal practice with which Bacon was professionally well acquainted.

Laws of the Subject

We will now turn to a second judicial feature operative in philosophical thinking, especially in the writings of Kant and Freud: the relation of laws to the thinking subject. In Kant's critical philosophy the composition of features becomes reshuffled and displaced. Kant denies that all claims of metaphysics have been lawfully decided with empiricist philosophy. The skeptical position according to which human reason is incapable of going beyond the empirical, can never bring to an end 'the controversy about what is lawful in human reason'.[27] It cannot decide against the expectation of reason to 'make claims' about this. Instead the way empiricists resort to experience as the foundation actually makes their claims rather 'suspicious'. In this light Kant famously sets out the task of philosophy:

> reason should take on anew the most difficult of all its tasks, namely, that of self-knowledge, and set up a ***tribunal*** that will make reason secure in its ***rightful claims*** and will dismiss all baseless pretensions not by fiat, but in accordance with reason's eternal and immutable ***laws***. This tribunal is none other than the critique of pure reason itself (Kant, 1998, A XI, pp. 6–8).

When we compare this judicial feature of the tribunal with the judicial features raised in Plato or Bacon, the interesting thing is not the novelty of the feature itself (other philosophers also deployed it), but the locus where it is installed with regard to thought. The tribunal becomes internalized into the transcendental subject where it becomes erected as the site where thought comes to turn to the investigation of its own possibilities. The forum, framing and criteria of the debate have hereby shifted. First the philosophical debate is framed as a dispute on what is lawful in human reason in which different philosophers have become claimants with regard to this dispute. Philosophy is hereby sent off in search of the laws of reason. Second, this controversy will have to be judged according to the laws that reason will itself discover as governing its own operations. Third, the forum where these claims will be judged is the tribunal erected by reason within the transcendental subject.[28] This is also the unifying locus where the laws of reason will have to be sought since 'laws exist just as little in the appearances, but rather exist only relative to the subject in which the appearances inhere' (*ibid.*, B 164, p. 202). The discovery of these

---

[27] Kant, 1998, A 764, p. 655.

[28] This gives a different meaning to the 'juridical subject' of Enlightenment (Foucault, 1991). It here does not refer to individuals of a social contract, but to the judicial subject of thought itself.

laws will take place according to the new Kantian method of a critique by reason of its own powers.

Thinking becomes further juridified when Kant makes it pass through these different cognitive powers of the subject. The critical philosopher here assumes the role of the constitutional thinker in specifying the separate judicial jurisdictions of each cognitive power. First, the understanding (*Verstand*) is the power of rules and laws that cannot be induced from experience, but makes all experience possible and provides all phenomena with their lawfulness. This leads to a radical reversal, since understanding is even 'the source of the laws of nature' itself[29] and is thus instituted as the legislative power whose laws provide a unity in the manifold of empirical phenomena. Second, reason (*Vernunft*) is the power of principles, which provides a unity in the laws of the understanding and is thus instituted as what we could call the constitutional power.[30] Third, judgment (*Urteilskraft*) is the power that subsumes cases under the laws of the understanding and of practical reason (*casus datae legis*).

In Freud we can also see a mobilization of the juridical feature of the law in the construction of philosophy and for the very possibility of thought by the subject. Whereas in Kant the laws were evoked before the tribunal of human reason internalized in the transcendental subject, in Freud this very act of internalization of the law leads to a splitting of the subject and will thereafter be the law that will govern his unconscious, realm of irrationality. The law is also mobilized in two settings very different from Kant's tribunal of reason. Instead Freud displaces us first to a quasi-historical context of the primal horde of mankind in which the Oedipus complex finds its birth. Through the primordial acts of parricide and cannibalism the tribal band of brothers incorporates the dominant father and enters into a 'covenant' with him. The acts that he once prevented through his physical presence now become psychically prohibited as 'the first law' against murder and incest (Freud, 2001, pp. 162–70; Freud, 1961b, p. 58). Morality and societal organizations are born in these acts that put cultural limitations on seeking satisfaction for physical needs.

Freud reintroduces this Oedipal complex in the familial setting of the small boy who desires his mother, but is also faced with the paternal prohibition of incest. Under the threat of castration, he incorporates these cultural paternal demands and the Oedipal ideas become repressed. In

---

29 Kant, 1998, A 127, p. 252.

30 Kant deploys a direct legal metaphor here: 'It is an ancient wish [. . .] that in place of the endless manifold of civil laws, their principles may be sought out; for in this alone can consist the secret, as one says, of simplifying legislation' (*ibid.*, B 358, p. 388).

this process there is a 'splitting of the I' into a conscious part that forms a synthetic unity and an unconscious part that becomes inaccessible to the conscious I.[31] The father's authority is introjected in the I where it forms the core of the critical Super-I or conscience, which is also split off from the synthetic I.[32] These processes *subject* the I to the internalized Law of the Father. This law has hereby become transcendent and will govern his unconsciousness and install it within the jurisdiction of cultural reality.

***

The juridical feature of the trial is deployed in different ways by philosophers (Plato, Bacon, Kant) in order to construct a way to deal with the philosophies of their opponents and to subsequently construct new ways of thinking.[33] In Plato the jury trial is deployed as the arena for dialectical thought. In this trial the philosopher has to convince his interlocutors of his propositions by providing arguments and by defending himself against their charges. In these proceedings the concept of the constant idea is developed as a standard of judgment. In Bacon, the trial with its many procedural rules, devices and maxims, provides the model for the construction of a new procedure of scientific investigation of things that can be used to reach a verdict on older philosophies and intellectual notions. In Kant, the tribunal of reason becomes installed in the transcendental subject in order to judge the claims of other philosophers in the controversy on what is lawful in human reason. Thought becomes reason in search of its own laws and principles which have become transcendental due to their internalization in the subject of thought. In Freud this juridical feature of the law also becomes internalized into the subject. Here it becomes transcendent (or rather 'subscendent') not from above, so to speak, in the operations of reason, but from below from the realm of unconsciousness and unreason.

A philosophical thought that will have constituted itself in advance through such juridical features runs the risk of moving in self-enclosed circles of recognition. When the philosopher comes to study legal phenomena as a subject of thought preformed by figures like the transcendental 'tribunal', the 'laws' of the subject, the 'principles' of reason,

---

[31] Freud, 1961a.

[32] Freud, 1949.

[33] Of course as *historical phenomena* jury trials in ancient Athens were quite different from seventeenth century common law trials in England and eighteenth century continental law trials in Germany. It remains to be studied whether such differences influenced the subsequent roles of this *philosophical feature* of the trial in thinking.

subsuming 'judgments' and *a priori* 'conditions' of things, or when the proceedings in legal disputes have already been determined in advance by an axiology of legal subjectivity and legal objectivity that have been pre-modelled upon such judicial features, then our turn in philosophical thinking will have been in vain. Instead of traversing, we will have jumped over the middle of things – *medias res* – where law has its happening and its becoming. We will have either become caught in a circle of presuppositions and conclusions that turns around a middle of propositions with regard to law and conditions, or have confused the beginnings of a process dynamics for its outcomes in legal subjects and objects.

First, in this case the legal subject is prefixed from the start as the autonomous judicial subject of rights and contracts whereas the legal object is already modelled in a relation to this subject within the very concept of subjective rights. The thing here is either constituted as an object in its material or physical exteriority (*Sache*), the object of a certain right of a subject (*Gegenstand*), or the object incorporated in the subject as its capacity (*Vermögen*) (Thomas, 1980, p. 414). Instead, we have argued that the thing in its primordial sense as a *res* is neither necessarily a physical object nor an object for a subject but the whole process of a matter of dispute. Through the dispute protagonists are drawn into its antagonistic dynamics as opponents united in a common relation. From within the event of this dispute, legal subjects and legal objects can themselves become constituted. The matters of dispute and the actors involved can become transformed throughout the adversarial play of qualification, proving, authorization, application, conviction and imputation. Within these processes what it means to be an inventor of an invention, an author of a work, or a holder of a mark or a model is up for continuous re-invention, re-creation, re-marking or re-modelling.

Second, how can we pretend to study the act of raising grounds in legal practices when philosophy has already constituted itself beforehand as the discipline that will provide the grounds of things independent of any empirical approximation, or has already pre-constituted the concept of a ground as an *a priori* condition of everything empirical?[34] How can we hope to understand the laws and conditions raised or laid down throughout these practices, in ways different from the transcendental schemes of the subject of thought, of which concrete things are mere copies or instantiations? We would have brought along everything beforehand that we might want to take out after our analysis. Our turn to the productive positivities of legal practices has been a way to try to escape this circle

[34] See Kant, 1998, A 95–6, pp. 226–7.

of auto-recognition of a desk philosophy of law. Far from being the presuppositions and conclusions of investigation, conditions and law are themselves drawn into dispute in which they are granted the power to check hidden presuppositions or to terminate as grounds of judgment. When we unravel some of these judicial features in philosophical thought and downplay their transcendental dimension, we create an openness for a transversal turn through legal practices in which these features can become relocated on the new planes emerging in this process. This is a shift from ideas and observations on trial, tribunals of reason and laws of the subject, to the observations of reasoning in trials and the legal constitution of ideas and subjects.

6.2 PRACTICE OF LEGAL THEORY AND THEORIES OF LEGAL PRACTICE

After this analysis of the juridical features in philosophical thought, we will turn to the creation of paths and concepts of law within legal theory. The way in which law is approached is very important here and we need to inquire into the different ways in which such access has been secured. We will study the constructions of philosophies of law and how they have created paths, concepts and conceptions of law.[35] The focus will be on the elements that bear on the turn to legal practices explored in this book. We will explore how these legal theories construct the paths of thinking, the relation between philosophy and law, the approach to practices, the role of things, the status of disputes, the formation of alliances with other practices, the creation of concepts, the unfolding of presupposed planes of consistency, the introduction of conceptual personae and even the confrontation with chaos. These will be confronted with the findings in this book both with regard to the practice turn for legal thinking explored in Chapter 2 and the empirical accounts of legal practices at law firms and courts provided in Chapters 3 and 4. This treatment primarily endeavours to re-establish an openness for an encounter between philosophy and law in which both can engage in a mutual becoming when dealing with new emerging issues. Nevertheless, the confrontations with past philosophies of law often force one to think about what is involved in these very processes of becoming in order to learn from them. This knowledge can be useful in mobilizing different conceptual figures (the idiot, Iolaus),

---

[35] They will be treated comparable to the ways in which philosophers construct their general theories (Deleuze & Guattari, 1994).

opening up different paths or practical alliances and assembling different elements for a concept of law (facts, things, disputes, points of view). These can provide a counterweight against the figures, paths, alliances and elements identified in the legal theories analyzed and, when pushed further into their domain, re-align and tinker with the constellation of forces they have established. The three legal theories that we will study are those by the Legal Realists, H.L.A. Hart and Ronald Dworkin.

The Paths and Crossroads of Law

We will start with the movement known as 'Legal Realism' and will focus on two tracks. First, we will have a look at Hohfeld's relativistic account of law as relations between subjects and the role it assigned to things in legal theory. Second, we will turn to the writings of Llewellyn and, especially, Holmes. We will study the role assigned to disputes in an account of law and its alliance established with practices of prediction of legal behaviour in order to approach these disputes.

Bundles without things

Hohfeld is a precursor to, and an important influence on the Legal Realist movement. His two seminal articles on the fundamental legal conceptions applied in judicial reasoning (Hohfeld, 1913; Hohfeld, 1917) have had an important effect on the role and status of things in legal theory. At stake in these articles is an analysis of all possible kinds of jural interests and relations. This account will provide 'a solution to everyday problems of law, by providing the basic conceptions of law – the legal elements that enter into all types of jural interests' (Hohfeld, 1913, p. 20). These elements are a set of eight fundamental legal relations that can be exhibited in a core scheme of opposites and correlatives. Hohfeld calls these eight conceptions 'the lowest common denominators of the law' constituting 'the lowest generic conceptions to which any and all "legal quantities" may be reduced'. This 'depth' analysis makes possible a comparison of all concrete legal relations and the discovery of the common principles of justice and policy underlying various jural problems (pp. 58–9).[36] We can call this a *fractional* conception of law in which legal relations are reduced to generic underlying legal quantities

[36] Hohfeld's scheme of fundamental relations has a strange similarity to the deep level semiotic squares in Greimassian semiotics that manifest themselves in legal discourse (Greimas, 1976). It can also be said to suffer from the same problems relating to the concept of virtuality.

as the fundamental elements of law.[37] In this sense, it is different from Troller's static axiology that assumes two poles (object and subject). Hohfeld's account is not axiological but elemental, the fundamental elements being relations.

In working out this account Hohfeld distinguishes between legal conceptions and non-legal quantities in a given problem. One of the false contrasts he detects in legal theory is that of corporeal and incorporeal property, which he traces back to Blackstone's distinction we encountered in Chapter 1. Hohfeld thinks this distinction confuses the physical or corporeal objects of property with the legal interests involved, which are incorporeal and invisible. In fact, he states that 'all legal interests are "incorporeal" – consisting, as they do, of more or less limited aggregates of abstract legal relations' (p. 24). Incorporeality is thus not something restricted to intellectual rights, but constitutes the nature of law itself![38] The real contrast is not between incorporeal and corporeal but between the degrees of extension of an aggregate of legal relations.

Hohfeld thinks the legal and non-legal quantities are especially confused in the concept of property. He criticizes the distinction between rights *in rem* and rights *in personam*. The fact that a right *in personam* is a right against a person, does not symmetrically imply that a right *in rem* is a right against a thing.

> A man may indeed sustain close and beneficial physical relations to a given physical thing. [. . .] But obviously, such purely physical relations could as well exist quite apart from, or occasionally in spite of, the law of organized society: physical relations are wholly distinct from jural relations. The latter take significance from the law; and since the purpose of the law is to regulate the conduct of human beings, all jural relations must, in order to be clear and direct

---

[37] 'Ten fractions (1–3, 2–5, etc.) may superficially seem so different from one another as to defy comparison. If, however, they are expressed in terms of their lowest common denominators (5–15, 6–15, etc.) comparison becomes easy, and fundamental similarity may be discovered. The same thing is of course true as regards the lowest generic conceptions to which any and all "legal quantities" may be reduced' (Hohfeld, 1913, pp. 58–9).

[38] We find this conception in a great variety of legal thinking of very different character. It goes back to the study of Roman law. In his discussion of the difference between *res corporales* and *res incorporales*, concrete social institutions and abstract relations, Thomas remarks that 'le monde du droit, en particulier, est tout entier situe du cote de l'incorporel' (Thomas, 1978, p. 112). MacCormick distinguishes the plane of existence of law characterized by its non-physical institutional nature, from the existence of 'brute facts' (MacCormick, 1986). Deleuze and Guattari call law the semiotic regime of enunciation that brings about incorporeal transformations (Deleuze & Guattari, 1987, pp. 80–81, 88).

in their meaning, be predicated of such human beings. [. . .] all rights *in rem* are against persons (Hohfeld, 1917, pp. 721–2).

According to Hohfeld both rights *in rem* and rights *in personam* are thus 'intrinsically considered, of the same general character'; they are both against persons. The difference between them is rather extrinsic, relating to the number of people against which they can be mobilized and the kind of companion rights attached. Rights *in rem* should thus not be understood as a single absolute relation of a right and a thing. Instead they involve a 'relativity' of distinct elemental legal relations.

Hohfeld's relativistic analysis of legal phenomena in terms of aggregates of legal relations, or what will later be called 'bundles of rights',[39] has stimulated a dominant image of property in Legal Realism, or even of law in general, where things have become filtered out of the bundle.[40] This image of law is not without its normative effects. Textbooks and articles on property that operate from this presupposition qualify those who think of ownership as a relation between a person and an object as 'laymen', since 'rights, liberties, and duties are the basic stuff of ownership' and these hold between people.[41] Mentioning this relation in discussions of property or intellectual rights on conferences also leads to habitual reactions of automatic rejection. The fact that things do not figure in these theories of law however, does not mean they do not operate underneath their surface of representation. Quite the contrary, this picture of law stands in stark contrast with what has become visible in the studies in this book on intellectual 'property' proceedings in which things play a prominent role. In what sense can we still talk about a 'realism' about law and legal practices when this crucial aspect is filtered out?[42]

Hohfeld's shift away from classical theories that assume a single relation

---

[39] Although this image is disputed since property does not only deal with rights but with a whole range of other incidents like prohibitions and limitations (Honoré, 1961). Property is rather a bundle of legal relations as Hohfeld already insisted.

[40] This conception of property as a bundle of rights between people has become the dominant image of law (in the Wittgensteinian sense) not as an explicit theory but rather an unexamined perspective which implicitly guides our approach to the subject (Penner, 1995–1996, pp. 714–15).

[41] Waldron, 1985, p. 314.

[42] In this sense we can agree with Penner who states that 'the bundle of rights picture obscures more than it illuminates, [. . .] presenting without foundation the view that we can have a workable idea of property without having a workable idea of the 'things' that can be owned' (Penner, 1995–1996, p. 724). For a mapping of several relations between law and thingness, see Madison, 2005.

of a right with a thing, has the advantage of opening up legal theory towards a relativity of legal relations.[43] However, it comes at the cost of subjecting all these relations to an anthropocentric theory of law that only allows for jural relations between people and in which things are left out of the account. Society only consists of humans and order in society is conceived as legally regulated human behaviour. This de-reified view can be disputed in several ways. Such anthropocentric views of society, supported by the strong conception of the subject of law, are very misleading since they ignore the crucial role played by non-humans in stabilizing and constituting society.[44] First of all, law is just one of the many ways in which the behaviour of people can become affected. Other important factors in the disposition of human behaviour are (the design of) things, apparatuses, architectures.[45] Second, as we have seen in the previous chapters, law itself has its own things, apparatuses and architectures at the heart of its practices that play a crucial role in the performance of legal operations. In this sense we could even reverse Hohfeld's image and state that things are always involved in all law and in every legal relation. These are not the physical objects that Hohfeld mobilizes in order to disqualify the role of things in law. Even in science itself this physical object is barely ever something given, but rather has a precarious existence as an achievement that is the outcome of elaborate processes of scientific construction.[46] In law things play a very different role, one that is much more proper to the very notion of thingness itself. As a *res* the thing is the matter of dispute at the core of legal practice. What kind of object this matter of dispute constitutes and whether there is such an object at all (or even the proposition that there is a legal 'claim without matter') can all be part of the dynamics of such a dispute. Furthermore, the materiality or immateriality, corporeality or incorporeality, physicality or intangibility of this thing is not given in advance but is the result of the legal processes of proceeding and grounding, especially in the cases of patents and copyrights.[47]

All of this does not diminish the force of Hohfeld's relativity thesis of

---

[43] We can compare this to a parallel move in the philosophy of language that criticizes the view of language as an image of reality in which words refer to things in the world. Wittgenstein criticized this image of language. If we want to know the meaning of a word we should focus on the multiple ways in which it is used in specific practices (Wittgenstein, 2009).

[44] Latour, 1993; Latour, 2005.

[45] See the notion of the '*dispositif*' or 'apparatus' in Foucault (Foucault, 1991). See also Lessig's notion of code as a behavioural regulator (Lessig, 2006).

[46] Latour, 1999.

[47] To which Hohfeld also refers (Hohfeld, 1917, p. 725).

legal relations. Quite the contrary, a removal of this physical object as the model for a single absolute legal relation between rights and things and as a negative unifying principle for excluding things from law in classical legal theory, opens a broader space for a multiplicity of legal relations that are not limited to humans only, but also can take account of the plurality of ways that things make their ingression in law. This raises the question about the place of things in legal relations and the consequences for the legal research required. Hohfeld himself primarily calls his schematic account 'a matter of analysis and exposition' and adds that this account is 'also a matter of great practical consequence and economic significance' that can 'be applied in judicial reasoning to the solution of concrete problems of litigation' (Hohfeld, 1917, pp. 747, 713). The question of things in law might well reverse this relation between the analytics and pragmatics of law by making us turn to the matters at stake in legal practices.[48] Instead of providing a *fractional* approach to judicial reasoning that analytically reduces law to its most atomistic common elements, this more truly legal 'pragmatic' approach could be called *fractal* to the extent that it deals with generative entities that have the power to reconstitute the axiological systems of dimensions that are projected in order to grasp it.

The predictive alliance

These last remarks by Hohfeld about the relation between the pragmatics of law and economic significance open a second avenue of questioning of Legal Realism, concerning the relation of the legal scholar with law and disputes and the alliances of legal philosophy. Within the Legal Realist movement Karl Llewellyn had a sensibility for describing the processes of law with which our present account has some affinity. For one, he cherished the deep relation between law and disputes. In asking the question: 'What, then, is this law about?' he answers that 'it is about the fact that our society is honeycombed with disputes'. When arguing about the nature of law, Llewellyn rejects a focus on abstract legal rules and propositions. These concepts belong to the repertoire of self-representation of what judges say they do. Instead a study of law has to focus on what these judges in fact do in their work of adjudication: 'to my mind the main thing is seeing what officials do, do about disputes', which leads to a definition of law as 'what officials do about disputes' (Llewellyn, 2008, p. 5). From

[48] In the context of Thomas' writings on the relations between the things in nature and legal institutions (in Roman law), we could state that these Hohfeldian schematic elements are overly general, utopian '*didactic categories*' and 'not a qualification that can be produced in legal action [*en justice*]' (Thomas, 2011, p. 31).

this perspective he provides an interesting short overview of the selections and legal translations that are involved in the process of adjudication when a case proceeds from 'the raw facts' to the decisions in appeal.

Rules might play a role in this process but cannot serve as an adequate description of what judges have done in the process of adjudication. They are only important to the extent they help one predict what the courts will do, or help you get judges to do something. He formulates this as a widespread point of common departure for the whole Legal Realist movement: 'Distrust of traditional legal rules and concepts insofar as they purport to describe what either courts or people are actually doing. Hence the constant emphasis on rules as "generalized predictions of what courts will do"' (Llewellyn, 1962, p. 56).

There is much to agree with in Llewellyn's account of law, like the deep relation he sketches between law and disputes and the rejection of the focus on abstract rules in the description of what law is about. His focus on what judges do about disputes is also interesting, but provides an overly narrow maxim for the study of legal disputes. In our conflict-based approach we have tried to cast the net of study wider in both spatio-temporal and actorial dimensions, by focusing on the work done by actors like lawyers, clients, engineers, secretaries, registrars, experts, witnesses, the work done by all the things, apparatuses and architectures as described above, and the different sites through which the matter of dispute circulates and is transformed, all of this before reaching the judges. In this sense this study has made visible all the things that precede and make possible legal judgment at all. A second and related point of discussion is the angle of study from which the importance of disputes looms into focus. In Llewellyn's writing it becomes clear that the sketches of the nature of disputes, the role of rules in them and what judges do about them, are mobilized as an instrument for the prediction of the judge's future behaviour and for 'the study of how to make the official do what you would like to have him'.[49] Apart from the relation of mutual distrust between lawyer and judge that we discussed in the previous chapter, there is a broader issue at stake here about the alliances of legal practice and legal philosophy with other practices.

The predictive view of the law in Legal Realism is most strongly associated with the work of Holmes, especially *The Path to the Law*. Holmes is concerned with the direction of legal philosophy in his time, thinking

[49] There is a relation with the methodological individualist approach in Weberian sociology aimed at reconstructing social phenomena as the chance or probability of occurrence of a certain type of social behaviour (Weber, 1947).

it restricts itself to trotting 'the narrow path of legal doctrine' (Holmes, 2009, p. 16). Instead, he wants legal thought to change direction and open up the broad path of a new legal philosophy. In this sense, Holmes is not concerned with the creation of a concept of law by contracting certain legal features, but rather with an articulation of law through its directions and its alliances. This move is interesting and it is worthwhile to pay close attention to how he progressively describes the path of law in terms of its boundaries, its pitfalls, its first and further steps and its principles of progression.

Holmes presents the narrow path of law as an itinerary of doctrine through the combined territories of morality, history and logic.[50] He discusses the relation between law and ***morality*** to raise the issue of the limits and boundaries of law. He states that lawyers often use many legal concepts like right, duty, intent or negligence in a moral sense: 'law is full of phraseology drawn from morals, and by the mere force of language continually *invites us to pass from one domain to the other without perceiving it*, as we are sure to do unless we have the *boundary* constantly before our minds' (Holmes, 2009, pp. 7–8, my italics). Law and morality are presented as two territorial domains and the role of the legal philosopher is that of the customs officer who has to ensure the border is not crossed from the one to the other. Holmes subsequently occupies the philosophical position thus prepared, by introducing the conceptual figure of the bad man.

> If you want to know the *law and nothing else*, you *must look at it as a bad man*, who cares only for the *material consequences* which such knowledge enables him to *predict*, not as a good one, who finds his reasons for conduct, *whether inside the law or outside of it*, in the vaguer sanctions of conscience (Holmes, 2009, p. 7, my italics).

This figure of the bad man is indifferent to moral rules, but sensitive to the practical effects that law can have for him. For this reason he plays an important demarcating role since his 'point of view is the test of legal principles'. This conceptual figure offers a different perspective on law. It is set up against the point of view of the figure of the good man, assumed by existing legal doctrine, who due to his sensitivity to morality, mixes the concepts from both domains. This perspective has consequences for certain concepts that travel between the two domains, because 'you see how the *vague circumference* of the notion of duty shrinks and at the same time

---

[50] In short, we could call this an alliance of law with the humanities and mathematics.

grows more precise when we wash it with cynical acid and expel everything except the object of our study, the *operations of the law*' (p. 11). Concepts like 'right' and 'duty' have different meanings in law and morality and should be distinguished. In this book, something similar was argued about the concept of the 'idea' with regard to art, philosophy and intellectual rights. In this sense, Holmes is quite right to insist on the distinction and the focus on the operations of law as its lever is also interesting. Some caution is needed however in presenting this as a distinction between 'domains' due to their static territorial overtones and fixed boundaries.[51] This is why in this book the more dynamic concept of practice was chosen, which is always related to an actual practic*ing* in action. Similar reservations pertain to how Holmes occupies the demarcation position with the figure of the bad man (the customs officer with the acid shower for travelling concepts) and to the specific 'pragmatic' approach to law that is hereby opened up. 'Legal operations' are first approached in terms of their material consequences. Here Holmes follows the pragmatists, especially to the extent that these consequences can be predicted.[52] Here we again encounter the predictive position. This move is essential for the alliance of legal philosophy that Holmes will propose. We will turn to this later; here we maintain our focus on the configuration of legal doctrine.

Holmes calls the confusion of law and morality one of the two '*pitfalls*' that 'lie perilously near to' the narrow path of law. The second pitfall does not deal with the boundaries of the legal domain, but with the forces that determine the growth and content of the law itself, the principles of its mode of development. Here Holmes tackles the tendency in law schools to exclusively train lawyers in ***logic*** in order to develop legal arguments. He denies that there is a fixed quantitative relation between legal phenomena and that a legal system could be worked out mathematically from the axioms of conduct, thus seemingly diverging from Hohfeld's image of law. Holmes states that 'behind the logical form lies a judgment as to the relative *worth* and importance of competing legislative grounds' (p. 18).

Last in the doctrinal configuration is the relation between law and ***history***. Holmes states that 'history must be a part of the study [. . .of rules . . .] because it is the *first step* toward an enlightened skepticism, that is, towards a deliberate reconsideration of the *worth* of those rules' (p. 24). Nevertheless, tradition has played a too dominant role as the basis for

---

[51] For an argument against the conception of law as a domain, territory or sphere, see Latour, 2010, pp. 263–4.

[52] Peirce first formulated the pragmatist maxim that focused on the practical effects of certain ideas or concepts (Peirce, 1878).

legal principles, making history more important than it is for the study of law. Since tradition is justified by the mere fact of acceptance and custom, this provides a rather shaky basis for legal development. History often obscures and obstructs the real worth of legal rules, which is their *social end* in terms of which they can also be reshaped. This social teleology provides the path of law with a destination and a direction and allows Holmes to reconfigure the relation of law with the practices of logic and history, calling the former a 'pitfall' and the latter merely a 'first step'.[53] From here onwards the space is opened for a new broad path of legal philosophy:

> Now let us consider the present condition of the law as a subject for study, and the ideal toward which it tends. We still are far from the *point of view* which I desire to see *reached*. No one has reached it or can reach it as yet. We are only at the *beginning* of a *philosophical* reaction, and of a *reconsideration of the worth of doctrines* which for the most part still are taken for granted without any deliberate, conscious, and systematic questioning of their *grounds* (Holmes, 2009, pp. 22–3).

Holmes then assigns social ends the status of 'the very ground and foundation of judgment' that judges have 'failed to recognize' in their reasoning and which will determine the worth of legal doctrines. At the ideal state at the end of the path of legal philosophy, each legal rule in the body of law would be articulated in terms of the social end it serves. In this account of law, a lot will thus depend on the conception of the social. What kind of social ends are conceived of here and how can we find them? For answering this question we have to take one step back and look at how Holmes sketches the approach of the philosopher to law. It is closely related to the figure of the bad man who looks at legal concepts or rights from the point of view of predicting their material consequences. This enables him to define law as 'the prophesies of what the courts will do'. The task of the legal philosopher then becomes to lay down the first principles of law as 'the body of systemized prediction [. . .] for men who want to use it as the instrument of their ***business*** to enable them to prophesy' (pp. 5–6). Holmes' broad path of legal philosophy involves a new configuration of practices that exhibits a most curious double instrumentality. First, law as applied by the courts is approached as the instrument of public force whose incidence can be predicted. Second, legal philosophy is the discipline that is to systematize these predictions in a coherent body and, as such, becomes the instrument for commerce by providing a 'businesslike

53 He already took this position on the relations between law, logic and history in Holmes, 1881.

understanding' of law. We can see a link here with Llewellyn's writings, but in Holmes' prediction becomes even more fundamental. Furthermore, where morality and logic have been sidestepped and history downgraded, the path is now open for a new alliance and Holmes establishes connections with the practices of ***statistics*** and ***economics***. Where history might have been a first step towards the present state of law, economics and statistics would be a step towards the future in reaching the ideal of tying each rule to a social end.

> I look forward to a time when the part played by ***history*** in the explanation of dogma shall be very small, and instead of ingenious research we shall spend our energy on a *study of the ends* sought to be attained and the reasons for desiring them. As *a step toward that ideal* it seems to me that every lawyer ought to seek an understanding of ***economics***. The present divorce between the schools of political economy and law seems to me an evidence of how much progress in ***philosophical*** study still remains to be made. In the present state of political economy, indeed, we come again upon history on a larger scale, but there we are called on to consider and *weigh the ends of legislation, the means of attaining them, and the cost* (Holmes, 2009, p. 33, my accents).

This sheds a different light on his concept of the worth of legal rules. In the alliance that Holmes proposes with business, economics and statistics this worth can be statistically quantified as an economical cost that permits the weighing of social ends. The consequences of legal actions can now be calculated in order to provide insight into whether they are effective. Holmes' proposal has certainly itself not been without its effects on (Anglo-Saxon) law. The law and economics movement that arose in the 1960 could be seen as the economic turn of Holmes' proposition in the application of economic methods to legal problems.[54] Furthermore, the advent of information technologies of mass data storage and data mining might well give rise to a 'computational turn' for law that could provide law with all the statistics Holmes would ever have required about its own operations.[55] Economics and statistics have become configured within the knowledge economy and information society in ways that indeed try to make law the instrument of their practices.[56]

Holmes' writings incite us to think about the paths of law and legal

---

[54] Apparent for instance in the title of Coase's foundational article: *The Problem of Social Cost.*

[55] Hildebrandt & De Vries, 2013.

[56] Tribe discusses the consequences of the Holmesian utilitarian approaches to law in the US. Interestingly, he discusses crucial new 'paths of law' that call for new alliances, leading away from both economics and statistics that have become too dominant, and from history and its unreflected appeal to past authority. Instead

philosophy and the alliances forged at their crossroads. Whereas one could well consent to the path legal philosophy is leaving behind, there is considerably more hesitation with regard to the path that is to be taken.[57] Legal philosophy should be extremely reluctant in accepting a proposition that makes it the instrument of another practice. The problem with mobilizing the perspective of the everyday citizen and its relation to social ends as the test for legal principles, is that it always raises the issue of representation. To whom does one delegate the power to represent this point of view of the citizen and to define these social ends? Holmes' answer seems clear: he delegates this power to the practices of economics and statistics. This alliance might have been useful in establishing the limits of law and untying it from morality (and logic), but it comes at the cost of delivering law into the hands of other practices beyond its bounds. Now, where pragmatism has been invaluable in orienting thinking towards the consequences it produces, it does not imply that these consequences need to be defined as 'social', especially when the social is supported by the vaguely assembled construct of society of which that law is supposed to become the instrument.[58] For the same reason, legal philosophy should be reluctant in casting its own fate in the service of the members of the public, where it is re-aligned as an aid in predicting the social consequences of law for their actions. By being mobilized in advance by external definitions of its utility for society or for the public, legal thought would have lost the crucial power to name its own issues and to invent the paths of thinking that these require.[59]

In this sense, an important step for legal thinking is the understanding of techniques and 'operations of law' deployed in legal practices for

---

Tribe proposes a re-engagement with morality when discussing the 'moral vacuum' left by cost-benefit analysis in legal argumentation (Tribe, 1985).

[57] We should be skeptical of downplaying history to the point that (Anglo-Saxon) legal thought has become quite ahistoric. We only need to turn to the studies by a legal historian like Yann Thomas to see what a good study of Roman law can do for legal philosophy!

[58] For critiques of this badly assembled notion of society, see Dewey, 1957, pp. 185–94 and especially Latour, 2005.

[59] The point is analogous to the mobilization of social science in the service of the public by another great pragmatist thinker: John Dewey. According to Dewey, the task of the social sciences is to assist the publics that are emerging around certain issues in society, in identifying and organizing themselves by continuous inquiry into these issues (Dewey, 1957). What links social scientists is not a general public interest in working in the service of democracy, but their own practical ways of assigning importance to, dealing with, and hesitating about the issues at stake (Stengers, 2006).

resisting such mobilizations. In the previous chapter we have become acquainted with some of the ways in which judges themselves resisted the kind of Holmesian case law predications, based either on the statistical regularities of their judging behaviour, or on a database of case law with extracted general criteria. An approach to case law decisions that is fundamentally linked to the singularity of the dispute in which they were passed, thwarts their easy mobilization in another dispute. Instead this requires a lot of judicial work in establishing reasonances between the disputes. This position is fundamentally at odds with Holmes' conception of case law as a body of systematized prediction.[60]

Creating a Concept of Law: Practice Theory and Legislative Observers

We will now turn to Hart's seminal *The Concept of Law*.[61] This book provides a rewarding example of the work of legal philosophy in creating a concept of law. Hart constructs his theory of law by unfolding a plane of consistency (implicit presuppositions), introducing conceptual personae (gunman, game participant, external observer), and creating a concept of law by contracting and excluding several elements. His investigations are guided by the classical question 'What is law?' Hart's goal is 'to advance legal theory by providing an improved analysis of the distinctive structure of a municipal legal system and a better understanding of the resemblances and differences between law, coercion, and morality, *as types of social phenomena*' (Hart, 1997, p. 17, my italics).

He turns to the history of speculation about the nature of law to identify a set of 'central elements in the concept of law'. Hart takes some of the ideas earlier legal theorists had used, like orders, obedience, habits, coercion, obligations and morality. These are raised on a new plane of consistency on which they will become centred around different ideas like that of a rule, a concept (general descriptive), legal theory and sociology. This new centring allows him to select certain of these elements and contract them in a different concept of law, and simultaneously unties it from others like morality and coercion that become separate concepts.

---

[60] Furthermore, the present use of information technologies by big institutions in intransparent data processing practices for predicting human behaviour might actually thwart the Holmesian path of law with its client-centred predictive perspective on law. 'Having bathed the law in "cynical acid", cleansing it of any and all moral stain, Holmes undermines any normative basis of complaint for citizens who wish to ensure predictability and fairness in decisions being made about them' (Kerr, 2013, p. 111).

[61] Parts of this analysis have appeared before in De Vries & van Dijk, 2013.

Moreover, these three concepts become reconstituted as social phenomena, transposing them onto a new plane of social consistency on which new directions for approaching them are opened up and new connections become possible between them.[62] Hart also introduces several conceptual figures that allow new points of view on these phenomena and mediate between the creation of the concept of law and the unfolding of this social plane.

The kind of legal theory that Hart proposes oscillates between two methodological perspectives. He qualifies his book as both 'an essay in analytical jurisprudence' that is 'concerned with the clarification of the general framework of legal thought' and has to provide a legal theory that is both general and descriptive, but also as 'an essay in descriptive sociology' (p. vi) that takes the existence of law as a question of concrete social fact determined by empirical research. There is a tension between these two perspectives that perhaps comes out best in his practice-oriented approach to law. Hart describes his own enterprise as a 'practice theory of rules', which 'treats the social rules of a group as constituted by a form of social practice' (Hart 1997, p. 255). The elements of 'practice' and 'rule' are here intricately woven together in a mutually constitutive way. This is related to an earlier distinction that Hart made between the two ways in which these can generally be approached:

> it is possible to be concerned with the rules, either merely as an observer who does not himself accept them, or as a member of the group which accepts and uses them as guides to conduct. We may call these respectively the 'external' and the 'internal points of view' (Hart 1997, p. 89).

Once rules are framed as the core of a social practice, Hart sets up two observer positions on them, which he calls an internal and an external perspective,[63] and occupies these by introducing two conceptual figures. The internal perspective on rules is that of the practitioner who accepts the validity of a rule, regards it as a guide for his or her conduct and for whom deviations of the rule are a reason for legitimate criticism. Hart illustrates this by introducing the figure of the participant to a game like chess who 'has views' about the moves in the game. The external perspective on rules is assumed by what Hart calls an 'external observer'. This observer looks at the practice in question as a pattern of regular

---

[62] 'MY aim in this book has been to further the understanding of law, coercion, and morality as different but related social phenomena' (Hart, 1997, p. vi).

[63] Hart calls this distinction of 'great importance for the understanding not only of law but of the structure of any society' (Hart, 1997, p. 89).

behaviour. On the basis of his observations he can record the existence of a rule of behaviour as an empirical social fact. The legal theory that Hart proposes about law as a social phenomenon takes account of the internal perspective of participants, which for instance enables Hart to sidetrack the predictive approaches to law and rules by Legal Realist writers like Llewellyn and Holmes (and the figure of the bad man mobilized by the latter). Nevertheless, in the last instance Hart's account situates itself at the external point of view of a 'morally neutral descriptive jurisprudence'. In the end this internal perspective can be recorded as a fact on which the theorist can base his general descriptive conclusions (pp. 243–4).

Several remarks can be made about these points. First, with regard to the phrase cited, Hart presents a rather binary model of 'concern' and of the ways in which one can let oneself be addressed by rules. The territorial way in which the structure of concern is framed does not leave any room for the many diverse possibilities to be concerned with the rules, i.e. for someone who is not a practitioner, but who is engaged by the rules of a practice, like the activist, the ethicist, the philosopher, the anthropologist, the ethnographer, etc. We could say that Hart does not take serious what it means when something is a matter of concern to somebody,[64] but ultimately subjects all perspectives to the introduced figure of the external observer who would himself be indifferent to the rules observed and merely records them as facts from his morally neutral perspective. We could further ask what is involved in this process of recording such complex phenomenon as a 'matter of fact' by observers. This question becomes especially pertinent in the case of rules which are not observable on the basis of behaviour at all, but which have rather to be deduced from observation, like Hart's crucial rules of recognition.[65] Hart assumes a strong separation between facts and values and, on this basis, states that values can be registered as facts. Latour, to the contrary, shows how matters of fact are a particular modality of matters of concern. They are a particular way in which concerns are canalized and in which values can never be so clearly separated.[66]

---

64 For a good account of all the dimensions involved in a 'matter of concern', see Latour, 2005.

65 Turner argued that from the sociological observation of regular behaviour, one cannot deduce the fact that people follow the same rule. He called this the sociologist imposition of 'the tacit rule book' (Turner, 2001).

66 Fleck already, in 1935, observed 'an excessive respect' within sociology and the humanities for scientific facts as something fixed, as given objective realities. He instead describes facts as entities with a genesis and a life-cycle in which social conditions and cultural processes play an important role (Fleck, 1981).

In the second chapter, two ways of turning to legal practice were discussed: practice theory and practice approach. Hart explicitly calls his account a 'practice theory' and, like the practice theorists, he distinguishes between regular patterns of conduct and a normative attitude of acceptance. We could say that Hart's account suffers from the same infelicities as other practice theories, especially with regard to the status of rules and norms in relation to the role of the sociologist as a legislative observer.[67] The way Hart frames practices as a factual given and pinpoints their identity by fixing their rules of behaviour, confounds their crucial dynamic character. The concept of a practice here rather functions as an abstract notion that forms the object of a general theory and is necessary to constitute the concept of rules. Hart in this context speaks of a 'general social practice' of the acceptance of a rule. Practices however are not something general or theoretical but have their existence in the concrete activity of being practiced. By mobilizing the figure of the external social observer in this way, the legal theorist is manoeuvred into the position of the legislator who authoritatively identifies and codifies the norms and rules that the practitioners would be following.[68] S/he hereby imposes a 'tacit rule book' on the practices that s/he is studying (Turner, 2001). Furthermore, this external observer is at several occasions staged not as someone who has actually done empirical observations in practice, but as an abstract figure of thought, who is nevertheless capable of registering all kinds of facts about practices and making important deductions from such 'observations'.

Later, in response to criticisms, Hart nuanced his methodological stance by saying that *The Concept of Law* should itself not be seen as descriptive sociology but as 'providing the tools for descriptive sociology' (Sugarman & Hart, 2005, p. 291). This shift of positioning further pushes the observation of the already highly abstract figure of the 'external observer'

Interestingly, more recent studies have shown the legal features involved in the historical development of the epistemological conception of the modern fact itself (Poovey, 1998; Shapiro, 2000).

67 Hart has a practice theory without a clear concept of practices, which is curious since they are introduced to 'constitute' or 'underlie' his crucial notion of a rule. He only gives a few examples throughout his book (stopping for a red traffic light, playing chess, taking one's hat off in church), but it could be seriously questioned if these are adequate for a full-fledged notion of practice, since these are all models with rather binary options for the correctness of behaviour. Turner has criticized the use of such simplistic examples as the way to approach practices. He opposes them with several examples of ordinary social practices in which practitioners cannot at all be said to be following the same tacit rule (Turner, 2001).

68 On this role of the sociologist as legislator, see Bauman, 2003.

to binocular range. Hart further states that all the important distinctions about law as a social phenomenon come from analytical philosophy and are supposedly vital for engaging in any unambiguous project of sociology of law. He also remarked that he 'said far too little in my book about the topic of adjudication and legal reasoning' (Hart, 1997, p. 259) and that he was not really engaged by studies of law in practice and sociology of law (Sugarman & Hart, 2005, p. 292).

In this sense we could say that Hart posits what the observer sees if he *would* observe practice – i.e., the very concepts of analytical jurisprudence that according to him *should* be the starting point of empirical sociological observation – independently of what any actual observer of concrete legal practices *does* in fact see. In this way, the plane of law and the manner in which it is to be approached has already been unfolded in such a way that one *could* only recognize what is already put in as a presupposition from the start.[69] Why should one prefer an 'approach' to law based on the conceptual 'observations' of a figural external observer above the actual observations made from up close by empirical research of these very processes and operations of legal reasoning and adjudication? Why prefer such a distant 'practice theory' of law through descriptive armchair sociology, above a transversal approach of law in practice?[70] In the latter case, one actually encounters a plurality of different *points of view* that are laboriously set up by legal practitioners on the proceeding of the matter of dispute at stake: the enactment of monadic visibilities, optic devices to 'make things visible' in documents, fictive persona of the (mind of the) public and the creator, evidential observer positions of witnesses and experts, jurisprudential characters, legal positions raised by legal practitioners. This dispute is the event that allows certain loci to be assumed as points of view on legal processes in the first place. This point would be lost when this pluriformity of observer positions is subsumed under the single perspective of the figure of the legislative external observer that would be imposed by the legal theorist. Furthermore, this approach shows how the

---

[69] A person who has not already grasped what law is (like the Deleuzian idiot) is not taken very seriously in *The Concept of Law*. Hart for instance depicts the rule-skeptic as simply in denial or confused.

[70] Galligan says about 'an analysis of law avowedly grounded in social reality' of actions of officials that 'Once we examine those actions, it is plain that acceptance of law, for instance, while capable of precise description analytically, is entwined in practice with other social factors from which it cannot readily be separated and which affect the very idea. A law and society approach needs to go beyond the analytical concept of acceptance and consider how officials behave in practice' (Galligan, 2007, p. 15).

registering of facts about the behavioural regularities of practitioners is itself an act within the antagonistic dynamics of the dispute, according to the specific legal concepts of proof and facts proper to legal practices. In this sense, we could say that *matters of fact* are an integral part of the legal proceedings of *matters of dispute*.

Taking Disputes Seriously? Hercules, Iolaus and the Hydra of Legal Practice

One could argue that the dimension of concern of legal practitioners for disputes would put us in the same camp as Dworkin with his account of law and his criticism of Hart's concept of law. Several of Dworkin's insights have indeed been important for legal theory, like the focus on disputes and the liberation of the activity of judges from a prior understanding of the activities of legislators (Dworkin, 1997, p. 82). The debate between Hart and Dworkin has been to an important extent about the positioning of the legal philosopher with regard to law or legal practice. Dworkin tries to construct a different concept of law. He unties law from certain ideas proposed by Hart, like those of rules, facts and discretion, and centres the concept on principles and rights and on different ideas of concepts (as contested *within* legal practice and as existing in different conceptions) and legal theory (as interpretive not descriptive, and as useful for judges). In this way, he separates law from sociology and reties it with morality. Although Dworkin criticizes Hart's practice theory of rules, he retains the goal of providing a theory of legal practice. On this theory however, the concept of legal practice changes significantly and so does its relation to the legal theorist.

Dworkin accepts the distinction between internal and external points of view on legal practice that Hart introduced. He however changes the balance of power delegated to both perspectives in approaching the question about the nature of law. Dworkin side-tracks the conceptual figure of the external observer who makes factual statements about practices, and increases the role of the figure of the game participant (or rather the referee) who has to interpret the purpose of the practice. In this sense his legal theory purports to occupy 'the internal, participants' point of view' by 'joining that practice' and struggling with the issues that the participants face (Dworkin, 1998, p. 14). We will need to trace the specific way in which Dworkin occupies this internal perspective in order to become the spokesperson for legal practices. Dworkin states that his approach of legal practice 'centers on formal adjudication, on judges in black robes' (pp. 12–13). He hereby partakes in the tendency in legal theory to narrowly focus on the work of judges in arriving at judgment that we have criticized.[71] Curiously however, Dworkin explicitly disqualifies the accounts that legal practitioners actually give of their own activities, in which they conceive of judgment as an art that combines analogy, craft and political wisdom. He calls these accounts 'too unstructured' and states that 'we need to throw discipline over the idea of law as a craft' (p. 10).[72] Instead, he aims to show 'the hidden structure of their judgments' (p. 265) by proposing a legal theory about 'the interpretive questions a judge should put to himself' (p. 412) about their legal practice. He will call this legal theory 'law as integrity'.

These remarks are closely related to the different concept Dworkin constructs of the legal practice, which has to be captured by legal theory. This concept explicitly 'neglects' both issues of fact and 'the practical politics of adjudication, the compromises judges must accept'. Instead, what crucially characterizes law is that 'legal practice, unlike many other social phenomena, is argumentative' (p. 13). This cannot be read independently from Dworkin's statements that 'law as integrity is the idea of law worked pure' (Dworkin, 1998, p. 400). In order to attain a purified image of law, this conception has to filter out all these 'entropic' elements of noise that would plunge the substantive coherence of law back in 'chaos'. There are however many ways to confront the chaos in philosophy and law, as was argued in the previous section. Large parts of this book carefully accounted for the many things that happen between the moment a particular conflict is first brought into contact with attorneys and the moment it is decided by the judges, in order to make visible all the things that precede and make possible legal judgment in the first place. All these things will remain invisible behind the limited image of law as the macroscopic act of judgment with the sword of justice or morality that Dworkin will draw as we will see hereafter. These things include the crucial 'impure' elements of facts and meta-accounts of legal actors on their actions, which are all purified in Dworkin's account.

We could compare these 'undisciplined' elements of friction to the paradigms of classical mechanical physics that searched for the laws and principles of nature through setting up experiments and by disregarding the messy bits of noise and irregularity that disturbed the neat pure image of

---

71 Dworkin does state however that judges are 'not the only or even the most important actors in the legal drama' and cites a list of other actors (Dworkin, 1998, p. 12), without indicating, however, why these are more important.

72 These accounts of legal practitioners pose more of a nuisance for Dworkin than he might like to admit, especially since the new interpretive picture of law he proposes would have 'the signal merit of allowing us once again to believe what our judges say' (Dworkin, 1998, p. 90).

science. Chaos theory however has shown the fundamental importance of noise, or what in our setting we could call '*practical friction*', in the eventual generation of order.[73] Practical friction is not some nuisance that has to be eliminated from the start in an account of law. Law becomes what it is within the rich processes of dealing with practical friction, by plunging into the chaos that each matter of dispute presents and by deploying the diverse techniques in legal practice of gradually eliminating this chaos in the course of proceedings. Practices are the sites where the mediations between the confrontational forces of chaos and order, consistency and inconsistency, or disruptive hidden ideologies and unifying holistic ideals play themselves out; they are their constitutive chaotic mixers.[74]

Dworkin makes an important point about the role of disputes in legal practice when he introduces the idea of disagreement. He states that in the Hartian image of law, legal philosophers 'try to identify the hidden grounds that must be there, embedded, though unrecognized, in legal practice' but this image 'does not hold when members of particular communities who share practices and traditions make and *dispute* claims about the best interpretation of these – when they disagree, that is, about what some tradition or *practice actually requires in concrete circumstances*. These claims are often controversial, and the *disagreement is genuine*' (Dworkin, 1998, pp. 45–6, my italics). Disagreement in those cases does not only pertain to empirical facts about law, but also to the theoretical grounds of law. Dworkin here ties practice to dealing with the concrete circumstances and requirements of a particular dispute, instead of to some kind of general theory. Within these interpretive processes, facts about the existence of a social practice mix with the values and purposes that this practice is taken to serve. Dworkin here uncouples the concept of law from the factual element that Hart infused into it and reconstitutes it: 'law is an interpretive concept' (Dworkin, 1998, pp. 87, 410). Legal reasoning consists of providing the best interpretation of 'legal practice as a whole' (p. vii). Processes of interpretation thus become crucial in defining the nature of law.

Unlike Hart, Dworkin no longer conceives of legal practice in terms of the concept of 'rules' but of 'principle', 'purpose' and 'character'. He in fact states that 'all genuine interpretation is purposive' (p. 51). Importantly, he follows Gadamer in stating that all interpretation consists in the interpreter imposing his own meanings on the object that he

---

[73] Gleick, 1998, pp. 39–45.

[74] Phrased differently, when Dworkin repeatedly states that 'adjudication is a matter of principle', he says a lot about the 'principle' but very little about this 'matter'. Adjudication is all about dealing with the practical frictions of matters of dispute.

interprets, in this case legal practice. Dworkin proposes the theory of law as integrity as the 'best interpretation of what lawyers, law teachers, and judges do and much of what they say' (p. 94).

In order to work out the complex structure of legal interpretation that a judge faces when dealing with a controversy, Dworkin introduces the figure of Hercules, the philosophical judge whom he describes as a 'lawyer of superhuman skill, learning, patience and acumen' (Dworkin, 1997, p. 105) and as 'an imaginary judge of superhuman intellectual power and patience who accepts law as integrity' (Dworkin, 1998, p. 239). This figure will replace the figure of the game referee in the occupation of the internal perspective on legal practice. Hercules is mobilized in order to accomplish the magnificent task of constructing the interpretive theory that captures the whole of legal practice in a consistent overall set of principles. Hercules is a good example of a conceptual personae in the sense in which Deleuze and Guattari have used the term: a figure that simultaneously helps in constructing the concept of law and in unfolding the plane of presuppositions. In fact Hercules is full of presuppositions. The most important of these is the Kantian assumption that 'law is structured by a consistent overall set of principles about justice and fairness and procedural due process' (p. 243) just mentioned. Dworkin further stages Hercules in a range of interpretational exercises of different cases throughout which he imbues him with a spectrum of presupposing imperatives. Hercules 'must begin by asking', 'his answer must take some form such as' he 'must then ask', he 'must take into account only the arguments', he 'must suppose that it is understood' (Dworkin, 1997, pp. 105–23) and finally, once all these assumptions are in place, there are 'the types of judgment he must make and tensions he must resolve in deciding a variety of cases' (Dworkin, 1998, p. 239).

Many things can and have been said about Dworkin's theory. Here the focus will be on the role of the concepts of dispute, practice and legal philosophy. First, Gadamer himself explicitly rejects the idea that the meaning the interpreter applies to the object of interpretation is in any way 'better'.[75] He merely calls it 'different'. The conception of

---

[75] What does this notion of 'better' mean in the context of legal practice? One could argue that lawyers want to do better than their opponent within the *agon* of the dispute. Are judges however necessarily competing, and with whom? Is life in court an exam, a contest? An approach that addresses legal practitioners in terms of doing their work well steers a course between the two extremes of showing law in the best light possible (Dworkin) or in the worst light possible (Dworkin's version of Legal Realism). Both versions eventually bypass legal practice in favour of its domination by other practices, be they morality, or sociology and psychoanalysis.

better interpretation is related to the erroneous idea that there would be something hidden in the object of interpretation that the interpreter has to uncover and that would constitute the criterion of superiority. This is for instance the case when Dworkin aims to show 'the hidden structure' of the judgments of judges. In fact Gadamer states that the interpreter can never separate in advance the prejudices that will enable or hinder the interpretation, but that such separation can only take place within the process of interpretation itself (Gadamer, 1999, pp. 295–7). This is all opposed to Dworkin's attempt to infuse the Herculean interpreter at the outset with all the concrete imperatives of what he must have already understood in order to interpret and the idea to 'work out this entire scheme [of coherent principles and presuppositions] in advance, so that he would be ready to confront litigants with an entire theory of law' (Dworkin, 1997, p. 117). The Gadamerian project does not multiply the number of presuppositions needed in general to interpret something, but assigns the concrete object of interpretation at stake the power to pull an interpreter back in her projections and presumptions, so that these can become foregrounded and modified. This is a very different philosophical move in the delegation of power in framing a (interpretive) theory. The way in which philosophy clears a path for itself through legal practices and the points of view it sets up on them, is of crucial importance and will weigh upon the balance of forces involved. Instead of imposing such conceptual figures like the Legislator (Hart) or the Judge (Dworkin) in advance, it is instructive to find out what is involved in the act of attaining such points of view in the first place and how this is achieved within legal practice itself.

At this point we could introduce two different conceptual personae in order to provide a counterweight against the figure of Hercules. The first is that of the idiot as introduced by Deleuze in order to again open up a space for approaching legal practice that Hercules had closed down. The second is that of Iolaus in order to rethink the relation of philosophy to legal practice. When Deleuze discusses the philosophical problem of where to begin, he mobilizes the figure of the idiot against those who appeal to a pre-conceptual common sense in stating what everybody would already know.[76] The idiot instead is a figure who does not manage to know what everybody knows and modestly denies what everybody is supposed to

[76] Dworkin for instance states that 'every actor in the [legal] practice understands that what it permits or requires depends on the truth of certain propositions that are given sense only by and within the practice' (Dworkin, 1998, p. 13).

recognize (Deleuze, 2004a, p. 155).[77] Thinking with this figure retains an openness of thought in dealing with problems encountered in a way that can no longer rely on the comfort of previous presuppositions, but forces us to give birth to a different thinking that has to confront what this encounter requires. Hercules is a figure infused with the logic of presuppositions, who knows how to begin in approaching legal practice, knows what everyone else must know and which conclusions to draw. I would prefer to mobilize the figure of the idiot here in order to create space for a philosophical approach to law not impregnated by what we must have already understood about legal practice, but rather what we may come to understand about what it requires when addressing the exigencies a concrete matter of dispute poses to its practitioners.[78]

One can thus question whether Dworkin's theory really gives account of what a legal practice requires in concrete circumstances of solving a (hard) dispute. Where it seemed that he took disputes seriously, he does not *nearly* take them seriously enough. In fact Dworkin states that all approaches to legal practice, be they of philosophical jurisprudence or of adjudication, 'are distinctly legal because they are dominated by the adjudicative principle of inclusive integrity' (Dworkin, 1998, p. 410). When we read this in combination with his statement that theories about the nature of law should be useful to judges and that 'no firm line divides jurisprudence from adjudication or any other aspect of legal practice' but rather that 'jurisprudence is the general part of adjudication' (p. 90), we get a definite image of a philosophy *of* law *of* morality. Questioning the line between legal philosophy and adjudication in itself is interesting.[79] It becomes suspicious however when their boundaries are blurred in order to constitute both on a single plane of a new territory in which jurisprudence is subjected to adjudication (for which it has to be useful) and both

---

77 Two idiotic characters figure in Deleuze's work. First, Melville's Bartleby defies any request of common sense about what a sensible person is bound to do or know with the short utterance 'I would prefer not to', a formula that has the performative effect of shattering each logic of presuppositions (Deleuze, 1998a, p. 73). Second, Dostoyevsky's idiot does not manage to think or know how to proceed in the way his general environment presupposes.

78 There is a similarity here with Wittgenstein's warning against the use of the 'must' verb in philosophy and his instruction not to approach practices with an *a priori* 'image of thought' of what they must necessarily have in common, but instead to empirically look (*schau!*) at many concrete different practices in action.

79 This chapter pursued this issue in the light of the hypothesis of the becoming legal of philosophy. This becoming however, takes place through the continuous differentiation of two planes instead of only taking place on one.

jurisprudence and adjudication are subjected to the principles of political morality (by which they are dominated).

This 'disciplinary' constellation can be countered with the concepts of an 'ecology of practices' or a 'cosmopolitics' as proposed by Stengers. The approach of a particular practice cannot be separated from its relation to other practices. In fact this is part of what constitutes a practice as a practice. As Stengers has remarked 'talking of practices, that's immediately talking of an ecology of practices' (Stengers, 2004, p. 31). The ecological question forces us to think the power relations between different practices with regard to the way these are to mutually co-exist in a common world. The practices of law and philosophy are both part of such an ecology in which they have important interactions. We could say that Dworkin's proposal of integrity will not render this ecology of practices sustainable, in the sense that certain practices are instrumentally made to serve others, or are even assimilated in the sense argued above. Instead, a practice and its practitioners require the capacity to invent their own questions and define their own problems in order to maintain their proper way of existing and making things matter, which will not be the case when another practice sets its goals and speaks in its name. This is why we rejected a philosophy *of* law and argued for a mutual becoming of philosophy and law in which each retains its own vital thrust. The same goes for the practice of morality. A philosophy that turns to legal practice cannot let itself at the outset be dominated by the imposition of moral political principles, but needs rather to think their mutual relations through cosmo-political concepts in which the relations of power (politics) of their possible mutual becoming (the cosmos) are the question at stake.[80]

Whereas it might no longer be possible to rely upon pre-drawn boundaries in order to distinguish legal philosophy from practices of adjudication, this does not preclude that within the course of legal practice all kinds of practical differentiations between such different strands of activity do continuously occur. In Chapter 3 it became clear that the guiding questions of the lawyers and the philosopher were very different, i.e. 'Is the plaintiff the co-inventor of the disputed machine?' v. 'How is immateriality legally constituted?' These eventually led us to quite different accounts of things. Is a philosophical account that addresses this question 'useful' or 'helpful' to the lawyer? That of course depends. It could have this effect for legal practitioners[81] in

---

[80] For the relation between the ecology of practices and the cosmo-political question, see Stengers, 1997.

[81] In this sense, the opposite conclusion that philosophy has nothing to teach the lawyer (De Sutter, 2009, p. 112) also has to be rejected.

a variety of different ways.[82] This, however, should not be its primary goal. Such a philosophy needs to safeguard its capacity for inventing its own questions and defining its own problems and thus of enacting its own becoming.

Hercules the half-god is a purifier. With the divine golden sword of moral justice he cuts off the heads of the Hydra of legal practice. He thus defeats the chaos the Hydra presents but at the price of killing its vital force of life. This violence of purification is not sustainable. As in the myth, the purified often returns through the backdoor, as is the case when Hercules is eventually killed by the poison extracted from the slain creature. We can here introduce the figure of Iolaus in the new openness that the figure of the idiot has created, in order to re-engage with legal practice. Iolaus applies the ancient medical art of cauterizing through firebrand to the Hydra. It is an art of minimizing potential medical harmful possibilities through applying fire to tissue. These are tissue-based operations of new life that require close contact with the problem to be solved. Iolaus can thus be seen as the master in performing the small deaths of the chaotic extensions that constitute the legal life of a dispute. As a human operator, skilled in working with practical friction, he provides a philosophical counter-weight against the Herculean model of superhuman purifications in engaging the Hydra of legal practice.

***

This section has turned to legal theory to study the work of several legal thinkers and has studied how they constituted their theories of legal practice by constructing paths of thinking, the role of things, the status of disputes, the formation of alliances with other practices, the creation of concepts, the unfolding of presupposed planes of consistency, the introduction of conceptual personae and the confrontation with chaos. In this way we have also tried to shed light on the practice of legal theory itself as it establishes its relations with legal and other practices.

---

[82] When I confronted the attorney Mrs Blanchard with the question why, as a legal practitioner, she was interested in the account I provided of her practice, she answered: '*In the first place, I want to understand how I function when working without being aware of it. When you are working on a case, you are engulfed in the process, busy with your part of the story. You don't know how your clients prepare the process and how the judges are busy with it afterwards. You do not have an overview of the whole trajectory. You are caught between the client and the judge. Secondly, as a lawyer you never have the time to think about these things, to extract the outlines of the process and understand the map. A good lawyer needs to know where she is on the map and what the country looks like and its history*.' This is a quite different conception of usefulness than that of Dworkin.

Although the paths to law and the paths of law are distinct, they cannot be clearly separated as they gradually pass over into each other. This also holds for a philosophical approach to law. Through traversing the grounds of legal practices this philosophy can gradually become capable of further unfolding its own plane of consistency on which it can first become a legal philosophy. At certain early points along these trajectories the philosophical traveller can encounter the most curious figures ranging from the most wicked to the most noble, from the most involved to the most detached. Some point out that one has arrived at a crossroads and they are full of good will to provide the explanation of how to proceed from here, even offering maps with all the borders, paths and pitfalls of the terrain and provident tour guides to direct one to one's destination. Sometimes, when asked about different directions they answer that there are no stable paths but only tracks that lead into the chaos of the wilderness in which one will inevitably get lost, that it is full of rival tribes in whose disputes one will become entangled so that one will never reach one's goal. Others assure that their route has no-thing that might pose an obstacle, that it is much safer and that arrival is guaranteed. They say that although their path leads across different territories and that the permission of its authorities must be acquired before proceeding, one will in the end be led up to points with good panoramic views of what one is looking for. If the traveller, after all these warnings, still persists in confronting the chaos, he is urged to take a golden sword along on the voyage, which is guaranteed to clear the right path through the wilderness and to provide protection in solving any conflict encountered. What happens however when the traveller is idiotic enough not to follow this advice and pursues the tracks of legal cognition in the wild? This is the proposal for an approach to legal practice that this book has tried to explore.

In this way it has tried to create an openness for thought[83] in which the legal question can both be restated and re-explored anew. This question is not 'What is law?' but has been 'How does something become legal?'[84]

---

[83] This openness is partially created by untying law from some other legal features (laws of the subject), figures (predictive bad man, legislative observer, teleological Hercules), and practices (statistics, economics, morality, structuralist sociology, information science, axiological doctrine, deconstructivist history).

[84] Would the legal theorist object 'But you use the word "legal" so you must already presuppose what law is'? This move has been resisted by refusing the theoretical obligation of having to assume ('you must presuppose') a certain systematic totality of law when approaching legal practice. The present approach has experimented with a conceptual delegation of power that grants the singularity of what is practically at stake to re-constitute what law can be on different levels, and

This question sends philosophical enquiry off in a different direction. The response does not necessarily consist in the creation of a concept of law, although it definitively involves the raising and creation of many other concepts that condense what is encountered underway. The confrontation with legal practices has instead more immediately resulted in a range of trajectories of and for thought.[85] The philosophical differentiations along these movements have unfolded the legal plane of grounding and its many figures, paths and concepts and might have provided a direction for a becoming legal of philosophy itself.

---

opens new vistas on how such legal totalities become assembled in the first place (van Dijk, 2015).

[85] As movements they have a certain affinity to the idea of a path of thought. This idea of a path however is also misleading in suggesting that the path is already there for the movement to follow, whereas the tracks of thought are actually cleared by these very movements.

Bibliography

Abélès, M. (2000). *Un ethnologue à l'Assemblée*. Paris, Odile Jacob.

Akrich, M. (1992). The De-Scription of Technical Objects. In W.E. Bijker & J. Law (Eds), *Shaping Technology/Building Society: Studies in Sociotechnical Change*. (pp. 205–24). Cambridge: MIT Press.

Austin, J.L. (1976). *How to do Things with Words*. Oxford: Oxford University Press.

Bacon, F. (2000). *The New Organon*. Cambridge: Cambridge University Press.

Bakker, J.H. (2011). *Grond*. Amsterdam: Atlas.

Barthes, R. (1977). The Death of the Author. In S. Heath (Ed.), *Image-Music-Text*. (pp. 142–8). Glasgow: Fontana/Collins.

Bauman, Z. (2003). *Intimations of Postmodernity*. London: Routledge.

Benjamin, W. (2008). *The Work of Art in the Age of Mechanical Reproduction*. London: Penguin.

Bently, L. (2008). The Making of Modern Trade Marks Law: The Constitution of the Legal Concept of Trade Mark (1860–1880). In L. Bently, J. Davids & J.C. Ginsburg (Eds), *Trade Marks and Brands: An Interdisciplinary Critique*. (pp. 3–41). Cambridge: Cambridge University Press.

Bently, L. & Sherman, B. (2009). *Intellectual Property Law*. Oxford: Oxford University Press.

Biagioli, M. (2006). Patent Republic. *Social Research*, *73*(4), 1129–72.

Blackstone, W. (1897). *Commentaries on the Laws of England*. St. Paul: West Publishing Co.

Blanchette, J.-F. (2011). A material history of bits. *Journal of the American Society for Information Science and Technology*, *62*(6), 1042–57.

Blenko Jr., W.J. (1990). The Doctrine of Equivalents in Patent Infringement. *JOM*, *42*(5), 59.

Bowrey, K. (2011). The New Intellectual Property. Celebrity, Fans and the Properties of the Entertainment Franchise. *Griffith Law Review*, *20*(1), 188–220.

Boyle, J. (1996). *Shamans, Software, and Spleens. Law and the Construction of the Information Society*. Cambridge, Massachusetts: Harvard University Press.

Boyle, J. (1997). A Politics of Intellectual Property: Environmentalism for the Net? *Duke Law Journal*, *47*(87), 87–116.
Brenninkmeijer, A.F.M. (1995). *Rechtspleging*. Nijmegen: Ars Aequi Libri.
Buydens, M. (1993). *La protection de la quasi-création*. Brussels: Larcier.
Buydens, M. (2012). *La propriété intellectuelle. Évolution historique et philosophique*. Brussels: Bruylant.
Callon, M. (1986). Elements of a sociology of translation: Domestication of the Scallops and the Fishermen of St Brieuc Bay. In J. Law (Ed.), *Power, Action and Belief: A New Sociology of Knowledge?* (pp. 196–233). London: Routledge.
Cambrosio, A., Keating, P. & Mackenzie, M. (1990). Scientific Practice in the Courtroom: The Construction of Sociotechnical Identities in a Biotechnology Patent Dispute. *Social Problems*, *37*(3), 275–93.
Cardozo, B.N. (1924). *The Growth of the Law*. New Haven: Yale University Press.
Carroll, L. (1994). *Alice's Adventures in Wonderland*. London: Penguin.
Cayla, O. (1993). La qualification ou la vérité du droit. *Droits*, *18*, 3–18.
Condorcet, N. (1776). Fragments on the Freedom of the Press. In L.B.M. Kretschmer (Ed.), *Primary Sources on Copyright (1450–1900)*. www.copyrighthistory.org.
Coquillette, D.R. (1992). *Francis Bacon*. Stanford: Stanford University Press.
Crommelin, R.W.J. (2007). *Het aanvullen van de rechtsgronden*. Alphen aan den Rijn: Kluwer.
d'Héricourt, L. (1725). Memorandum. In L.B.M. Kretschmer (Ed.), *Primary Sources on Copyright (1450–1900)*. www.copyrighthistory.org.
De Preter, C. & Roox, K. (2008). De interpretatie van octrooien aan de hand van het verleningsdossier en andere extrinsieke elementen. *Intellectuele Rechten*, 134–48.
De Sutter, L. (2009). *Deleuze. La pratique du droit*. Paris: Michalon.
De Vries, E. & van Dijk, N. (2013). A Bump in the Road. Ruling out Law from Technology. In M. Hildebrandt & J. Gakeer (Eds), *Human Law and Computer Law: Comparative Perspectives* (25 ed.). (pp. 89–121). Dordrecht: Springer.
Deazley, R. (2008). Commentary on Tonson v. Collins (1762). In L.B.M. Kretschmer (Ed.), *Primary Sources on Copyright (1450–1900)*. www.copyrighthistory.org.
Deleuze, G. (1993). *The Fold. Leibniz and the Baroque*. London: Athlone.
Deleuze, G. (1995). *Negotations 1972–1990*. New York: Columbia University Press.
Deleuze, G. (1998a). *Essays Critical and Clinical*. London: Verso.

Deleuze, G. (1998b). Qu'est-ce que l'acte de création? (Avoir une idée en cínema). *TRAFIC*, *27*, 133–42.

Deleuze, G. (2004a). *Difference and Repetition*. London: Continuum.

Deleuze, G. (2004b). The Method of Dramatization. In *Desert islands and other texts, 1953–1974*. (pp. 94–116). Los Angeles: Semiotext(e).

Deleuze, G. & Guattari, F. (1987). *A Thousand Plateaus*. Minneapolis: University of Minnesota Press.

Deleuze, G. & Guattari, F. (1994). *What is Philosophy?* New York: Columbia.

Dennett, D.C. (1996). *Darwin's Dangerous Idea*. London: Penguin.

Depreeuw, S. (2011). *The variable scope of the exclusive economic rights in copyright. Exploring the articulation of law and technology through the case of Web search engines.* VUB, Brussels.

Derrida, J. (1988). *Limited Inc*. Evanston: Northwestern University Press.

Derrida, J. (1992a). Before the Law. In D. Attridge (Ed.), *Acts of Literature* (pp. 181–220). New York: Routledge.

Derrida, J. (1992b). Force of Law. The "Mystical Foundation of Authority". In D. Cornell, M. Rosenfeld & D.G. Carlson (Eds), *Deconstruction and the Possibility of Justice.* (pp. 3–67). New York: Routledge.

Dewey, J. (1924). Logical Method and Law. *The Philosophical Review*, *33*(6), 560–72.

Dewey, J. (1957). *The public & its problems*. Athens: Swallow Press.

Diderot, D. (1763). Letter on the book trade. In L.B.M. Kretschmer (Ed.), *Primary Sources on Copyright (1450–1900)*. www.copyrighthistory.org.

Dölemeyer, B. (2005). Thing Site, Tie, Ting Place. Venues for the Administration of Law. In B. Latour & P. Weibel (Eds), *Making Things Public*. (pp. 260–67). Cambridge, Massachusetts: The MIT Press.

Drescher, T.D. (1992). The Transformation and Evolution of Trademarks – From Signals to Symbols to Myth. *The Trademark Reporter®*, *82*(301), 301–40.

Ducrot, O. (1991). *Dire et ne pas dire*. Paris: Hermann.

Dworkin, R. (1997). *Taking Rights Seriously*. Cambridge, Massachusetts: Harvard University Press.

Dworkin, R. (1998). *Law's Empire*. Oxford: Hart.

Eisenstein, E. (2005). *The Printing Revolution in Early Modern Europe*. New York: Cambridge University Press.

Eldredge, N. & Gould, S.J. (1972). Punctuated equilibria: an alternative to phyletic gradualism. In T.J.M. Schopf (Ed.), *Models in Paleobiology*. (pp. 82–115). San Francisco: Freeman Cooper.

Fichte, J.G. (1793). Proof of the Unlawfulness of Reprinting. In L.B.M. Kretschmer (Ed.), *Primary Sources on Copyright (1450–1900)*. www.copyrighthistory.org.

Fleck, L. (1981). *Genesis and Development of a Scientific Fact*. Chicago: The University of Chicago Press.
Foucault, M. (1979). What is an Author? In J. Harari (Ed.), *Textual Strategies: Perspectives in Post-Structuralist Criticism*. (pp. 141–60). Ithaca, N.Y.: Cornell University Press.
Foucault, M. (1982). The Subject and Power. In H.L. Dreyfus & P. Rabinow (Eds), *Michel Foucault: Beyond Structuralism and Hermeneutics*. (pp. 208–27). New York: Harvester Weatsheaf.
Foucault, M. (1991). *Discipline and Punish*. London: Penguin.
Freud, S. (1949). *Group Psychology and the Analysis of the Ego*. London: The Hogart Press and the Institute of Psychoanalysis.
Freud, S. (1961a). *Beyond the Pleasure Principle*. New York: W W Norton & Company.
Freud, S. (1961b). *Civilization and its Discontents*. New York: W W Norton & Company Inc.
Freud, S. (2001). *Totem and Taboo*. London: Routledge.
Gadamer, H.-G. (1999). *Truth and Method*. New York: The Continuum Publishing Company.
Galligan, D. (2007). *Law in Modern Society*. Oxford: Oxford University Press.
Garfinkel, H. (1984). *Studies in Ethnomethodology*. Cambridge: Polity Press.
Gleick, J. (1998). *Chaos*. London: Vintage.
Goethe, J.W. (2003). *Faust*. A.S. Kline (Trans). Poetry in Translation. http://www.poetryintranslation.com.
Goetting, H.-P. (2006). Der Begriff des geistigen Eigentums. *GRUR*, *108*(5), 353–8.
Goody, J. (2000). *The Power of the Written Tradition*. Washington: Smithsonian Institution.
Goody, J. & Watt, I. (1963). The Consequences of Literacy. *Comparative Studies in Society and History*, *5*(3), 304–45.
Greimas, A.J. (1976). Analyse sémiotique d'un discours juridique. In A.J. Greimas (Ed.), *Sémiotique et sciences sociales*. (pp. 79–128). Paris: Le Seuil.
Gruter, M. & Bohannan, P. (Eds). (1983). *Law, Biology & Culture. The Evolution of Law*. Santa Barbara: Ross-Erikson, Inc.
Gutwirth, S. (1993). *Waarheidsaanspraken in recht en wetenschap*. Brussels: VUBPress.
Gutwirth, S., De Hert, P. & De Sutter, L. (2008). The trouble with technology regulation from a legal perspective. Why Lessig's 'optimal mix' will not work. In R. Brownsword & K. Yeung (Eds), *Regulating Technologies*. (pp. 193–218). Oxford: Hart Publishers.

Hart, H.L.A. (1997). *The Concept of Law*. Oxford: Oxford University Press.

Heidegger, M. (1962). *Time and Being*. Oxford: Basil Blackwell.

Heidegger, M. (1997). Der Satz vom Grund. In *Gesamtausgabe*. I.10. Frankfurt am Main: Vittorio Klostermann.

Heidegger, M. (2004). Das Ding. In *Vorträge und Aufsätze*. (pp. 157–80). Stuttgart: Klett-Cotta.

Heller, M.A. & Eisenberg, R.S. (1998). Can Patents Deter Innovation? The Anticommons in Biomedical Research. *Science*, *280*(698), 698–701.

Hermitte, M.-A. (1998). Le droit est un autre monde. *Enquête*, *7*, 17–37.

Hesse, C. (1990). Enlightenment Epistemology and the Laws of Authorship in Revolutionary France, 1777–1793. *Representations*, *30*, 109–37.

Hight, M.A. (2008). *Idea and Ontology. An Essay in Early Modern Metaphysics of Ideas*. Pennsylvania: The Pennsylvania State University Press.

Hildebrandt, M. & De Vries, K. (2013). *Privacy, Due Process and the Computational Turn. The Philosophy of Law Meets the Philosophy of Technology*. London: Routledge.

Hohfeld, W.N. (1913). Some fundamental legal conceptions as applied in judicial reasoning. *Yale Law Journal*, *23*(16), 16–59.

Hohfeld, W.N. (1917). Fundamental legal conceptions as applied in judicial reasoning. *Yale Law Journal*, *28*(2), 710–70.

Holmes, O.W. (1881). *The Common Law*. Boston: Little, Brown, and Company.

Holmes, O.W. (2009). *The Path of The Law*: The Floating Press.

Honoré, A.M. (1961). Ownership. In A.G. Guest (Ed.), *Oxford Essays in Jurisprudence*. (pp. 107–47). Oxford: Oxford University Press.

Hugenholtz, P.B. (2005). *Auteursrecht op Informatie*. Amsterdam: Amsterdam Academic Archive.

Hume, D. (1740). *An Abstract of a Book Lately Published, Entitled, A Treatise of Human Nature, &c.* C. Borbet: London.

Hutchins, E. (1995). *Cognition in the Wild*. Cambridge: MIT Press.

James, W. (1995). *Pragmatism*. New York: Dover Publications.

James, W. (2003). *Essays in Radical Empiricism*. New York: Dover Publications.

Jasanoff, S. (1997). *Science at the Bar*. Cambridge: Harvard University Press.

Jaszi, P. (1991). Towards a Theory of Copyright: The Metamorphoses of "Authorship". *Duke Law Journal*, *455*, 485–91.

Jefferson, T. (1905). Thomas Jefferson to Isaac McPherson. In A.A. Lipscomb & A. Ellery Bergh (Eds), *The Writings of Thomas Jefferson*. Vol. 13. Washington: Thomas Jefferson Memorial Association.

Juarróz, R. (1958). *Poesía Vertical* (Antología ed.): http://elciruja.unlugar.com.

Kabel, J. (2006). *Rechter en publieksopvattingen: feit, fictie of ervaring?* Amsterdam: Vossiuspers UvA.

Kafka, F. (2005). *The Trial*. London: Vintage.

Kafka, F. (2009). *The Castle*. London: Wordsworth.

Kang, H.Y. (2013). Science Inside Law. The Making of a New Patent Class in the International Patent Classification. *Science in Context*, *25* (4), 551–94.

Kant, I. (1785). Von der Unrechtmäßigkeit des Büchernachdrucks. *Berlinische Monatschrift*. 1783–1811. 1785, 403–17.

Kant, I. (1998). *Critique of Pure Reason*. Cambridge: Cambridge University Press.

Kerr, I. (2013). Prediction, Preemption, Presumption: The Path of Law After the Computational Turn. In M. Hildebrandt & K. De Vries (Eds), *Privacy, Due Process and the Computational Turn*. (pp. 91–120). London: Routledge.

Kittler, F. (1986). *Gramophone, Film, Typewriter*. Stanford: Stanford University Press.

Kohler, J. (1880). *Das Autorrecht*. Jena: Verlag von Gustav Fischer.

Kohler, J. (1894). Die Idee des geistigen Eigentums. *AcP*, *32*, 99–167.

Kohler, J. (1900). *Handbuch des deutschen Patentrechts in rechtsvergleichender Darstellung*. Mannheim: J. Bensheimer Verlag.

Kozin, A.V. (2007). The Legal File. *International Journal for the Semiotics of Law*, *20*, 191–216.

Kozinski, A. (1992–1993). What I Ate for Breakfast and Other Mysteries of Judicial Decision Making. *Loyola of Los Angeles Law Review*, *26*(993), 993–9.

Kripke, S. (1980). *Naming and Necessity*. Oxford: Blackwell.

Kuhn, T.S. (1996). *The Structure of Scientific Revolutions*. Chicago: University of Chicago Press.

Laenens, J., Broeckx, K., Scheers, D. & Thiriar, P. (2008). *Handboek Gerechtelijk Recht*. Antwerpen: Intersentia.

Latour, B. (1986). Visualization and Cognition. *Knowledge and Society*, *6*, 1–40.

Latour, B. (1993). *We Have Never Been Modern*. Cambridge: Harvard University Press.

Latour, B. (1996). *Aramis or the love of technology*. Cambridge: Harvard University Press.

Latour, B. (1999). *Pandora's Hope. Essays on the Reality of the Science Studies*. Cambridge: Harvard University Press.

Latour, B. (2005). *Reassembling the Social. An Introduction into Actor-Network-Theory*. Oxford: Oxford University Press.

Latour, B. (2010). *The Making of Law. An ethnography of the conseil d'état*. Cambridge: Polity.

Lefebvre. (2008). *The Image of Law. Deleuze, Bergson, Spinoza*. Stanford: Stanford University Press.

Leibniz, G.W. (2010). *The Principles of Philosophy Known as Monadology*. J. Bennett (Trans). Early Modern Texts. http://www.earlymoderntexts.com.

Lemley, M. (1997). Romantic Authorship and the Rhetoric of Property. *Texas Law Review*, *75*, 873–906.

Lessig, L. (2006). *Code* (2nd ed.). New York: BasicBooks.

Lippmann, W. (2009). *The Phantom Public*. New Brunswick: Transaction Publishers.

Llewellyn, K.N. (1962). Some Realism about Realism. In *Jurisprudence. Realism in Theory and Practice*. (pp. 42–76). Chicago: University of Chicago.

Llewellyn, K.N. (2008). *The Bramble Bush*. New York: Oxford University Press.

Locke, J. (2005). *Two Treatises of Government*. Cambridge: Cambridge University Press.

MacCormick, N. (1986). Law as Institutional Fact. In N. MacCormick & O. Weinberger (Eds), *An institutional theory of law: new approaches to legal positivism*. (pp. 49–76). Dordrecht: Reidel.

Madison, M.J. (2005). Law as Design: Objects, Concepts and Digital Things. *Case Western Reserve Law Review*, *56*(2), 381–478.

Maturana, H.R., & Varela, F.J. (1998). *The Tree of Knowledge. The Biological Roots of Human Understanding*. Boston & London: Shambhala.

McLuhan, M. (1994). *Understanding Media. The Extensions of Man*. Cambridge, Massachusetts: MIT Press.

Mill, J.S. (1981). *A System of Logic Ratiocinative and Inductive*. Toronto: University of Toronto Press/Routledge.

Mol, A. & Law, J. (1994). Networks and Fluids, Anaemia and Social Topology. *Social Studies of Science*, *24*(4), 641–71.

Murphy, P. (Ed.). (2003). *Evidence, Proof, and Facts*. Oxford: Oxford University Press.

Nietzsche, F. (2005). Homer's Contest. In M.W. Grenke (Ed.), *Prefaces To Unwritten Works*. St. Augustine's Press.

Nordmann, A. (2004). *Converging Technologies – Shaping the Future of European Societies*. Luxembourg: European Communities.

Norman, D.A. (1988). *The Psychology of Everyday Things*. New York: Basic Books.

Panofsky, E. (1968). *Idea. A Concept in Art Theory*. London: Harper & Row.
Peirce, C.S. (1878). How to Make Our Ideas Clear. *Popular Science Monthly*, *12*, 286–302.
Penner, J.E. (1995–1996). The "Bundle of Rights" Picture of Property. *UCLA Law Review*, *43*, 711–820.
Peukert, A. (2011). Intellectual Property. In J. Basedow, K. Hopt & R. Zimmermann (Eds), *Encyclopedia of European Private Law*. Oxford: Oxford University Press.
Plato (1999). *Phaedo*. Oxford: Oxford University Press.
Poovey, M. (1998). *A History of the Modern Fact*. Chicago: The University of Chicago Press.
Posner, R.A. (2008). *How Judges Think*. Cambridge: Harvard University Press.
Pottage, A. (2009). Fiction Science and Proprietary Effect. In J.-P. Gaudilliere & D. Kevles (Eds), *Living properties* (pp. 225–39). Berlin: Max Planck Institute for the History of Science.
Pottage, A. (2011). Law machines: Scale models, forensic materiality and the making of modern patent law. *Social Studies of Science*, *41*(5), 621–43
Pottage, A. & Sherman, B. (2010). *Figures of Invention*. Oxford: Oxford University Press.
Prakken, H. (2006). AI & Law, Logic and Argument Schemes. *Augmentation*, *19*, 303–16.
Rancière, J. (2005). L'affect indécis. Entretien avec Jacques Rancière réalisé par Patrice Brouin, Elie During et Dork Zabunyan. *Critique*, LXI (692–3), 142–3.
Riles, A. (2005–2006). A New Agenda for the Cultural Study of Law: Taking on the Technicalities. *Buffalo Law Review*, *53*, 973–1033.
Riles, A. (2011). *Collateral Knowledge: Legal Reasoning in the Global Financial Markets*. Chicago: University of Chicago Press.
Rorty, R. (1980). *Philosophy and the Mirror of Nature*. Princeton: Princeton University Press.
Rose, M. (1988). The Author as Proprietor Donaldson v. Becket and the Genealogy of Modern Authorship. *Representations*, *23*, 51–85.
Rouse, J. (2001). Two Concepts of Practice. In T.R. Schatzki, K. Knorr Cetina & E. von Savigny (Eds), *The Practice Turn in Contemporary Theory*. (pp. 198–208). London: Routledge.
Schatzki, T.R. (1996). *Social Practices, A Wittgensteinian Approach to Human Activity and the Social*. Cambridge: Cambridge University Press.
Schatzki, T.R., Knorr Cetina, K. & von Savigny, E. (Eds). (2001). *The Practice Turn in Contemporary Theory*. London: Routledge.

Schechter, F. (1927). The Rational Basis of Trade Mark Protection. *Harvard Law Review*, *40*(813), 813–33.
Scheffer, T. (2004). Materialities of Legal Proceedings. *International Journal for the Semiotics of Law*, *17*, 365–89.
Scheffer, T. (2007). Event and Process: An Exercise in Analytical Ethnography. *Human Studies*, *30*(3), 167–97.
Schmidt, A.H.J. (1986). Rechtsinformatica. *Computerrecht*, *1*, 15–19.
Schopenhauer, A. (1864). Zur Rechtslehre, Politik, Geschichte und Volkerkarakteristik. In Arthur Schopenhauer's *Handschriftlichem Nachlaß*. (pp. 375–88). Leipzig: J.A. Brockhaus.
Schopenhauer, A. (1954). *World as Will and Representation*. New York: Dover.
Shapin, S. & Schaffer, S. (1985). *Leviathan and the Air-Pump*. Princeton: Princeton University Press.
Shapiro, B.J. (2000). *A Culture of Fact*. Ithaca: Cornell University Press.
Sherman, B. (1991). Patent Claim Interpretation: The Impact of the Protocol on Interpretation. *The Modern Law Review*, *54*(4), 499–510.
Sherman, B. & Bently, L. (1999). *The Making of Modern Intellectual Property Law*. Cambridge: Cambridge University Press.
Sloterdijk, P. (2004). *Schäume* (Vol. III). Frankfurt am Main: Suhrkamp.
Smith, R. & Wynne, B. (1989). *Expert Evidence. Interpreting Science in Law*. London: Routledge Chapman & Hall.
Spinello, R.A. & Bottis, M. (2009). *A Defense of Intellectual Property Rights*. Cheltenham: Edward Elgar.
Stallman, R. (2006). Did You Say "Intellectual Property"? It's a Seductive Mirage. *Policy Futures in Education*, *4*(4), 334–6.
Stein, P.A. & Rueb, A.S. (2002). *Compendium Nieuw Burgerlijk Procesrecht*. Deventer: Kluwer.
Stengers, I. (1997). *Pour en finir avec la tolerance* (Vol. VII). Paris: La Découverte.
Stengers, I. (2004). Une pratique cosmopolitique du droit est-elle possible? Entretien avec Laurent de Sutter. In F. Audren & L. De Sutter (Eds), *Pratiques cosmopolitiques du droit*. (pp. 14–33). Paris: Cosmopolitiques.
Stengers, I. (2006). *La Vierge et le Neutrino*. Paris: Les Empêcheurs de penser en rond.
Stengers, I. (2007). Une approache impressioniste de la question de la théorie de droit. (Unpublished).
Stiegler, B. (2012). *Die Aufklärung in the Age of Philosophical Engineering*. Paper presented at the World Wide Web conference 2012, from http://www2012.wwwconference.org/documents/Stiegler-www2012-keynote.pdf.

Strathern, M. (1996). Cutting the Network. *The Journal of the Royal Anthropological Institute*, *2*(3), 517–35.
Sugarman, D. & Hart, H.L.A. (2005). Hart Interviewed: H.L.A. Hart in Conversation with David Sugarman. *Journal of Law and Society*, *32*(2), 267–93.
Thomas, G. & James, D. (2006). Reinventing grounded theory: some questions about theory, ground and discovery. *British Educational Research Journal*, *32*(6), 767–95.
Thomas, Y. (1978). Le droit entre les mots et les choses. *Archives de philosophie du droit*, *23*, 93–114.
Thomas, Y. (1980). Res, chose et patrimoine. *Archives de philosophie du droit*, *25*, 413–26.
Thomas, Y. (2011). *Les Opérations du Droit.* Seuil/Gallimard.
Tribe, L.H. (1985). Seven Deadly Sins of Straining the Constitution Through a Pseudo-Scientific Sieve. *Hastings Law Journal*, *36*, 155–72.
Troller, A. (1978). *Précis du droit de la propriété immatériele*. Bâle: Helbing & Lichtenhahn.
Troller, A. (1983). *Immaterialgüterrecht*. Basel: Helbing & Lichtenhahn.
Turner, S. (2001). Throwing out the tacit rule book. In T.R. Schatzki, K. Knorr Cetina & E. Von Savigny (Eds), *The Practice Turn in Contemporary Theory*. (pp. 129–39). London: Routledge.
Ulmer, E. (1960). *Urheber- und Verlagrecht*. Berlin: Springer.
Upton, F.H. (1860). *A Treatise on the Law of Trade Marks, with a Digest and Review of the English and American Authorities*. Albany: Weare C. Little.
van Dijk, N. (2011). Approaching Law through Conflicts. *Law and Method*, *1*, 44–63.
van Dijk, N. (2013). *Grounds of the Immaterial. A Transversal Approach of Legal Philosophy in Intellectual Rights.* Ph.D Thesis. VUB. Brussels.
van Dijk, N. (2015). The Life and Deaths of a Dispute. An Inquiry into Matters of Law. In K. McGee (Ed.), *Latour and the Passage of Law*. (pp. 160–96). Edinburgh: Edinburgh University Press.
Venturini, T. (2010). Diving in magma: how to explore controversies with actor-network theory. *Public Understanding of Science*, *19*(3), 258–73
Vismann, C. (2008). *Files | Law and Media Technology*. Stanford: Stanford University Press.
Wald, P.M. (1992). Some Real-Life Observations About Judging. *Indiana Law Review*, *26*(1), 173–86.
Waldron, J. (1985). What is Private Property? *Oxford Journal of Legal Studies*, *5*(3), 313–49.
Weber, M. (1947). *The Theory of Social and Economic Organization*. New York: Oxford University Press.

Whitehead, A.N. (2004). *The Concept of Nature*. Mineola: Dover Publications.
Wichers Hoeth, L. (2007). *Kort begrip van het intellectuele eigendomsrecht*. Deventer: Kluwer.
Wittgenstein, L. (1975). *On Certainty*. Oxford: Blackwell.
Wittgenstein, L. (2009). *Philosophical Investigations*. Wiley-Blackwell.
Woodmansee, M. (1984). The Genius and the Copyright: Economic and Legal Conditions of the Emergence of the "Author". *Eighteenth-Century Studies*, *17*(4), 425–48.
Yarn, D.H. (2000). Law, Love, and Reconciliation: Searching for Natural Conflict Resolution in Homo Sapiens. In F. Aureli & F. De Waal (Eds), *Natural Conflict Resolution.* (pp. 54–70). Berkeley: University of California Press.
Young, E. (1918). *Conjectures on Original Composition*. (Modern Language Texts) Manchester: At the University Press.
Zilsel, E. (1942). The Genesis of the Concept of Physical Law. *The Philosophical Review*, *51*(3), 245–79.

Index